ATHEISTS AND ATHEISM BEFORE THE ENLIGHTENMENT

Anxiety about the threat of atheism was rampant in the early modern period, yet fully documented examples of openly expressed irreligious opinion are surprisingly rare. England and Scotland saw only a handful of such cases before 1750, and this book offers a detailed analysis of three of them. Thomas Aikenhead was executed for his atheistic opinions at Edinburgh in 1697; Tinkler Ducket was convicted of atheism by the Vice-Chancellor's court at the University of Cambridge in 1739; whereas Archibald Pitcairne's overtly atheist tract, *Pitcairneana*, though evidently compiled very early in the eighteenth century, was first published only in 2016. Drawing on these, and on the better-known apostacy of Christopher Marlowe and the Earl of Rochester, Michael Hunter argues that such atheists showed real 'assurance' in publicly promoting their views. This contrasts with the private doubts of Christian believers, and this book demonstrates that the two phenomena are quite distinct, even though they have sometimes been wrongly conflated.

MICHAEL HUNTER is Emeritus Professor of History at Birkbeck, University of London, and a Fellow of the British Academy. He is well known for his publications on Robert Boyle and on the early Royal Society and its milieu. His most recent book is *The Decline of Magic: Britain in the Enlightenment* (2020).

ATHEISTS AND ATHEISM BEFORE THE ENLIGHTENMENT

The English and Scottish Experience

MICHAEL HUNTER

Birkbeck, University of London

For David Meets & Michel Moor

With best wishes

from Michael Hunter

13 August 2023

CAMBRIDGE
UNIVERSITY PRESS

Shaftesbury Road, Cambridge CB2 8EA, United Kingdom

One Liberty Plaza, 20th Floor, New York, NY 10006, USA

477 Williamstown Road, Port Melbourne, VIC 3207, Australia

314–321, 3rd Floor, Plot 3, Splendor Forum, Jasola District Centre, New Delhi – 110025, India

103 Penang Road, #05-06/07, Visioncrest Commercial, Singapore 238467

Cambridge University Press is part of Cambridge University Press & Assessment, a department of the University of Cambridge.

We share the University's mission to contribute to society through the pursuit of education, learning and research at the highest international levels of excellence.

www.cambridge.org
Information on this title: www.cambridge.org/9781009268776

DOI: 10.1017/9781009268790

First published 2023

Printed in the United Kingdom by CPI Group Ltd, Croydon CR0 4YY

A catalogue record for this publication is available from the British Library.

Library of Congress Cataloging-in-Publication Data
NAMES: Hunter, Michael, 1949– author.
TITLE: Atheists and atheism before the Enlightenment : the English and Scottish experience / Michael Hunter.
DESCRIPTION: Cambridge ; New York, NY : Cambridge University Press, 2023. | Includes bibliographical references and index.
IDENTIFIERS: LCCN 2023008157 (print) | LCCN 2023008158 (ebook) | ISBN 9781009268776 (hardback) | ISBN 9781009268769 (paperback) | ISBN 9781009268790 (epub)
SUBJECTS: LCSH: Atheism–England–History. | Atheism–Scotland–History. | Atheists–England. | Atheists–Scotland. | Great Britain–History–1066-1687. | Great Britain–Religion.
CLASSIFICATION: LCC BL2765.G7 H86 2023 (print) | LCC BL2765.G7 (ebook) | DDC 211/.80942–DC23/eng/20230322
LC record available at https://lccn.loc.gov/2023008157
LC ebook record available at https://lccn.loc.gov/2023008158

ISBN 978-1-009-26877-6 Hardback

Contents

Acknowledgements   *page* vi

1 Introduction: The Nature of Atheism and the Assurance
   of Atheists   1

2 The Problem of 'Atheism' in Early Modern England   33

3 Atheism among the Godly: The Covert History of
   Religious Doubt   57

4 'This degenerate Age ... so miserably over-run with
   Scepticism and *Infidelity*': The Culture of Atheism after 1660   73

5 'Aikenhead the Atheist': The Context and Consequences of
   Articulate Irreligion in the Late Seventeenth Century   94

6 An Atheist Text by Archibald Pitcairne: Introduction to
   Pitcairneana   123

7 The Text of *Pitcairneana*: Houghton Library, Harvard, MS
   Eng 1114   144

8 The Trial of Tinkler Ducket: Atheism and Libertinism in
   Eighteenth-Century England   158

9 Conclusion   178

Bibliography   190
Index   218

Acknowledgements

The publishing status of the chapters of this book is as follows:

1   Hitherto unpublished
2   Previously published in *Transactions of the Royal Historical Society*, 5th series 35 (1985), 135–57. Updated with revised notes and comments
3   Hitherto unpublished
4   Hitherto unpublished
5   Originally published in Michael Hunter and David Wootton (eds.), *Atheism from the Reformation to the Enlightenment* (Oxford: Clarendon Press, 1992), pp. 221–54, and reprinted in Michael Hunter, *Science and the Shape of Orthodoxy: Intellectual Change in Late Seventeenth-Century Britain* (Woodbridge: Boydell Press, 1995), pp. 308–32.
    © Oxford Publishing Limited. Reproduced with permission of the Licensor through PLSclear. In the current version, the footnotes have been slightly updated
6   Largely published in the *Historical Journal*, 59 (2016), 595–607.
    © Cambridge University Press; reprinted with permission. Material has been added from Michael Hunter, 'Archibald Pitcairne: Heterodoxy and Its Milieu in Late Seventeenth- and Early Eighteenth-Century Edinburgh', in Anja-Silvia Goeing, Glynn Parry and Mordechai Feingold (eds.), *Early Modern Universities: Networks of Higher Learning* (Leiden: Brill, 2021), pp. 281–94; this appears here with due acknowledgement
7   Published in the *Historical Journal*, 59 (2016), 607–21. © Cambridge University Press; reprinted with permission
8   Hitherto unpublished; to appear in Alex Barber and Katherine A. East (eds.), *Politics and Religion: Republicanism, Radical Ideas, and the Crisis of Christianity c. 1640–1740. Essays in Honour of Justin A. I. Champion* (Woodbridge: Boydell & Brewer, forthcoming)
9   Hitherto unpublished

Acknowledgements are recorded at the start of each chapter that has already been published and in Chapter 8. In addition, I am indebted to Peter Anstey, David Bebbington, Stephen Brogan, Callum Brown, Sue Dale, Edward B. Davis, Claire Foster-Gilbert and Anthony Turner for comments on hitherto unpublished material. I am also grateful to various of these for discussions of related topics that have helped shape my ideas; to Gerard Willemsen for an illuminating conversation about atheism some years ago, and to Frederick and Margaret Lock for perceptive comments on the project. Tristram Clarke's assistance with Scottish source material has been invaluable. At Cambridge University Press, I am greatly indebted to Liz Friend-Smith and, through her, to the Press's anonymous readers. Robert Holden has been an effective copy editor. I have also benefitted from advice from such colleagues and friends as the late lamented Justin Champion, Mark Goldie, Wayne Hudson, Will Poole and Alex Walsham.

Note: Quotations from manuscripts retain original spelling, capitalisation and punctuation; standard contractions (e.g. the thorn with superscript 'e' for 'the') have been silently expanded. Underlining in the original is shown by the use of italic. Editorial insertions have been denoted by square brackets. Words or phrases inserted above the line in the original have been denoted ‹thus›, and deletions are recorded in footnotes. However, in cases where a full transcription is already available in print, insertions and deletions have sometimes been silently ignored.

CHAPTER I

Introduction
The Nature of Atheism and the Assurance of Atheists

a   The Nature of Atheism

My Lord, if any heere can proove there is a God, I will beleeue it.

So, it was claimed, an unnamed 'atheist' 'openly and impudently' challenged Richard Bancroft, Bishop of London, at a London court in 1599.[1] It is a striking statement, bold, provocative and enticing. Unfortunately, it is impossible retrospectively to elucidate it. The episode was recorded in passing, in connection with the controversy over the exorcisms carried out in the late Elizabethan period by the Puritan cleric, John Darrell. The author was one of Darrell's sympathisers, who referred briefly to the incident in order to illustrate how atheists like this should have been the target of Bancroft's zeal, as a means of criticising him and other members of the establishment for their persecution of Darrell for his supposed gifts.[2] Sadly, however, this passing reference is all that we will ever know about it.

Yet it introduces the issue that lies at the heart of the current volume. In contrast to the man who confronted Bancroft, about whom we know virtually nothing, there are a handful of cases in the early modern period where we are fortunate enough to have full information about the views and milieu of 'atheists', men who launched an explicit attack on the Christian religion and offered an alternative, irreligious view of the world. In two instances, these involved trials: one of the student Thomas Aikenhead, whose case was decided by the Scottish Privy Council and who was executed for his atheist views in 1697; the other of the youthful cleric Tinkler Ducket, who was arraigned before the Vice-Chancellor's court at the University of Cambridge in 1739. The third example involves the medical savant Archibald Pitcairne, who flourished in Edinburgh at the

---

[1] *The Triall of Maist. Dorrell* (Middelburg, 1599), p. 88.
[2] Marion Gibson, *Possession, Puritanism and Print: Darrell, Harsnett, Shakespeare and the Elizabethan Exorcism Controversy* (London, 2006), esp. pp. 66–8.

same time as Aikenhead and who left behind him an extraordinary dialogue, *Pitcairneana*, which advocates a fully atheistic viewpoint. In these rare instances, sufficient evidence survives to provide the basis for a detailed case study of the episode involved, and this is provided in various of the chapters that follow, using the micro-history approach that I have already fruitfully adopted in various articles and books.[3] From these examples, one arguably learns much about the rationale and setting of the irreligious views to which the individuals in question gave expression. Moreover, such fully documented cases may be supplemented by tantalising clues concerning other, more shadowy figures who we will encounter in the pages that follow, and by similar accusations made against better-known individuals like Christopher Marlowe in Elizabethan England and the Earl of Rochester after the Restoration.

Such men were undoubtedly responsible for assertive, destructive statements of anti-Christian sentiment, which make it is easy to understand why contemporaries thought it appropriate to use the term 'atheist' to describe them. We may start with Marlowe's view 'that the first beginning of Religioun was only to keep men in awe' or his knowing assertion that the Jews knew best who to crucify.[4] We continue to Rochester's opinion that devotions were 'the Inventions of Priests, to make the World believe they had a secret of Incensing and Appeasing God as they pleased', and his scepticism about the Bible and the 'boldness and cunning' of those responsible for it.[5] Then there are Aikenhead's gibes against 'the History of the Impostor Christ' and his dismissal of the Old Testament as 'Ezra's fables', which achieved real notoriety during the Enlightenment.[6] We also have his confident assertion that Christianity would be extinct by 1800.[7] In the case of Tinkler Ducket, he gloried in reaching 'the Top, the *ne plus ultra*' of atheism and spoke with great assurance about the views that he had held while he was an atheist.[8] The climax is represented by the fully atheistic position with real coherence and sophistication put forward in

---

[3] For a brief account of the rationale, see Michael Hunter, *Science and the Shape of Orthodoxy: Intellectual Change in Late Seventeenth-Century Britain* (Woodbridge, 1995), Introduction, esp. pp. 1–2, 11–18; *The Decline of Magic: Britain in the Enlightenment* (New Haven and London, 2020), esp. pp. 4, 167–8.

[4] Constance B. Kuriyama, *Christopher Marlowe: A Renaissance Life* (Ithaca, 2002), p. 221.

[5] Gilbert Burnet, *Some Passages of the Life and Death of the Right Hon. John Earl of Rochester* (London, 1680), pp. 53, 72–3.

[6] See Noel Malcolm, *Aspects of Hobbes* (Oxford, 2002), pp. 383–6; this volume, pp. 97–8, 121.

[7] See pp. 98, 122. It is also worth noting the associated case of the apprentice, John Frazer, accused of expressing various irreligious opinions, 'And when asked what religion he could be off that held such principles he answered of no religion at all but was just ane Atheist', p. 111.

[8] See pp. 162, 166–7.

Pitcairneana, attributed to Archibald Pitcairne and presented in Chapter 7. Whereas the viewpoint presented there was clearly carefully thought out, some of the other recorded statements may not have been so systematic. Nevertheless, it is easy to understand the outrage that such incendiary utterances were bound to cause in the deeply theistic culture in which they were expressed, and the term 'atheist' well summarises their aggressive and confrontational manner.

Yet it needs to be emphasised at the outset just how rare such examples are. Obviously, the judicial execution of Aikenhead illustrated the dangers of publicly expressing such views, and others were clearly well advised to be more discreet in putting forward opinions of this kind. Yet the fact of the matter is that assiduous research has failed to bring to light more than scattered examples of other figures who fall into a similar category. The earliest work to be published in Britain which openly argued for a fully atheist position came out only in 1745: this took the form of a book titled *The Origin of Moral Virtue and Religion Arraigned*, of which Roger Maioli has recently discovered an apparently unique copy once owned by Horace Walpole, and which he has tentatively attributed to Lord Hervey.[9] Atheists in the early modern period turn out to be extremely hard to find.

This makes it all the more paradoxical that concern about the threat presented by atheism dominated the thought of British, as of European, intellectuals throughout the early modern period. Famously, the French Minim monk Marin Mersenne claimed in 1623 that there were 50,000 atheists in Paris alone, a claim that was echoed by Robert Burton in his encyclopedic *Anatomy of Melancholy* (1621 and subsequent editions).[10] There are comparable estimates as far as Britain is concerned. From the claim of the Elizabethan littérateur Thomas Nashe, that 'There is no Sect now in *England* so scattered as Atheisme' to the view of the Calvinist divine John Edwards in 1695 that 'there is scarcely a Town where there are not some that may justly be reckon'd in this number', contemporaries were unanimous in their sense of the scale and perniciousness of the threat

---

[9] See Roger Maioli, 'The First Avowed British Atheist: Lord Hervey?', *Eighteenth-Century Studies*, 54 (2021), 357–79. This supersedes the earlier claim by David Berman that the first openly atheist book was Matthew Turner's *An Answer to Dr Priestley's Letter to a Philosophical Unbeliever* (1782) (see Berman, *A History of Atheism in Britain: From Hobbes to Russell* (London, 1988), pp. 110–20), unless *The Origin of Moral Virtue* was in fact ironically intended, a possibility that Maioli does not discuss.

[10] Robert Burton, *The Anatomy of Melancholy*, ed. T. C. Faulkner, N. K. Kiessling and R. L. Blair, 6 vols (Oxford, 1989–2000), III, 405. For Mersenne's statement (and his removal of it from later editions of the book in question), see Adam Horsley, *Libertines and the Law: Subversive Authors and Criminal Justice in Early Seventeenth-Century France* (Oxford, 2021), p. 59 and n. 149.

that they faced.[11] Volume after volume poured from the press expounding and excoriating the supposed atheist menace, and this literature has been the subject of intense scrutiny by modern scholars.[12] It was also for this reason that the great scientist Robert Boyle made provision in his will for the endowment of what proved to be a highly influential series of Lectures 'for proving the Christian Religion against Atheists and Theists [i.e., Deists] descending no lower to any Controversies that are among Christians'.[13]

How, therefore, is this major discrepancy between the scale of concern and the evidence of actual irreligion to be explained? Here, various points need to be made. In the first place, it is necessary to understand that 'atheism' was at the same time a concept – almost an abstract one – and potentially a description of a phenomenon. For Richard Hooker in his classic *Laws of Ecclesiastical Polity* (1593–7), 'affected Atheism' was 'the most extreme opposite to true Religion', and it is important to appreciate the role of antitheses in early modern thought, the need to evoke and elaborate contrary positions to explicate and make sense of deeply held beliefs.[14] This has been demonstrated with particular clarity by Stuart Clark in his magisterial study of witchcraft, who has made clear the extent to which contemporaries used inversion to understand the witches' sabbat and related phenomena, elaborating a world of misrule to illustrate the virtues of order. As James I succinctly put it, 'since the Devill is the verie

---

[11] Thomas Nashe, *Works*, ed. R. B. McKerrow, 2nd ed., 5 vols (Oxford, 1958), II, 121–2; John Edwards, *Some Thoughts Concerning the Several Causes and Occasions of Atheism* (London, 1695), p. 132.

[12] Most recently, see Kenneth Sheppard, *Anti-Atheism in Early Modern England 1580–1720. The Atheist Answered and His Error Confuted* (Leiden, 2015). A general account is provided by *Atheism from the Reformation to the Enlightenment*, ed. Michael Hunter and David Wootton (Oxford, 1992). For earlier studies, see D. C. Allen, *Doubt's Boundless Sea: Skepticism and Faith in the Renaissance* (Baltimore, 1964); G. E. Aylmer, 'Unbelief in Seventeenth-Century England', in *Puritans and Revolutionaries: Essays in Seventeenth-Century History Presented to Christopher Hill*, ed. D. H. Pennington and Keith Thomas (Oxford, 1978), pp. 22–46; Berman, *History of Atheism*. See also Sarah Ellensweig, *The Fringes of Belief: English Literature, Ancient Heresy, and the Politics of Freethinking, 1660–1760* (Stanford, 2008) and Roger D. Lund, *Ridicule, Religion and the Politics of Wit in Augustan England* (Farnham, 2012). For France, see Horsley, *Libertines and the Law* and the works by Alan C. Kors listed in n. 16.

[13] Quoted from the memorandum in the hand of Gilbert Burnet which clearly represents the original notion for the lectureship in *Robert Boyle by Himself and His Friends*, ed. Michael Hunter (London, 1994), p. xxv. In Boyle's will, the rubric was slightly elaborated to include 'Pagans, Jews and Mahometans': see Michael Hunter, *Boyle: Between God and Science* (New Haven and London, 2009), pp. 240–1.

[14] Richard Hooker, *Of the Laws of Ecclesiastical Polity*, ed. A. S. McGrade, 3 vols (Oxford, 2013), II, 13.

contrarie opposite to God, there can be no better way to know God, then by the contrarie'.[15]

Much the same is true of atheism, as has been illustrated most brilliantly by Alan Kors in relation to late seventeenth- and early eighteenth-century France, where he has argued that, in the course of deploying such tactics, a whole armoury of atheist arguments was forged by orthodox thinkers. In Kors's words, such authors knew that there 'had to be an "atheism" in the form of atheistic argumentation, whether or not there were any minds who actually held to or proselytized for such a point of view ... If atheism in that sense did not exist, the members of the learned world would have had to invent it'.[16] There is a real sense in which the word was used in the period almost as an abstraction, a theoretical concept to describe a godless universe which, however unthinkable in practice, it was frighteningly possible to construct by means of the inexorable logic encouraged by scholastic modes of thought. The matter was well summarised by the English divine Thomas Barlow in a letter to Robert Boyle in which, discussing the assertion of another cleric, John Turner, that Descartes was an atheist (a claim often made at the time, which was as often refuted), Barlow explained: 'I suppose he does not meane, that Des Cartes is a profess'd Atheist, soe as to deny the beeinge of a Deity; but that it will follow from his avowed principles, that there is noe God'.[17]

On the other hand, the ancillary term 'atheists' was also used to describe people whom it was claimed actually held such views, and herein arises a degree of complication. There were those who denied that any 'true' atheists existed, including men against whom atheist accusations were made. Thus, Bishop Gilbert Burnet recorded how the Earl of Rochester 'professed often to me, That he had never known an entire *Atheist*, who fully believed there was no God', while John Wagstaffe, a Restoration freethinker who had to respond to accusations that he was an atheist, not only denied this but went on: 'Nor did I ever meet with an Atheist in all

---

[15] Stuart Clark, *Thinking with Demons. The Idea of Witchcraft in Early Modern Europe* (Oxford, 1997), p. 137.

[16] Kors, *Atheism in France 1650–1729. Volume 1: The Orthodox Sources of Disbelief* (Princeton, 1990), p. 81. See also his *Naturalism and Unbelief in France, 1650–1729* (Cambridge, 2016) and his ancillary study, *Epicureans and Atheists in France, 1650–1729* (Cambridge, 2016). For the related argument that apologists like the Boyle lecturer Samuel Clarke effectively sold the pass on religion by conducting their defence of it almost wholly in philosophical rather than theological terms, see Michael J. Buckley, *At the Origins of Modern Atheism* (New Haven and London, 1987); see also his *Denying and Disclosing God: The Ambiguous Progress of Modern Atheism* (New Haven and London, 2004).

[17] Barlow to Boyle, 29 November 1684, in *The Correspondence of Robert Boyle*, ed. Michael Hunter, Antonio Clericuzio and Lawrence M. Principe, 6 vols (London, 2001), VI, 93.

my life, as to my own knowledge; and therefore am apt to believe, that those who are recorded such in History, were rather reputed then, real Atheists'.[18] Other contemporaries agreed that the word could be used as a term of abuse, like the Latitudinarian divine Joseph Glanvill, who claimed that 'the Charge of *Atheism*, is like the bolt of one that throws *hard words* in *haste*, and without aim or judgment' – though this did not prevent him from frequently using the accusation himself.[19]

Glanvill's claim has been echoed by modern authors such as Leonard W. Levy, who has argued that 'the term "atheist" was little more than a dirty word', or Margaret C. Jacob, who has claimed that this and similar words 'were bandied about so much that they lost all useful meaning'.[20] Indeed, it is easy to understand the frustration concerning our knowledge of the nature and extent of the atheist threat in the period expressed by David Berman in the first book-length study of its subject, *A History of Atheism in Britain: From Hobbes to Russell* (1988). As he there pointed out concerning George T. Buckley's promising-sounding *Atheism in the English Renaissance*, published in 1932 and reprinted in 1965: 'Despite his title, Buckley is unable to find any atheism during the period', and Berman continued:

> A similar judgement can be passed on John Redwood's study of the period 1660 to 1750, *Reason, Ridicule and Religion* (London, 1976). Throughout the book we read of the 'atheist scare', 'atheist question', 'atheist plot'; but the author never examines the simple but central question: Were there any avowedly atheistic books published in the seventeenth or eighteenth centuries?[21]

It did not help that, for much of the twentieth century, a powerful historiography prevailed which denied that atheism existed at all in the sixteenth century, by extension also throwing doubt on the validity of the concept in relation to the seventeenth. This was associated particularly with the influential polemic by the annalist historian Lucien Febvre, *Le*

---

[18] Burnet, *Some Passages*, p. 22; Wagstaffe, *The Question of Witchcraft Debated*, 2nd ed. (London, 1671), pp. 151–2, quoted in Hunter, *Decline of Magic*, p. 41.

[19] Glanvill, *Plus Ultra* (London, 1668), sig. A7. For his use of the accusation, see Hunter, *Decline of Magic*, pp. 19, 24, 28–9, 39, 41, 103–4.

[20] Leonard W. Levy, *Blasphemy: Verbal Offense against the Sacred, from Moses to Salman Rushdie* (New York, 1993), p. 279; M. C. Jacob, *The Newtonians and the English Revolution 1689–1720* (Hassocks, 1976), p. 202.

[21] Berman, *History of Atheism*, p. 46, n. 37 ('there' is accidently misprinted as 'they'). It is perhaps worth pointing out that Redwood's *Reason, Ridicule and Religion: The Age of Enlightenment in England 1660–1750* was reprinted in 1996 with some of its more egregious misprints and other infelicities corrected, though its overall thrust is unchanged.

problème de l'incroyance au XVIe siècle: La religion de Rabelais (1942),
translated into English in 1982 as *The Problem of Unbelief in the
Sixteenth Century: The Religion of Rabelais*. This is undoubtedly a brilliant
and thought-provoking book, but it could be argued that in it Febvre was
himself guilty of the kind of anachronistic thinking that he castigated in
others in his presumption that the only possible route to atheism was post-
Cartesian philosophy and science. As David Wootton has pointed out, the
combination of Febvre's influence with a reaction against 'Whig' history
and an increased scrupulousness concerning evidence led to a diffidence on
the part of historians about labelling figures in the past as atheists, almost
as if this were a form of character assassination.[22]

On the other hand, the argument that atheists were non-existent is not
only at odds with the proliferation of anti-atheist polemic in the period
that has already been described; it was also specifically countered by
contemporaries themselves. A clear example is provided by the
Cambridge divine Ralph Cudworth in his magisterial work, *The True
Intellectual System of the Universe* (1678). In the concluding paragraph of
his 'Preface to the Reader', Cudworth wrote:

> We are not Ignorant, That some will be ready to condemn this whole
> Labour of ours, and of others in this Kind, Against *Atheism*, as altogether
> Useless and Superfluous; upon this Pretence, that an *Atheist* is a meer
> *Chimæra*, and there is no such thing any-where to be found in the
> World. And indeed we could heartily wish, upon that condition, that all
> this Labour of ours, were *Superfluous* and *Useless*. But as to *Atheists*, These so
> confident *Exploders* of them, are both Unskilled in the *Monuments* of
> *Antiquity*, and Unacquainted with the Present Age, they live in; others
> having found too great an Assurance, from their own *Personal Converse*, of
> the *Reality* of Them.[23]

Cudworth's allusion to 'the *Monuments* of *Antiquity*' provides us with
one crucial clue. There was a sense of contemporaneity with the classics,
and a proclivity to cross-reference to them at every point, which needs to
be borne in mind: as Alan Kors has pointed out in relation to French
writings in the period, 'it is difficult to exaggerate the "presence" in early-

---

[22] David Wootton, 'New Histories of Atheism', in Hunter and Wootton, *Atheism from the
Reformation to the Enlightenment*, pp. 13–53 (pp. 15–21). See also his important studies, 'Lucien
Febvre and the Problem of Unbelief in the Early Modern Period', *Journal of Modern History*, 60
(1988), 695–730; 'Unbelief in Early Modern Europe', *History Workshop Journal*, 20 (1985),
82–100, and *Paolo Sarpi: Between Renaissance and Enlightenment* (Cambridge, 1983).

[23] Ralph Cudworth, *The True Intellectual System of the Universe* (London, 1678), sig. ***2v. Cudworth
went on to assert his ancillary aim of helping in 'the Confirmation of *Weak, Staggering*, and
Scepticall Theists'.

modern minds of classical and patristic thought'.[24] This has more recently and fully been demonstrated in relation to the English state of affairs by Dmitri Levitin in his *Ancient Wisdom in the Age of the New Science* (2015), which has illustrated how passionately Cudworth and others revisited the literature of antiquity in their lengthy discussions of matter theory and related topics, and their pursuit of a view of nature that was at the same time safe and compatible with orthodox Christianity.[25]

On the other hand, Cudworth speaks equally knowingly of his acquaintance with 'the Present Age', including his '*Personal Converse*' with those who espoused opinions of the kind that caused him concern, and this presents us with more of a challenge. In order to understand this, and particularly his reference to views orally expressed, we need to look more deeply and imaginatively at his and his fellow authors' usage in order to understand the phenomenon in question and how it related to trends in the thought of the period more generally. In particular, it may be argued that the accusation of atheism could be used to denote extremes in the styles of naturalistic and secularist explanation that, in a less extreme form, were pervasive in the thought of the time, and this is a topic which it is particularly important to understand.

Thus, in his 1669 attack on atheism, the politician and author Sir Charles Wolseley had no doubt that a crucial factor in the growth of irreligion had been 'The general revival of, and the great applause that hath, of late, been given to such Philosophical notions, as broadly and directly lead this way'.[26] He was clearly referring to the flourishing new science of the period, and it is noteworthy how defensive in tone the writings on behalf of the new philosophy in the late seventeenth century often were, notwithstanding the deep piety of many of its practitioners. 'I cannot deny, but that some *Philosophers*, by their carelessness of a Future Estate, have brought a discredit on *Knowledge* itself', wrote Thomas Sprat in his *History of the Royal Society* (1667), and a concern about the potentially irreligious connotations of the study of nature was echoed by the scientists themselves.[27] Even Robert Boyle was anxious to show 'that, if I be a Naturalist, 'tis possible to be so, without being an Atheist, or of Kin to it'; he was equally clear in hoping that his work, *The Christian Virtuoso*

[24] Kors, *Atheism in France*, p. 197.
[25] Levitin, *Ancient Wisdom in the Age of the New Science. Histories of Philosophy in England, c. 1640–1700* (Cambridge, 2015), esp. ch. 5.
[26] Wolseley, *The Unreasonablenesse of Atheism Made Manifest* (London, 1669), p. 37.
[27] Sprat, *The History of the Royal Society of London* (London, 1667), p. 375. For background, see Hunter, *Science and Society in Restoration England* (Cambridge, 1981), ch. 7.

(1690–1), would demonstrate 'That there is no Inconsistence between a Man's being an Industrious *Virtuoso,* and a Good *Christian*'.[28] This placed an even greater premium on the Boyle Lectures that Boyle founded to use scientific findings to attack irreligion, an objective with which Richard Bentley and his successors obligingly complied.[29]

More broadly, accusations of atheism reflected concern about an overwhelming this-worldliness, an appeal to commonsensical values and to sceptical, reductionist principles. Here, a case in point is provided by John Wagstaffe, the very figure whose denial of the existence of atheists was quoted earlier in this chapter. Wagstaffe was a typical example of the culture of 'freethinking' that flourished in the Restoration period, and his book, *The Question of Witchcraft Debated* (1669), well illustrates the deflationary, rather cynical discourse that was often the target of atheist accusations like that made against him. Wagstaffe took the view that witchcraft beliefs had deliberately been promoted by rulers and priests in antiquity and the Middle Ages, the entire superstructure of such beliefs being encouraged by human deceit and misapprehension, 'the folly of some, or the knavery of others'.[30] He thus well exemplified the attitude excoriated by Joseph Glanvill, who took the view that 'those that dare not bluntly say, *There is NO GOD*, content themselves, (for a fair *step*, and *Introduction*) to deny there are *SPIRITS*, or *WITCHES*'. In Wagstaffe's case, he also held other questionable opinions, even expressing the view that 'the various Religions that have been in the world, are more than enough to convince one, how absurd and ridiculous the wisest of men are in matters of Opinion or Belief'.[31]

In terms of religious doctrine, it is hardly surprising that atheist accusations were often made against those who challenged Christian orthodoxy by espousing a religion that appealed to reason, rejecting components of doctrine which were seen as incompatible with this. A case in point are the Socinians, a radical group which originated in sixteenth-century Italy before becoming established in Poland and then spreading first to the Netherlands and thence to England, who argued for a scaled-down,

---

[28] Boyle, *Works*, ed. Michael Hunter and Edward B. Davis, 14 vols (London, 1999–2000), II, 389; XI, 283.

[29] For recent studies see Pierre Lurbe, 'La réfutation de l'athéism par Richard Bentley', in *La question de l'athéism au dix-huitieme siècle*, ed. Sylvia Taussig and Pierre Lurbe (Turnhout, 2004), pp. 157–72, and Paul C. H. Lim, 'Atheism, Atoms, and the Activity of God: Science and Religion in Early Boyle Lectures, 1692–1707', *Zygon*, 56 (2021), 143–67. On the genre of physico-theology as a whole see now Kaspar von Greyerz, *European Physico-Theology (1650–c. 1760) in Context: Celebrating Nature and Creation* (Oxford, 2022).

[30] Hunter, *Decline of Magic*, ch. 1, esp. p. 38.   [31] Ibid., pp. 24, 39.

rationalistic religion, denying both the Trinity and the divinity of Christ. In the view of John Edwards, there was a definite '*Atheistick* Tang' to Socinian views, and, from the early seventeenth century onwards, those who held such opinions were widely attacked as dangerously undermining the key precepts of the Christian faith.[32]

This was equally true of the movement in late seventeenth- and eighteenth-century England known as Deism, which has been the subject of extensive and ongoing scrutiny.[33] Undoubtedly, those described as Deists – such men as Charles Blount, John Toland and Anthony Collins – represented an extreme attack on accepted Christian principles which was often perceived at the time as a highroad to atheism. Indeed, Richard Bentley in his Boyle Lectures accused such men of fomenting overt irreligion, arguing that 'to avoid the odious name of *Atheists*, [such thinkers] would shelter and screen themselves under a new one of *Deists*, which is not quite so obnoxious'.[34] There is in fact some ambiguity concerning the extent to which certain of these men, notably Collins, might be accused of being actual, if concealed, atheists, a vexed question which it is probably in retrospect impossible to resolve.[35] On the other hand, matters are complicated by the breadth of usage of the word 'Deism', since those frequently described as Deists held a wide range of doctrines. Indeed, there is a sense in which both contemporaries and historians have used the term as a kind of 'fudge', 'a matter of convenience

---

[32] Edwards, *Some Thoughts*, p. 64. See H. J. McLachlan, *Socinianism in Seventeenth-Century England* (Oxford, 1951); Sarah Mortimer, *Reason and Religion in the English Revolution: The Challenge of Socinianism* (Cambridge, 2010); Paul C. H. Lim, *Mystery Unveiled: The Crisis of the Trinity in Early Modern England* (Oxford, 2012).

[33] For some of the principal studies see R. E. Sullivan, *John Toland and the Deist Controversy* (Cambridge, MA., 1982); Justin A. I. Champion, *The Pillars of Priestcraft Shaken: The Church and England and its Enemies, 1660–1730* (Cambridge, 1992) and *Republican Learning: John Toland and the Crisis of Christian Culture, 1696–1722* (Manchester, 2003); Isabel Rivers, *Reason, Grace and Sentiment: A Study of the Language of Religion and Ethics in England, 1660–1780*, 2 vols (Cambridge, 1991–2000), II, ch. 1; Wayne Hudson, *The English Deists: Studies in Early Enlightenment* (London, 2009) and *Enlightenment and Modernity: The English Deists and Reform* (London, 2009); and Jeffrey Wigelsworth, *Deism in Enlightenment England: Theology, Politics and Newtonian Public Science* (Manchester, 2009). The Deists also figure in Jonathan Israel's magisterial *Radical Enlightenment: Philosophy and the Making of Modernity 1650–1750* (Oxford, 2001); see also his *Enlightenment Contested: Philosophy, Modernity and the Emancipation of Man 1670–1752* (Oxford, 2006) and his *The Enlightenment that Failed: Ideas, Revolution and Democratic Defeat 1748–1830* (Oxford, 2019), esp. ch. 5.

[34] Bentley, *Works*, ed. Alexander Dyce, 3 vols (London, 1836–8), III, 4.

[35] See esp. Berman, *History of Atheism*, ch. 3, Pascal Taranto, *Du déism à l'athéisme: La libre-pensée d'Anthony Collins* (Paris, 2000) and Giovanni Tarantino, 'Collins's Cicero, Freethinker', in *Atheism and Deism Revalued: Heterodox Religious Identities in Britain, 1650–1800*, ed. Wayne Hudson, Diego Lucci and J. R. Wigelsworth (Farnham, 2014), pp. 81–99.

rather than an aid to analysis', to quote the words of Robert E. Sullivan in one of the most profound accounts of this topic.[36] Scholars have rightly expressed doubts about exaggerating the extent to which such men were on the highroad to atheism, as against expressing an outspoken hostility towards priestcraft and clerisy.[37] In particular, an important distinction has been made between so-called 'providentialist' Deists – men like William Wollaston, Matthew Tindal, Thomas Chubb and Thomas Morgan – who, while insisting on the existence of a universal natural religion, nevertheless claimed that this had been reasserted by Christ, as against others like Blount, Toland or Collins, whose thought tended more directly in an atheistic direction.[38] The existence of such 'Christian Deists' undoubtedly complicates the picture, even if they shared the overwhelming emphasis on the role of reason in religion, and the hostility to clerical power and pretensions, which characterised Deism as a whole.

Here, it is worth pausing on one specific figure, the Third Earl of Shaftesbury – sometimes classified as a Deist, sometimes not[39] – who, in his *Inquiry Concerning Virtue or Merit* (1699), questioned the dependency of morality on Christianity, thus echoing the argument earlier put forward by the Huguenot Pierre Bayle in his *Miscellaneous Reflections on the Comet of 1680* (1682) that a society of virtuous atheists was perfectly possible.[40] In this, both men took the important step of challenging the presumption that had previously been almost axiomatic among orthodox thinkers that atheism was as pernicious in its 'practical' as in its 'speculative' mode, in that it was inevitably associated with immorality. As the future Archbishop of Canterbury Thomas Tenison put it in 1691:

> Immorality is the beginning of Atheism, and Atheism is the strengthning of Immorality . . . . For Atheism begins, not from the Arguments of a sound

[36] Sullivan, *Toland and the Deist Controversy*, p. 232.

[37] See Wayne Hudson, Diego Lucci and J. R. Wigelsworth, 'Introduction: Atheism and Deism Revived', and Wayne Hudson, 'Atheism and Deism Demythologized', in Hudson, Lucci and Wigelsworth, *Atheism and Deism Revalued*, pp. 1–11, 13–23, esp. Hudson, 'Atheism and Deism Demythologized', pp. 20–1.

[38] See Diego Lucci and Jeffrey R. Wigelsworth, '"God does not act arbitrarily, or interpose unnecessarily": Providential Deism and the Denial of Miracles in Wollaston, Tindal, Chubb and Morgan', *Intellectual History Review*, 25 (2015), 167–89.

[39] His status as a Deist is questioned by Hudson, *Enlightenment and Modernity*, pp. 151–2, but this runs against the prevailing historiography as outlined in the next note.

[40] On Shaftesbury, including his relations with Bayle, see Sheppard, *Anti-Atheism in Early Modern England*, ch. 8; Rivers, *Reason, Grace and Sentiment*, II, esp. ch. 2–3, and Lawrence Klein, *Shaftesbury and the Culture of Politeness: Moral Discourse and Cultural Politics in Early Eighteenth-Century England* (Cambridge, 1994), ch. 2. See also A. O. Aldridge 'Shaftesbury and the Deist Manifesto', *Transactions of the American Philosophical Society*, n.s. 41 (1951), 297–385.

Mind in a sober Temper, but in a sensual Disposition, which inclines Men to seek out for colours, whereby they may deceive themselves into an opinion of the safety of living in a course that pleases them.[41]

Obviously, orthodox spokesmen had an incentive to emphasise this aspect of the phenomenon, whether or not it was justified by the actual behaviour of supposed atheists. By contrast, Bayle and Shaftesbury argued for the naturalness of a moral sense in all rational beings, a view with huge significance in the longer term.

Of course, the orthodox were not easily convinced of this, and the argument of the pernicious nature of 'practical' atheism continued for much longer – even into the nineteenth century.[42] Throughout our period, the term atheist was often used in an inclusive sense, to describe what was in effect immoral behaviour, on the grounds that a moral sense was dependent on Christianity, with its promise of a future state of rewards and punishments. Indeed, it is not surprising that a word that was often used as a virtual synonym for 'atheism' was 'libertinism', which in modern usage clearly denotes debauchery, but in its earlier emanations – for instance in seventeenth-century France – was often taken to denote the expression of anti-Christian sentiment as much as immoral behaviour, on the grounds of the interrelatedness of 'speculative' and 'practical' irreligion that has already been indicated.[43]

Through such usage, the concept of 'atheism' could become yet more invidious, since it might even be applied to believers, or those who thought that they were believers, themselves. At this point, the remit of the term extended almost infinitesimally, potentially being used to describe the misdemeanours and doubts even of practising Christians. Here, it is helpful to turn to an apologetic volume by an influential religious writer, the Presbyterian divine Richard Baxter, titled *The Reasons of the Christian Religion* (1667), which, tellingly, was furnished with three separate prefaces. One was 'To the Christian Reader', the second '*To the Doubting and the Unbelieving* Readers', and the third 'To the Hypocrite Readers; Who have the Name of *Christians*, and the Hearts and Lives of *Atheists* and *Unbelievers*', and it is worth analysing Baxter's rationale in this.[44] Perhaps the most striking is the third, to the 'Hypocrite Readers', whom he

---

[41] Tenison, *A Sermon Concerning the Folly of Atheism* (London, 1691), pp. 15–16.

[42] See Nathan Alexander, 'Defining and Redefining Atheism: Dictionary and Encyclopedia Entries for "Atheism" and their Critics in the Anglophone World from the Early Modern Period to the Present', *Intellectual History Review*, 30 (2020), 253–71 (p. 263).

[43] For a helpful recent discussion see Horsley, *Libertines and the Law*, ch. 1.

[44] Baxter, *The Reasons of the Christian Religion* (London, 1667), sigs A3–4, (a)–(b), (c)1–2.

excoriated for the fact that, notwithstanding 'the great Mercy of God to you, that you were born of Christian Parents, and in a Land where Christianity is the professed Religion, and under Governors and Laws which countenance it ... you banished it from your Hearts and Lives'. 'Believe it, Hypocrites', he continued: 'your fornications, gluttony, drunkennesse, idlenesse, covetousnesse, selfishnesse, or pride, will find no Cloak in the day of Judgement, from the Christian name'. For all their professed piety, therefore, it was imperative for such erring sinners to mend their ways.

In his preface to the 'Christian Reader' Baxter repeated much of this while also referring to the effect of the disputes among the religious that had characterised Europe since the Reformation and the Counter-Reformation of the sixteenth century, noting how 'we have had hot and scandalous Disputes among Christians, *de Resolutione Fidei;* each Party invaliding the others Foundations, as if it had been our work to perswade the Infidel World, that *they* are in the right.' Moreover, both here and in the preface to '*the Doubting and the Unbelieving* Readers', he referred to the extent to which believers might be plagued by doubt. In Baxter's words, 'Too many good Christians, especially if Melancholy surprise them, are haunted with such temptations, to Atheisme, blasphemy and unbelief, as make their lives a burden to them!' He even identified 'the most perilous age' for infidelity as between eighteen and twenty-eight years of age, when people 'first grow to a confidence of their own understandings ... and think that their unfurnished minds (because they have a natural quickness) are competent judges of all that they read'. He added: 'The imperfection of our Faith (even about the Gospel, and the Life to come) is the secret root of all our faults; of the weaknesse of every other grace, of our yielding to temptations; and of the carelessnesse, badnesse, and barrennesse of our Lives'.[45]

This, therefore, brings us to a somewhat different setting for the study of unbelief, which has come to the fore in recent investigation of the topic. For all the extent to which disbelief in the gods had existed in classical antiquity, while related attitudes prove to have been surprisingly prevalent in the Middle Ages, 'atheism' clearly played a particularly important role in the aftermath of the Reformation.[46] Not only did this open up a sharp disparity between different religious positions, thus increasing the

---

[45] Ibid., sigs A3–4, (a)–(b2).
[46] For the earlier periods see Tim Whitmarsh, *Battling the Gods: Atheism in the Ancient World* (New York, 2015); John H. Arnold, *Belief and Unbelief in Medieval Europe* (London, 2005), esp. ch. 6.

problems of deciding between them; it also placed a premium on genuine, as against merely formal and accepted, belief. Indeed, as Ethan Shagan has argued in a profound and ground-breaking study, at this stage the issue of atheism could almost be seen as beside the point: 'in order to figure out what atheism was ... early moderns had to wrestle with the problem of belief itself'.[47] Shagan lucidly and comprehensively analyses the way in which a far more intense burden was at this point placed on the believer, whether Protestant or Catholic, whose faith now required a new judgement and commitment.

His lead has been followed by Alec Ryrie in his *Unbelievers: An Emotional History of Doubt* (2019), a sequel to his exploration of the psychology of everyday belief in his masterly study, *Being Protestant in Reformation Britain* (2013).[48] As will be seen, Ryrie actually places 'doubt' in the subtitle to his book, much of which is devoted to the phenomenon of doubt as experienced by the godly during the early modern period. The implication is that when Baxter and similar spokesmen used the term 'atheism', they were referring to the same thing as the outspoken irreligion that we encountered at the start of this Introduction. And, of course, Ryrie has a pedigree for using 'doubt' in this way, in that he echoes Don Cameron Allen's 1964 study of atheism, titled *Doubt's Boundless Sea: Skepticism and Religion in the Renaissance*, or even Jennifer Michael Hecht's blockbuster, *Doubt: A History*, of 2003.[49]

b   The Assurance of Atheists

But is this correct? Doubt has certainly been a facet of the normal experience of ordinary Christians in all ages, as Ryrie rightly points out. To quote the father of the child whom Jesus exorcised in Mark 9. 24, 'Lord, I believe; help thou my unbelief', and (as Ryrie illustrates in his book) such sentiments were echoed particularly profusely in the context of seventeenth-century British Protestantism.[50] But, as will be argued more fully in Chapter 3 of the current book, there is an important distinction to be made between the doubts of the godly and those of the openly impious,

---

[47] Ethan H. Shagan, *The Birth of Modern Belief: Faith and Judgment from the Middle Ages to the Enlightenment* (Princeton, 2018), p. 110 and elsewhere in ch. 3–4.

[48] Alec Ryrie, *Unbelievers: An Emotional History of Doubt* (London, 2019) and *Being Protestant in Reformation Britain* (Oxford, 2013).

[49] D. C. Allen, *Doubt's Boundless Sea: Skepticism and Faith in the Renaissance* (Baltimore, 1964); Jennifer Michael Hecht, *Doubt: A History* (New York, 2003).

[50] Ryrie, *Unbelievers*, p. 139.

for all the extent to which the literature of atheism might capitalise on the congruity between reservations about Christian doctrine on the part of the pious and outright irreligion. As will there be argued, for the godly there was something apologetic and hesitant about the concept of 'doubt', which was experienced in private and often with a degree of embarrassment: this will become apparent particularly through an examination of the views of one of the greatest of Christian doubters, John Bunyan. The essential nature of the misgivings experienced by the godly was that they were private, confidential, almost a matter of shame.

By comparison, it is important to stress that the irreligion of true infidels – as represented by the individuals itemised at the start of this Introduction and as will be illustrated at greater length in the studies that follow – is that it was expressed openly and publicly. These men showed little sign of doubt: rather, they expressed their views with swagger and bravado, seeming sure of themselves, supremely confident in their outlook. Their opinions were expressed with a real assurance, which is striking and revealing in itself. Indeed, it is worth pausing here to consider that word, 'assurance', which I will repeatedly use in this book to describe the demeanour of atheists. And, since I deployed the same term without elucidation in *The Decline of Magic* (2020) to characterise those who were in the forefront of rejecting magical beliefs during the long eighteenth century, this seems an appropriate place to explain exactly what I mean by it.[51]

In fact, the term comes straight from Christian theology. It was originally used by the Calvinists to describe an individual's confidence that he or she was one of the elect, and in this connection it was the subject of much discussion in a Reformation context, particularly the question of how a believer could be certain that they had achieved this assured state, as is well illustrated by Ryrie in *Being Protestant in Reformation Britain*.[52] But, especially in the hands of John Wesley in the eighteenth century, it broadened into a wider sense of certainty, not just of salvation but of faith itself. As Wesley explained in a letter of 28 September 1738 to the divine Arthur Bedford: 'That assurance of which alone I speak, I should not choose to call an assurance of salvation, but rather (with the Scriptures) the

---

[51] Hunter, *Decline of Magic*, esp. pp. vi, 140, 175.
[52] Ryrie, *Being Protestant in Reformation Britain*, esp. pp. 44–8. See also the informative discussion in Ian Green, *The Christian's ABC: Catechisms and Catechising in England c. 1530–1740* (Oxford, 1996), ch. 9.

assurance of faith', and he cited Hebrews 10. 22 in support of this.[53] Obviously it is a somewhat vague concept, which is why it has inspired so much discussion among committed Christians.[54] But it is nonetheless a real one, and it seems to be me equally to apply to the apostates whom we will encounter in this book. 'Assurance' well captures the confidence and self-sufficiency of these spokesmen for irreligion.

What is more, this helps us to understand the commonplace view on the part of the orthodox that atheists were not really rational, that atheism was the product of 'interest' rather than reason, which might otherwise seem strange except as an explanation of the 'practical' aspects of irreligion that have already been noted. Tenison's claim that atheism stemmed from 'a sensual Disposition' rather than from 'the Arguments of a sound Mind in a sober Temper' has already been quoted, and Ralph Cudworth put it more strongly still in his *True Intellectual System of the Universe*, expostulating how: 'were there any *Interest of Life*, any *Concernment* of *Appetite* and *Passion*, against the *Truth* of *Geometricall Theorems* themselves . . . whereby mens Judgements might be Clouded and Bribed; Notwithstanding all the *Demonstrations* of them, many would remain, at least *Sceptical* about them'.[55]

Moreover, this belief that atheists were irrational, and the accompanying attempt to dismiss or disallow their arguments on the grounds that they were libertines and thus incapable of serious ratiocination, is widely found. Samuel Clarke in his 1706 Boyle Lectures, for instance, affirmed that 'Wickedness and ungoverned Lusts, are the only Causes of obstinate Infidelity'.[56] In fact, the orthodox were notably unclear concerning the mutual relationship between immorality and atheism, as to which was the cause and which was the effect. Did atheism make you immoral, or did immorality make you prone to atheism? These were distinct claims, but they were rarely differentiated. On the contrary, contemporaries seem to have postulated a kind of symbiosis between the two – 'like Water and Ice they produce one another', as another polemicist, Joseph Glanvill, put it –

[53] Wesley, *Letters*, ed. John Telford, 8 vols (London, 1931, reprinted 1960), 1, 255–6. Cf., for example, Henry D. Rack, *Reasonable Enthusiast: John Wesley and the Rise of Methodism*, 3rd ed. (London 2002), ch. 11; Rivers, *Reason, Grace and Sentiment*, 1, ch. 5.

[54] See, for instance, Kenneth J. Collins, 'Assurance', in *The Oxford Handbook to Methodist Studies*, ed. W. J. Abraham and J. E. Kirby (Oxford, 2009), pp. 602–17.

[55] Cudworth, *True Intellectual System*, sig. ***1.

[56] Clarke, *A Discourse Concerning the Unchangeable Obligations of Natural Religion* (London, 1706), p. 393.

on the grounds that 'mens *lusts* are the occasion of their scoffing; and . . . this again is a cause of the *greater heights*, and boldness of their *Lusts*'.[57]

Here it is interesting to consider the line taken by Francis Gastrell in his 1697 series of Boyle Lectures, in which he argued that 'the Belief and Patronage of the *Doctrines* of *Irreligion* is the *sole Result* of *Prejudice*, and not *deliberate Reason*', on the grounds that atheists' disbelief commonly came 'first before they enter upon any *Examination* or *Proof* of their *Principles*'. He continued:

> And thus, as *Irreligion springs* from *Prejudice*, so it is *nourished* and *fed* the *same way*: by a constant Application to such Books and Company as give it any countenance or colour of Defence; with an industrous avoiding and ridiculing the contrary; picking out such things as minister most occasion for Raillery; and magnifying every bold thing that is said by any Man, without any regard to his other Opinions, or the Consequences even of that that is liked.[58]

At this point we are again obviously close to the phenomenon of 'practical atheism', the concept that 'atheism' was manifested not by belief at all but by bad behaviour. On the other hand, if Gastrell's statement is examined carefully, it will be noted that it was not about practical atheism that he was complaining. Note in particular his reference to 'Books', to 'Company' and to 'Raillery' in his view of irreligion: he is clearly describing a consciously articulated attitude on the part of those responsible, which may often have been orally expressed but which also had printed sources. Though he is dismissive of its intellectual coherence, this is hardly surprising, typifying the insistence of the orthodox that their arguments were so self-evidently correct that only the wilful or the prejudiced could possibly resist them.

In this refusal to accept the legitimacy of atheistic argumentation there is perhaps an analogy to the 'repressive denial' of atheism in which the orthodox engaged, a phenomenon which David Berman has noted in an insightful study.[59] What is odd, as Berman points out, is that many authors writing on atheism in the seventeenth and eighteenth centuries

---

[57] Glanvill, *Seasonable Reflections and Discourses in Order to the Conviction, & Cure of the Scoffing, & Infidelity of a Degenerate Age* (London, 1676), p. 14.

[58] Gastrell, *The Certainty and Necessity of Religion in General* (London, 1697), pp. 239, 242, 244–5.

[59] Berman, *History of Atheism*, ch. 1, a reprint of 'The Repressive Denials of Atheism in Britain in the Seventeenth and Eighteenth Centuries', *Proceedings of the Royal Irish Academy*, 82 (1982), 211–46. See also his argument for the use of 'disclaimers' by freethinkers: 'Deism, Immortality, and the Art of Theological Lying', in *Deism, Masonry, and the Enlightenment*, ed. J. A. Leo Lemay (Newark, DE, 1987), pp. 61–78, and 'Disclaimers as Offence Mechanisms in Charles Blount and John Toland', in Hunter and Wootton, *Atheism from the Reformation to the Enlightenment*, pp. 255–72.

combined a denial that atheism existed – which should surely have ended the matter – with a comprehensive refutation of the very phenomenon that was supposed not to exist, an apparent contradiction. As he went on to illustrate, this behaviour can be explained in terms of a Freudian theory of repression, the denial of the existence of a phenomenon being used as a means of expressing the wish that it did not exist (hence constituting a sub-conscious rather than a conscious desire, in which case it would constitute suppression). Moreover, as Berman argued, this may itself have had some effect in inhibiting the rise of openly expressed atheism in Britain.[60]

Be that as it may, a further answer to this dilemma is clearly to be sought in the burgeoning field of the history of emotions.[61] Indeed, this is almost epitomised by the view expressed by Robert Boyle in his writings on atheism that 'the Will and Affections have so great an influence upon some mens Understandings, that 'tis almost as difficult to make them *believe*, as to make them *Love*, against their Will'.[62] Where therefore should one look? Here, a potential lead is provided by Alec Ryrie, who, in subtitling his volume 'an Emotional History of Doubt', explains that 'the term "emotion" here does not refer only to spontaneous or involun-tary passions. Indeed, it includes (but is not exhausted by) the conscious intellect'.[63] At the outset, I should state that I fully second his reservations about the 'intellectualist fallacy', the undue intellectualism which blights much of the study of ideas on atheism as on other topics in the history of thought.[64] On the other hand, what Ryrie actually offers by way of an 'emotional history' of the phenomenon is somewhat disappointing. He is surely right to characterise the feelings of his doubting believers as 'anxi-ety' – though, considering the prominence of the concept in his subtitle, his treatment of the matter from the viewpoint of emotional history is surprisingly cursory (and it has to be admitted that the phenomenon of doubt has not been much pursued by historians of the emotions).[65] But his contrasting characterisation of more articulate unbelievers as 'angry'

---

[60] Berman, *History of Atheism*, p. 41.

[61] For helpful accounts, see Thomas Dixon, *From Passions to Emotions: The Creation of a Secular Psychological Category* (Cambridge, 2003); Joanna Bourke, *Fear: A Cultural History* (London, 2005); and Barbara Rosenwein, *Generations of Feeling: A History of Emotions, 600–1700* (Cambridge, 2016).

[62] *Boyle on Atheism*, ed. J. J. MacIntosh (Toronto, 2005), p. 384.   [63] Ryrie, *Unbelievers*, p. 5.

[64] Ibid., p. 5, citing the important work of Dominic Erdozan, *The Soul of Doubt: The Religious Roots of Unbelief from Luther to Marx* (Oxford, 2016), which discusses the issue on p. 5 and p. 268 n. 14, with reference to Charles Taylor's influential study, *A Secular Age* (Cambridge, MA, 2007).

[65] For instance, this theme is disappointingly lacking from the recent survey of the field in *The Routledge History of Emotions in Europe, 1100–1700*, ed. Andrew Lynch and Susan Broomhall (London, 2020).

seems to me misleading, failing to do justice to the complexity and subtlety of the sentiments involved. I do not detect anger as the primary motivation of these men, and other concepts that Ryrie uses in assessing them in passing, such as 'defiance', 'insolence' and 'mockery', seem to me to express their attitude much better.[66]

In fact, I would like to turn to Robert Boyle himself to try to construct a kind of emotional profile of the atheist antagonists that caused him concern, using the profuse writings on the subject printed by J. J. MacIntosh in his *Boyle on Atheism*.[67] Unlike many other writers on the topic, who were often engaged simply in polemics, Boyle actually tried to reflect on the characteristics of his antagonists. His comments are shrewd, clearly based on a good deal of conversation with the men involved, and I will draw on these here, though largely omitting the counter-arguments in favour of his own, avowedly Christian viewpoint with which his remarks are interspersed. In particular, Boyle laid stress on the self-esteem of his opponents, seeing the quintessential 'atheist' as

> one that affects to have nothing above himselfe, that may not only ecclipse his Excellencys, but controul his Freedome, and crosses the radicated desire he has of liveing as an Independent Being & master of his owne Will without being obligd to give an account of its Volitions to any other than his owne Reason.

Indeed, he wrote:

> There is one thing more which tho not usually observ'd, I looke upon as a great Promoter of mens Indisposition to beleive there is a God, and it is this, That not only desperately wicked men as such, but the generality of men (I had almost added as they are men) are subject to an inbred Temptation upon the account of selfe Love. For man is generally a haughty Being & sufficiently sensible of the great Prerogatives he enjoyes in a Rational Intellect & a Freedome of Will. And on the account of his inbred haughtiness or selfe Love, he is not a little indisposed to admit the Beleife of a Deity.[68]

Thus, the essence of the matter comes down to a view of atheists as self-centred and narcissistic, and there is arguably a great deal of mileage in this. Indeed, the matter was succinctly summarised by the divine John

---

[66] Ryrie, *Unbelievers*, pp. 89, 93, 94, 104, 105, 106, 185–8.
[67] Boyle's atheists are in general anonymous, but for a clue to the identity of one man who caused his concern, note his reference to 'Atheism, as 'tis maintain'd by L.C.V.E.; and some other Libertines that ha[u]nt you', *Boyle on Atheism*, p. 51. I have not been able to identify this figure.
[68] *Boyle on Atheism*, pp. 54–5.

Harris in the title of the first of his 1698 series of Boyle Lectures: *Immorality and Pride, the Great Causes of Atheism.*[69]

In Boyle's case, he elaborated on this, itemising what he saw as the characteristics of such men, notably their dogmatism and intellectual complacency. He laid particular stress on their appeal to common sense and their refusal to conceive of difficult but, to him, essential concepts to do with God's nature and omnipotence. As he put it, 'God is not an Object of sense & therefore his Existence not to be directly demonstrated by that sort of Prooffes, which Atheists chieffly require, & which alone some of them will admit, & be impress'd by'.[70] He itemised the difficulty which such men had in conceiving a being who was at once powerful but also incorporeal and invisible, and their proneness to reject arguments along such lines as 'unintelligible impertinent or precarious'.[71] It is also worth noting that he was worried that such figures often adopted 'some smattering of Philosophy' to 'countenance the Irreligious Principles, they brought with them to the Study of it', thus returning us to the anxiety about excessive naturalism that we have already encountered as one of the symptoms of atheism, except that he moved the stimulus to this away from naturalism itself towards the attitude deemed to underly it.[72]

Above all, Boyle deprecated the easy recourse to irony on the part of such men in their attempt to discredit what failed to fit in with their preconceptions. 'There are thousands that can apprehend the force of a popular Objection or a witty Jest, that can not understand the force of a Metaphysical Demonstration or a Learned Answer', in Boyle's words.[73] It deeply concerned him that those who indulged in such sarcasm enjoyed the reputation of being 'great witts', celebrities of the coffee-house culture of his day in which such attitudes were thought to flourish: 'For it passes with the most for a mark of Superiority in point of Judgment to be able to find fault with that which others reverence or acquiesce in'.[74] He also sought to 'reprehend those scepticall Witts, that will rather seeke Truth, then find it, (like those that hunt foxes who aime more at the chase, than the Game)'.[75] Boyle was worried by the superficiality of those who espoused such attitudes, their failure to penetrate the true depth of the mysteries that were often involved. Again and again Boyle, like other

---

[69] Harris, *Immorality and Pride, the Great Causes of Atheism* (London, 1698).
[70] *Boyle on Atheism*, p. 55 (there is a superfluous 'on' before 'by').   [71] Ibid., pp. 55–69, 100.
[72] Boyle, *Works*, XI, 294.   [73] *Boyle on Atheism*, p. 63.
[74] Ibid., pp. 163–4. For the coffee-house milieu see *The Character of a Coffee-House, with the Symptomes of a Town-Wit* (London, 1673).
[75] *Boyle on Atheism*, p. 372.

contemporaries, deprecated wit and satire as the chief weapons used by atheists in their assault on Christianity.

Indeed, at one point he sought to reassure those who might be disquieted by such talk, 'That they may looke upon the boldness & seeming pleasantness of these Scoffers rather as an Effect of a Distemper then of a Vigor & inward pleasantness of Mind, as we looke upon the briske strugglings & loud Laughters of Hysterical Persons, not as true signs of Health & Joy, but symptoms of a Disease'.[76] That appropriately medical metaphor returns us to the thrust of the view held by Boyle – like so many of his contemporaries – that 'speculative' and 'practical' atheism were so intertwined that they were indistinguishable. In Boyle's words:

> If those of Your Friends that are growne Libertines, would but deal ingenuously with themselves, it would soon appear to them, that they did not first employ their Reason to make choyce of their Opinions about Religion, but to defend the choyce which their Prejudices and Vices had already made for them.[77]

We thus return once again to Boyle's and other polemicists' evident frustration at their opponents' unwillingness to accept the supposedly self-evident truths with which they were confronted, their 'confident and perhaps facetious way of derideing whatever they do not understand'.[78] But it is precisely that assurance on the part of their atheist opponents that lies at the heart of this book, and that it is important for us to understand.

c   The Current Volume

First, however, it is appropriate to outline the book's component parts, and to indicate the manner in which they have taken shape. The earliest comprises an attempt to do justice to the ways in which contemporaries defined and approached the phenomenon that they described as 'atheism' in the period when concern about this first became commonplace, namely before the Civil War, and Chapter 2 of this book deals with the period up to 1640 – though (as is there argued) many of its implications also extend to a later period. This essay was published in 1985 and since then has been widely cited:[79] I have therefore not attempted to tamper with it here,

---

[76] Ibid., pp. 375–6.   [77] Ibid., p. 377.   [78] Ibid., p. 376.

[79] See, for example, the lengthy quotations from it in Roger D. Lund, 'Introduction', in his *The Margins of Orthodoxy: Heterodox Writing and Cultural Response, 1660–1750* (Cambridge, 1995), pp. 1–27, on pp. 6, 25 n. 19, and 27–8, nn. 42–3. See also John Marshall, *John Locke, Toleration and Early Enlightenment Culture* (Cambridge, 2006), pp. 256–63.

simply updating its citations and references as appropriate. I should perhaps explain that this abnormal intervention in an earlier period than that
in which I have mainly specialised occurred in the aftermath of my book
Science and Society in Restoration England (1981), itself containing a
chapter on 'Atheism and Orthodoxy', which represents my first foray in
the field. My paper on atheism was delivered in 1982–3 at various
universities in England, Australia, New Zealand, the Unites States and
Canada, where it attracted a good deal of interest, not least from J. C.
Davis, then based at Wellington University, New Zealand, who acknowledged its stimulus for his notorious book on the Interregnum Ranters,
Fear, Myth and History, published in 1986.[80] However, it should be noted
that Davis insists on a stricter dichotomy between the imaginary and the
real than is argued for either in the current chapter or in the unpublished
but indistinguishable version of it on which he drew, picking up on the
idealised side and failing to discuss the case that is here made for an
interrelationship between that and the actual state of affairs.

In fact, as my paper was at pains to illustrate, the whole point about
'atheism' was the extent to which it represented an amalgam of the
imaginary and the real, and only in these terms can it properly be
understood. Its thrust is that the literature on atheism had various, overlapping purposes. To some extent, 'atheism' was a way of expressing
disquiet by exaggerating and idealising it. The stock character of the atheist
summed up all that contemporaries feared about irreligion in both its
philosophical and practical manifestations, enabling them to identify and
sensationalise tendencies that they observed around them which seemed to
lead in that direction, however mild, and however absurd this may in
retrospect appear to us. Atheism was an ideal type, and, like other ideal
types of the time, such as Puritanism, it served a broader role as a means of
voicing contemporary anxieties by depicting them in polarised form, thus
setting up a kind of continuum from the acceptable to the extreme along
which actual instances could be measured. To this needs to be added the
context of inversionary thinking typical of the period, as already alluded to:
atheism played an essential role in the world impregnated by Aristotelian
contraries and polarities that typified early modern thought. In a real sense,
therefore, the actual existence of atheists was almost irrelevant to the
literature of atheism, which served significant functions in its own right –

---

[80] J. C. Davis, *Fear, Myth and History: The Ranters and the Historians* (Cambridge, 1986), p. xi and
pp. 114–15, 118, and 120–1, which cites an unpublished version of the paper at length. See also
p. 34n.

though it was helpfully reinforced by spectacular examples of irreligion that occasionally came to light. Moreover, before the Civil War as later, one of the principal audiences of the anti-atheist literature were clearly the godly themselves. The personification of ungodliness in an extreme form was a means of alarming those who professed to be religious, encouraging them to display greater zeal and enabling preachers to conflate almost any deviance from godly commitment with extreme irreligion on the grounds that it was a slippery slope with an inevitable and pernicious endpoint; it also accommodated the godly's own anxieties about Christian doctrine in ways that we will examine in Chapter 3.

If that is the overall thrust of Chapter 2, it is worth noting that it encapsulates an examination of two episodes which are of great significance in their own right and to which it is worth drawing attention here. Both stemmed from a unique concern to root out heterodoxy that seized the English establishment in the early 1590s. The dissidence that caused concern was mainly of an extreme Protestant variety: the threat presented by the Presbyterian Movement and the Marprelate Tracts of the 1580s reached a climax with the case of the Messianic William Hacket in 1591, and in 1593 the authorities imprisoned the leading separatists, John Greenwood and Henry Barrow, and rounded up and questioned their followers.[81] It might have seemed as if Protestant extremism would be enough of a challenge, but at the same time investigations were also made concerning 'Atheisme; or Apostacye'. In 1594, a special commission was set up at Cerne Abbas in Dorset under direction from the 'High Commissioners in Causes Ecclesiastical', who were specifically instructed to investigate rumours of atheistic opinions associated with Sir Walter Ralegh and his circle. The previous year, separate enquiries had been authorised concerning a related matter, the outrageous views supposedly expressed by the poet and dramatist Christopher Marlowe.

The findings of these investigations were preserved alongside the interrogations of the sectaries – not the fullest set of depositions, which are now to be found among the papers of Lord Chancellor Ellesmere at the Huntington Library in California, but a subsidiary series in the papers of Sir John Puckering, Lord Keeper of the Privy Seal, which form part of the

---

[81] For the examinations of the separatists, see *The Writings of John Greenwood and Henry Barrow, 1591–3*, ed. Leland H. Carlson (Elizabethan Nonconformist Texts, VI, London, 1970). For background, see the classic account in Patrick Collinson, *The Elizabethan Puritan Movement* (London, 1967), part 8.

Harleian Manuscripts at the British Library.[82] In fact, this juxtaposition does not seem to have been noted prior to the publication of my paper on atheism in 1985: the Cerne Abbas and Marlowe enquiries had previously been of concern to literary historians, whereas the interrogations of the sectaries were the preserve of students of religious history. But the juxtaposition illustrates a real concern about the definition of the parameters of orthodoxy, including an anxiety about atheism, which seems to have come to a head in the early 1590s. Not only did the first four books of Richard Hooker's *Laws of Ecclesiastical Polity* appear in 1593, but so did the first full-length English book attacking atheism, Henry Smith's *Gods Arrowe against Atheists.*

The Cerne Abbas enquiry deserves to be better known, as much for what it does not reveal as for what it does. It did not bring to light the hotbed of simmering atheism that the authorities had evidently been expecting: instead, what it illustrates are the commonplaces of irreligious sentiment that were probably widespread in Elizabethan England, and it is for this that it is repeatedly cited in Chapter 2. Perhaps the most striking statement came from a local shoemaker, Robert Hyde, who reported that there was

> a companye aboute this towne that saye, that hell is noe other but povertie & penurye in this worlde; and heaven is noe other but to be ritch, and enioye pleasueres; and that we dye like beastes, and when we ar gonne there is noe more rememberance of vs &c and such like.

On examination, however, he claimed that these notions were derived from their confutation in a sermon by a local priest.[83] More typical was banter about the poor quality of local preaching, or about God's control of the weather, thus representing a questioning of the doctrine of providence that was so central to Calvinist orthodoxy.[84] Scepticism about the immortality of the soul was also reported, while a robust dinner-time discussion of the doctrine of the soul between Ralegh, his brother Carew and the local vicar illustrates a degree of orally expressed scepticism that may not have been unusual at the time but which suddenly appeared sinister when

[82] For the Cerne Abbas enquiry, see British Library Harleian MS 6849, fols 183–90, available in F.-C. Danchin, 'Etudes Critiques sur Christopher Marlowe', *Revue Germanique*, 9 (1913), 566–87, and in *Willobie His Avisa*, ed. G. B. Harrison (London, 1926), pp. 255–71 (citations are from the latter). The content of the text was first divulged in an article by the Catholic historian, J. M. Stone, 'Atheism under Elizabeth and James I', *The Month*, 81 (1894), 174–87. For background, see R. G. Usher, *The Rise and Fall of the High Commission* (Oxford, 1913; 2nd ed., introduced by P. Tyler, 1968), esp. ch. 13.
[83] *Willobie His Avisa*, pp. 264, 269–70.   [84] Ibid., pp. 259, 261, 264.

subjected to scrutiny of the kind that the enquiry represented.[85] Indeed, it is interesting that it was reported that Carew Ralegh had on some unspecified earlier occasion argued 'as like a pagan as euer you harde anye', but that 'the matter was soe shutt up' that it only came to light in conjunction with the enquiry. It is also revealing that one informant, 'a Barber in Warminster dwellinge in a bye Lane there ... did marvell', not at the anti-providentialist sentiment uttered by Ralegh's nephew, Charles Thynne, but 'that a gentleman of his credite shoulde deliver words to soe meane a man as him selfe tendinge to this sence'.[86] Much the same is true of the casual remarks that were recorded concerning Thomas Allen, Ralegh's lieutenant at Portland Castle, and his servant, Oliver, who apparently said 'manye other thinges in derogacion of God & the scriptures. and of the immortallitye of the soule', which were obviously shocking to the godly but which, again, would have remained unrecorded but for the unusual circumstances of the enquiry.[87] Indeed, what the episode mainly reveals is a degree of casual irreligion that was probably commonplace throughout the entire early modern period, but which is rarely so neatly encapsulated.

It remains possible that Sir Walter himself had gone further than this, as witness the Jesuit Robert Parsons's rather incendiary report on his 'schoole of Atheisme', at which 'both Moyses, and our Savior; the olde, and new Testamente are iested at, and the schollers taught amonge other thinges, to spell God backwarde': this evidently received wide circulation, and rumours of Ralegh's heterodoxy were echoed even by an English-born heretic in Italy.[88] It certainly seems unwise to reconstruct Ralegh's views on such subjects, as has often been done, from his *History of the World*, written in the chastened circumstances of his imprisonment in the Tower of London, as against 'the youthful and freer times' of his earlier years at court.[89] John Aubrey, as so often, has the last word here, recording how Ralegh 'was a bold man, and would venture at discourse, which was unpleasant to the Churchmen', and it was for this reason that he 'was

---

[85] Ibid., esp. pp. 265–8.

[86] Ibid., pp. 258–9. As to whether 'Mr Thinn' was in fact Charles or John, see p. 49.

[87] Ibid., pp. 260, 263.

[88] [Parsons], *An Advertisement Written to a Secretarie of My L. Treasurers of Ingland* ([Antwerp], 1592), p. 18. Cf. the quotation from Christopher Stremar in Nicholas Davidson, 'Christopher Marlowe and Atheism', in *Christopher Marlowe and English Renaissance Culture*, ed. Darryll Grantley and Peter Roberts (Aldershot, 1996), pp. 129–47 (p. 138).

[89] For the orthodox reading, see Ernest A. Strathmann, *Sir Walter Ralegh. A Study in Elizabethan Skepticism* (New York, 1951), and Pierre Lefranc, *Sir Walter Ralegh Ecrivain: l'oeuvre et les ideés* (Paris, 1968), ch. 12; for a more sceptical position, see Stephen J. Greenblatt, *Sir Walter Ralegh: The Renaissance Man and His Roles* (New Haven, 1973), p. 101. The quotation is from Joseph Hall, *The Balm of Gilead* (1646), quoted in Strathmann, p. 171.

scandalizd with Atheisme'.[90] That is probably about as much as can be said, while as for Ralegh's protégé, the mathematician Thomas Harriot, who was invoked both in the Cerne Abbas enquiry and also by Christopher Marlowe, the current thinking is that he was conventionally pious, but that his open-minded attitude towards the religious practices of the American Indians might have caused concern.[91]

Turning to the case of Marlowe, this is so familiar that it need only be briefly introduced. The documents describing Marlowe's heterodoxy have now been usefully brought together in print by Constance Kuriyama, and they may therefore be left to speak for themselves.[92] Once one has escaped the plethora of conspiracy theories surrounding Marlowe's death and its context, one may stand back and look at the allegations made by Richard Baines, and echoed by Thomas Beard and others, in their own right.[93] Various allusions are made to the Marlowe case in Chapter 2, but what needs to be emphasised strongly here is the breathtaking audacity and coherence of the statements that he was claimed to have made.[94] This has perhaps been lost sight of by some recent commentators, who have become obsessed by parallels with the anti-Catholic statements that were earlier attributed to the informer Richard Baines himself.[95] In many ways, the best account of the Baines note remains that of the scholar, Paul H. Kocher, although it was published as long ago as 1946 and seems to

---

[90] John Aubrey, *Brief Lives with an Apparatus for the Lives of Our English Mathematical Writers*, ed. Kate Bennett, 2 vols (Oxford, 2015), I, 238.

[91] *Willobie His Avisa*, pp. 258, 260; Kuriyama, *Christopher Marlowe*, p. 221; Scott Mandelbrote, 'The Religion of Thomas Harriot', in *Thomas Harriot: An Elizabethan Man of Science*, ed. Robert Fox (Aldershot, 2000), pp. 246–79 (pp. 267–9). It is perhaps also worth noting Aubrey's perceptive view that Harriot 'was a Deist': *Brief Lives*, I, 678. See also pp. 54–5.

[92] Kuriyama, *Christopher Marlowe*, Appendix. The citations have therefore been updated in ch. 2: in the 1985 version some had to come from C. F. Tucker Brooke, *The Life of Marlowe and the Tragedy of Dido Queen of Carthage* (London, 1930), and some from Danchin, 'Etudes Critiques sur Christopher Marlowe'.

[93] For conspiracy theories, see especially Charles Nicholl, *The Reckoning: The Murder of Christopher Marlowe* (London, 1992), rewritten in a second edition of 2002 to address some of the criticisms of it made in the interim. Nicholl also wrote the *Oxford Dictionary of National Biography (ODNB)* article on Marlowe, which is more restrained. A not dissimilar line is taken in David Riggs, *The World of Christopher Marlowe* (London, 2004). For a balanced account of Marlowe's views on such subjects, see Davidson, 'Marlowe and Atheism'.

[94] See pp. 34, 47–8, 49.

[95] See especially Roy Kendall, 'Richard Baines and Christopher Marlowe's Milieu', *English Literary Renaissance*, 24 (1994), 507–52, extended in Roy Kendall, *Christopher Marlowe and Richard Baines* (Madison, NJ, 2003), though this is also true to some extent of Nicholl, *The Reckoning*, esp. p. 129, and of Riggs, *World of Christopher Marlowe*, esp. pp. 132–3. Park Honan, *Christopher Marlowe: Poet and Spy* (Oxford, 2005) takes only a passing interest in this aspect of Marlowe's thought.

have escaped the radar of contemporary Marlowe scholars.[96] Kocher's verdict was that, although much of the dangerous ideology that Marlowe formulated can be paralleled in texts from the patristic period and in writings of his own time, in Marlowe's recorded statement we see 'the quintessence of it drawn together and revealed ... For revolutionary impact and scope it stands alone, an extraordinary document in the history of English free thought'.[97]

It is also revealing that Marlowe's sentiments remained scandalous long after his own time. The view of them taken by the antiquary Thomas Baker, from whose holdings the documents in question reached the Harleian Collection, was that 'These opinions are so horribly blasphemous, that I dare not transcribe them, or be any way Instrumentall in preserving them'.[98] Luckily, however, he *did* ensure their survival, and the Baines note was published by the scholar Joseph Ritson in 1782, though more for the sake of scoring a point off Thomas Wharton's *History of English Poetry* (1774–81) than out of any sympathy for Marlowe's views.[99] A century later, Marlowe's opinions still remained controversial. The writer Havelock Ellis included the Baines note in his edition of Marlowe in the popular 'Mermaid' series of 'The Best Plays of the Old Dramatists' in 1887, with an approving commentary seeing Marlowe's 'acute and audacious utterances' as in tune with the findings of 'students of science and of the Bible in our own days'. However, the edition had to be withdrawn so that the offending passages – including both Ellis's approving comments and Marlowe's sexual allegations against Christ – could be suppressed.[100]

As such reactions reveal, the views that Marlowe expressed were offensively irreligious, deliberately calculated to upset believers. More than any

---

[96] P. H. Kocher, *Christopher Marlowe: A Study of His Thought, Learning, and Character* (Chapel Hill, 1946), esp. ch. 3. This is cited by Davidson, 'Marlowe and Atheism', by William Urry, *Christopher Marlowe and Canterbury* (London, 1988), and by Riggs, but is not referred to by Kuriyama or Honan.

[97] Kocher, *Christopher Marlowe*, p. 68.

[98] British Library Harleian MS 7042, fol. 206. Concerning the Cerne Abbas enquiry, he also expressed himself 'unwilling to believe such a charge against so great a man as Sir Walter Rawleigh'.

[99] Ritson, *Observations on the Three First Volumes of the History of English Poetry* (London, 1782), pp. 39–42. It is perhaps worth noting the surprise of S. W. Singer in his edition of Marlowe's and Chapman's *Hero and Leander* (London, 1821), p. xxiiin., that 'Ritson, of all men' should have brought this to light.

[100] *Christopher Marlowe*, ed. Havelock Ellis (The Mermaid Series, London, 1887), pp. 428–31 (expurgated version in most extant copies of the book on pp. 428–30 only). John Addington Symonds had contributed a General Introduction to the edition, but he was complicit in the suppression of the passages of the Baines note: see Thomas Dabbs, *Reforming Marlowe: The Nineteenth-Century Canonisation of a Renaissance Dramatist* (Lewisburg, 1991), pp. 129–33.

other comparable episode in the period – with the possible exception of that involving Aikenhead – they display that aggressive certainty, that assurance, which has already been singled out as characterising the atheists with whom this book is concerned. This makes it all the more important to clarify the contrast between this confidence on the part of aggressive unbelievers and the doubts experienced almost furtively by the godly, by way of demarcation from the view put forward by Alec Ryrie in his *Unbelievers*: that task therefore falls to Chapter 3 of this book.

Continuing the history of the volume's component parts and their evolution, we then move to Chapter 4, which takes up the story of irreligion by examining the legacy of Thomas Hobbes and the 'Hobbism' that was perceived as widespread in the years after 1660. By way of background to this, it is perhaps appropriate to refer to two writings of mine from the mid-1980s which do *not* appear in the current volume – an essay on 'Science and Heterodoxy: An Early Modern Problem Reconsidered', and my account of John Wagstaffe as a case study of Restoration free-thought. The latter, which originated as a conference paper given in Leeds in September 1985, ultimately appeared in print in my *Science and the Shape of Orthodoxy* in 1995, from which it was reprinted in *The Decline of Magic* in 2020. As for the former, completed in 1983, this appeared after various delays in 1990 in a volume titled *Reappraisals of the Scientific Revolution*, edited by David C. Lindberg and Robert S. Westman, from which it was reprinted in *Science and the Shape of Orthodoxy*. Thereafter, much of its treatment of atheism was spliced into the introduction to *The Decline of Magic*, whereas the section dealing with the theme of science and irreligion was abandoned as a slightly dated relic of the culture wars of the 1980s.[101] Instead, it has here seemed appropriate to give a fresh account of such well-known freethinkers from Restoration England as Charles Blount and the Earl of Rochester, combining this with an attempt to confront the continuing elusiveness of atheists in the historical record in this period; the chapter ends with reflections on the significance of the career of a reformed atheist in the form of 'Burridge the Blasphemer'.

---

[101] Michael Hunter, 'Science and Heterodoxy: An Early Modern Problem Reconsidered', in *Reappraisals of the Scientific Revolution*, ed. David C. Lindberg and Robert S. Westman (Cambridge, 1990), pp. 437–60, reprinted in Michael Hunter, *Science and the Shape of Orthodoxy* (Woodbridge, 1995), pp. 225–44. See also Michael Hunter, *The Decline of Magic*, pp. 17–25, and pp. 28–48 (and *Science and the Shape of Orthodoxy*, pp. 286–307) for the Wagstaffe essay.

Chapter 5 moves on to one of the most spectacular examples of articulate irreligion in the early modern period, that of Thomas Aikenhead, which had the shocking outcome of its perpetrator being hanged in 1697, the last of the relatively few executions for the crime of blasphemy ever to take place in Britain.[102] The depositions concerning the case had long been available in *State Trials*, but this essay, originally published in the volume, *Atheism from the Reformation to the Enlightenment* (1992), attempted to go beyond such readily accessible material to give a detailed examination of the sources of Aikenhead's irreligious ideas and to assess the significance of the manner and milieu in which he expressed them. In particular, it is argued that his ideas had a coherence and power which is somewhat comparable to Marlowe's utterances a century earlier, thus perhaps making sense of the extremity of the authorities' reaction to him.

Since my essay was published, there has been further work on Aikenhead in the form of a book-length study by Michael F. Graham and an important pair of articles by John S. Warren.[103] Graham goes into much greater detail than I did on the background to the case in terms of Presbyterian infighting in Edinburgh in Aikenhead's period, while Warren offers extra information about the academic milieu of the affair, particularly the availability of books by Spinoza and others on which Aikenhead might have drawn, also reflecting on the aftermath of the case in the period leading up to David Hume. In addition, no book on Scotland in the period prior to the Enlightenment seems complete without some reference to the Aikenhead case;[104] it also naturally figures in histories of the crime of blasphemy, and has even been made the subject of an essay in its own right by one such author, David Nash.[105] It might be felt, however, that

---

[102] For the earlier ones, see Levy, *Blasphemy*, pp. 94–9.

[103] Michael F. Graham, *The Blasphemies of Thomas Aikenhead: Boundaries of Belief on the Eve of the Enlightenment* (Edinburgh, 2008); John S. Warren, 'Shining a Light in Dark Places, Parts I and II', *Global Intellectual History*, 2 (2017), 268–307; 3 (2018), 1–46. See also Graham's essay, 'Kirk in Danger: Presbyterian Political Divinity in Two Eras', in *The Impact of the European Reformation*, ed. Bridget Heal and O. P. Grell (Aldershot, 2008), pp. 167–86.

[104] In addition to the instances cited on p. 94–5, n. 4, see especially John Robertson, *The Case for Enlightenment: Scotland and Naples 1680–1760* (Cambridge, 2005), ch. 3; D. G. Mullan, *Narratives of the Religious Self in Early-Modern Scotland* (Farnham, 2010), pp. 300–7; and Alasdair Raffe, *The Culture of Controversy: Religious Arguments in Scotland, 1660–1714* (Woodbridge, 2012), pp. 57–61.

[105] Levy, *Blasphemy*, pp. 232–5 (a reprint of the relevant section of his *Treason against God: A History of the Offense of Blasphemy* [New York, 1981], pp. 325–7); David Nash, *Acts against God: A Short History of Blasphemy* (London, 2020), pp. 104–10; and Nash, 'The Uses of a Martyred Blasphemer's Death: The Execution of Thomas Aikenhead, Scotland's Religion, the Enlightenment and Contemporary Activism', in *Law, Crime and Deviance since 1700: Micro-*

none of this supersedes my initial account, which raised issues to do with the nature of Aikenhead's blasphemy and the contrast between his outspoken irreligion and the private doubts of men like the divine Thomas Halyburton, with which no subsequent author has really engaged; my essay is therefore reprinted here with only trivial modifications.[106]

It is perhaps worth noting that, since writing it, I have come across a strange analogue slightly earlier in the 1690s to which I was initially alerted by a passage in the *Life and Times* of the Oxford antiquary Anthony Wood. Under the year 1694 he writes:

> 'March 9, F[riday], Dr. Eliot hang'd at Edinburgh in the Grassmarket': so letters dated 17 March, S[aturday]. His confession read, because he could not speak it, his mouth being no bigger than the bowle of a tobacco pipe head, which he said had been contracted by a judgment of God for ridiculing the Scriptures. Eliot was an apothecary.[107]

This case occasioned the issue of a pamphlet by the Edinburgh printer George Mosman, which provided a rather heightened account of it in conjunction with a copious profession of contrition on Eliot's part. It turns out that he had become involved in a rather murky fraud case involving Daniel Nicolson and Mrs Pringle, who were conducting an adulterous affair and who sought Eliot's help in poisoning Nicolson's wife (both were also executed). In his *Last Speech*, Eliot revealed that earlier, while travelling abroad (perhaps to England), he had been caught up in a 'Cabal' of '*Witts*' where the existence of God was denied, the Trinity declared irrational, and the scriptures mocked. All of this was reported in slightly clichéd terms, along with his account of God's punishment of him for his apostasy by a defect to his mouth, the whole being framed by the profuse expression of contrite repentance.[108] The case merits fuller attention, but

---

Studies in the History of Crime, ed. Anne-Marie Kilday and David Nash (London, 2017), pp. 19–35.

[106] The most notable concerns my misattribution of *Macaulay on Scotland* to Hugh Miller in n. 3: in fact, it was by Thomas McCrie. Also, I perhaps overstated the suggestion that Aikenhead might have had legal representation on the basis of a report in the London papers: see p. 99, and Graham, *Blasphemies*, p. 102.

[107] Wood, *Life and Time*, ed. Andrew Clark, 5 vols (Oxford, 1891–1900), III, 447.

[108] *Mr John Eliot, Called, Doctor of Medicine, His Last Speech and Advice to the World, At His Suffering, March 9, 1694* (Edinburgh, 1694). The element of cliché is suggested by the fact that the views of the apostate circle in which Eliot moved are recounted in virtually identical terms on pp. 3 and 10. The pamphlet thus fits into the sensationalist and slightly questionable genre of the *Second Spira* (see pp. 83–4), of which Mosman published the Edinburgh edition, which is advertised on p. 15. For the case in which Eliot, Nicolson and Pringle were involved, see National Records of Scotland, JC2/19, High Court Books of Adjournal, fols 38v–74v. There is an account of it in David Hume, *Commentaries on the Law of Scotland*, 2 vols (Edinburgh, 1797), I, 246–9 (it is also referred to, e.g.,

here it is significant not least because Mosman, who published the pamphlet, was to be one of the assize at Aikenhead's trial, while the merchant, Adam Brown, who served on the assize at the earlier trial, was clerk at Aikenhead's.[109] This makes it the more surprising that Michael Graham fails to record this episode in his book, despite all the extra detail that he includes about Edinburgh in the 1690s. As with the case of the apprentice John Frazer, with which both Graham and I *did* deal, it appears that more heterodoxy lurked in Scotland than was hitherto known, although it seems unlikely that anything as striking as the Aikenhead case has yet to be discovered.

One revealing analogous case, however, is that of the Scottish medical theorist, satirist and poet Archibald Pitcairne (1652–1713), to whom Chapters 6 and 7 of the current volume are devoted. Pitcairne is, of course, notorious as a scourge of the Presbyterian establishment, whom he ridiculed from a staunchly Episcopalian viewpoint. He also wrote a convoluted anti-religious satire, a Latin *Epistle* purporting to be written by Archimedes to his patron, King Gelo of Syracuse, which was printed in the Netherlands in the early eighteenth century.[110] But what was extraordinary was my discovery of an overtly atheist text attributed to Pitcairne which had been completely unknown prior to 2016, when it was first presented to the public in the *Historical Journal*, from which it is here reprinted in full as Chapter 7. The document survives in manuscript in the Houghton Library at Harvard University, to which it was presented in 1841, and Chapter 6 provides an evaluation of its atheistic content, at the same time examining in detail its claimed links with Pitcairne and filling in the background in terms of Pitcairne's career and milieu.

We will return in the Conclusion to the extent to which further examples of freethinking were in evidence in Scotland in the early eighteenth century, by which time, of course, the tradition of Deism that has already been briefly surveyed was well established in England in the hands of figures like Toland, Collins and Tindal. The ferment of ideas associated with the Deists provides the setting for the final discussion of a case of atheism contained in this book, Chapter 8, which gives a detailed account

---

in R. A. Houston, *Social Change in the Age of Enlightenment: Edinburgh 1660–1760* (Oxford, 1994), pp. 145–6). Eliot's medical credentials seem questionable in view of the way in which they are referred to in the title of the pamphlet; that his medical knowledge was limited is also suggested by the fact that he aspired to have his mouth treated by the famous physician Thomas Willis, although Willis had died in 1675 (JC2/19, fol. 43v). I am indebted to Tristram Clarke for the archival reference and for his extensive assistance in this matter.
[109] Graham, *Blasphemies*, p. 112.   [110] See pp. 132–4.

of the trial of Tinkler Ducket at Cambridge in 1739, a hitherto neglected episode. The background to this is provided by a prologue dealing with a comparable case that occurred at Oxford a few years earlier, involving a man named Nicholas Stevens, who was accused of stirring up disquiet by drawing attention to the ideas of Pierre Bayle and others. As for Ducket, in the course of the proceedings he gave a surprisingly articulate exposition of his atheistic views, but this was largely ignored in contemporary accounts of the case because it was drowned out by the charges of immorality that were made against him. It appears that, by rather lazily invoking the smear of 'practical atheism', the orthodox could avoid discussion of the serious philosophising in which Ducket indulged. Once again, therefore, the fact that the supposed promiscuity of atheists meant that their ideas were greeted with outrage rather than given serious attention struck home with unfortunate effects.

There is therefore much to be digested in the pages that follow, both concerning the anti-Christian statements made by the various figures whom we will consider and concerning the strategies used in dealing with these on the part of their orthodox antagonists. Quite apart from the intrinsic interest of the detail that is provided, readers will be at liberty to form their own opinions as to just what was at stake. In a Conclusion, however, we will take stock, reiterating the 'assurance' displayed by the heterodox spokesmen involved and assessing the reaction towards this on the part of the orthodox. These, it will be argued, showed a combination of complacency and disdain towards the threat presented by such men which is not only revealing in itself but may unwittingly also have contributed to the growth of a more pluralist religious culture in Britain since the Enlightenment.

CHAPTER 2

The Problem of 'Atheism' in Early Modern England[*]

To speak of 'atheism' in the context of early modern England immediately invites confusion, and it is for this reason that I shall place the word in inverted commas throughout this chapter. On the one hand, I intend to deal with what a twentieth-first century reader might expect 'atheism' to imply, namely overt hostility to religion. On the other, I want to consider at some length the profuse writings on 'atheism' that survive from the period: in these, as we shall see, the word is often used to describe a much broader range of phenomena, in a manner typical of a genre which often appears frustratingly heightened and rhetorical. Some might argue that this juxtaposition displays – and will encourage – muddled thought. But, on the contrary, I think that it is precisely from such a combination that we stand to learn most. Not only are we likely to discover how contemporaries experienced and responded to the threat of irreligion in the society of their day. In addition, by re-examining the relationship between the real and the exaggerated in their perceptions of such heterodoxy, we may be able to draw broader conclusions about early modern thought.

I intend to limit myself to the period before the Civil War, largely for the sake of clarity: an attempt to generalise about the whole period from the 1580s to the 1690s, say, would create more problems than it would solve. Much of what I shall be saying is, however, equally applicable to the late seventeenth century,[1] while there is arguably also something to be

[*] Previously published in *Transactions of the Royal Historical Society*, 5th series 35 (1985), 135–57, where the heading included the information that the paper was read at a meeting of the society on 12 October 1984. For comments on an earlier draft of this paper, I am indebted to various seminar audiences and to Stuart Clark, Patrick Collinson, Margaret Spufford and Keith Thomas. [In the subsequent notes to this chapter, added material is enclosed in square brackets.]
[1] See Chapter 4 and Michael Hunter, 'Science and Heterodoxy: An Early Modern Problem Reconsidered', in *Reappraisals of the Scientific Revolution*, ed. David C. Lindberg and Robert S. Westman (Cambridge, 1990), pp. 437–60, reprinted in Hunter, *Science and the Shape of Orthodoxy: Intellectual Change in Late Seventeenth-Century Britain* (Woodbridge, 1995), pp. 225–44.

learnt about how we should interpret the contemporary views of Interregnum radicalism that have come down to posterity.[2]

At the outset, I should define what it is that I wish to consider in the context of contemporary perceptions of it, and this is irreligion in the sense of a more or less extreme attack on orthodox Christianity from a cynical or Deistic viewpoint. This cynical, iconoclastic attitude towards religion represents a genuine historical phenomenon which was consistently described at the time as 'atheism'. Moreover, it can be distinguished from sectarian heresy – as it was, for instance, by Francis Bacon, who devoted separate essays to 'Atheisme' and 'Superstition'[3] – although some views might be shared by heretics and infidels, and despite the fact that there was a suspicion at the time that sectarianism could encourage outright disbelief.[4]

Undoubtedly the best-known case of such heterodoxy in England in the period we are considering is that of Christopher Marlowe, whose fertile speculations were retailed in depositions by Thomas Kyd and Richard Baines, besides being reported by godly authors like Thomas Beard and William Vaughan.[5] The context of the official investigation of Marlowe seems to have been a broader heresy hunt which took place in 1593, since

---

[2] For example, the characterisation of 'The Ranters' in Ephraim Pagitt, *Heresiography* (5th ed., London, 1654), pp. 143–4, has many echoes of the stock figure of the 'atheist' outlined in this chapter, and Pagitt's book shares other features with the anti-atheist literature. [See further p. 76. Here it should be noted that profuse, if selective, citations of and quotations from an unpublished version of this chapter were deployed by J. C. Davis in his *Fear, Myth and History: The Ranters and the Historians* (Cambridge, 1986), pp. xi, 114–15, 118, and 120–1. However, as noted above (p. 22), Davis picks up only on the negative side of the characterisation of the 'atheist' here outlined, ignoring the ambivalence that is here stressed. For the controversy aroused by his book and for much background information on Interregnum radicalism as a whole, see the debate, 'Fear, Myth and Furore: Reassessing the "Ranters"', *Past & Present*, 129 (1990), 79–103, and 140 (1993), 155–210.]

[3] Francis Bacon, *The Essayes or Counsels, Civill and Morall*, ed. Michael Kiernan (Oxford, 1985), pp. 51–6.

[4] For shared opinions, see Thomas Rogers, *The Catholic Doctrine of the Church of England*, ed. J. J. S. Perowne (Parker Society, Cambridge, 1854), pp. 78, 147–8, 246. On heresy as a route to 'atheism', see, for example, Thomas Heywood, *A True Discourse of the Two Infamous Upstart Prophets* (London, 1636), p. 7.

[5] Thomas Beard, *The Theatre of Gods Judgements* (London, 1597), pp. 147–8; William Vaughan, *The Golden-Grove, Moralised in Three Books* (London, 1600), sigs C4v–5. The relevant papers from British Library Harleian MSS 6848, 6849 and 6853 are most conveniently available in Constance B. Kuriyama, *Christopher Marlowe: A Renaissance Life* (Ithaca, 2002), Appendix [In 1985 they had to be cited via F. C. Danchin,'Etudes Critiques sur Christopher Marlowe', *Revue Gemanique*, 9 (1913), 566–87 (with commentary in *Revue Gemanique*, 10 [1914], 52–68), and C. F. Tucker Brooke, *The Life of Christopher Marlowe and the Tragedy of Dido Queen of Carthage* (London, 1930), each of which had some material not included by the other.] On the context of the accusations, see, in addition to these works, John Bakeless, *The Tragicall History of Christopher Marlowe*, 2 vols (Cambridge, MA, 1942), ch. 5, P. H. Kocher, *Christopher Marlowe* (Chapel Hill, 1946), ch. 2–3, and this volume, pp. 26–8.

the depositions concerning him are preserved among the papers of Sir John Puckering, Lord Keeper of the Great Seal, alongside examinations of sectaries and recusants carried out at the same time, a juxtaposition not hitherto noted.[6] In the same context – and therefore probably inspired by the same concern – survives a record of the only known official enquiry into 'Atheisme; or Apostacy' in the period, the special commission held at Cerne Abbas in Dorset in 1594 to investigate the supposed heterodoxy of Sir Walter Ralegh and his circle: this brought to light various more or less extreme irreligious utterances which would evidently normally have gone unrecorded.[7]

Apart from this, we know of isolated cases of anti-religious talk, as with a man who said to Richard Bancroft, then Bishop of London, at the London sessions in 1599: 'My Lord, if any heere can proove there is a God, I will beleeue it', or one John Baldwin, a witness in a 1595 Star Chamber case,

> who questioned whether there were a god; if there were, howe he showld be knowne; if by his worde, who wrote the same; if the prophetes & the Apostles, they were but men, et humanum est errare; & such like most damnable doubtes, & not suffered to be reade in the hearinge of this Courte.[8]

A scattering of cases of more or less extreme utterances of a clearly sceptical rather than sectarian variety have also come to light in local ecclesiastical records.[9]

But even allowing for the disappearance of relevant records that would have dealt with such matters, such as those of the High Commission based in London, not many instances of this kind ever seem to have come before the courts. Moreover, aside from the exceptional episode in 1593–4 when

[6] This juxtaposition is made particularly plain by the transcripts and abstracts of the material by the antiquary Thomas Baker, from whom Harley acquired the documents, in British Library Harleian MS 7042, fols 193–236. For the material relating to the sectaries, see *The Writings of John Greenwood and Henry Barrow, 1591–3*, ed. L. H. Carlson (Elizabethan Nonconformist Texts, VI, London, 1970).

[7] British Library Harleian MS 6849, fols 183–90, printed in Danchin, 'Etudes Critiques', pp. 578–87, and *Willobie His Avisa*, ed. G. B. Harrison (London, 1926), pp. 255–71. See also E. A. Strathmann, *Sir Walter Ralegh: A Study in Elizabethan Skepticism* (New York, 1951), pp. 46–52, and Pierre Lefranc, *Sir Walter Ralegh, Ecrivain: l'oeuvre et les idées* (Paris, 1968), pp. 379–93 (which stresses the local context of the enquiry).

[8] *The Triall of Maist. Dorrell* (Middelburg, 1599), p. 88; John Hawarde, *Les Reportes del Cases in Camera Stellata, 1593–1609*, ed. W. P. Baildon (London, 1894), p. 17. [The quotation, 'It is human to make mistakes', is from Seneca.]

[9] A selection of such cases will be noted in the course of this chapter. See also Keith Thomas, *Religion and the Decline of Magic* (London, 1971), pp. 168–72.

irreligion became peripherally involved in the government's general clampdown on religious extremism, it is also telling how often cases came to light by accident, arising only in connection with assessing the character of witnesses or of defendants who were primarily in trouble on other charges. And it goes almost without saying that nearly all the accusations were based on hearsay evidence: only in the case of Marlowe was it claimed that he wrote an irreligious treatise, and the uniqueness of this is plain from the almost incredulous tone of Thomas Beard's report of the fact.[10]

What makes this the more surprising is the unanimity of contemporary commentators on the seriousness of the threat that 'atheism' presented, and the need for rigour in dealing with this 'sinne of all sinnes'.[11] As will become apparent from my citations in the course of this chapter, this was a topic in which there was considerable consensus among figures covering a spectrum of affiliations and status: churchmen who wrote on the subject ranged from Richard Hooker and Joseph Hall through Thomas Fuller to 'puritans' like Richard Greenham, William Perkins and Thomas Adams, while lay authors included both the godly country gentleman Sir George More of Loseley and the incendiary litterateur Thomas Nashe. Fuller's paraphrase of Greenham's claim – 'That Atheisme in England is more to be feared then Popery' – is not so different from Nashe's sentiment: 'There is no Sect now in *England* so scattered as Atheisme'.[12] Similarly, Hooker's view that his contemporaries should follow Nebuchadnezzar in their treatment of these infidels was echoed by William Perkins's opinion that they deserved the death penalty or Thomas Adams's conviction that they should be branded.[13]

What are the reasons for this disparity? One might be that the authorities were too lax, a view certainly held by the divine John Dove, who would have liked his countrymen to emulate the rigour of the Spanish Inquisition.[14] It is revealing that the case of the 1599 London 'atheist' is

[10] Beard, *Theatre*, p. 148. For the hypothesis that the Baines note is based on a written text by Marlowe, see Kocher, *Marlowe*, ch. 3.
[11] Adam Hill, *The Crie of England* (London, 1595), p. 32.
[12] Thomas Fuller, *The Holy State and the Profane State* (Cambridge, 1642), p. 383 (cf. Richard Greenham, *Workes*, ed. H. Holland, 3rd ed. [London, 1601], p. 3); Thomas Nashe, *Works*, ed. R. B. McKerrow, 2nd ed., 5 vols (Oxford, 1958), II, 121–2.
[13] Richard Hooker, *Of the Laws of Ecclesiastical Polity*, ed. A. S. McGrade, 3 vols (Oxford, 2013), II, p. 15 (cf. Daniel 3. 29); William Perkins, *Workes*, 3 vols (Cambridge, 1608–9), I, 130, II, 527; Thomas Adams, *A Commentary or Exposition Upon the Divine Second Epistle Generall, [of] St. Peter* (London, 1633), p. 1179. On More's views, see p. 42.
[14] John Dove, *A Confutation of Atheisme* (London, 1605), p. 14.

known only because the author who recorded it shared Dove's view,[15] and this is a point to the implications of which we will return. More pertinent, however, is a question of terminology. Was what contemporaries described as 'atheism' and said was common anything that we would recognise as irreligion according to the criteria so far outlined?

In fact, from the time of its introduction into English in the middle years of the sixteenth century onwards, the word 'atheist' was frequently used to mean 'godless' in a rather broad and loose sense.[16] Thus the word was commonly employed to describe a failure to espouse the new Protestant creed in a positive as against a merely negative way, and in this connection lack of enthusiasm for the new religion was often conflated with a continued attachment to the old. 'Papistes, Atheistes, and all wicked enemies of the Ghospell' was Josias Nichols's inclusive formula, while another godly divine, Samuel Smith, saw as 'atheists' those 'that thinke it lost labour to bee Religious, and that there is no good got by hearing Sermons, and leading of a godly life'.[17] From this, it is easy to see how the word's currency could be extended to imply a lack of commitment in the eyes of the beholder even in those ostensibly devoted to pursuing the good of the national church, as when Elizabeth I was accused of being 'an atheist, and a maintainer of atheism'.[18] By a similar process of elision, Roman Catholicism could also be condemned as – if no worse – 'the high way to Atheisme'.[19]

Broader still was the usage of the word to describe godlessness in the sense of evil living, as expounded by the religious writer Thomas Palfreyman in a helpful lexicographical note on 'the accursed': 'whome the *Hebricians* doe call *Reshaim:* that is to say, *Sinners:* the Latine menne *Impios,* that is, Wicked: the Grecians, *Atheos,* which is, Ungodlie or

---

[15] *The Triall of Maist. Dorrell,* p. 88.

[16] For early examples of the use of the word, see, for example, John Veron, *A Frutefull Treatise of Predestination* (London, [1561]) (where it is used as a synonym for 'anabaptists') or H. S. Bennett, *English Books and Readers, 1558–1603* (Cambridge, 1965), p. 148. Other early instances of usage are included in Friedrich Brie, 'Deismus und Atheismus in der Englischen Renaissance', *Anglia,* 48, (1924), 54–98, 105–68, and G. T. Buckley, *Atheism in the English Renaissance* (Chicago, 1932; reprinted New York, 1965). See also *Oxford English Dictionary (OED),* s.v. 'atheism', 'atheist', and, on the continental background, Henri Busson, 'Les Noms des Incrédules au XVIᵉ Siècle', *Bibliothèque d'Humanisme et Renaissance,* 16 (1954), 273–83, and Concetta Bianca, 'Per la Storia del Termine "Atheus" nel Cinquecento: Fonti et Traduzioni Greco-Latine', *Studi Filosofici,* 3 (1980), 71–104 (I owe this reference to the late Charles Schmitt).

[17] Josias Nichols, *The Plea of the Innocent* (London, 1602), p. 221 (bis); Samuel Smith, *The Great Assize,* 3rd impression (London, 1618), p. 263. Cf. Patrick Collinson, *The Religion of Protestants* (Oxford, 1982), p. 200.

[18] *Calendar of State Papers Domestic, 1601–3,* p. 23.

[19] John Hull, *The Unmasking of the Politike Atheist,* 2nd ed. (London, 1602), p. 42 and elsewhere.

without God'.[20] This appropriation of the word to describe 'the generall prophanenesse of mens liues' is perhaps particularly to be found in sermons and the like, though it is also in evidence in accusations against certain individuals.[21] 'Many that shall read this title', wrote the preacher John Wingfield in his book, *Atheisme Close and Open, Anatomised* (1634), 'will be ready to say, Is there any such? that dare say, or dare thinke, that there is no God?' 'Let me tell you', he continued, '& tel you that it is truth, and let these few lines witnesse against you: the hypocrite is a close Atheist: the loose wicked man is an open Atheist, the secure, bold, and proud transgressour is an Atheist: he that will not be taught & reformed, is an Atheist'.[22]

Such inclusive rhetoric has led some to dismiss 'atheism' as an empty term of abuse, but the difficulty is that this co-existed with the use of the word to signify overt irreligion of the kind manifested by Marlowe and others. Descriptions of 'atheism' of the latter kind go back to the years around 1570, and perhaps particularly to Roger Ascham's tirade in *The Scholemaster* against Machiavellian, Italianate Englishmen, 'Epicures in liuing, and `ἄθεοι in doctrine', who 'counte as Fables, the holie misteries of Christian Religion. They make Christ and his Gospell, onelie serue Ciuill pollicie'.[23] An equally well-known early specimen is John Lyly's dialogue between Euphues and Atheos of 1578, while, more unexpectedly, the State Papers have filed among them under the year 1571 a 'confutation of the atheists opynyon as Aristotle etc: who foleshely doeth affyrme the world to be wythout begynnyng'.[24]

If the latter, particularly, is rather crude in its evocation of an 'atheist' threat, a series of works from the 1580s onwards deal at length with 'atheism' in the sense of overt hostility to Christianity, elaborating a godless view of the world which is then duly refuted. This is seen, for instance, in sections of Robert Parsons's *Christian Directorie* or Sir Philip Sidney's *Arcadia*, while in chapter 2 of book 5 of Hooker's *Laws of Ecclesiastical Polity*, 'atheism' appears in polarisation to superstition in a

---

[20] Thomas Palfreyman, *The Treatise of Heavenly Philosophie* (London, 1578), p. 83.

[21] Pierre de la Primaudaye, *The Second Part of the French Academie*, trans. Thomas Bowes (London, 1594), sig. b3v. For accusations against individuals, see, for example, C. T. Prouty, *George Gascoigne* (New York, 1942), p. 61.

[22] John Wingfield, *Atheisme Close and Open, Anatomized*, 2 pts (London, 1634), II, 20–1.

[23] Roger Ascham, *English Works*, ed. W. A. Wright (Cambridge, 1904), pp. 228–36.

[24] John Lyly, *Euphues: The Anatomy of Wit and Euphues & His England*, ed. M. W. Croll and H. Clemons (London, 1916), pp. 147–62; The National Archives, SP 12/83, fols 114–15.

passage which should be pondered by all inclined to dismiss Elizabethan writings about 'atheism' as unworthy of serious attention.[25]

By the early seventeenth century, England could boast a number of books devoted exclusively to the subject, such as John Dove's *A Confutation of Atheisme* (1605) or the unfinished *Atheomastix* (1622) of Martin Fotherby, Bishop of Salisbury.[26] Somewhat livelier than these solemn treatises is Jeremy Corderoy's dialogue, *A Warning for Worldlings, or, a Comfort to the Godly and a Terror to the Wicked* (1608), which presents a disarmingly vivid portrait of a traveller who not only states at one point, 'I am fully perswaded, that there is no God', but also divulges a whole series of heterodox opinions and attitudes in discussion with a godly Scholar who has been taken to represent Corderoy – chaplain of Merton College, Oxford – himself.[27]

In these and other books, a profile emerges of the 'atheist' as the kind of freethinker we might expect, denying the existence of God and supporting this position with a fairly standard battery of arguments. Prominent was the questioning of the authority of the scriptures and drawing attention to inconsistencies within them: indeed, Corderoy's traveller averred that 'the Scripture was it, that first draue me to these opinions. For I find in it so many falshoods and vntruthes, so many absurdities, so many vnreasonable things, that he is a sencelesse man that perceaueth it not, and a foole that beleeueth it'.[28] Equally central, it was believed, was a preference for natural as against supernatural explanations, the view that 'all things come to passe by nature, or fortune'.[29] Hence God's active supervision of the world came under challenge, while it was also axiomatic that 'atheists' questioned the doctrine of the creation on the basis of a view of the world as eternal derived 'from Aristotle his schoole'.[30]

[25] Robert Parsons, *A Christian Directorie Guiding Men to Their Salvation* ([Louvain], 1585), ch. 2, 4 (these chapters do not appear in the 1582 edition; they recur in the 1598 edition but are omitted from that of 1607); cf. Ernest A. Strathmann, 'Robert Parsons's Essay on Atheism', in *Joseph Quincy Adams Memorial Studies*, ed. J. G. McManaway, G. E. Dawson and E. E. Willoughby (Washington, D.C., 1948), pp. 665–81. Sir Philip Sidney, *The Countess of Pembroke's Arcadia*, ed. Maurice Evans (Harmondsworth, 1977), pp. 487–92; cf. D. P. Walker, 'Atheism, the Ancient Theology and Sidney's *Arcadia*', in *The Ancient Theology* (London, 1972), pp. 132–63. Hooker, *Laws of Ecclesiastical Polity*, II, 13–16.

[26] For an account of various of these books, see Strathmann, *Ralegh*, ch. 3. See also G. E. Aylmer, 'Unbelief in Seventeenth-Century England', in *Puritans and Revolutionaries*, ed. Donald Pennington and Keith Thomas (Oxford, 1978), pp. 22–46.

[27] Jeremy Corderoy, *A Warning for Worldlings* (London, 1608), p. 37; C. M. Dent, *Protestant Reformers in Elizabethan Oxford* (Oxford, 1983), p. 159.

[28] Corderoy, *A Warning*, pp. 202–3.   [29] Perkins, *Workes*, II, 451.

[30] Henry Cuffe, *The Differences of the Ages of Mans Life* (London, 1607), p. 24.

A denial of the immortality of the soul was seen as a further common trait of 'atheists'; this was thought to lead to a dismissal of the Last Judgment as 'ridiculous and fabulous', and to the belief 'that vertue, innocence, and craftie dealing be alike rewarded', while an overriding worldliness was also presumed to be quintessential.[31] Lastly, 'atheists' were supposed to hold a cynical view of religion itself as 'nothing else but a certaine humane inuen- tion and politike rule of mans wit', intended 'to keepe men within the compasse of humane lawes', a view that was frequently associated with Machiavelli, of whose ideas 'atheists' were habitually seen as devotees.[32]

There is also consensus on the milieu and characteristics of 'atheists'. That Corderoy's was a traveller was symptomatic – since Ascham's time, Italy had been seen as the source of heterodoxy of this kind – while it was also a commonplace that such free-thought was associated with education and with verbal agility in the form of 'wit'. Martin Fotherby thought that the doubts that he refuted in his *Atheomastix* 'neuer creepe into the heads of simpler and vnlearned persons', while Thomas Nashe averred that 'it is the superaboundance of witte that makes Atheists'.[33] In manner, 'atheists' were thought to be 'always confident beyond reformation', speaking their ideas 'openly and boldly', promoting their ideas with almost missionary zeal in the oral milieux in which they were thought to express them, appealing to 'sence, experience [and] reason', and having recourse to 'vnsauourie scorne' in propounding their opinions.[34] Indeed, 'scoffing' was seen as a typical irreligious trait, its apparently increased incidence being seen by Hooker as confirming St Peter's prophecy about the latter days.[35]

I have separated this recognisably modern concept of 'atheism' from the broader usage of the word to mean in effect godlessness, and contempo- raries themselves recognised that this was a word 'of a very large extent', being employed to describe more things than one.[36] This is shown by a series of more or less convoluted attempts to classify different types of 'atheist', and to distinguish 'atheists' proper from such other classes of person as hypocrites, temporisers, Epicures and 'Common Profane

---

[31] Samuel Gardiner, *Doomes-Day Booke* (London, 1606), p. 1; John Stephens, *Satyrical Essayes Characters and Others* (London, 1615), p. 212.

[32] John Carpenter, *A Preparative to Contentation* (London, 1597), p. 233; Corderoy, *A Warning*, p. 12.

[33] Martin Fotherby, *Atheomastix* (London, 1622), sig. A2v; Nashe, *Works*, II, 124.

[34] Stephens, *Satyrical Essayes*, p. 216; Robert Burton, *The Anatomy of Melancholy*, ed. T. C. Faulkner, N. K. Kiessling, and R. L. Blair, 6 vols (Oxford, 1989–2000), III, 404; Corderoy, *A Warning*, p. 38; Cuffe, *Differences*, p. 20. On atheists as proselytisers, see Bacon, *Essayes*, p. 52.

[35] Hooker, *Laws of Ecclesiastical Polity*, II, 14–15. Cf. II Peter 3. 3.   [36] Fuller, *Holy State*, p. 378.

persons'[37] – in other words, the uncommitted Protestants and evil-doers whom we have already seen the word being used to describe.

It would be possible to write at length about the varying definitions used by different authors and the inconsistencies between them, and sometimes even within the works of a single author, as to what should or should not be described as 'atheism' – whether hypocrisy was to be seen as part of it or as a separate phenomenon, for instance[38] – and as to what terminology should be used to convey the degrees of seriousness of irreligion. A certain consensus emerges in distinguishing between 'inward' and 'outward atheism' – irreligious views openly expressed and those that their holders kept to themselves – and between 'atheism in judgment' and 'practical atheism', heterodoxy expressed through immoral actions.

But though differing degrees of infidelity were distinguished, there was a constant tendency to conflate them and to argue that in fact they inevitably led to one another. In particular, a kind of circular connection was presumed between theoretical irreligion and bad behaviour. As the divine William Ames put it: 'such wicked opinions or imaginations do let loose the raines of all concupiscence, and therefore are the cause of increasing that wickednesse, whereof at the first they were the effect'.[39] Moreover free-thought was itself seen as progressive, with mild positions inexorably giving way to more extreme ones. In his portrait of an 'atheist' in *The Profane State* (1642), Thomas Fuller considered that articulate irreligion grew from quarrelling and scoffing at sacred things, which 'by degrees abates the reverence of religion, and ulcers mens hearts with profanenesse', a view expressed more rhetorically by Thomas Adams: 'The Chayre of the Scorner, is the seate of Sathan, the lowest staire and very threshold of Hell'.[40]

In addition, Fuller saw anti-providentialism as a preliminary step to outright 'atheism', and it was doubtless because they thought the same that others simply elided the difference between the two, like the Catholic writer Thomas Fitzherbert, who pointed out 'that I take Atheists, not only for those, who deny that there is a God, but also for such, as deny the particuler prouidence of God in the affaires of men: who are no lesse to be counted Atheists, then the other'.[41] It is similarly symptomatic that the

---

[37] Thomas Adams, *Workes* (London, 1630), p. 16.
[38] Compare Perkins, *Workes*, I, 479 with II, 526.
[39] William Ames, *An Analyticall Exposition of Both the Epistles of the Apostle Peter* (London, 1641), pp. 237–8.
[40] Fuller, *Holy State*, p. 379; Adams, *Workes*, p. 14.
[41] Fuller, *Holy State*, p. 380; Thomas Fitzherbert, *The Second Part of a Treatise Concerning Policy, and Religion* ([Douai], 1610), pp. 69–70.

word 'Epicure' was used as a label both for 'A lover of pleasure, more then of God' and also for the man 'which denieth his prouidence'.[42]

Hence, though our inclination might be to try to separate the two, there is an overlap between the portrayal of 'philosophical atheism' and the attack on godlessness. Authors like John Wingfield or Josias Nichols whose main thrust is an attack on sinfulness or lack of commitment also allude to the phenomenon of philosophical doubt.[43] More serious, it is apparent that even some of those who portrayed and attacked articulate irreligion were really concerned about 'practical atheism'. Thus, for all the apparent verisimilitude of Jeremy Corderoy's portrait of an 'atheist' in his *A Warning for Worldlings*, in his 'To the Reader' he paradoxically claimed that 'fewe or none there are, who now in words deny God', continuing: 'But the Scripture forewarneth vs of a more dangerous kind of Atheist, who wil not in words deny God, but by their deeds'.[44]

Indeed, though all agreed on the menace presented by 'practical atheism', there is a frustrating lack of consensus among contemporaries as to whether 'philosophical atheists' were common at all. To some extent this depends on what 'common' is taken to mean, and matters are further complicated by contemporaries' fastidiousness in their definition of true 'atheism'. Thomas Fuller, for instance, thought that 'to give an instance of a speculative Atheist, is both hard and dangerous' – a view similar to that of Francis Bacon – but this was partly because 'we cannot see mens speculations otherwise then as they cloth themselves visible in their actions, some Atheisticall speeches being not sufficient evidence to convict the speaker an Atheist'.[45] Moreover, while some asserted that 'I can assure you of my owne experience, that there are such, that denie not onely the prouidence, but euen the very nature and existence of God', other writers were simply vague or inconsistent, like Sir George More, who alternated between expressing amazement that anyone should disbelieve in God and asserting that open 'atheists' actually existed.[46]

But he was not thereby prevented from entering into a refutation of irreligious views, which might appear to suggest that what orthodox writers attacked was not necessarily very closely related to any phenomenon in

---

[42] Adams, *Workes*, p. 498; John Spicer, *The Sale of Salt* (London, 1611), p. 32. See also W. R. Elton, *King Lear and the Gods* (San Marino, 1966), ch.1.

[43] Wingfield, *Atheism*, esp. 1, 66–7; Nichols, *Plea*, pp. 208–9 (bis).

[44] Corderoy, *A Warning*, sig. A6v.   [45] Fuller, *Holy State*, p. 383; Bacon, *Essayes*, p. 52.

[46] Thomas Morton, *A Treatise of the Nature of God* (London, 1599), p. 30 (a statement by the gentleman who acts as an interlocutor in the dialogue); Sir George More, *A Demonstration of God in His Workes* (London, 1597), sig. A2v, pp. 20, 25–6 and elsewhere.

contemporary life, despite the existence in England at this time of occasional cases of outright infidelity of the kind already noted.

Certainly, the anti-atheist literature displays a number of features which suggest artificiality. In these books as a whole, there is a disquieting shortage of instances of native 'atheists', and instead a reliance on examples from classical antiquity or Renaissance Europe. The names of Diagoras, Epicurus, Lucian, Lucretius, Pliny, Protagoras and Theodorus recur again and again, and more recent specimens are equally standard, the commonest being Machiavelli and – perhaps more surprisingly – Pope Leo X. Even when native instances are given, there is often a distinctly folklorish quality about them, as with the 'gentleman of Barkshire, whose name I forebeare to express, a man of great possessions', who figures in Thomas Beard's *Theatre of God's Judgements*. This person was said to be an open 'atheist', given over to swearing and to 'all sensualitie of the flesh', who wanted the name 'Beelzebub' to be given to a child whose christening he attended. He was struck dead while out hunting and 'discoursing of many vaine matters', 'and became a terrible example to all wicked Atheists, of Gods justice'.[47]

Equally disturbing is the derivative and clichéd nature of the argument with 'atheists' in which orthodox polemicists engaged. To some extent their sources lay in recent continental writings, and especially French ones, including such works as Phillippe Duplessis Mornay's *De la Verité de la Religion Chrestienne,* of which an English translation by Sir Philip Sidney and Arthur Golding appeared in 1587. Perhaps more significant, however, were classical, patristic and biblical texts, as is clear from the frequency with which passages from the Bible and the names of the Fathers and of classical authors like Cicero are cited. As Thomas Nashe put it as he ended his breathless summary of the design argument in *Christs Teares over Jerusalem* (1593): 'O why should I but squintingly glance at these matters, when they are so admirably expatiated by auncient Writers?'[48] Even within the literature itself, there is a substantial derivative element. Roger Ascham's 'atheist' profile was quoted verbatim by Thomas Palfreyman in his *Treatise of Heauenly Philosophie* (1578) and was repeatedly paraphrased thereafter.[49] More surprisingly, Nashe's evocation of 'atheism' in *Christs Teares* was cited as an authority in Thomas Rogers's *Catholic Doctrine of*

[47] Thomas Beard, *The Theatre of God's Judgements* (3rd ed., London, 1631), pp. 150–1.
[48] Nashe, Works, II, 121.
[49] Palfreyman, *The Treatise*, pp. 702–4, and see, for example, Primaudaye, *Second Part*, sig. b4v; John Hull, *Saint Peters Prophesie of These Last Daies* (London, 1610), p. 127; Thomas Jackson, *London New-Yeeres Gift* (London, 1609), fol. 18.

the Church of England (1607), apart from being reworked by Thomas Adams along with other existing accounts of infidelity.[50] In addition, folklorish accounts of 'atheism' were borrowed by one author from another.[51]

The element of cliché emerges perhaps particularly in the views that 'atheists' were supposed to hold. John Hull's summary of the presumed arguments of infidels in his *Saint Peters Prophesie of these Last Daies* (1610) – 'making Christ an imposter, Moyses a deceiuer, the Gospell a tale, and the Law a fable'[52] – recites formulae that had been used time and time again, in particular the notion of all or part either of the scriptures or the Christian religion being a 'fable', and the accusation that Moses and Christ were cozeners, which in fact echoes the views of Celsus as refuted by Origen.[53] This also applies to such aspects of the profile of the 'atheist' already outlined as the naturalism, or the view of religion as a device of policy.

Moreover, the arguments used to 'refute' infidels are markedly lacking in originality, though some expositions are more ingenious than others. We hear again and again the design argument, rehearsed in greater or lesser detail, or the argument from man's conscience, or the 'consent of nations', the innate religiosity of mankind. Equally frequent is the argument that 'atheists' come to a bad end, a theme epitomised by the relevant section of Beard's *Theatre of God's Judgements.*

All this artificiality is compounded by a distinctly complacent and self-congratulatory tone about the literature. It was a commonplace that 'atheists' were unreasonable, that true rationality could only underwrite an orthodox religious outlook. As John Lyly's Euphues put it in his dialogue with Atheos: 'But why go I about in a thing so manifest to use proofs so manifold? If thou deny the truth who can prove it; if thou deny that black is black, who can by reason reprove thee when thou opposest thyself against reason?' It goes almost without saying that the dialogue ends

---

[50] Rogers, *Catholic Doctrine*, pp. 78, 148; Adams, *Commentary*, pp. 1159–66: other sources include Bacon.

[51] For instance, Richard Greenham's account of an 'atheist' (*Workes*, p. 3) was reused in Miles Mosse, *Ivstifying and Saving Faith Distinguished from the Faith of the Devils* (Cambridge and London, 1614), pp. 17–18, and in Adams, *Commentary*, p. 16.

[52] Hull, *Saint Peters Prophesie*, p. 8.

[53] *Origen: Contra Celsum*, trans. Henry Chadwick (Cambridge, 1953), esp. pp. 22, 28, 37, 297. For an instance of a typical formulaic description of 'atheism', see Daniel Price, *Sauls Prohibition Staide* (London, 1609), sig. E3.

with Atheos in a state of gushing repentance, and there was a widespread tendency to presume that those who resisted theistic arguments could not be so much men as 'brute beasts'.[54]

To a large extent, these books were clearly aimed at the godly rather than the ungodly, as is shown by their effusive dedications or by passages where authors break off from their anti-atheist polemic to include asides for the orthodox.[55] Quite apart from the actual existence of 'atheism', the spectre of it undoubtedly allowed authors to rehearse arguments on matters 'most needefull to be beleeued; yet least laboured in by *Diuines*'.[56] By visualising unbelievers who 'must be refuted by the principles of nature onely, for all other arguments they scorne', writers were given an excuse to expound the principles of natural theology, while the gentleman who acts as interlocutor in Thomas Morton's *Treatise of the Nature of God* (1599) sought comfort even in matters 'which are most certaine, manifest, and without all question ... that I may knowe and hold that more firmly, which I doo alreadie both beleeue, and also know in part'.[57]

The notion of 'atheism' served other intellectual functions which it is important for us to understand. In part, it stemmed from an a priori assumption that anti-Christian behaviour must be linked to anti-Christian belief, that there must be as articulate a rationale for evil as for good. And, both for this reason and more generally, the evocation and elaboration of an image of irreligion played an important part in a world percolated by Aristotelian contraries, rather comparable to the significance of statements about witchcraft which has been demonstrated by Stuart Clark.[58] Hooker saw 'affected Atheism' as 'The most extreme opposite to true Religion', and others used the concept of 'Antipodes'.[59]

The sense of contrariety is confirmed by the overlap between the attacks on 'atheism' and the Theophrastan character literature which was so popular in early seventeenth-century England.[60] 'The Atheist' is one of the stock characters of these books, and, in the typical moralistic manner of the genre, he is presented as an ideal type of the 'most badde man', to quote the synonym for 'An Atheist' in Nicholas Breton's *The Good and the*

---

[54] Lyly, *Euphues*, pp. 150, 161–2; More, *Demonstration*, p. 34.

[55] For example, Dove, *Confutation*, p. 70.   [56] Fotherby, *Atheomastix*, sig. A2.

[57] John Weemes, *A Treatise of the Foure Degenerate Sonnes* (London, 1636), p. 7; Morton, *Treatise*, p. 7.

[58] Stuart Clark, 'Inversion, Misrule and the Meaning of Witchcraft', *Past & Present*, 87 (1980), 98–127. [See also his *Thinking with Demons: The Idea of Witchcraft in Early Modern Europe* (Oxford, 1997).]

[59] Hooker, *Laws of Ecclesiastical Polity*, II, 13; Burton, *Anatomy*, III, 395–6; Weemes, *Treatise*, p. 6.

[60] See Benjamin Boyce, *The Theophrastan Character in England to 1642* (Cambridge, MA, 1947), and C. N. Greenough, *A Bibliography of the Theophrastan Character in English* (Cambridge, MA, 1947).

Badde, or Descriptions of the Worthies, and Vnworthies of this Age (1616).[61]
The function of polarities of this kind was explained by a divine who
himself wrote a character-book, Bishop Joseph Hall, who claimed that 'this
light contraries give to each other in the midst of their enmity, that one
makes the other seem more good or ill'.[62] Josias Nichols had earlier
pointed out the value, in expounding Christian doctrine, of noting 'errors
which are contrarie to these trueths ... and so it wil much further them;
euen as by all contraries, euery good thing is the more perceiued, felt and
esteemed'.[63]

It would be quite possible, therefore, to argue that 'atheism' would have
had to be invented in the early modern period even if it had not existed,
that the anti-atheist literature served purposes in its own right to which the
actual incidence of articulate irreligion was barely relevant. Undoubtedly,
there is an element of truth in this, but the question to which we must
address ourselves is whether this is the whole of the story, or whether there
was in fact more interconnection between fiction and the actual phenomenon of infidelity than has so far been apparent.

For one thing, we must be careful not to impose modern standards on
our early modern forebears. The fact that their categorisation may seem to
us rather artificial does not mean that they were not trying to make sense of
real phenomena in such terms, while the dependence on written sources
for 'atheist' instances is equally easily misconstrued. Though we may find
the most recent and local examples the most telling, for them classical ones
offered at the same time authority and an established typology of unbelief.
The proclivity to cite antique instances was encouraged by the sense of
virtual contemporaneity with the classics and the Fathers shown by these
writers, so that it seemed quite natural to cite opinions and statements
from such sources as if they were of universal validity and hence to conflate
'all Atheistes of olde, and of our tyme'.[64]

There is also the nature of the genre to consider, for an envenomed
tirade against free-thought would have been weakened by pausing to name
nonentities, particularly when the commonness of the phenomenon was
all along being asserted. Even concerning God's vengeance, where
individual cases were most relevant, there was a premium on spectacular
examples rather than ordinary ones. Hence most of the specimens in

---

[61] Nicholas Breton, *The Good and the Badde* (London, 1616), p. 20.
[62] Joseph Hall, *Works*, new ed., ed. Philip Wynter, 10 vols (Oxford, 1863), VI, 106
[63] Josias Nichols, *An Order of Houshold Instruction* (London, 1596), sig. E5.
[64] Parsons, *Christian Directorie*, p. 25.

Beard's *Theatre of God's Judgements* came from books rather than experience – even when he extended the work with extra material – and Marlowe's case was virtually the only local one which seemed to Beard 'Not inferiour to any of the former in Atheisme & impiety, and equall to all in maner of punishment'.[65]

But, as the instancing of Marlowe by Beard and by William Vaughan in his *Golden-Groue* reveals, these authors were concerned to document a connection between their stock 'atheist' figure and real phenomena in the society of their day, and it would be wrong to see the erudition of such writers as in any way precluding empirical experience. In Nicholas Gibbens's *Questions and Disputations Concerning the Holy Scripture* (1601), for instance, the margins are mainly filled with learned patristic citations, but among these appears at one point the rather incongruous note, 'My selfe hath bin an eye and an eare witnes', to document the fact that 'there are of this our age, which will demaunde, more curious then wise, where these skins were had so sodainelie, which made *Adam* clothing ... yea they will be so madde as to demaund, where *Adam* had a thred to sew his figge leaues'.[66]

Moreover, when one returns to the actual instances of irreligion recorded in contemporary documents after soaking oneself in the anti-atheist literature, one finds in the descriptions of those accused echoes of the 'atheist' stereotype which, because of its pedigree and presentation, one might otherwise have been tempted to dismiss. This suggests a more complex relationship between the imaginary and the real than has so far been allowed for.

Thus, in one of the instances of heterodox talk that came up at Star Chamber, the 'heretical and execrable words' which one Robert Fisher was accused of uttering – 'that Christe was no saviour & the gospell a fable' – repeat almost verbatim one of the commonplaces of anti-atheist writings.[67] The same is true of some of what was said in our best-documented case, that of Marlowe. Even parts of the informers' reports about him fall into this category – for instance, the view retailed by Richard Baines, 'That the first beginning of Religioun was only to keep men in awe' – while there is a strong element of cliché in Thomas Beard's account of Marlowe's supposed writings, 'affirming our Sauiour to be but a deceiuer, and *Moses* to be

---

[65] Beard, *Theatre* (1597), p. 147. For Beard's additions, see the 1631 edition, esp. pp. 548–9.
[66] Nicholas Gibbens, *Questions and Disputations Concerning the Holy Scripture* (London, 1601), pp. 168–9.
[67] Hawarde, *Reportes*, p. 41.

but a coniurer and seducer of the people, and the holy Bible to be but vaine and idle stories, and all religion but a deuice of pollicie'.[68]

This might be taken to suggest that the accusations merely represented an attempt at character assassination by projecting conventional expectations onto those suspected of irreligion, though the originality of some of the opinions attributed to Marlowe suggests that this cannot be the whole truth.[69] It might show that the orthodox tended to perceive the heterodoxy they heard in hackneyed terms, as is certainly suggested by Beard's description, which – though bearing sufficient relationship to the more detailed informers' reports on Marlowe not to be dismissed – nevertheless ignores Marlowe's more ingenious speculations.

But it is surely no less likely that the vocabulary of irreligion itself comprised commonplaces of heterodoxy picked up from orthodox sources. Paul H. Kocher has painstakingly demonstrated how many of the views said to have been expressed by Marlowe can be paralleled in writings against 'atheism',[70] and such books may well have helped to create the very phenomenon which they sought to refute. There are hints of this in our sources, and it is certainly revealing that anti-atheist authors felt the need to defend themselves against those

> more scrupulous, then rightly zealous; who thinke it not conuenient, that any question should be made, whether there be any God or no, (because as they say) there are very fewe, who doubt of it, and the very calling of it in question, breedeth scruples in the mindes of those, who made no question of it before.[71]

Whichever of these things is true – or whether they all are to some extent – we nevertheless have to visualise a kind of symbiotic relationship between 'atheism' as imagined and irreligion as it existed. It is therefore

---

[68] Kuriyama, *Christopher Marlowe*, p. 221; Beard, *Theatre* (1597), p. 148. Compare Robert Parsons's accusation against Ralegh (Lefranc, *Ralegh*, p. 356), or the allegations against the Earl of Oxford in 1581, in which appear such cliches as 'The trinity a fable' and 'Scriptures for pollicye': see Lefranc, *Ralegh*, pp. 340–1, and The National Archives, SP 12/151, fols 102, 109, 118.

[69] For such a suggestion in a comparable context, see David Wootton, *Paolo Sarpi: Between Renaissance and Enlightenment* (Cambridge, 1983), p. 143. On Marlowe's originality, see Kocher, *Marlowe*, ch. 3.

[70] Kocher, *Marlowe*, p. 30n. and ch. 3.

[71] Corderoy, *A Warning*, sig. A6. For examples – though more of heretical than atheistic ideas – see the manuscript owned by Kyd in which an anti-Arian work was eviscerated for heretical opinions (Kuriyama, *Christopher Marlowe*, pp. 217–18; Danchin, 'Etudes Critiques', pp. 568–70; and W. D. Briggs, 'On a Document concerning Christopher Marlowe', *Studies in Philology*, 20 (1923), 153–9) or the claim of the Sherborne shoemaker Robert Hyde, at the Cerne Abbas hearing, to have derived his notions from reports of a local priest's sermon attacking sectarian views: *Willobie His Avisa*, pp. 264, 269–70.

hardly surprising to find that the cases of irreligious talk that came to light duplicate in piecemeal form elements of the stock atheist figure that I have already outlined.

Thus one finds doubts about the scope of God's providential intervention in the world, as reported of 'Mr Thinn' at the Cerne Abbas enquiry of 1594 – probably Charles Thynne, Ralegh's nephew, though it might have been John Thynne of Longleat – who spoke 'as though godes providence did not reach ouer all creatures or to like effecte'.[72] Similarly, William Gardiner, a Surrey landowner and Justice of the Peace, was accused in the 1580s of claiming – if not 'that there was no God' – 'that He had no government in the world'.[73] Antiscripturalism was spectacularly manifested by Marlowe, who was said to have denounced Moses, Christ and St Paul, questioned the biblical age of the world, jested at the scriptures and compiled a collection of 'contrarieties' in them.[74] But at a humbler level, comparable sentiments were also attributed to one Robert Blagden of Keevil in Wiltshire, who was alleged in 1619 to have 'made doubt ... whether the prophetts and Appostles writinges were true or not'.[75]

The denial of the immortality of the soul from an atheistic standpoint was imputed to Thomas Allen, Lieutenant of Portland Castle, and his servant Oliver at the Cerne Abbas hearing, to Marlowe's protegé, Thomas Fineaux or Finis of Dover, and also to a Wiltshire gentleman, John Derpier, who was accused in 1607 of maintaining the 'most hereticall & damnable opinion (that there was noe god & noe resurrection, & that men died a death like beastes)'.[76] With this might go a cynicism about the

---

[72] *Willobie His Avisa*, p. 259. For the possibility that this was Charles Thynne, see Lefranc, *Ralegh*, p. 387; on John Thynne, to whom Carew Ralegh was gentleman of horse and whose widow Carew married, see ODNB s.v. 'Sir Walter Ralegh'. Thynne's view was possibly heretical rather than atheistic; see the different positions distinguished in Stephen Gosson, *The Trumpet of Warre* (London, 1598), pp. 52–4.

[73] Leslie Hotson, *Shakespeare versus Shallow* (London, 1931), pp. 54–8, 198, 202, 228–9.

[74] Kuriyama, *Christopher Marlowe*, pp. 220–2. According to Simon Aldrich, Marlowe's 'booke' was 'against the Scriptur'; ibid., pp. 239–40.

[75] The National Archives, STA 8/59/11, memb. 2. [For background, see Martin Ingram, *Church Courts, Sex and Marriage in England, 1570–1640* (Cambridge, 1987), pp. 117–18, which illustrates the complex inter-personal rivalries lying behind this accusation.]

[76] *Willobie His Avisa*, pp. 262–3; Kuriyama, *Christopher Marlowe*, pp. 239–40; Wiltshire Record Office, Diocese of Salisbury Dean's Presentments, 1607–9 (10), fol. 66. This is another case to which I was alerted by Ingram, *Church Courts*, p. 95; he does not, however, note the circumstances in which Derpier was accused of uttering these words as referred to below [though these *are* included in the reference to the case in Christopher Haigh, *The Plain Man's Pathways to Heaven* (Oxford, 2007), p. 169 (where the name is give as 'Deryner')]. Such cases seem to me distinct from the non-atheistic mortalism dealt with in N. T. Burns, *Christian Mortalism from Tyndale to Milton* (Cambridge, MA, 1972).

function of religion and the motives of the clergy, expressed not only by Marlowe but also by a Yorkshire gentleman, Peter Vavasour, who was accused before the York High Commission in 1637 of having

> held, uttered and vented diverse and sundrye hereticall and damnable opinions and sayings touchinge the mysteries of faith, and especiallye ... beinge talkeinge of the Resurrection of the dead, said in a most impious and hereticall manner tush tush. that is but a tricke of the clergye, to cause the people to beleeve that to gett money and to catch fooles withall, and that prayers weere noe better then the barkeinge of doggs.[77]

In their manner, too, there is evidence of that confidence, that sense almost of proselytising, which anti-atheist authors stress. The 'atheist' who challenged Bancroft at the London sessions in 1599 did so, we are told, 'openly and impudently', while Richard Baines reported of Marlowe that 'almost into every company he cometh he perswades men to Atheism'.[78] It is perhaps also in this light that one should interpret the case of John Derpier, since the deposition against him reveals that it was only after he affirmed his views 'in disputation' with a local vicar in front of his scholars in church that Derpier was presented by the churchwardens. In addition, the sarcastic wit imputed to 'atheists' is borne out by some of these instances, while the orthodox would hardly have been surprised by the view of another alleged 'atheist', Brian Walker of Bishop Auckland, County Durham: 'neyther will I beleive anie thinge but what I see'.[79]

More significant still, these cases substantiate what might otherwise seem perhaps the most frustrating feature of the literature, that conviction of the progressive nature of infidelity, the difficulty of distinguishing between mild and extreme irreligious traits. The very manner in which such opinions came to light was prone to confirm presumptions about the link between theoretical and practical 'atheism'. As already noted, it was often only because people had been accused of other misdemeanours that their irreligious views were disclosed – in Vavasour's case, of interfering sexually with a servant, for instance, or in Gardiner's of trying to defraud his son-in-law. This kind of presumption was made explicit in the case of Robert Fisher, another figure whose 'blasphemous heresy' was recorded in conjunction with other offences at the Court of Star Chamber, who was

---

[77] Borthwick Institute, York, HC CP 1637/3: I am indebted to Bill Sheils for his help with this case. Cf. Kuriyama, *Christopher Marlowe*, pp. 221–2, 231.

[78] *The Triall of Maist. Dorrell*, p. 88; Kuriyama, *Christopher Marlowe*, p. 222.

[79] *The Acts of the High Commission Court within the Diocese of Durham*, ed. W. H. D. Longstaffe (Surtees Society, xxxiv, Durham, 1858), p. 116: I am indebted to Pete Rushton for his advice on this case. On wit, see Kocher, *Marlowe*, pp. 48, 56–7, and *Willobie His Avisa*, esp. pp. 266–8.

condemned 'by his outrage and impudence' despite there being 'not much testimony', Lord Treasurer Burghley observing: 'He who is once evil in the highest degree is always presumed to be evil, and [Fisher's] previous acts and subsequent life declare his impiety'.[80]

These instances also bear out the idea of a spectrum from mild to graver irreligion. The way in which horseplay could merge into something more serious is illustrated by the case of Robert Blagden, who was accused not only of antiscripturalism but also of having 'procured one Francis the Tapster of the George in Warminster to stand on a stoole and preache', 'in disgrace of gods worde & the ministrie',[81] and the same kind of juxtaposition is in evidence from the Cerne Abbas hearing. Against Thomas Allen, for instance, the allegations ranged from the serious claim that he had denied the immortality of the soul to such matters as his tearing two leaves out of a Bible to dry tobacco on, or expostulating when it rained while he was out hawking: 'if there be a god A poxe on that god which sendeth such weather to marr our sporte'.[82]

With Sir Walter Ralegh's brother, Carew, we again have a spectrum from mild anticlericalism to more serious heresy, from facetiously telling a local priest that his horse could preach as well as he could to maintaining the heterodox position that 'there was a god in nature' and arguing about the godhead in a manner said to be 'as like a pagan as euer you harde anye'. Ralegh was also said to have admitted 'that he had in deade sinned in manye thinges but what hurte had come vnto him for it?', asserting that death came to sinners and righteous alike, thus giving expression to exactly the kind of cynical attitude which caused concern at the time.[83]

None of this casual talk may seem very significant or dangerous, and it is perhaps not surprising that such cases were rarely pursued very far. It must have been hard to obtain a conviction on hearsay reports of table-talk, particularly when – as happened even in some of these instances – those accused denied that they had uttered the words imputed to them, and particularly with people of high status. Indeed, it is worth noting parenthetically here that, though the survival of accusations is far too random for

---

[80] Hawarde, *Reportes*, p. 42. See above, p. 47.   [81] The National Archives, STA 8/59/11, memb. 2.
[82] *Willobie His Avisa*, pp. 262–3, 256 (these, like other words cited in the 'Interrogatories', are clearly based on hearsay reports of those accused: cf. p. 264, for a slightly different version of the same story about Allen).
[83] *Willobie His Avisa*, pp. 258, 260, 261, 262, 266. It is interesting that Ralegh's opinion on the godhead had been uttered on an earlier occasion but was 'shutt up' till brought to light by the enquiry (p. 258).

any serious conclusions to be drawn concerning the social affiliations of articulate irreligion, gentlemen are disproportionately represented, even in cases from local ecclesiastical records. In addition, this random element makes it difficult to be sure how common such heterodoxy was, while, in the bulk of instances, we do not know how systematically thought-out even extreme-sounding statements were: one could easily believe that the most outspoken of these men were not outright 'atheists' in a modern sense.

But here we must again beware of being too literal-minded in searching for 'real' phenomena and return to an attempt to understand how anxiety about irreligion actually functioned. Allowance must be made for the ease with which oral evidence can be misconstrued, for the conviction that mild and extreme atheistic traits were inextricably linked, and for the intellectualist character of early modern thought – its tendency to extrapolate directly from premises to conclusions, from piecemeal evidence to a complete 'atheist' stereotype.[84] In these circumstances – and particularly in the light of the overlap of characteristics between real and imaginary 'atheists' – it is easy to see how scattered cases of irreligion like those I have surveyed fed a belief in a serious threat of the kind depicted in the literature.

Moreover, the juxtaposition of an exaggerated 'atheist' stereotype with the sense of an inexorable continuum from mild to extreme infidelity had a wider significance. For it may be argued that through the concept of 'atheism' it was possible to express disquiet about tendencies in contemporary ideas and attitudes which were commonplace and ultimately had irreligious implications, but which were rarely found in so extreme a form. It is thus possible to see a certain rationale even in the broad usage of 'atheism' to mean godlessness that I alluded to earlier in this chapter, if due allowance is made for the preacherly exaggeration to which its exponents were prone.

The threat of 'atheism' sensationalised the religious doubt that was widely experienced by the devout, which, it was feared, could all too easily develop into articulate irreligion if not kept in check. Many, like the politician and antiquary Sir Simonds D'Ewes, were attacked by 'unruly thoughts of atheism',[85] and one important function of the anti-atheist

---

[84] Cf. the suggestive remarks in Lucien Febvre, *The Problem of Unbelief in the Sixteenth Century: The Religion of Rabelais*, trans. Beatrice Gottlieb (Cambridge, MA, 1982), pp. 142–51, though my disagreement with the general thrust of Febvre's argument should have become apparent in the course of this chapter.

[85] Sir Simonds D'Ewes, *Autobiography and Correspondence*, ed. J. O. Halliwell, 2 vols (London, 1845), I, 253. Cf. Thomas, *Religion and the Decline of Magic*, pp. 167–8, 474–5, and this volume, Chapter 3.

literature was to act 'as a stablishment to such as any way eyther by their owne infirmitie or through the wilinesse of wicked persons are made to wauer and hang in suspense'.[86]

To some extent, the seeds of 'atheism' were seen as the inheritance of natural man, and it is not surprising to find the appearance of 'atheism' as a symptom of melancholy in Robert Burton's treatise on that subject.[87] But 'atheism' also illustrated the new situation inaugurated by the Reformation, epitomising in extreme form the fuller awareness of alternatives in religious outlook between which, for the first time, people had to choose. It was a commonplace of anti-atheist writings that unbelief had been encouraged by religious schism, something which Richard Greenham illustrated by a story of a man who moved from Catholicism, through Protestantism, to the Family of Love before throwing religion over altogether.[88] In addition, recorded cases of heterodoxy reveal an open-minded attitude towards different religions of precisely the kind deprecated by the devout.[89]

More serious – in view of the intellectual character of the stock 'atheist' figure – was the ambivalence that the fear of infidelity induced in the educated, particularly on topics which overlapped with elements in the stereotype, where usage of the word could express anxiety about even mild instances of the secularist tendencies which 'atheism' exemplified in exaggerated form. Here the fear of 'atheism' arguably had a negative effect, inhibiting heterodoxy and underwriting orthodoxy: many would have shared Thomas Kyd's anxiety, writing to Sir John Puckering in 1593, 'to cleere my self of being thought an *Atheist* . . . a deadly thing'.[90]

Wit itself could be seen to have its dangers – as Francis Meres averred in his *Palladis Tamia* (1598), 'impiety doth infect the wisest wit, if it be giuen to idlenes' – while the perils of speculation in areas where the boundary between correct and incorrect opinion was ill-defined, such as the doctrine of the soul, were noted by John Woolton, Bishop of Exeter, in his book on that subject.[91] Such problems were perhaps borne out in the case of Sir Walter Ralegh, for, though views differ on his orthodoxy in religious

---

[86] Phillippe Duplessis Mornay, *A Woorke Concerning the Trewnesse of the Christian Religion*, trans. Sir Philip Sidney and Arthur Golding (London, 1587), sig. *3.

[87] Burton, *Anatomy of Melancholy*, III, 395–408 (pt 3, sect. 4, memb. 2, subsect. i).

[88] Greenham, *Workes*, p. 3.

[89] For example, the case of Richard Barker in W. H. Hale, *A Series of Precedents and Proceedings in Criminal Causes* (London, 1847), p. 176.

[90] Kuriyama, *Christopher Marlowe*, p. 229.

[91] Francis Meres, *Palladis Tamia. Wits Treasury* (London, 1598), fol. 303v; John Woolton, *A Treatise of the Immortalitie of the Soule* (London, 1576), Ep. Ded., fol. 26.

matters, the evidence of the Cerne Abbas enquiry illustrates the imprudence of venting sceptical opinions on fundamental doctrinal issues at dinner parties.[92]

Anxiety focussed on two areas, both of them well known, where a challenge was presented to the providentialist and moralistic worldview of the day. One was a secular attitude to politics of the kind habitually associated with Machiavelli, whose centrality to the 'atheist' stereotype has been indicated. Much has been written about anti-Machiavellianism, but here we may note the good evidence that exists of concern on the part of those interested in Machiavellian writings to try to devise a Christian version of 'policy' to avoid finding themselves on the highroad to irreligion.[93] In addition, naturalism and systems of scientific explanation seen as implicitly atheistic caused misgivings: 'Young Naturalists oft Atheists old doe proue', as Sir William Alexander put it in a dedicatory poem to a work by John Abernethy in which 'atheism' bulked large.[94] It is against the background of such orthodox presumptions that one should see the almost unreasonably touchy attitude of a man like Thomas Harriot, arguably as much under suspicion for the character of his interests as for anything he actually said.[95]

Moreover, since naturalistic views had been set out most fully by classical authors like Pliny, it is hardly surprising that the orthodox should experience particular anxiety in connection with these, as epitomising the milder tendencies that they observed in contemporaries. It is thus symptomatic that when Philemon Holland translated Pliny's *Natural History* into English, he felt concern about the possible danger of Pliny's 'attributing so much unto Nature', which might derogate from the power of

---

[92] Strathmann, *Ralegh*; Lefranc, *Ralegh*, ch. 12; Stephen J. Greenblatt, *Sir Walter Ralegh: The Renaissance Man and His Roles* (New Haven, 1973), pp. 99–101; *Willobie His Avisa*, pp. 266–8.

[93] For example, Stuart Clark, 'Wisdom Literature of the Seventeenth Century: A Guide to the Contents of the "Bacon Tottel" Commonplace Books', *Transactions of the Cambridge Bibliographical Society*, 6 (1976), 291–305 (p. 300). See also particularly G. L. Mosse, *The Holy Pretence* (Oxford, 1957) and Felix Raab, *The English Face of Machiavelli* (London, 1964), ch. 3.

[94] John Abernethy, *A Christian and Heavenly Treatise Containing Physicke for the Soule* (3rd ed., London, 1630), sig. A7v. On this theme, see also P. H. Kocher, *Science and Religion in Elizabethan England* (San Marino, 1953), esp. ch. 5.

[95] See particularly D. B. Quinn and J. W. Shirley, 'A Contemporary List of Hariot References', *Renaissance Quarterly*, 22 (1969), 9–26, esp. pp. 18–24. But see also Jean Jacquot, 'Thomas Harriot's Reputation for Impiety', *Notes and Records of the Royal Society*, 9 (1952), 164–87, and Stephen Greenblatt, 'Invisible Bullets: Renaissance Authority and Its Subversion', *Glyph; Johns Hopkins Textual Studies*, 8 (1981), 40–61, reprinted in Greenblatt, *Shakespearean Negotiations: The Circulation of Social Energy in Renaissance England* (Berkeley and Los Angeles, 1988), ch. 2 (a reference I owe to Moti Feingold): Harriot almost certainly had Deistic tendencies. [See further p. 26.]

God. 'Farre be it from me, that I should publish any thing to corrupt mens manners, and much lesse to prejudice Christian religion', he wrote, and, after conferring with 'sundrie divines' on the subject, he actually appended a letter from one of them to his preface, to 'settle the minds of the weake, and free my labours from the taint of irreligion'.[96]

It would, of course, be naive to conflate secularism and naturalism with outright 'atheism', though it did not help that ideas of a secularist and naturalistic kind were expressed by outspoken freethinkers like Marlowe, who also specifically alluded to Harriot.[97] What is significant, in reconstructing contemporary anxieties, is to see how such incipiently irreligious tendencies appeared in the light of contemporaries' conviction of the progressive nature of 'atheism' and their proclivity to conflate mild manifestations into an extreme image. It is worthy of note that at this time no alternative word like 'Deist' caught on to describe such milder heterodoxy, despite the existence of this word in English at an earlier date than has hitherto been suspected.[98] Instead, in a manner typical of the thought of the day, people preferred to use the inclusive concept of 'atheism' to encapsulate a range of phenomena that were believed to present a threat to religion by sensationalising them in a single, pervasive stereotype.

Indeed, 'atheism' is by no means the only example of this. One can draw a parallel with other genres in which real and exaggerated components were brought together into an idealised whole that we find distastefully artificial, but which clearly served significant descriptive and prescriptive functions at the time and coloured contemporary perceptions of reality. There are the writings on witchcraft and on sodomy; the Protestant onslaught on Roman Catholicism and the attack on the radical sects from the mid-Tudor period onwards; the vexed questions of Puritanism and Arminianism; even ideas about enclosers, or about Court and Country. In each case, as with 'atheism', though it would be quite wrong to take the contemporary concept completely seriously, it would be equally mistaken to write it off altogether. Some of these genres have received sympathetic attention in which this has been illustrated, as in

---

[96] *The Historie of the World. Commonly called, The Naturall Historie of C. Plinius Secundus*, trans. Philemon Holland (London, 1601), 'The Preface to the Reader'.

[97] See Kuriyama, *Christopher Marlowe*, pp. 221, 229; Kocher, *Marlowe*, esp. pp. 61–3. On this aspect of Marlowe's ideas see, for instance, D. J. Palmer, 'Marlowe's Naturalism', in *Christopher Marlowe*, ed. Brian Morris (London, 1968), pp. 151–75.

[98] The word is used by Josias Nichols in his *Order of Houshold Instruction* (London, 1596), sig. E7, although the earliest usage given in *OED* is Burton's of 1621; it is symptomatic, however, that Nichols uses the word as a synonym for 'atheist'. On its (rare) use in sixteenth-century France, see Busson, 'Les Noms', pp. 278–9.

Carol Z. Wiener's stress on the element of projection in anti-Catholicism, or Patrick Collinson's note of the overlap between the literature on Puritanism and the Theophrastan character tradition.[99] Others, however, deserve more scrutiny than they have yet received, from a standpoint similar to that which I have adopted here.

As with more recent 'moral panics',[100] hostility to a specific stock figure could encapsulate a wider range of anxieties, and only a sensitive appraisal can do justice to the mixture of real and exaggerated phenomena involved. As historians we have to be able to handle contemporary statements in which the imaginary and the real have a kind of symbiotic relationship, understanding the meaning of constructs that seem to us fantastic. Such heightened effusions may provide us with important information about anxieties of the day which is not available from more direct statements, while their mode of presentation throws significant light on contemporary thought.

---

[99] C. Z. Wiener, 'The Beleaguered Isle. A Study of Elizabethan and Early Stuart Anti-Catholicism', *Past & Present*, 51 (1971), 27–62; Patrick Collinson, 'A Comment: Concerning the Name Puritan', *Journal of Ecclesiastical History*, 31 (1980), 483–88, and *English Puritanism* (Historical Association, 1983), pp. 7–11. [This passage was otherwise left knowingly unannotated and it is perhaps now too late to attempt a comprehensive account, though it seems worth mentioning Clark, *Thinking with Demons* (already cited), Alan Bray, *Homosexuality in Renaissance England* (London, 1982; new ed., New York, 1995) and the writings of Peter Lake, including his 'Anti-Popery: The Structure of a Prejudice', in *Conflict in Early Stuart England*, ed. Richard Cust and Ann Hughes (London, 1989), pp. 72–106; 'Anti-Puritanism: The Structure of a Prejudice', in *Religious Politics in Post-Reformation England*, ed. Lake and Kenneth Fincham (Woodbridge, 2006) pp. 80–97; and 'The Historiography of Puritanism' in *The Cambridge Companion to Puritanism*, ed. Paul C. H. Lim and John Coffey (Cambridge, 2008), pp. 346–71.]

[100] Cf. Stanley Cohen, *Folk Devils and Moral Panics: The Creation of the Mods and Rockers* (London, 1972). See also K. T. Erikson, *Wayward Puritans: A Study in the Sociology of Deviance* (New York, 1966).

CHAPTER 3

Atheism among the Godly
The Covert History of Religious Doubt

This chapter considers the experience of doubt among the highly religious in early modern Britain. What was the nature of this, and how did it relate to the 'atheism' that forms the subject of the bulk of this book? This may seem like a digression from the volume's main theme, but it is a necessary one because the issue has been raised with peculiar clarity by Alec Ryrie in his recent book, *Unbelievers* (2019), which is subtitled *An Emotional History of Doubt*, and it is on that volume and its claims that this chapter is mainly focussed.[1] We have already considered Ryrie's book in the Introduction, where we examined the value of the history of emotions as a means of approaching religious and irreligious experience in the early modern period. In particular, we emphasised the 'assurance' that characterised atheists, the sense of certainty which led them to proselytise on behalf of their beliefs. On the face of it, such activity seems rather different from the doubt experienced by anxious believers, despite the conflation of the two in Ryrie's book, and this matter therefore deserves fuller attention. Just how *did* the two phenomena relate to one another? What can be said about the doubts experienced by believers, and what were the similarities and differences between these and the overt irreligion expressed by Christopher Marlowe and others?

First, however, it is worth pointing out that much the same issue had received an earlier exposition in a brief, but disproportionately influential, section of Keith Thomas's seminal work, *Religion and the Decline of Magic*, published in 1971. Chapter 6 of that book, titled 'Religion and the People', starts by considering the local role of the church, including the function of the clergy in providing advice, but it goes on to a section on 'Ignorance and Indifference' which has proved highly persuasive because (in the words of one commentator) it 'famously argued that "a substantial proportion" of the population was hostile to organised religion and rarely if

---

[1] Alec Ryrie, *Unbelievers: An Emotional History of Doubt* (London, 2019).

ever went to church'.[2] This is followed by a further section titled 'Scepticism', and it is that which concerns us here. It opens with a paragraph on the atheism associated with intellectuals and aristocrats like Marlowe and Sir Walter Ralegh, whose sceptical views on religious topics have already been outlined. Having noted that historians are perfectly familiar with such infidelity, Thomas continues: 'But they have paid less attention to the evidence of scepticism among humbler members of the population', noting:

> One of the most striking features of the spiritual biographies of the time is their revelation that atheistical thoughts could trouble even 'persons of eminent and singular holiness'. Many future Puritan saints seem to have temporarily doubted the existence of God and the Devil, the reality of Heaven and Hell, and the truthfulness of the Scriptures.

Thomas then cites various examples of this, both from famous authors like John Bunyan and Richard Baxter and from less well-known men and women, a number of whom are itemised in a footnote. After this, he goes on to provide a paragraph on late medieval examples of blasphemy and atheism, followed by two more on post-Reformation instances and another on the Interregnum, which 'brought much of this endemic scepticism into the open'. Some broader comments follow on the growth of secularism, and Thomas finally reaches the conclusion that 'we do not know enough about the religious beliefs and practices of our remote ancestors to be certain of the extent to which religious faith and practice have actually declined'.[3]

During the past few decades I have often pondered on these telling remarks and have discussed them with other historians, many of whom found them as striking as I did; occasionally, I have cited them and commented on them.[4] But the theme has undoubtedly been given a new lease of life by Ryrie's *Unbelievers*, which devotes a disproportionate amount of attention to this very phenomenon. In particular, in chapter 4 of his book, titled 'The Puritan Atheist', Ryrie gives a whole sequence of examples of such expressions of doubt on the part of the godly, illustrating the background to this in the 'Acknowledgements' at the end of his book, where he points out:

---

[2] Christopher Marsh, *Popular Religion in Sixteenth-Century England* (Basingstoke, 1998), p. 43.
[3] Keith Thomas, *Religion and the Decline of Magic: Studies in Popular Beliefs in Sixteenth and Seventeenth Century England* (London, 1971, reprinted Harmondsworth, 1978), pp. 179–206.
[4] For example, Chapter 2, n. 9; Michael Hunter, *Boyle Studies: Aspects of the Life and Thought of Robert Boyle (1627–91)* (Farnham, 2015), pp. 120–1 and n. 60.

Like many of the stories of doubt it tells, this book began as a niggling afterthought: a surprised observation, when I was preparing my 2013 book *Being Protestant in Reformation Britain*, that so many of the earnestly pious believers I was studying had consciously wrestled with atheism.[5]

As with Thomas's earlier account, Ryrie's examples range from celebrities like Baxter to relative non-entities whose autobiographies have come down to us, both in Britain and in New England. For instance, we learn of a woman known to us only as 'M. K.' who became convinced 'that there was no heaven, no God, no Jesus, no good angels, only a hell there was, and devils to carry me thither', or the New England Puritan Michael Wigglesworth who questioned the authority of the scriptures, and such doubts perhaps reached their climax in the classic instance of John Bunyan. In his *Grace Abounding to the Chief of Sinners* (1666), Bunyan wrote of the 'whole floods of blasphemies' by which he was afflicted,

> such as stirred up questions in me against the very Being of God, and of his only beloved Son: As, whether there were in truth, a God, or Christ? And whether the holy Scriptures were not rather a fable, and cunning story, than the holy and pure Word of God.[6]

Earlier, in chapter 2 of his book, Ryrie had looked at the scruples experienced by such well-known intellectuals of the sixteenth and seventeenth centuries as Michel de Montaigne, William Chillingworth and Sir Thomas Browne.[7] On the other hand, doubt hardly appears in chapter 3, which deals with figures like Ralegh and Marlowe and with the drama of the Elizabethan and Jacobean periods, surveying what might be described as the more assertive aspects of the rejection of religion in the period. Chapter 5 then takes a slightly different tack, developing the theme of chapter 4 by looking at examples of the extremes of religious radicalism that came to the fore in the aftermath of the Civil War, when hostility to traditional religious forms boiled over and men like Gerrard Winstanley and Lawrence Clarkson engaged in spiritual odysseys, which Ryrie briefly chronicles. Ryrie sees these as 'Seekers', men and women who were looking (in the words of one of them, Mary Springett) to 'be without a religion until the Lord manifestly taught me one'. The chapter reaches the bizarre climax – after briefly introducing the secularist thinker Francis Osborne

---

[5] Ryrie, *Unbelievers*, p. 207. Cf. his *Being Protestant in Reformation Britain* (Oxford, 2013), though the index entries under 'atheism' are perhaps surprisingly inexplicit.
[6] Ryrie, *Unbelievers*, ch. 4, esp. pp. 114, 116, 120.
[7] These also form the principal subject of his 'Reformation', in *The Cambridge History of Atheism*, ed. Stephen Bullivant and Michael Ruse, 2 vols (Cambridge, 2021), I, 183–201.

and his *Advice to a Son* (1656) – that 'As we look from Seeker to libertine, and from libertine to Seeker, already it is becoming difficult to say which is which'.[8]

Yet, this theme is not pursued. Chapter 6 of Ryrie's book, which surveys the entire period from the mid-seventeenth century to the present, focusses on a more traditional pantheon of atheistic figures and only alludes in passing to the well-documented doubts of the highly religious at a more recent date.[9] By the author's own admission, his book has 'an hourglass shape', focussing to a disproportionate extent on the Protestant world in the early modern period and arguably stimulating many questions about the significance of doing so.[10] In particular, Ryrie's account, like Thomas's earlier one in *The Decline of Magic*, raises issues concerning the nature and significance of the phenomena they are describing. Just how *is* one to interpret the doubts and anxieties of the godly in this critical period? Can one presume, as Thomas did, that if 'even' Puritan saints experienced doubts, then these were widespread among the population at large, reinforcing the evidence of ignorance and indifference that had been the subject of his previous section, and thus leading on to the issue of secularisation that he goes on to discuss?

Equally important, particularly in light of the subject matter of the current volume, is the question of how such dubitation related to the openly expressed atheism that we have already come across and that, as we will see in subsequent chapters, became all the commoner after 1660 – the period when it is unfortunate that (by his own admission) Ryrie's 'main story ends: for this is when unbelief finally came out into the open and claimed philosophical respectability for itself'.[11] Whether that *was* in fact an appropriate place for him to end is far from clear, since debates about the nature and significance of atheism, and even about the extent of the phenomenon, continued into the eighteenth century and beyond. Here, however, we are concerned with the significance of the phenomenon of

---

[8] Ryrie, *Unbelievers*, ch. 5, esp. pp. 166, 172. See also his 'Seeking the Seekers', *Studies in Church History*, 57 (2021), 185–209.

[9] See Ryrie, *Unbelievers*, ch. 6, esp. p. 192. On such doubts, see *Doubting Christianity: The Church and Doubt*, ed. Frances Andrews, Charlotte Methuen and Andrew Spicer, *Studies in Church History*, 52 (2016). See also, for example, Susan Budd, 'The Loss of Faith. Reasons for Unbelief among Members of the Secular Movement in England, 1850–1950', *Past and Present*, 36 (1967), 106–25, reprinted as ch. 5 of her *Varieties of Unbelief: Atheists and Agnostics in English Society 1850–1960* (London, 1977); Timothy Larsen, *Crisis of Doubt: Honest Faith in Nineteenth-Century England* (Oxford, 2006); David Hempton, *Evangelical Disenchantment: Nine Portraits of Faith and Doubt* (New Haven and London, 2008).

[10] Ryrie, *Unbelievers*, p. 5.   [11] Ibid., p. 181.

religious doubt as dealt with particularly in his chapter on 'The Puritan Atheist'. Exactly what was the nature of such doubt, and how did it relate to open infidelity?

There are in fact echoes here of one of the themes dealt with in the Introduction and in Chapter 2 of the current volume. Among the various usages of 'atheism' there dealt with was the proneness of contemporary commentators to deploy the word to exemplify ungodliness in an extreme form as a means of alarming the godly and encouraging them to show more clearly their allegiance to the true faith. This was the thrust of a work like John Wingfield's *Atheisme Close and Open, Anatomised* (1634), for instance, and of many other earnest tracts of the type that Ryrie deploys in the course of his book. It was a device that enabled zealous preachers to conflate almost any deviance from godly commitment with extreme irreligion, a rhetorical device that could hardly be bettered, while the expression of anxiety in this way helped the godly to identify themselves and close ranks against the wiles of Satan through the righteous self-examination and moral demeanour to which they were exhorted. Hence, one finds a steady flow of exhortatory manuals, together with stories of the successful vanquishment of doubts in the minds of believers of the kind that Ryrie is able to document at length.

Almost endless examples could be cited of godly figures who experienced periods of acute doubt, such as the late seventeenth-century divine George Trosse, who penned a graphic account of his repeated tribulations, or, to take an example almost at random, Elizabeth, wife of the nonconformist minister Oliver Heywood, who died in 1661: 'For a great part of her life she had sharp conflicts with the prince of darknes, and the unbeleefe of her own heart.'[12] We find the same phenomenon in Scotland, in the experience of the Edinburgh servant Elizabeth West, who was assailed with the view that 'There is no God; there is no Christ; no Holy Ghost; it is but a Fancy[;] the Bible, it is not Gods Word; it is but a Contrivance of Man', or of the divine Thomas Halyburton, whom we will encounter below in connection with his contemporary, Thomas Aikenhead.[13] Here, I would like to focus on a figure of whom I have made a particular study, the scientist Robert Boyle, who unfortunately falls outside the period on which Ryrie's book is focussed and therefore does

---

[12] *The Life of the Revd. George Trosse*, ed. A. W. Brink (Montreal, 1974); Oliver Heywood, *Autobiography and Diaries*, ed. J. H. Turner, 4 vols (Brighouse/Bingley, 1882–5), 1, 69.

[13] Elizabeth West [Wast], *Memoirs, or Spiritual Exercises* (Edinburgh, 1724), pp. 19–20. For Halyburton, see pp. 115–16.

not appear in it. We have already come across Boyle in the Introduction as the author of profuse writings on atheism, where we fruitfully investigated his comments on the motivation of those who espoused such attitudes.[14]

Here, Boyle is relevant on two counts. First, contrary to a misleading historiography that saw him as engaged in a hostile 'dialogue with the sects', which has now long been discredited, it turns out that, on the contrary, Boyle was deeply fascinated by 'enthusiasts' in search of a purer, more spiritualistic religion.[15] In particular, he patronised Adam Boreel, the radical Dutch Collegiant who features in Ryrie's chapter on 'Seekers'; in addition, Boyle had links with Quakers and others who followed the promptings of the spirit in their religious life and who feature in the same chapter.[16] There is even evidence of a muted endorsement on Boyle's part of the extreme hostility towards oath-taking that characterised the Quakers, thus typifying their iconoclastic attitude towards orthodox doctrine. Though Boyle did not wholly reject the taking of oaths, he seems to have experienced abnormal scruples about the practice on scriptural grounds, which prevented him from becoming president of the Royal Society in 1680 and led to his resignation from his governorship of the New England Company in 1689. It may well be significant that Bishop John Gauden actually dedicated to Boyle his attack on Quaker attitudes to oaths in 1662.[17]

More significant, however, are the acute scruples on religious topics that plagued Boyle throughout his life. His case provides a revealing record of intense religious doubt among the godly of the kind that Thomas and Ryrie have documented, the nature of which therefore merits investigation. We initially hear of these perturbations during Boyle's adolescence, as recorded in his autobiographical *Account of Philaretus during His Minority*: travelling in the Alps, he suffered 'such distracting Doubts of some of the Fundamentals of Christianity; that tho his looks did little betray his Thoughts, nothing but the Forbiddenesse of Selfe-dispatch, hindred his

---

[14] See pp. 19–21.

[15] See Michael Hunter, 'Appendix: Boyle and the Sects', *History of Science*, 33 (1995), 86–92, reprinted in *Robert Boyle (1627–91): Scrupulosity and Science* (Woodbridge, 2000), pp. 51–7. The principal author critiqued is J. R. Jacob, *Robert Boyle and the English Revolution* (New York, 1977).

[16] See Ryrie, *Unbelievers*, pp. 146–7, 164–5, 167, 169.

[17] See Michael Hunter, 'The Conscience of Robert Boyle: Functionalism, "Dysfunctionalism" and the Task of Historical Understanding', in *Renaissance and Revolution*, ed. J. V. Field and F. A. J. L. James (Cambridge, 1993), pp. 147–59 (pp. 153–7), reprinted in Hunter, *Scrupulosity and Science*, pp. 58–71 (pp. 64–8) (on the New England Company, see also Hunter, *Boyle: Between God and Science* [New Haven and London, 2009], pp. 226–7).

acting it'.[18] In his later years, such disturbances recurred, and Boyle took up the matter in recorded interviews with his ecclesiastical advisers, Bishops Thomas Barlow, Gilbert Burnet and Edward Stillingfleet. He complained of his inclination whenever he referred to God to add '*whom I renounce*, or, *defye*, or the like'; he also alluded more generically to the 'Impious or Blasphemous Suggestions or Injections' by which he was assailed.[19] Indeed, in an early work, his *Essay of the Holy Scriptures* of *c.* 1653, Boyle went so far as to see doubts of the kind that he suffered as part of the normal experience of the godly, stating: 'I have ever esteemed, that He whose Fayth hath never had any Doubts, hath some cause to Doubt whether he hath ever had any Fayth.'[20] On the other hand, there were also times when he feared that he had committed the unforgiveable Sin against the Holy Ghost: in the words of St Mark, 'he that shall blaspheme against the Holy Ghost hath never forgiveness, but is in danger of eternal damnation'.[21]

In Boyle's case, his doubts seem to have extended beyond a direct temptation to disbelieve in God to a more general vacillation concerning the possibility of certain knowledge about religious matters – in essence, about the validity of his own spiritual experience. This was dealt with by Thomas Barlow in one of the lengthy treatises on related matters that he compiled at Boyle's behest, 'about a doubting Conscience', in which he discussed the case of a cleric who had consulted him because he was worried that he failed to meet the criteria of true faith and therefore found difficulty even in praying. Barlow extrapolated from this example to Boyle himself, affirming the ubiquity of doubt even in the best of Christians and urging Boyle to take solace in God's promises, which formed 'a most firme and Infallible ground of assurance and confidence, and abundantly able to exclude all feares and doubtings'.[22]

It is interesting – apropos what has already been said about the continuity of a concern with doubt among Christians long after the period on which Alec Ryrie focusses – that Boyle forms one of the principal subjects of a

[18] *Robert Boyle by Himself and His Friends*, ed. Michael Hunter (London, 1994), pp. 15–18 (p. 17): duplicated words/spaces have been ignored.

[19] Michael Hunter, 'Robert Boyle's Blasphemous Thoughts and "Flashy Emanations": Newly Discovered Evidence', *The Seventeenth Century*, 34 (2019), 601–14 (p. 603); Michael Hunter, 'Casuistry in Action: Robert Boyle's Confessional Interviews with Gilbert Burnet and Edward Stillingfleet, 1691', *Journal of Ecclesiastical History*, 44 (1993), 80–98 (pp. 90, 97), reprinted in Hunter, *Scrupulosity and Science*, pp. 72–92 (pp. 83, 90).

[20] Boyle, *Works*, ed. Michael Hunter and Edward B. Davis, 14 vols (London, 1999–2000), XIII, 181. For an earlier version of this aphorism as entry 24 in the first of Boyle's workdiaries, see *The Workdiaries of Robert Boyle* (www.livesandletters.ac.uk//wd/view/text_ed/WD1_ed.html).

[21] Mark 3. 29; Hunter, 'Casuistry in Action', esp. pp. 90/83.

[22] Hunter, *Boyle Studies*, pp. 112, 119–20.

two-volume collection titled *Converts from Infidelity; or Lives of Eminent Individuals Who Have Renounced Libertine Principles and Sceptical Opinions, and Embraced Christianity*, published by the Presbyterian divine and journalist Andrew Crichton, in 'Constable's Miscellany' in 1827. The essay in question opens with an extraordinary diatribe against irreligion (not paralleled in other lives in the same collection) before going on to deal with Boyle, noting his doubts as recorded in *Philaretus* and continuing to give an account of his conversion experience and his subsequent career as a great and good man, based largely on Thomas Birch's eighteenth-century life of him.[23]

Here, it is worth reflecting on the fact that Boyle not only experienced such doubts himself but also participated in the onslaught on atheism that we have already encountered in this book, devoting page after page to a systematic refutation of atheist principles.[24] It is notable – if hardly surprising – that in these texts Boyle makes no reference at all to his own doubts: the atheists whom he there dealt with are reported on and characterised in the third person in terms that one cannot imagine Boyle ever feeling it appropriate to apply to himself. In particular, such men are presented as open and antagonistic in their onslaught on Christianity, in contrast to the almost apologetic tone of Boyle's account of the 'Suggestions or Injections' which he himself evidently suffered. This contrast is surely worthy of note in itself, giving pause to any simplistic conflation of believers' doubt with the aggressive irreligion of atheists.

In a recent attempt to elucidate Boyle's 'Blasphemous Thoughts and "Flashy Emanations"', I considered the analogous case of Richard Baxter, another godly figure who was assailed by acute religious scruples, and, since Baxter arguably wrote about such doubts as fully as almost any other contemporary, it is appropriate to look at his views on the subject here.[25] The topic is much in evidence throughout Baxter's writings, perhaps particularly his *Christian Directory* (1673), a manual of casuistry which grew out of a joint initiative stimulated by Archbishop James Ussher and is often seen as a classic of its kind.[26] Here, however, I shall focus on the

---

[23] Andrew Crichton, *Converts from Infidelity*, 2 vols (Edinburgh, 1827), II, 7–99.

[24] See *Boyle on Atheism*, ed. J. J. MacIntosh (Toronto, 2005), together with various texts in Boyle's *Works*. For a valuable recent discussion of these and related writings on Boyle's part, see Edward B. Davis, 'Boyle's Philosophy of Religion', in *The Bloomsbury Companion to Robert Boyle*, ed. Jan-Erik Jones (London, 2020), pp. 257–82.

[25] Hunter, 'Boyle's Blasphemous Thoughts', p. 605.

[26] N. H. Keeble, *Richard Baxter: Puritan Man of Letters* (Oxford, 1982), ch. 4 (see also Hunter, *Boyle Studies*, p. 117n). For an appraisal of the work, see Nathan Johnstone, *The Devil and Demonism in Early Modern England* (Cambridge, 2006), esp. pp. 69–70.

account of Baxter's doubts given in his autobiography, posthumously published by Mathew Sylvester in 1696 as *Reliquiae Baxterianae*: the matter is there introduced in connection with Baxter's training for the ministry, when he explained how at that point he was seriously tempted to 'a setled doubting of Christianity'.[27]

What is particularly interesting is that his doubts appear to have been 'graded' according to his ability to deal with them. 'Whereas in my younger Days I never was tempted to doubt of the Truth of Scripture or Christianity', now he faced 'more pernicious temptations, especially to question the Certaine truth of the sacred scriptures; & also the life to come & the immortality of the soule'. Baxter explained how

> Though formerly I was wont when any such temptation came to cast it aside, as fitter to be abhorred than considered of, yet now this would not giue me satisfaction, but I was faine to dig to the very foundations, & seriously to examine the Reasons of Christianity, & to giue a hearing to all that could be said against it, that so my faith might be indeed my owne.

He then enumerated the scruples that he experienced, and the 'diverse things that in this assault proved great assistances to my faith'; the result was ultimately to lead him to the conclusion 'that It is our *Beliefe of the truth of the word of God & the Life to come*, which is the spring that sets all grace on worke'. Baxter returned to comparable themes in many of his other writings, for instance his *Reasons of the Christian Religion* (1667), in which he frankly commented in his prefatory material: 'Had I felt as strong assaults against my Faith while I was young, as I have done since, I am not sure it would have scap'd an overthrow'.[28] Here as elsewhere, he is frank and honest about the severity of the crises of belief that he suffered.

In *Reliquiae Baxterianae*, Baxter reassuringly asserted that 'at last I found that *nil tam certum quam quod ex dubio certum:* Nothing is so firmly believed, as that which hath bin sometime doubted of' (though his editor, Matthew Sylvester, tells of doubts he was said to have experienced about the future state on his deathbed).[29] The great Presbyterian thus echoed the sentiments of Boyle, who claimed in *Philaretus* that as a result of the perturbations that he suffered as an adolescent he achieved 'the Advantage of Groundednesse in his Religion'.[30] Although (as we have seen) Boyle

---

[27] Baxter, *Reliquiae Baxterianae: Or, Mr Richard Baxter's Narrative of the Most Memorable Passages of His Life and Times*, ed. N. H. Keeble, John Coffey, Tim Cooper and Tom Charlton, 5 vols (Oxford, 2020), I, 257–62, 505–6.

[28] Baxter, *The Reasons of the Christian Religion* (London, 1667), sig. (a1v).

[29] Baxter, *Reliquiae Baxterianae*, I, 258; IV, 437.   [30] *Boyle by Himself and His Friends*, p. 17.

continued to suffer from similar doubts later in his life, his struggles with them undoubtedly enhanced his strength and conviction as a religious polemicist. Indeed, I have only respect and awe for such lucubrations on the part of these obviously deeply pious men. One can fully sympathise with Boyle's comment to Bishop Barlow on the effect of his mental agitations on him, which induced 'such Sadness & Disquiets of mind, as, besides other Inconveniences, *sometimes* even Discourage, & *often* Distract & interrupt his Devotions'.[31] When reading texts such as the manuscript ones by Boyle that I have here discussed, one often feels that one is eavesdropping on confidential matters. It is notable that Baxter writes of the 'shame' involved in such mental disturbances, and his concern lest 'many others may be as weak as I' but felt unable to admit it.[32]

For all that, however, I think that one needs to be clear about the nature of – and sensitive to the potential limitations to – these dubitations, however fundamental they may have seemed to the godly believers who suffered them. I have already referred to Baxter's awareness of a kind of 'control' on what was appropriate at different stages of his emotional development – in that God apparently spared him such doubts until he was ready to handle them – and in such writings there is a clear sense of divine discretion as to just what anxieties the godly should suffer. Here, the role of the Devil as the archetypal tempter was crucial, and the Revd. Richard Gilpin, in his omnibus account of tribulations of this kind, explained clearly how 'God (who will not suffer his Children to be tempted *above what they are able*) doth *not permit* Satan to molest the *weaker* sort of Christians with such dangerous assaults'.[33] There was thus a limit to the extent to which the Devil, as the direct source of such temptations, was permitted to inflict them, and Alec Ryrie puts this well in noting how 'to call your blasphemous thoughts *temptations* was an indispensable distancing technique'.[34]

Even more crucial was the fact that such doubts tended to be suffered in private, in the confidentiality of a believer's secret thoughts, a point that Ryrie perhaps rather underplays. As Baxter put it: 'There is many a one that hideth his Temptations to Infidelity, because he thinketh it a shame to open them, and because it may generate doubts in others'.[35] Gilpin concurred, noting how such impious thoughts 'are by some thought to be rare and extraordinary; but this mistake ariseth from the *concealment* of these kind of Troubles, those that are thus afflicted, are often *ashamed* to speak to others

---

[31] Hunter, 'Boyle's Blasphemous Thoughts', p. 604.   [32] Baxter, *The Reasons*, sig. A3.
[33] Richard Gilpin, *Daemonologia Sacra; or, A Treatise of Satan's Temptations* (London, 1677), p. 315.
[34] Ryrie, *Unbelievers*, p. 118.   [35] Baxter, *Reliquiae Baxterianae*, I, 506.

what they find in their own hearts'.[36] In this, such authors were echoed by many of the godly doubters themselves. For instance, Hannah Allen, who suffered for many years from scruples of this kind, initially kept her doubt to herself, 'not so much as acquainting my Mother with it . . . thinking with my self that never any was like me'.[37] Similarly, Elizabeth Wilkinson, who was also afflicted with atheistic thoughts, felt that she 'could not acquaint any with my condition. I did not think that it was so with any other, as it was with me'.[38] Subsequently, on the other hand, both she and Hannah Allen *did* communicate their feelings to a limited family circle, and this helped, and there is a good evidence of doubts being shared to this restricted extent, usually within the believer's immediate milieu.[39] Insofar as they *were*, however, this was in the context of a kind of mutual therapy session – of a shared shock and horror that such pernicious questioning of the truth of essential doctrines could have occurred at all. On the other hand, it is striking that Alec Ryrie observes that 'I have found no accounts of being tempted into unbelief by others'.[40] We are stuck in the same, embarrassed and almost secretive world of doubt.

By contrast, it is salutary to return to the outspoken, public expression of irreligion that we have come across in previous chapters. What about the man whom we encountered at the very start of this book who 'openly and impudently' said to Bishop Bancroft at the 1599 London sessions: 'My Lord, if any heere can proove there is a God, I will beleeue it'? Or Christopher Marlowe, of whom Richard Baines reported that 'almost into every company he cometh he perswades men to Atheism'?[41] In these, we encounter a quite different picture, which will also be borne out by some of the irreligious utterances documented in the later chapters of this book, not least those of Thomas Aikenhead. Not only were such 'atheists' characterised by an assurance verging on arrogance in expressing their opinions that at the same time infuriated and frustrated their orthodox antagonists. It is also clear that such men gloried in their open propagation of atheistic views; they completely rejected the diffidence of godly spokesmen like Baxter or Boyle, with their sense of guilt and anxiety about even holding opinions of this kind.

---

[36] Gilpin, *Daemonologia Sacra*, p. 312.
[37] *Satan His Methods and Malice Baffled* (London, 1683), pp. 3–4, 23.
[38] Edmund Staunton, *A Sermon Preacht at Great Milton, 1654, at the Funeral of Elizabeth Wilkinson* (Oxford, 1659), p. 27.
[39] Ibid., p. 32; *Satan His Methods*, pp. 25–30, 42–3. Cf. the various instances given in Ryrie, *Unbelievers*, pp. 112–19, and in Johnstone, *The Devil and Demonism*, pp. 135–41.
[40] Ryrie, *Unbelievers*, p. 119.   [41] See pp. 1, 35, 50.

Let us turn to one further narrative of unbelief, that of John Bunyan in his *Grace Abounding*, perhaps the most telling account of such experiences from the period. A flavour of this has already been provided by the brief quotation from the work given by Alec Ryrie, and readers should study this readily available text for themselves in order fully to appreciate Bunyan's relentless and repeated questioning of his faith.[42] It is in fact interesting that Bunyan illustrates the overlap between the subject matter of the fourth and fifth chapters of Ryrie's book, since at an early stage in his spiritual odyssey Bunyan records meeting Ranters and reading their books, after which developed a more sustained questioning of his faith and its basis (in which, interestingly, he also invoked Martin Luther and the renowned Italian apostate, Francesco Spira).[43]

In the course of his tribulations Bunyan often invoked biblical texts for reflection or consolation – from the gospels, the epistles and the Old Testament – and it was through these that he ultimately found a route out of his despair. In particular, a key facet of his deliverance seemed to lie in his realisation of the fact that his apostasy had not been openly or publicly expressed, and this is a point on which he dwells. Citing the Epistle to the Hebrews about those who were guilty of 'falling away' from Christ, Bunyan protested: 'I found that this falling away must be openly, even in the view of the World, even so as *to put Christ to an open shame*'. Then again, of the sin 'which doth throw off Christ, and then his Commandments too', this 'must also be done openly, before two or three witnesses, to answer that of the Law, *ver.* 28'. In his own case, on the other hand, Bunyan 'confessed that I had put Jesus Christ to *shame* by my sin, but not to open *shame*. I did not deny him before men, nor condemn him as a fruitless one before the World'.[44]

The concept of publicly shaming Christ raised the issue of the Sin against the Holy Ghost, since it was this ultimate and unforgiveable sin that Bunyan invoked in this connection.[45] As already noted, Robert Boyle

---

[42] Although a definitive edition is available in *Grace Abounding to the Chief of Sinners*, ed. Roger Sharrock (Oxford, 1962), reprinted with *The Pilgrim's Progress* in the Oxford Standard Authors series in 1966, I have preferred to use the World's Classics edition, *Grace Abounding with Other Spiritual Biographies*, ed. John Stachniewski and Anita Pacheco (Oxford, 1998), which clearly differentiates passages of the work added to the third and later editions.

[43] Bunyan, *Grace Abounding*, pp. 16–17 (sects 44–5), 37–8 (sects 129–30), 45–6 (sect. 163), 51 (sect. 179). All these passages were added to the third edition, but this does not appear to be of any particular significance.

[44] Ibid., pp. 63–4 (sects 223–4). Cf. Hebrews, ch. 6, 10.

[45] For background, see Baird Tipson, 'A Dark Side of Seventeenth-century English Protestantism: The Sin against the Holy Ghost', *Harvard Theological Review*, 77 (1984), 301–30.

also feared that he had committed this mysterious but unpardonable apostasy, and the same was true of Elizabeth Wilkinson and others.[46] In Bunyan's case, he focussed on the case of the Old Testament figure of Esau, whose selling of his birthright to his elder brother, Jacob, is presented in the Epistle to the Hebrews as the 'type' of this sin. Here too Bunyan made the point that what was important about this was not least its public nature: 'it was a publick and open action, even before his Brother, if not before many more; this made his sin of a far more hainous nature then otherwise it would have been'.[47] By comparison, Bunyan took solace in the knowledge that his own apostasy had been kept to himself and not publicly advertised, and he found this reassuring: though his doubts returned, they were never as severe as they had been during the most intense of his trials.

Of course, I am here failing to do justice to the sheer intensity of Bunyan's spiritual crisis – I leave the reader to study his work and experience that for themselves – but this issue of the 'publick and open' nature of the act committed does seem crucial. The point is that the doubts experienced by the godly were overwhelmingly private and confidential. They tended to be kept to the security of a believer's heart and the privacy of his or her chamber, and were released only posthumously, as in the *Reliquiae Baxterianae* or Staunton's funeral sermon for Elizabeth Wilkinson, or long in retrospect, as with Hannah Allen's tribulations, divulged some twenty years after they had actually occurred. Similarly, one cannot imagine Robert Boyle ever giving public expression to the religious doubts that he suffered, the evidence concerning which was left to be discovered by his biographers first in the eighteenth century and then in the twentieth.

These were intensely private, personal matters, which were the subject of guilt and remorse on the part of those who suffered them, even if in retrospect they could become ostentatious symbols of a believer's triumph over them. Indeed, though the godly often tried to confront these pernicious thoughts, they frequently took the view that they were 'not to be dallied withal or disputed, but to be avoided, prayed against, and resisted by a strong and lively faith', to quote the words in a similar connection of the scholar and parliamentarian, Sir Simonds D'Ewes.[48] Richard Gilpin comparably invoked 'those who know 'tis the best way *not to dispute*

---

[46] Hunter, 'Casuistry in Action', pp. 90–3/83–5; Staunton, *A Sermon*, p. 27; *Satan His Methods*, pp. 4, 42; *Life of George Trosse*, pp. 88–9, 109. Cf. Gilpin, *Daemonologia Sacra*, p. 314.

[47] Bunyan, *Grace Abounding*, p. 64 (sect. 225). Cf. Hebrews, ch. 12.

[48] D'Ewes, *Autobiography and Correspondence*, ed. J. O. Halliwell, 2 vols (London, 1845), I, 253.

Fundamentals with Satan, but with abhorrency to reject him' – invoking Christ's 'Get thee behind me, Satan'.[49] Either way, however, it was all done in private, in the fetid atmosphere of the believer's cogitations and in the intimacy of his or her closet or immediate family circle. Indeed, there is a real danger here of unwitting anachronism on the part of historians, of forgetting that, due to the retrospective publication of the intimate texts in which such trials were divulged, we are privy to the inner thoughts of believers of which their contemporaries were completely ignorant.

To this it might be objected in the case of *Grace Abounding* that it was a public document, in that it was printed during Bunyan's lifetime, in 1666, being often reprinted thereafter. This is because Bunyan's book is an example of the rather different genre that is dealt with in chapter 5 of Alec Ryrie's book, namely the literature produced by 'Seekers', to use his term. These were men and women who sought to vindicate their spiritual superiority by providing evidence of the intense trials that they had experienced and overcome in their search for religious enlightenment, which often involved questioning the very foundations of orthodox doctrine. This was associated with groups like the Ranters and the Quakers, and perhaps particularly the latter. Such writings become commonplace in the 1650s, when the divine John Rogers, and others, started to collect on behalf of such believers 'some *experimental* Evidences of the work of *grace* upon his *soul*... whereby he (or she) is *convinced* that he is *regenerate* and *received* of God' – almost as a kind of membership card of one of the radical sects.[50] Figures like these, as Ryrie points out, were sometimes accused of being 'atheists' by heresy-hunters like the Presbyterian Thomas Edwards, and very occasionally they *did* appear to reject religion altogether.[51] A case in point is provided by the Ranter, Lawrence Clarkson, whose *The Lost Sheep Found* (1660) contains (in the words of one author) what 'may well be the first overt confession of atheism to be printed in English' – though by the time it was published Clarkson had rejected such ideas and become a devotee of another sect, Muggletonianism.[52] In general, however, the quest of such figures was for a greater level of commitment to the pure life of the spirit

---

[49] Gilpin, *Daemonologia Sacra*, p. 317. Cf. Matthew 16. 23.

[50] John Rogers, *Ohel or Beth-Shemesh. A Tabernacle for the Sun* (London, 1653), p. 354, quoted in Owen Watkins, *The Puritan Experience* (London, 1972), p. 29. Watkins's book bears out the predominance of Quakers among such writings.

[51] Ryrie, *Unbelievers*, pp. 155–68 and the references cited on pp. 243–6.

[52] Paul Delany, *British Autobiography in the Seventeenth Century* (London, 1969), p. 87. On the complexities of Clarkson's text see J. C. Davis, *Fear, Myth and History: The Ranters and the Historians* (Cambridge, 1986), pp. 64–75.

rather than a rejection of it, as seen in such books as Jane Turner's classic *Choice Experiences* (1653). These men and women were intent on collecting the '*soule-whisperings*' that they experienced (to use a further phrase from Rogers's collection), and only rarely does one find substantively atheistic sentiments among their recorded utterances.[53]

If at this point, therefore, one *does* find a marginal overlap between the assertiveness of the highly religious of the Interregnum and the 'true' atheists with whom the rest of this book is concerned, the overall picture remains one of a contrast between the public and private expression of heterodox views – between the privacy and embarrassment of the godly and the sheer openness of unbelievers. Indeed, it could be even argued that such public and overt expression of irreligious views was what Christ had in mind in the passages in the gospels in which He spoke of the Sin against the Holy Ghost. Gilbert Burnet evidently had an inkling of this when he confronted Boyle's anxiety that he had committed this most heinous of sins, assuring Boyle, almost with a tone of irritation, that 'it was scarse possible it could be committed in our Age', especially by a godly figure like Boyle. In the careful notes that Boyle kept on his 1691 interview with Burnet, he recorded how Burnet 'seemd not to thinke that any Christian remaining' could be 'guilty of the Unpardonable Sin', on the grounds that such behaviour would align him with the apostates of Christ's own time. These (like such latter-day apostates as Marlowe or Aikenhead) 'did as much as in them lay expose Christ to open Shame by approveing those that Crucifyed him as a Seducer & an Imposter, & much more by joyning themselves to the Jews who in those times cursed him publickly in their Synagogues'. Boyle's other confessor, Edward Stillingfleet, agreed that the Sin against the Holy Ghost involved 'a Deliberate & settled Resolution to oppose & oppress the Truth of the Gospel what evidence soever as by Miracles & other strong Arguments, should be brought to evince or establish it'. Hence 'none that is affraid of haveing committed that Sin are guilty of it; since one cannot commit it without haveing a full Intention to do it'. Like Burnet, moreover, he then had recourse to a 'psychological' explanation of the doubts of a godly man like Boyle that seems perhaps surprisingly modern.[54]

To summarise, the point thus surely is that, whatever doubts the godly experienced in their private lucubrations, the open, public expression of

---

[53] Quoted in Nigel Smith, *Perfection Proclaimed: Language and Literature in English Radical Religion 1640–60* (Oxford, 1989), p. 28; see also elsewhere in ibid., ch. 3.

[54] Hunter, 'Casuistry in Action', pp. 95–8/88–92.

atheistic sentiment by such figures was simply unthinkable. We need to restore the crucial distinction between the *private* and the *public* in the articulation of such views that has been explored here. It was all very well for a man like George Trosse to use the hyperbole that in his youth he had been 'a *very Atheist*', but he was using the term in the more elastic, nebulous meaning that we encountered in the Introduction and in Chapter 2, aimed primarily at the edification of the godly.[55] Arguably, he was a million miles away from being a *true* apostate like Thomas Aikenhead. The extrapolation from an inappropriately literal reading of the term has arguably misled the likes of Keith Thomas and Alec Ryrie. 'Atheism' among the godly turns out not to be what, on the face of it, it may seem.

[55] *Life of George Trosse*, p. 48. Cf. ibid., pp. 60, 132.

CHAPTER 4

'This degenerate Age ... so miserably over-run with Scepticism *and* Infidelity*

The Culture of Atheism after 1660

There are many similarities between the state of affairs concerning atheism after 1660 and the situation before the Civil War as surveyed in Chapter 2. Much of the ambivalence concerning the phenomenon – the sliding and inclusive definitions, the overlap between the real and the imaginary, the ambivalence, the element of cliché – remain as true in the Restoration period as they had done before 1640. In particular, it is important to do justice to the extent to which the anti-atheist literature erected a stereotype that idealised and sensationalised deviance from orthodoxy.[1] Within this, various tendencies in contemporary life were conflated, even if it is apparent to us in retrospect that the actual connection between these phenomena and irreligion was weaker than contemporaries believed. The components included naturalism – an emphasis on secondary causes in the working of nature, to the potential exclusion of primary ones – together with what might be called secularism, a cynical and this-worldly attitude to politics and religion. But hardly less important was 'wit' and what was labelled 'scoffing' – the iconoclastic manner in which such ideas were often presented, together with the informal and irreverent venues, such as coffee-houses, in which they were voiced. In the background lay an anxiety about immorality which itself seemed to provide evidence for the practical effects of the disregard for the sanctions of an afterlife that was perceived as closely linked to more theoretical irreligion. This composite 'atheist' stereotype enhanced concern about each of the components that made it up; it was

---

[*] The quotation in the chapter title is taken from John Tillotson's preface to John Wilkins, *Of the Principles and Duties of Natural Religion* (London, 1678), sig. A4.

[1] This paragraph represents a paraphrase of Michael Hunter, 'Science and Heterodoxy: An Early Modern Problem Reconsidered', in *Reappraisals of the Scientific Revolution*, ed. David C. Lindberg and Robert S. Westman (Cambridge, 1990), pp. 437–60, reprinted in Hunter, *Science and the Shape of Orthodoxy* (Woodbridge, 1995), pp. 225–44. See also Hunter, *The Decline of Magic: Britain in the Enlightenment* (New Haven and London, 2020), pp. 17–25, and *Science and Society in Restoration England* (Cambridge, 1981), ch. 7.

successful precisely because it played on genuine anxieties of the time, the threat as a whole making each of its perceived parts seem the more menacing. By bringing disparate trends together in this way, 'atheism' focussed such concerns and made them easier to express.

It is no less important to stress that the axiomatic presumption of a link between evil living and the adoption of pernicious principles remained commonplace. If anything, this traditional concern about immorality received a new emphasis in orthodox doctrine at this time due to a growing stress on what has been described as 'a least common denominator Christianity in which moral rectitude, rather than doctrinal orthodoxy, was the litmus test of inclusion', to quote the historian, Ethan Shagan. This position was put forward most influentially by the divine Jeremy Taylor in his Θεολογια Σχλεκτικη. *A Discourse of the Liberty of Prophesying* (1647), in which he 'reframed the legitimate scope of religious coercion around what he termed "practical impiety" rather than doctrinal error'.[2] With this went a deep anxiety about the practical effects of irreligion that inspired various attempts during the Restoration period to get parliamentary legislation passed against 'atheism, blasphemy, and prophaneness'.[3] None of these proved successful: instead, the initiative in this regard was taken from the early 1690s onwards by the Societies for the Reformation of Manners, which sought to root out immorality by less formal means.[4]

This therefore needs to be borne in mind in relation to J. G. A. Pocock's observation, cited by Kenneth Sheppard in his book, *Anti-Atheism in Early Modern England* (2015), that 'between the Reformation and the Enlightenment in England the primary emphasis of anti-atheist concern switched from "vulgar" to "learned" atheism' (as Sheppard explains, by 'vulgar' Pocock meant 'practical' atheism of the kind already noted).[5]

---

[2] Ethan H. Shagan, *The Rule of Moderation: Violence, Religion and the Politics of Restraint in Early Modern England* (Cambridge, 2011), ch. 8, esp. pp. 300, 302.

[3] See John Marshall, *John Locke, Toleration and Early Enlightenment Culture* (Cambridge, 2006), pp. 124–33, 452–3. See also John Spurr, *The Restoration Church of England 1646–89* (New Haven and London, 1991), esp. ch. 5.

[4] See D. W. R. Bahlman, *The Moral Revolution of 1688* (New Haven, 1957); T. C. Curtis and W. A. Speck, 'The Societies for the Reformation of Manners: A Case Study in the Theory and Practice of Moral Reform', *Literature and History*, 3 (1976), 45–64; Robert B. Shoemaker, *Prosecution and Punishment: Petty Crime and the Law in London and Rural Middlesex, c. 1660–1725* (Cambridge, 1991), ch. 9; and Shelley Burtt, 'The Societies for the Reformation of Manners: Between John Locke and the Devil in Augustan England', in *The Margins of Orthodoxy: Heterodox Writing and Cultural Response 1660–1750*, ed. Roger D. Lund (Cambridge, 1995), pp. 149–69. For a recent appraisal, see Brent S. Sirota, *The Christian Monitors: The Church of England and the Age of Benevolence 1680–1730* (New Haven and London, 2014), esp. pp. 92–101.

[5] Kenneth Sheppard, *Anti-Atheism in Early Modern England 1580–1720. The Atheist Answered and His Error Confuted* (Leiden, 2015), p. 4. This observation is there explicitly attributed to Pocock. For a

There is undoubtedly an element of truth in the contrast that he discerns, in that the period after *c.* 1650 certainly saw a proliferation of weighty tomes like Ralph Cudworth's massive and sophisticated *True Intellectual System of the Universe* (1678). Indeed, less full an account of this extensive literature will be given here than might otherwise have been the case due to the coverage of it provided by Sheppard in his very capable book. But it is important to point out how such apologetic writings related to what was perceived as the real problem, the objective of such authors being (in the words of the divine William Wotton) 'to leave the unbelieving World without Excuse'.[6] Such polemics sought comprehensively 'to refute all possible explications that the Atheists have or can propose', to quote the author of one of the classics of such writing, Richard Bentley, whose *The Folly and Unreasonableness of Atheism Demonstrated* formed the first series of Boyle Lectures, founded to refute atheism from a bequest in the great scientist's will.[7] But it was made no less clear, in the words of the Lectures' founder, that this attempt 'to disable the grounds whereon the Atheists cheife Arguments are built' was only in case 'it be Error rather than vice that has made him an Unbeliever'.[8] We have already encountered in the Introduction this interrelationship between 'Heart' and 'Head' (to continue the paraphrase of Boyle), and it needs to be borne in mind throughout what follows.

What had been the effect of the Civil War and Interregnum? It is of course well known that this period saw an extraordinary outburst of religious speculation and innovation, with a widespread rejection of the discipline that first the Church of England and then the Presbyterians tried to impose, and the emergence of a bewildering variety of sects, such as the Ranters and the Quakers. The orthodox reaction was sometimes to invoke the concept of 'atheism', as in the Act published by Parliament in August 1650 against 'Atheistical, Blasphemous and Execrable Opinions, derogatory to the honor of God, and destructive to humane Society'.[9] On the other hand, it is important to stress that the concept was often used more as an extreme expletive rather than anything more specific, along the lines of the

---

comparable view, see Jeffrey R. Collins, 'Early Modern England', in *The Cambridge History of Atheism*, ed. Stephen Bullivant and Michael Ruse, 2 vols (Cambridge, 2021), I, 202–22 (pp. 213–14).

[6] William Wotton, *Reflections upon Ancient and Modern Learning* (London, 1694), sig. a6.

[7] Richard Bentley, *Works*, ed. Alexander Dyce, 3 vols (London, 1836–8), III, 131–2. On the Boyle Lectures, see above, pp. 4, 9.

[8] *Boyle on Atheism*, ed. J. J. MacIntosh (Toronto, 2005), p. 105.

[9] *Acts and Ordinances of the Interregnum, 1642–1660*, ed. C. H. Firth and R. S. Rait, 3 vols (London 1911), II, 409–12.

almost theoretical 'atheism' that we encountered in the Introduction. This is well exemplified by the heresy-hunting divine Thomas Edwards in his *Gangraena: Or a Catalogue and Discovery of Many of the Errours, Heresies, Blasphemies and Pernicious Practices of the Sectaries of this Time* (1646), who spoke of his horror at the idea of a '*Toleration* of all Religions, Poperie, Blasphemie, Atheisme'.[10] Very occasionally, Edwards cited statements by radicals which sound fully atheistic, but these are generally mixed in with more miscellaneous utterances which are heterodox but essentially theistic.[11] Other accounts of Interregnum radicalism – for instance, Ephraim Pagitt's in his *Heresiography* (1645 and subsequent editions) – closely echo the evocation of the stock atheist in the character books referred to in Chapter 2.[12] The epithets and phrases that such authors used to describe their antagonists sometimes directly paraphrase the earlier anti-atheist literature, not least in the association of heterodox opinion with evil living: the works in question evidently provided a readily accessible rhetorical arsenal which was deemed as appropriate to use to describe extremes in religious novelty as to decry actual irreligion.

Beyond that, rather folklorish stories circulated of a direct link between the proliferation of religious heterodoxy during the Interregnum and the prevalence of 'atheism' after 1660. Thus the divine Joseph Glanvill, in his *Blow at Modern Sadducism* (1668), averred the reality of men 'who deny the *existence* of a *Deity*' on the basis of meeting 'one such some years since in *London*, who confidently, and without mincing, denied that there was any such being, and bid me prove it'. According to Glanvill, it turned out 'that he had run through the several stages of *modern Sects*, not stopping till he came down to that *sink* of *Folly*, and *madness*, Quakerism, and thence made a step into *Atheism*, which is no great leap'.[13] He could almost have been describing the trajectory of Lawrence Clarkson, the Ranter whom we came across in Chapter 3, except that Clarkson ended up as a member of yet another sect, the Muggletonians.[14] In fact, as we there saw, sectarians were more often spiritualists than atheists, notwithstanding the attempt of Christopher Hill to find precursors for the materialist proletarians of the Russian Revolution among their English forebears three centuries earlier.[15]

---

[10] Thomas Edwards, *Gangraena*, 3 pts (London, 1646; reprinted Exeter, 1977), I, 121; cf. III, 185–7.

[11] For example, ibid., I, 54[bis], 82; III, 187.

[12] Pagitt, *Heresiography* (5th ed., London, 1654). Cf. J. C. Davis, *Fear, Myth and History* (Cambridge, 1986), ch. 5, though see also this volume, pp. 22, 34n.

[13] Glanvill, *A Blow at Modern Sadducism* (London, 1668), pp. 154–9.   [14] See p. 70.

[15] Christopher Hill, 'Irreligion in the "Puritan" Revolution', in *Radical Religion in the English Revolution*, ed. J. F. McGregor and Barry Reay (Oxford, 1984), pp. 191–211; see also his 'Freethinking and Libertinism: The Legacy of the English Revolution', in Lund, ed., *Margins of Orthodoxy*, pp. 54–70. For a thoughtful survey of Interregnum radicalism in the context of atheism,

A more significant development was the publication in 1651 of Thomas Hobbes's *Leviathan*, which, directly or indirectly, was held responsible for a proliferation of atheistic views in the decades that followed. Of course, Hobbes's own religious views were controversial in his own time and have remained so ever since.[16] But his combination of a materialist outlook with a cynical and manipulative view of human nature was widely seen as dangerously influential. The Oxford academic John Wallis put the matter rather perceptively in a letter reflecting on Hobbes and his role that he wrote to the future bishop Thomas Tenison in 1680. Though dismissive of Hobbes's mathematical prowess, Wallis wrote tellingly of his pernicious impact on contemporaries due to his 'bold daring phansy, which, with his magisterial way of speaking, did (not convince, but) please those that loved to be Atheists, and were glad to hear any body boldly to say what they wish'd to be true'.[17]

The result was a proliferation during the Restoration period of what was commonly referred to as 'Hobbism', a convenient shorthand used by contemporaries to describe the relativist and implicitly irreligious outlook that Hobbes was thought to have spawned. A case in point is provided by the witchcraft sceptic John Wagstaffe, whom we encountered in the Introduction, who had absorbed Hobbes's cynical attitude towards divine and human affairs and whose *The Question of Witchcraft Debated* (1669) provided a caustic and effective critique of traditional witch beliefs. Indeed, it is revealing that, as we have already seen, Wagstaffe was himself accused of being an atheist, an accusation to which he responded in the enlarged, second edition of his book, which came out in 1671: although he there described this as 'a ridiculous slander', 'not worthy to be answered', it is not difficult to see why such suspicions should have arisen.[18]

We then come to the notorious case of Daniel Scargill, expelled from the University of Cambridge in 1669 for his Hobbist views, of which a full account has been given by Jon Parkin.[19] As Parkin points out, Scargill

---

see Nigel Smith, 'The Charge of Atheism and the Language of Radical Speculation, 1640–60', in *Atheism from the Reformation to the Enlightenment*, ed. Michael Hunter and David Wootton (Oxford, 1992), pp. 131–58.

[16] For a helpful discussion, see Jeffrey R. Collins, *The Allegiance of Thomas Hobbes* (Oxford, 2005), esp. pp. 26–32.

[17] Wallis to Tenison, 30 November 1680, Bodleian Library, Oxford, MS Add D 105, fols 70–1 (70v) (within the quotation, 'that loved to be' is altered from 'who would fain be' and 'boldly' is inserted). For the mathematical debate between Wallis and Hobbes, see Douglas M. Jesseph, *Squaring the Circle: The War between Hobbes and Wallis* (Chicago, 1999).

[18] Hunter, *Decline of Magic*, ch. 1, esp. pp. 41–2. See this volume, pp. 5–6, 9.

[19] See Jon Parkin, *Taming the Leviathan: The Reception of the Political and Religious Ideas of Thomas Hobbes in England 1640–1700* (Cambridge, 2007), pp. 244–52, a revised version of his article, 'Hobbism in the later 1660s: Daniel Scargill and Samuel Parker', *Historical Journal*, 42 (1999),

defended controversially heterodox theses in the university exercises in which he participated, thus causing concern among his colleagues. But what really did for him was the claim that he was not only a Hobbist but also a libertine – thus playing to the increased stress on moral rectitude in the religious orthodoxy of the day that has already been referred to. Not only was it claimed that Scargill had 'lately vented and publickly asserted in the said University, diverse wicked, blasphemous, and Atheistical positions' relating to religious doctrine and its interpretation which stemmed from Hobbes. In addition, his *Recantation*, which was published in print and widely circulated, continued:

> Agreeably unto which principles and positions, I have lived in great licentiousness, swearing rashly, drinking intemperately, boasting myself insolently, corrupting others by my pernicious principles and example, to the high Dishonour of God, the Reproach of the University, the Scandal of Christianity, and the just offence of mankind.[20]

As Parkin shows, this was something of a propaganda coup for the orthodox, and poor Scargill was consigned to an impoverished Norfolk living for the rest of his days. On the other hand, it is ironic that, as Parkin points out, a codicil added to his *Recantation* rendered its sincerity doubtful 'by drawing attention to the fact that recanting Hobbists are intrinsically unreliable'.[21]

In any case, concern about irreligion only increased over the subsequent decades. Here, we come particularly to the controversial figure of Charles Blount, of whose *Oracles of Reason* (1693) a contemporary specifically commented that it was 'the first Book I ever saw which did openly avow Infidelity'.[22] Blount had been linked with attempts to propagate Hobbesian opinions in the aftermath of the great philosopher's death in 1679: he seems to have had at least some association with various broadsheets produced at that point which set out a succinct group of opinions on religious and other topics from Hobbes's writings, presenting the great philosopher's iconoclastic views in an approachable, almost aphoristic form.[23] One of these

---

85–108. See also J. L. Axtell, 'The Mechanics of Opposition: Restoration Cambridge v. Daniel Scargill', *Bulletin of the Institute of Historical Research*, 38 (1965), 102–11.

[20] *The Recantation of Daniel Scargill, Publickly Made before the University of Cambridge, in Great St Maries, July 25, 1669* (Cambridge, 1669), pp. 3–4.

[21] Parkin, *Taming the Leviathan*, pp. 249–50.

[22] William Nicholls, *A Conference with a Theist* (London, 1696), sig. A5v.

[23] There are difficulties about the authorship of these works, often accepted as genuine and by Blount (e.g., by Roger D. Lund, *Ridicule, Religion and the Politics of Wit in Augustan England* [Farnham, 2012], p. 49). See *The Correspondence of Thomas Hobbes*, ed. Noel Malcolm, 2 vols (Oxford, 1994), II, 793–4, for evidence from Blount's commonplace book that he was not in fact the author,

(which includes a striking etched portrait of Hobbes, derived from the plate produced by Wenceslaus Hollar in 1665) is titled *Memorable Sayings of Mr. Hobbes in His Books and at the Table*; the final phrase of the title is itself telling, in view of the extent to which atheistic sentiment was believed at the time to be predominantly orally expressed.[24]

More significantly, Blount also produced a series of 'sustainedly destructive' publications that were clearly intended to antagonise the orthodox through the heterodox opinions that they purveyed, even if the exact nature of his stance remains controversial.[25] These began with his *Anima Mundi: Or, an Historical Narration of the Opinions of the Ancients Concerning Man's Soul After This Life: According to Unenlightened Nature* (1679) and his *Great is Diana of the Ephesians: Or, The Original of Idolatry, together with the Politick Institution of the Gentiles Sacrifices* (1680), which deliberately stirred things up by drawing parallels between Christian and pagan doctrine and attributing both to the cynical manipulation of priests. He also produced a quasi-learned edition of *The First Two Books, of Philostratus, Concerning the Life of Apollonius Tyaneus* (1680), which paralleled Apollonius's miracles with Christ's, thereby covertly undermining the latter. Equally controversial was Blount's *Miracles, No Violations of the Laws of Nature* (1683), which presented to an English audience the naturalistic critique of miracles contained in chapter 6 of Spinoza's *Tractatus Theologico-Politicus*, thus offering a direct challenge to arguments for the key role of miracles in vindicating Christianity as presented by Robert Boyle and others.[26] Then there was Blount's *Religio Laici* (1683), which sought to revive the Deistic doctrines of Lord Herbert of Cherbury, and his *Oracles of Reason* (1693), the latter a kind of freethinking miscellany comprising various letters and texts of clearly subversive intent,

---

although he seems to have been linked with them. See also Parkin, *Taming the Leviathan*, pp. 346–53, who even argues (p. 349) that at least one of these items might in fact be a 'counter-radical' work asserting Hobbes's heterodoxy, though this seems slightly fanciful.

[24] *Memorable Sayings of Mr. Hobbes* ([London, 1680]). For the image, see Richard Pennington, *A Descriptive Catalogue of the Etched Work of Wenceslaus Hollar, 1607–77* (Cambridge, 1982), p. 244 (no. 1417) and Simon Turner, ed. Guilia Bartram, *The New Hollstein: German Engravings, Etchings and Woodcuts 1400–1700: Wenceslaus Hollar*, parts 1–9 (Ouderkerk aan den IJssel, 2009–12), VI, 241–2 (no. 1843).

[25] Robert E. Sullivan, *John Toland and the Deist Controversy* (Cambridge, MA, 1982), p. 220. For appraisals, see Justin A. I. Champion, *The Pillars of Priestcraft Shaken: The Church of England and Its Enemies, 1660–1730* (Cambridge, 1992), pp. 140–8; Wayne Hudson, *The English Deists: Studies in Early Enlightenment* (London, 2009), ch. 4; and Sheppard, *Anti-Atheism*, pp. 247–57.

[26] For Boyle's views on such subjects, see *Boyle on Atheism*, esp. pp. 261–97; and Michael Hunter, *Boyle Studies: Aspects of the Life and Thought of Robert Boyle (1627–91)* (Farnham, 2015), pp. 121, 166–7.

for instance one addressed by one Ralph Richardson to his 'Dear Friend Mr Harvey Wilwood', a professed Epicurean, arguing 'that Felicity consists generally in Pleasure'.[27]

There can be no doubt that Blount fulfilled orthodox expectations of what an atheist might be expected to publish, fuelling fears that the content of a book like *The Oracles of Reason* merely represented the tip of an iceberg of heterodox literature that was presumed otherwise to circulate clandestinely. Indeed, in the preface to *Anima Mundi*, Blount had defended himself against the accusation that he was an atheist, associating such attacks with 'some haughty Pedant', inspired by 'Ignorance and Malice'.[28] Blount provided an obvious target for orthodox writers, who were only too happy to respond to him as an archetypal atheist. For instance, the cleric John Harris, in his 1698 Boyle Lectures, published under the title *The Atheistical Objections, Against the Being of a God*, returned again and again to different parts of Blount's writings, seeing them as deeply pernicious. He was hardly less outspoken in his objections to the views of Hobbes, while at various points he also took issue with such notorious continental apostates as Guilio Cesare Vanini and Spinoza.[29]

Two of the letters in Blount's *Oracles of Reason* were addressed to John Wilmot, Earl of Rochester, and this brings us to another notorious libertine and freethinker of the period, whose views became all the more notorious when they were given wide circulation through a much-reprinted account of Rochester's final days by Bishop Gilbert Burnet in his *Some Passages of the Life and Death of the Right Honourable John, Earl of Rochester, Who Died the 26th of July, 1680*.[30] A sample of Rochester's views is provided by Burnet's exposition of them. In his words, Rochester sought to 'fortifie his Mind . . . by dispossessing it all he could of the belief or apprehensions of Religion'. The Earl acknowledged that there appeared to be some kind of 'vast power' behind the universe, but it did not seem appropriate to worship this, such devotions being 'the Inventions of Priests, to make the World believe they had a Secret of Incensing and Appeasing God as they pleased'. 'The belief of Mysteries', Rochester considered, 'made way for all the Juglings of Priests', and, even if there were an afterlife, 'he doubted much of Rewards or Punishments'. His yardstick of morality was 'that he should do nothing to the hurt of any other, or that might prejudice his own health: And he

---

[27] Blount, *The Oracles of Reason* (London, 1693), pp. 106–10.
[28] Blount, *Anima Mundi* (London, 1679), sig. A2.
[29] Harris, *The Atheistical Objections, Against the Being of God and His Attributes* (London, 1698).
[30] The letters from Blount are most conveniently available in *The Letters of John Wilmot Earl of Rochester*, ed. Jeremy Treglown (Oxford, 1980), pp. 206–16.

thought that all pleasure, when it did not interfere with these, was to be indulged as the gratification of our natural Appetites'. His reason for rejecting revealed religion as divulged in the scriptures was not least the inadequacy of the sacred text itself, with its internal contradictions, its 'Incoherences of Stile' and its retailing of miracles and other strange stories: 'for the boldness and cunning of Contrivers meeting with the Simplicity and Credulity of the People, things were easily received; and being once received passed down without contradiction'. Moreover, he rejected the counter-arguments that Burnet put forward as 'the effect of Fancy'; these 'sounded to him like *Enthusiasme*, or *Canting*', at odds with 'the Dictates of *Reason* and *Philosophy*'.[31]

Related views are to be found in Rochester's poetry, which circulated at the time both in manuscript and in print, his love lyrics being interspersed by such works as his 'Upon Nothinge', with its astonishing nihilism, or his 'Satyre against Reason and Mankind', which explored the shortcomings of the naturalistic ethics that he had derived from Hobbes, though excoriating 'vain Prelatick pride' in doing so.[32] Indeed, on the basis of painstaking analysis of such compositions, complex readings have been put forward, some of them suggesting a degree of ambivalence on Rochester's part concerning the role as a spokesman for the culture of libertinism that he was widely seen to represent.[33] Of course, Burnet engineered a deathbed conversion, which the former Bishop of Oxford and many others have found convincing.[34] But one might harbour the suspicion that, had he recovered, Rochester would have reverted to his old sceptical principles, and certainly this is what his drinking companions and other cronies believed.[35] Reflecting on Rochester's death in the letter to Tenison that has already been cited, Wallis pointed out how Rochester 'could talk Atheistical things with as much briskness & as much witt as Mr Hobbes, & with more a sense

---

[31] Burnet, *Some Passages of the Life and Death of the Right Hon. John, Earl of Rochester* (London, 1680), esp. pp. 15, 22, 38, 45, 51–4, 72–3, 100.

[32] *The Works of John Wilmot, Earl of Rochester*, ed. Harold Love (Oxford, 1999), pp. 46–8, 57–63.

[33] See Gillian Manning, 'Rochester's *Satyr Against Reason and Mankind* and Contemporary Religious Debate', *The Seventeenth Century*, 8 (1993), 99–121; Christopher Tilmouth, *Passion's Triumph over Reason: A History of the Moral Imagination from Spenser to Rochester* (Oxford, 2007), ch. 7–8; and Sarah Ellensweig, *The Fringes of Belief: English Literature, Ancient Heresy, and the Politics of Freethinking, 1660–1760* (Stanford, 2008), ch. 1.

[34] Richard Harries, 'Rochester's "Death-Bed Repentance"', in *That Second Bottle: Essays on John Wilmot, Earl of Rochester*, ed. Nicholas Fisher (Manchester, 2000), pp. 191–6. More recently, see *Lord Rochester in the Restoration World*, ed. Matthew C. Augustine and Steven N. Zwicker (Cambridge, 2015).

[35] Treglown, *Letters of Rochester*, pp. 35–7.

of reason'; on the other hand, he perhaps predictably added that Rochester 'could not thoroughly beleive it' due to the pangs of conscience which ultimately brought about his repentance.

The example particularly of Rochester meant that from the 1670s onwards the association of atheism, 'Hobbism' and libertinism became almost axiomatic.[36] Yet, considering the level of orthodox outrage that poured from the press, actual instances of atheistic opinion remain hard to find, evidently due to the fact that such views were predominantly orally expressed. Here, it is helpful to quote at length from a revealing letter written in May 1692 by Richard Bentley, the Boyle Lecturer whom we have already come across, to the Oxford don, Edward Bernard, concerning the proper target of the lecture series that was by then under way. Having dismissed the Jews (another of the potential antagonists mentioned in Boyle's will), who 'do us little hurt', Bentley went on:

> And then for Theists [i.e., Deists], you say, they have books written, but Atheists have only talk. Must we then pass by the Atheists, against the judgment and command of my Honourable Benefactor, who hath put them in the very first place as the most dangerous enemies? Atheism is so much the worse that it is not buried in books; but is gotten εἰς τὸν βίον [into life], that taverns and coffee-houses, nay Westminster-hall and the very churches, are full of it. A sermon therefore must be *contra malos mores* [against bad manners], not *malos libros* [bad books]. But are the Atheists of your mind, that they have no books written for them? Not one of them but believes Tom Hobbes to be a rank one; and that his corporeal God is a meer sham to get his book printed. They understand the Cabbala well enough: that all that is but Juggle; and that a corporeal infinite God is downright nonsense. I have said something to this in my first sermon; and I know it to be true by the conversation I have had with them. There may be some Spinosists, or immaterial Fatalists, beyond seas. But not one English Infidel in a hundred is any other than a Hobbist; which I know to be rank Atheism in the private study and select conversation of those men, whatever it may appear to be abroad.[37]

Bentley was clearly well acquainted with the atheist clientele that caused him concern, as his knowing remarks both here and throughout his Boyle Lectures show. Yet is it frustratingly difficult to give substance to what usually remains a vaguely defined and nameless threat.

---

[36] See Parkin, *Taming the Leviathan*, pp. 304–11. See also Samuel I. Mintz, *The Hunting of Leviathan: Seventeenth-Century Reactions to the Materialism and Moral Philosophy of Thomas Hobbes* (Cambridge, 1962), ch. 7.

[37] Bentley to Bernard, 28 May 1692, in *The Correspondence of Richard Bentley*, ed. Christopher Wordsworth, 2 vols (London, 1842), I, 39–40. Cf. Bentley's Boyle Lectures in his *Works*, III.

It might have been hoped that we would gain help in this respect from contemporary memorialists or even from hints to be found in the anti-atheist literature itself. For instance, the Oxford antiquary Anthony Wood tells of a group of four 'notorious atheists' at St John's College, Oxford, in 1682, but when it came to filling in their names in his notes, he became rather sketchy.[38] He cites one as '. . . Smith son of Dr John Smith, a phisitian' (such a man did indeed matriculate at St John's in 1679, later becoming a Fellow of the college and dying in 1715, though of his irreligious tendencies nothing is otherwise known); for the names of the other three, however, Wood leaves their names blank except for vaguely noting one 'Comby', whose identity is unclear.[39] In any case, it might be felt that Wood's concern was not really with these individuals at all, but with doing down St John's, as 'a most debauched colledg, over which presides a peevish and proud president'.[40]

A further clue might hopefully have been provided by the tantalising case of *The Second Spira*, being (to quote the title of the book in question) *A Fearful Example of An Atheist, Who Had Apostacised from the Christian Religion, and Dyed in Despair at Westminster December 8. 1692*. This work, published in 1693 by the bookseller John Dunton and generally attributed to the miscellaneous writer Richard Sault, was an immediate bestseller which went through a print run of 30,000 copies in six weeks. Its title alluded to the story of the sixteenth-century Italian apostate who converted to Protestantism, apostacised and suffered religious despair, a popular story in Puritan circles in seventeenth-century England. The tract told of a country gentleman associated with the Inns of Court who fell in with a 'club' of notorious libertines whose tenets included the claim that

> 'tis the Habit and Custom of Education that creates the *formidable Notions of Conscience, Heaven, Hell, Futurity* and the *Immortality of the Soul*, all which are but the politick Inventions of Priests and cunning Magistrates, to enrich themselves and keep the Vulgar in Awe, who are naturally Superstitious and Fearful.[41]

---

[38] *The Life and Times of Anthony Wood*, ed. Andrew Clark, 5 vols (Oxford, 1891–1900), III, 3.

[39] See J. Foster, *Alumni Oxonienses, 1500–1714*, 4 vols. (Oxford, 1891–2), IV, 1375. 'Comby' could be intended for Edward Combe, who matriculated at St John's in 1679, later becoming rector of St Martin's, Worcester, and dying in 1737/8: ibid., I, 313.

[40] Wood, *Life and Times*, III, 3. He added that the President, William Levinz, had been 'a good-natur'd man when fellow, "magistratus indicat virum"'.

[41] Richard Sault (attrib.), *The Second Spira: Being A Fearful Example of An Atheist, Who Had Apostacised from the Christian Religion, and Dyed in Despair at Westminster December 8. 1692* (London, 1693), title page and p. 5. The work was said to be by 'J. S., A Minister of the Church of England'.

Needless to say the man subsequently 'dyed in Despair' to the accompaniment of 'dreadful Expressions and Blasphemies', thus providing an opportunity for a lengthy refutation of atheist principles, which was published 'for an Example to others, and recommended to all young Persons, to settle them in their Religion'; this was continued even more fully in a subsequent work published later in the same year.[42] In a further sequel to the original *Second Spira*, the atheist in question was actually named as 'Mr F. N.', and the late Gerald Aylmer, in his essay on 'Unbelief in Seventeenth-Century England', actually went to the trouble to establish that this could conceivably have been Francis Newport, third son of the second Baron Newport, later Earl of Bradford, and grandson of the fourth Earl of Bedford – though unfortunately the date of his burial (which Aylmer carefully investigated) failed to tally with the date of death given on the title page of the original book.[43] Matters are complicated, however, by the fact that the publisher of the tract, John Dunton, in his *Life and Errors* (1705), was to claim that the apostate in question was none other than the author Richard Sault himself – though whether the notoriously mendacious Dunton can be trusted in this is anyone's guess.[44] This rather inconclusive state of affairs again leaves one frustrated in the search for 'real' atheists.

Yet, it could be argued that it is slightly naive to expect orthodox spokesmen to give actual instances at all, rather than to complain in general terms about a threat that they perceived as epidemic. This state of affairs is similar to that noted in Chapter 2 concerning the period before the Civil War. It rather reduced the power of a tirade complaining of the prevalence of the phenomenon to descend to naming particular individuals, especially if they were otherwise nonentities – quite apart from the

---

[42] [Sault, Richard], *A Conference Between a Modern Atheist, and His Friend. By the Methodizer of the Second Spira* (London, 1693). For a full account, see Kenneth Sheppard, 'Atheism, Apostasy, and the Afterlives of Francis Spira in Early Modern England', *The Seventeenth Century*, 27 (2012), 410–34, reprinted in Sheppard, *Anti-Atheism*, ch. 5. See also Michael MacDonald's profound account of the Spira case and its legacy in '*The Fearful Estate of Francis Spira*: Narrative, Identity and Emotion in Early Modern England', *Journal of British Studies*, 31 (1992), 32–61.

[43] *The Second Spira, Being a Fearful Example of F. N. An Atheist, Part the Second* (London, 1693), by 'H. L., a Lay-Man, Mr N's particular Acquaintance and frequent Visitor of him in his Sickness'. See G. E. Aylmer, 'Unbelief in Seventeenth-Century England', in *Puritans and Revolutionaries: Essays in Seventeenth-Century History Presented to Christopher Hill*, ed. D. H. Pennington and Keith Thomas (Oxford, 1978), pp. 22–46 (p. 35 and 35–6n).

[44] John Dunton, *The Life and Errors* (London, 1705), pp. 218–22, and see also the '30th edition' of *The Second Spira* (London, [1719]). For a further account, see Gilbert D. McEwen, *The Oracle of the Coffee House. John Dunton's 'Athenian Mercury'* (San Marino, 1972), ch. 6. See also Stephen Parks, *John Dunton and the English Book Trade* (New York, 1976), pp. 57–9, 277, 289–90, 385.

fact that naming names invited protestations of innocence from those so identified. As Thomas Beard had put it in the earlier period concerning the renegades who caused him concern: 'Many such like examples I could adjoyne, with their names and places of abode, but I forebeare, least by reporting Gods judgements vpon the dead, I should offend some that are aliue'.[45] Moreover, the experience of the Societies for the Reformation of Manners suggested the difficulty of convicting those of elite status of the kind of libertinism about which there was so much concern at the time.[46] The sleuth in pursuit of individual cases of atheism is therefore destined to be disappointed.

There are, nevertheless, occasional telling survivals that are worthy of attention. Take, for example, a written text which professes to be the statement of an atheist's views dating from the year 1700. In fact, this bears some resemblance to the letters included in Blount's *Oracles of Reason* that have already been referred to, while the existence of such 'Papers' is also indicated by the cleric Edward Stillingfleet in his *Letter to a Deist* (1677), in which he responded to arguments that he had come across in similarly ephemeral form.[47] In this instance, the document in question forms part of a tract titled *The Judgment of God upon Atheism and Infidelity, in a Brief and True Account of the Irreligious Life and Miserable Death of Mr. George Edwards* (1704), by John Smith, a graduate of All Souls College, Oxford, who since 1690 had been Vicar of West Ham. Mostly, this provides a rather clichéd and typically heightened narrative of the apostacy of the man involved and his ultimate suicide, accompanied by a lengthy vindication of Christian doctrine against his supposed objections to it. But what is intriguing about this particular work is that it prints verbatim an apologetic statement ostensibly produced by the atheist George Edwards himself, which may be quoted at length here. In his narrative, Smith records how 'upon *Munday*-night following, which was *Sept.* the 9th, 1700, Mr *Edwards* brought me the following Paper, written with his own Hand, and which I have still lying by me'.[48] The document is as follows:

[45] Thomas Beard, *The Theatre of God's Judgements* (London, 1631), pp. 316–17. See also this volume, pp. 43–4, 46–7.

[46] Curtis and Speck, 'Societies for the Reformation of Manners', pp. 55–6, 58; Shoemaker, *Prosecution and Punishment*, pp. 250–2.

[47] Edward Stillingfleet, *A Letter to a Deist in Answer to Several Objections against the Truth and Authority of the Scriptures* (London, 1677), pp. 1–2.

[48] Smith, *The Judgment of God upon Atheism and Infidelity* (London, 1704), pp. 18–22. It is perhaps revealing that, when Smith's book was included in a rather sensationalist reprint of Bacon's *Relation of the Fearfull Estate of Francis Spira* by B. Harris from 1706 onwards, this text was omitted.

Of the Being, or not Being of GOD.

The Being of GOD, you say, is, and hath been acknowledged by all Ages and Nations; it hath likewise been denied by particular Persons, and publick Societies and Nations in most Ages; so there is no Universal Consent, because denied by several Nations, as many Historians report of the *Cannibals* in *America,* and of *Soldania* in *Africk*; and many great Philosophers, as *Diagoras, Theodorus,* and others. Further, if Universal be granted, and enough to prove a Deity, and Existence of GOD, it may also prove Polytheism, and Idolatry, for which, like Consent may be pleaded. Many take up their Belief of GOD, and the Creation, as part of their Education and Notion, more than any Conviction in their Minds and Consciences; and without being Censorious or Uncharitable, it may be said of most Part of Mankind, witness the daily Enormities and Executions among Men pretending to Religion, which also take off the Force of Universal Consent, it being in the Tongue only, and not in the Heart. This Belief may be introduced thro' Ignorance, as a great Philosopher observes in his Time, *the Illiterate believe more than the Philosophers*;[49] or thro' Policy, Fear, Interest, and such like. We find many Persons well disposed to Justice and Goodness, Love and Mercy, meerly by the Nobleness of their Nature, with the help of Education, and but small Friends to Religion; when others, by all the Care and Education that may be, for all the Fear they pretend of GOD, and future Punishments are not able to restrain them from the worst of Actions. Why should not this Almighty signalize himself to us by Miracles? Did he not know so long time would produce many Contradictions and Disputes, and question his Being? Supposing it is the World that governs the World, and is supplied from that great Orb of Nature, this Power had never more need to appear than now in Vindication of himself, when Men question his very Being. His Worship is become the Fancy of most Mens Brain; as *Luther* in his Book, *de potestate Papæ,* teaches 7 Sacraments; *de captivate Babylonica,* that there are only 3, and in his Book *ad Waldenses,* but 2. Also, sometimes having owned Purgatory, and since deny'd it, and Transubstantiation, and after deny'd it: To be brief, there are almost Threescore such Contradictions in this Author, and as many of *Beza* and *Calvin,* the first and great Lights of the Reformation. If I have a Soul to save, to which of these must I go? *Zuinglius* presents me with a Volume called *The Word of Life*; *Luther* says he is a Fool, Antichrist, and Deceiver; much to the same purpose says *Calvin, Beza,* and *Castellio,* of one another; what will be the product, I pray you judge.

---

[49] Var. *Hist.,* 2.31.[A footnote in the original. The impressive, quasi-learned reference is perhaps to Varro's *Divine Antiquities.*]

Of the Eternity of the World.

From the natural Prospect of Things, the Sun and Moon keep their constant Courses as ever, without any decay or diminution. There is also a fresh and flourishing Continuance or Existence of all natural Things. Besides the Judgment of several eminent and ancient Philosophers, as *Aristotle*, saith, *The World was Eternal, and a necessary Emanation from GOD, as Light from the Sun*: Epicurus, *That by Coalition of Atoms*, it came *into this Fabrick*; which is a later Edition than Eternity (which I believe not;) others, *That the World always was, and is of it self existing*; and why not as well as the Author? The Account the Chaldeans give, is 43000 Years from the Creation, to the time of *Alexander*. You say, *The Improvement of Arts evince the World's Beginning*; which might come in and go out as occasion, the Fashion of Times, and Humour of People; as these last twelve Years fully declare, and make good *Solomon*'s Saying, *There is no new thing under the Sun*. I wonder so Wise a Being, did not make the World from Eternity, or long before the *Caldeans* Account, and manifest his Glory and Praise in so great a Work, which he himself saw *very Good*.

Of the Origination, or Eternity of Man.

If all Men were Sons of *Adam*, whence came so many different Sorts of People, especially as to produce *Black Men*? If a married Woman here should bring forth such a Child, let her Reputation be as clear as may be, what would the World say, or to what Cause ascribe it, judge ye. If there were no Men, Arts, or Trade before, or in the beginning with *Adam*, with what Utensils or Implements did he and *Abel* Till the Ground? We read of none while *Tubalcain*, an Artificer in Brass and Iron; which make it probable, that Men were from all Eternity, with the World, as several Authors have observ'd. The Complaint of *Cain*, supposeth popularity of People, that every one finding him should kill him; his taking a Wife; where should he have her? We read of no more Children of *Adam*, especially Daughters, a great while. And that Cain should build a City with so little help, and for so few Inhabitants, is to me strange.

Sir, Tho' I have mentioned Probabilities, and the Judgment of several Authors in these Matters, I think the thing you desired, was an Account of my Belief, which is, That the World is eternal, and of Matter, existing without any more Power than Matter and Motion; and that all Men go to their Mother the Earth, and there end. Whatsoever some may say of *Transmigration* of *Souls*, no doubt it was the Judgment or Belief of those who ask'd our Saviour, *Who did sin, this Man or his Parents, that he was born blind*? This Question must suppose the Soul to have existence, and capable of contracting Guilt, before the coming into this Body, else a Man could not sin before born; this was the Opinion of the *Pythagoreans*, and of some among the *Jews*, but no more of that. I shall therefore beg your Pardon for all Offences past, and any in these presents; and give you many Thanks for all your Kindness to me, tho' provoked to the contrary, and hope to receive that satisfaction from you, as may, thro' Mercy of that Almighty you profess, bring me to that Peace and Comfort I believe you to enjoy here, and may to all Eternity hereafter; which all the Power of Heaven and Earth grant, if it be but for the Happiness of such Professors, and for the Commodity of the World. Assure your self, it shall be received into an unprejudic'd and honest Mind, and condescending and obedient Will.

> *Your humble Servant, well known; therefore I say no more,*
> *nor set my Name.*

What is one to make of this? It is, of course, possible that it is simply an artefact of the author of the tract in which it is contained, but it has an air of verisimilitude. In particular, it invokes some of the arguments that atheists might have been expected to use, notably the disagreements among Christians since the Reformation and the inconsistencies and illogicalities to be found in the narratives recorded in the Bible. It is interesting that it develops an eternalist argument rather similar to that put forward by Archibald Pitcairne in his *Pitcairneana* a decade or so later, to which we will come later in this book; it also takes up the argument from the inhabitants of Soldania (following Locke) and disagrees with the progressivist argument which was evidently associated with orthodox polemic at this stage, as it also was in Pitcairne's time.[50] Though it would be possible to annotate it in detail, this seems superfluous; in any case, needless to say, John Smith devoted page after page to refuting the views that it contained.[51] It nevertheless retains a certain vividness and potency which is telling in itself.

The final source of evidence on which is it is appropriate to draw here concerns a reformed atheist – a man who fully admitted that he had been an atheist of the most egregious kind, but who repented his errors and then capitalised on this in ways that we will explore. The figure in question is 'Burridge the Blasphemer' – to quote the title of the only extant essay on him, an early work by the august literary scholar, Sir James Sutherland – but the principal source for Burridge's life is the autobiographical account that he himself published in 1712 as *Religio Libertini: Or, The Faith of a Converted Atheist*.[52] Let us therefore give a brief account of his story, which is as complex and dramatic as any from his period.

---

[50] See pp. 140, 142, 156.   [51] See Sheppard, *Anti-Atheism*, pp. 196–9.

[52] James Sutherland, 'Burridge the Blasphemer', in his *Background for Queen Anne* (London, 1939), pp. 3–32; Richard Burridge, *Religio Libertini: Or, The Faith of a Converted Atheist* (London, 1712). For other brief references to Burridge, see D. C. Allen, *Doubt's Boundless Sea* (Baltimore, 1964), p. 212n., where Burridge's book is described as 'unbelievably pompous and vulgar', and Lund, *Ridicule, Religion and the Politics of Wit*, pp. 65n, 87n, and 98.

Burridge was born in 1670 and was initially expected to pursue a career as a churchman, being sent to study at Magdalen College, Oxford. Matters were complicated, however, by the Catholicising policies then in progress under James II; instead, he attended a Catholic seminary at the Savoy and became a Catholic convert. But with the Glorious Revolution he was placed at something of a loose end, being left to indulge in the pleasures of the town and to writing lascivious verse: indeed, he became known as the '*Young Rochester*'.[53] At this stage he married, and he also enlisted in the force raised to attempt the capture of the French possession of Martinique in the West Indies. It was now that he actually admitted to being an atheist. While others were frightened by the thunder and lightning by which their ship was assailed, Burridge coolly played cards and dice, and he wrote:

> Now, the Occasion of my turning *Atheist* proceeded from the great Delight I took in reading *Lucretius* and *Lucian*'s Dialogues; which pernicious Authors so poison'd my Reason, that publickly denying the Being of a Deity, and the Tenets of a Resurrection, Judgment, Heaven, or Hell, I have made my Auditors stand amaz'd, and not able to confute my impious Assertions, they have ceas'd any further Disputation.[54]

He explained his rationale more fully later in the book:

> whereas others were frighten'd at the terrible Meteors of Thunder and Lightning, it was my Delight always to hear and see it, as knowing by the reading of *Physicks* or Natural *Philosophy*, that such Effects proceeded only from Natural Causes. Besides, that which hath also strengthened me in the atheistical Notions, was the several Rents and Divisions which I have seen made in the establish'd Church of this Land; for how many Opinions have I seen broach'd every Day, that argue'd no less than a Spiritual Madness?[55]

The Martinique expedition ended in failure, despite a display of bravery on Burridge's part; its aftermath was made worse by the fact that he and his wife (who had camp-followed him to the West Indies) nearly died of the spotted fever, as he recounted in his narrative of his career. Back in England and following an abortive trip to the continent, Burridge again found himself on his uppers, so he took to writing to make a living. Indeed, for a time he became a successful hack writer, penning a poem commiserating with Princess Anne on the death of the Duke of Gloucester in 1700, in addition to a number of other pieces. But one of the lampoons that he wrote sailed too close to the wind, satirising the Dutch by burlesquing the church

---

[53] Burridge, *Religio Libertini*, p. 4.   [54] Ibid., p. 9.   [55] Ibid., p. 35.

catechism, and he was condemned to the pillory for his 'most diabolical and malicious' crime. The pamphlet in question does not appear to survive, but another that he wrote led to further problems, necessitating Burridge's absence from London for a while, time that he spent in Ireland and Scotland, where he 'was most civilly entertain'd' at the universities of Glasgow and Edinburgh.[56] On his return to London, however, Burridge was imprisoned for debt in 1711, getting into further trouble by drunkenly proposing 'a Health *to the Confusion of Almighty God*; a Health *to the Devil our Master*; and *Damnation to the Resurrection*', which led to a prosecution for blasphemy.[57] In his defence, Burridge claimed various mitigating circumstances, not least the malign practices of his gaoler and the transvestism and sodomitical proclivities of certain of his fellow prisoners; he also rather ingeniously protested that, since he had invoked the Devil, he was not really a blasphemer at all. He was, however, condemned and it was in the aftermath of this that, on 6 July 1712, he made his recantation to the Ordinary of Newgate, Paul Lorrain, who took the opportunity to publish a sermon celebrating the reclamation of the soul of this converted sinner.

Lorrain's sermon, it has to be said, is something of a disappointment. He rather sidestepped Burridge's atheism to focus on his Catholicism, devoting his remarks to a standard anti-Catholic polemic. The sermon was titled *Popery Near A-Kin to Paganism and Atheism*, and it invoked St James's definition of true religion as echoed by Luther to demarcate Protestantism from Catholicism and paganism, emphasising the authority of scripture and the relative purity of the reformed churches; atheism played only a minor role in his presentation.[58] Indeed, Lorrain's prioritisation was perhaps significant. It was unusual for the issues of anti-Catholicism and atheism to be juxtaposed, since the two literatures usually subsisted separately, and in this case anti-popery trumped anti-atheism.[59]

---

[56] Ibid., pp. 16–19. For Burridge's writings, see the listings in English Short Title Catalogue, estc.bl.uk, and D. F. Foxon, *English Verse 1701–1750: A Catalogue of Separately Printed Poems with Notes on Contemporary Collected Editions*, 2 vols (Cambridge, 1975), s.v 'Burridge, Richard'. Though the 1702 parody of the church catechism does not appear to survive, there is a 1703 *Recantation* of it: Foxon B588 (see also F124).

[57] Burridge, *Religio Libertini*, pp. 19–33.

[58] Lorrain, *Popery Near A-Kin to Paganism and Atheism* (London 1712). In his lengthy *ODNB* article on Lorrain, Tim Wales mistakenly states that the occasion of the sermon was 'the abjuration of a Catholic priest accused of blasphemy'.

[59] For comments on the mutual relationship between the two, see Shagan, *Rule of Moderation*, pp. 310–25. See also Peter Lake, 'Anti-Popery: The Structure of a Prejudice', in *Conflict in Early Stuart England*, ed. Richard Cust and Ann Hughes (London, 1989), pp. 72–106, esp. p. 102 n. 24. For a rare discussion linking them, see Thomas Manningham, *Two Discourses* (London, 1681), pp. 107–72.

This is perhaps hardly surprising in 1712, when the ongoing Jacobite threat was intense and the rising by the Old Pretender imminent. Indeed, it could be seen as a tribute to the power of the atheist stereotype that in his own defence of himself in *Religio Libertini*, Burridge capitalised so strongly on that, rather than on his conversion from Catholicism.

Lorrain's sermon was accompanied by Burridge's formal abjuration 'of the Errors of the Church of Rome, and of all Atheistical Principles, in which he did formerly live'.[60] To find a full elaboration of Burridge's views, however, one has to return to *Religio Libertini*, also published in 1712 (the tract was advertised at the end of Lorrain's printed sermon, and it was evidently issued to accompany it).[61] Rather predictably, Burridge there explained that Catholicism appealed to him 'because it gave me greater Latitude in Sin, than any Religion whatsoever', thus enabling him 'to be fashionably Prophane with the greatest Sinners'.[62] This forms part of a lengthy 'Recantation' in which Catholicism makes only a fairly brief appearance for the 'pious Frauds' which deluded its devotees, but was overwhelmed by an almost garrulous account of the atheism and blasphemy in which Burridge had long indulged and which he now profusely and wordily repented. To this was attached an even longer section comprising an almost unbelievably prolix and rather vacuous diatribe in favour of the Protestant religion and the spiritual and moral rectitude that Burridge professed that he had now espoused, the final few pages of which had to be set in increasingly small type in order to accommodate them. Burridge's activity as a hack writer had made him a facile wordsmith, and his skills were here all too evident.

What is important, however, is that he evidently relished the reputation he had by now acquired for being 'so long an *Atheist*, nay, the very greatest of *Atheists*', and he seems to have capitalised on this by arranging to meet eminent churchmen to discuss religious matters with them.[63] Such encounters went back to his atheist phase, when he recounts a similar encounter with the 'Collegians' of Jesus College, Cambridge, while his warm entertainment at the universities at Glasgow and Edinburgh has already been mentioned. But later in *Religio Libertini* he refers to a whole series of discussions that he evidently had with leading clerics – with John Williams, Bishop of Chichester, about the potential 'salvability' of well-intentioned heathens in antiquity; with William Moreton, Bishop of

---

[60] Lorrain, *Popery*, pp. 41–4.
[61] Both works were printed for Sam. Briscoe and sold by John Graves and John Morphew.
[62] Burridge, *Religio Libertini*, pp. 8, 35 and elsewhere.   [63] Ibid., p. 35. Cf. p. 20.

Kildare, about the doctrine of the soul; with Henry Compton, Bishop of London, about the extent of the destruction caused by the Flood; with Peter Mews, Bishop of Winchester, about the advantages of a good conscience; and even with Thomas Tenison, Archbishop of Canterbury, to whom he claimed to have 'upon several Demonstrations prov'd ... without Contradiction' the location and timing of the punishment of the damned.[64]

In many ways these conversations seem to me better to reveal Burridge's incorrigible self-esteem than the episodes in his later career that James Sutherland was able to document from archival sources and newspaper reports. In 1718 Burridge had a further brush with the authorities over a drunken outburst and was again condemned for blasphemy, thus earning him the sobriquet 'Burridge the Blasphemer', which provided the title for Sutherland's essay. He was also involved in various squabbles with newspaper proprietors and editors over writings for which he was responsible and related matters, so that (as Sutherland puts it) 'by this time Burridge's reputation was so scandalous that he could safely be blamed for anything'.[65] It is clear that, one way or another, Burridge enjoyed the notoriety of being a reformed (or imperfectly reformed) atheist, and that he capitalised on it.

This therefore returns us to the link of atheism with immorality which has been in evidence throughout this chapter. Moreover, this arguably helps to explain some of the more censorious remarks made by contemporary polemicists like Richard Bentley, who at one point in his Boyle Lectures broke off from an elaborate demonstration of the implausibility of materialism to exclaim: 'Tis a vigorous execution of good laws, and not rational discourses only, either neglected or not understood, that must reclaim the profaneness of those perverse and unreasonable men.'[66] Equally revealing are the comments with which one of his most eminent successors as Boyle Lecturer, Samuel Clarke, introduced his sermon series in 1705. Clarke explained how, in attacking the kind of 'Speculative Reasoning' that led to atheism, he was dealing with only part of a broader problem. He distinguished three kinds of atheists: first, 'such as are wholly ignorant and stupid'; second, 'such as through habitual Debauchery have brought themselves to a Custom of mocking and scoffing at all Religion, and will not hearken to any fair Reasoning'; and third,

---

[64] Ibid., pp. 15, 19, 49–50, 63 (the name is incorrectly given as 'Moulton'), 65, 79.
[65] Sutherland, 'Burridge the Blasphemer', pp. 24–32, esp. p. 29.   [66] Bentley, *Works*, III, 43.

those who in the Way of Speculative Reasoning, and upon the Principles of Philosophy, pretend that the Arguments brought against the Being or Attributes of God, do, upon the strictest and fullest Examination, appear to them to be more strong and conclusive, than those by which these great Truths are attempted to be proved; These [the third], I say, are the only Atheistical Persons, to whom my present Discourse can be supposed to be directed, or indeed who are capable of being reasoned with at all.[67]

One almost senses the frustration of a man like Clarke about the difficulty that he faced in dealing with these renegades driven by 'interest' rather than reason. Such polemicists must often have felt annoyed by the sheer obtuseness of their antagonists, their refusal to be convinced by the clear and evident principles so fully set out in the profuse anti-atheist literature. Matters were only made worse by the problems of pinning atheists down that have been indicated in the course of this chapter, notwithstanding the severity of the threat that the orthodox regularly insisted that they presented. What a relief it must have been to the Scottish Presbyterians when they were at last confronted by an outrageous apostate in the form of Thomas Aikenhead. To his story we must now turn.

---

[67] Samuel Clarke, *A Demonstration of the Being and Attributes of God* (London, 1705), pp. 1–5.

CHAPTER 5

'Aikenhead the Atheist'
The Context and Consequences of Articulate Irreligion in the Late Seventeenth Century

Thomas Aikenhead, a student at the University of Edinburgh, was executed for blasphemy on 8 January 1697. His fate was briefly a matter of controversy in Scotland, and it also 'made a great Noise' in London, where it was widely reported in the newspapers of the day.[1] Thereafter the case attracted some attention in the late eighteenth and early nineteenth century, when the main sources concerning it were published.[2] But interest in Aikenhead was dramatically revived in 1855, when Lord Macaulay devoted a lengthy passage to the affair in the fourth volume of his *History of England*, describing the youth's execution as 'a crime such as has never since polluted the island'. Macaulay's scathing view of clerical intolerance inspired a flurry of activity in Edinburgh, as the pros and cons of the great historian's views were debated between evangelicals and others.[3] Since then, the case has often been alluded to, usually as a means of taking the pulse of the state of Scottish culture at the end of the seventeenth century.[4]

Originally published in *Atheism from the Reformation to the Enlightenment*, ed. Michael Hunter and David Wootton (Oxford: Clarendon Press, 1992), pp. 221–54. © Oxford Publishing Limited. Reproduced with permission of the Licensor through PLSclear. For the quotation, see this volume, p. 109. I am greatly indebted to Tristram Clarke of the National Records of Scotland for his unstinting assistance in the preparation of this essay. David Berman, James K. Cameron, Roger Emerson, Trevor Pateman, George Rosie and Paul B. Wood read a draft and made helpful suggestions for its emendation.

[1] *Flying Post*, 28 January 1697 (no. 267). Other newspaper reports of the affair are mentioned in subsequent notes.

[2] See esp. Hugo Arnot, *A Collection and Abridgement of Celebrated Criminal Trials in Scotland* (Edinburgh, 1785), pp. 324–7, and *A Complete Collection of State Trials*, ed. W. Cobbett, T. B. Howell et al., 34 vols (London, 1809–28), XIII, 917–40 (no. 401).

[3] T. B. Macaulay, *The History of England*, 5 vols (London, 1849–61), IV, 781–4; [anon: almost certainly Thomas McCrie rather than Hugh Miller, as stated in earlier recensions of this study], *Macaulay on Scotland: A Critique Republished from 'The Witness'* (Edinburgh, n.d.), esp. pp. 21–7; John Gordon, *Thomas Aikenhead: A Historical Review*, 3rd ed. (London, 1856).

[4] For recent examples, see e.g. A. L. Drummond and James Bulloch, *The Scottish Church, 1688–1743: The Age of the Moderates* (Edinburgh, 1973), pp. 13–15; N. T. Phillipson, 'Culture and Society in

In the course of this chapter, I shall consider who was responsible for Aikenhead's death, and why, adducing some previously unknown evidence on the question, but I also wish to devote attention to Aikenhead's apostacy in its own right. For this episode has greater significance for the history of early modern irreligion than has hitherto been appreciated. In general, cases in this period where people were accused of 'atheism' or blasphemy are highly frustrating. The charges are often generalised and vague; even when specific individuals are denounced, the accusations against them frequently comprise unsubstantiated hearsay; and we hardly ever have a response by those challenged to their accusers. In the Aikenhead case, on the other hand, the materials available are almost as rich as those deployed by Carlo Ginzburg in his celebrated account of the Friuli sceptic, Mennochio.[5] Not only do we have a full account of the aggressively anti-Christian views which Aikenhead was accused of publicly expressing, which indicate their unusual range and ingenuity, but we also have a written account by Aikenhead of the rationale of his apostacy. This juxtaposition of blasphemy with serious philosophising provides a rare opportunity to probe at the relationship between two phenomena that were commonly seen as integral to the phenomenon of 'atheism' that caused such anxiety at the time, but that otherwise remain frustratingly distinct in the historical record.

* * *

Thomas Aikenhead was baptised on 28 March 1676. He was the son of James Aikenhead, an Edinburgh apothecary and burgess, who in 1667 had married Helen, daughter of Thomas Ramsey, former Minister of Foulden; the quality and number of witnesses at the baptism is a tribute to the family's evident respectability.[6] Thereafter the Aikenheads are heard of in

---

the Eighteenth-Century Province: The Case of Edinburgh and the Scottish Enlightenment', in *The University and Society*, ed. Lawrence Stone, 2 vols (Princeton, 1974), II, 407–48 (p. 431); G. E. Davie, *The Scottish Enlightenment* (London, 1981), pp. 9–10; J. K. Cameron, 'Scottish Calvinism and the Principle of Intolerance', in *Reformatio Perennis*, ed. B. A Gerrish (Pittsburgh, 1981), pp. 113–28 (pp. 123–5); and J. K. Cameron, 'Theological Controversy: A Factor in the Origins of the Scottish Enlightenment', in *The Origins and Nature of the Scottish Enlightenment*, ed. R. H. Campbell and A. S. Skinner (Edinburgh, 1982), pp. 116–30 (pp. 117–18). See also L. W. Levy, *Treason against God: A History of the Offense of Blasphemy* (New York, 1981), pp. 325–7, and this chapter, n. 12.

[5] Carlo Ginzburg, *The Cheese and the Worms: The Cosmos of a Sixteenth-Century Miller*, English trans. (London, 1980).

[6] National Records of Scotland (hereinafter NRS), OPR 685/1/8, fol. 23r: Baptism Register, Parish of Edinburgh, 1675–80. I am indebted to Tristram Clarke for this reference and for his advice on the Aikenhead family. See also *Roll of Edinburgh Burgesses and Guild-Brethren 1406–1700* (Scottish

connection with various legal cases, one of them, in 1682, involving a love potion sold by James that nearly poisoned someone; within a year of this, he was dead, and his wife was buried on 3 May 1685.[7] The orphaned Thomas matriculated as a student at the University of Edinburgh in 1693; he then proceeded to follow the standard curriculum of the Arts course, first, for his 'bajan' or first-year class, under the regent, Alexander Cunningham, and then under William Scott for the remainder of the course.[8]

Exactly when Aikenhead achieved notoriety as a freethinker is uncertain, though the indictment against him late in 1696 stated that the offences had been committed 'now for more than a twelvemoneth by past', while a contemporary pamphlet confirms that his views were well known in the early months of that year.[9] What we do know is that on 10 November 1696 he was summoned before the Scottish Privy Council, charged with blasphemy, and remitted for prosecution in the courts. The records of the Privy Council specifically note that Aikenhead was sent 'to be tryed for his life', which shows how seriously the matter was taken; the Privy Council could have dealt summarily with Aikenhead, but the death penalty could only be imposed through the justiciary. The reason for this may have been a defiance on his part of which we will hear more later: a newspaper report of his arrest specifically notes how Aikenhead responded to the charge by 'owning [it] in part, and maintaining his Principles'.[10]

The impious statements which Aikenhead was charged with having made are itemised in the indictment, which is evidently based on the depositions of four witnesses, most of them fellow students. These also separately survive, and they display a considerable degree of unanimity, though with sufficient variation to instil faith in their essential

Record Society, 59; Edinburgh, 1929), p. 23, and Hew Scott, *Fasti Ecclesiae Scoticanae,* new ed., 7 vols (Edinburgh, 1915–28), II, 48.

[7] *Historical Notices of Scotish Affairs. Selected from the Manuscripts of Sir John Lauder of Fountainhall,* ed. D. Laing, 2 vols (Edinburgh, 1848), I, 343, 353, 451. For James Aikenhead's will, proved 30 March 1683, see NRS CC8/8/77, fols 126v–8; on Helen's burial, see Scott, *Fasti,* II, 48.

[8] See 'Matriculation Roll of the University of Edinburgh. Arts, Law, Divinity. Transcribed by Dr Alexander Morgan, 1933–4' (typescript, Edinburgh University Library), I (1623–1774), 104; Edinburgh University Library MS Da. 1.33, fol. 120; and Christine Shepherd, 'Philosophy and Science in the Arts Curriculum of the Scottish Universities in the Seventeenth Century' (Edinburgh PhD thesis, 1975), p. 369.

[9] *State Trials,* XIII, 919; Mungo Craig, *A Lye is No Scandal* ([Edinburgh], 1697), pp. 8–9, 15.

[10] NRS, PC1/51, p. 29; PC4/2, fol. 29v (10 November); *Protestant Mercury,* 18 November 1696 (no. 109). The latter states that 'the Crime against him was for being a Priest', which immediately makes sense if it is presumed that 'Priest' is a misprint for 'Deist'. For the letters of diligence against Aikenhead and the petition asking that these be granted, dated 27 November 1696, see NRS JC26/78/1/2–3; for the execution of summons against him, dated 28 November, see JC26/78/1/4.

verisimilitude.[11] Theology, Aikenhead was said to have affirmed, 'was a rapsidie of faigned and ill-invented nonsense, patched up partly of the morall doctrine of philosophers, and pairtly of poeticall fictions and extravagant chimeras'. In one of the witnesses' statements, he was reported to have condemned theology as 'worse than the fictiones of the poets, for they had some connexione, but the Scriptures had none', and this perhaps represented a conflation with the next accusation against Aikenhead, namely, that 'you scoffed at, and endeavoured to ridicule the holy scriptures', claiming them to be 'so stuffed with maddness, nonsense, and contradictions, that you admired the stupidity of the world in being soe long deluded by them'. The Old Testament he was said to have described as

> Ezra's fables, by a profane allusione to Esop's fables, and saying that Ezra was the inventer thereof, and that being a cunning man he drew a number of Babylonian slaves to follow him, for whom he made up a feigned genealogie as if they had been descended of kings and princes in the land of Canaan, and therby imposed upon Cyrus who was a Persian and stranger, persuading him by the devyce of a pretendit prophecy concerning himself.

The same theme continued in a lighter vein in the accusation that one day Aikenhead had felt so cold that he had 'wished to be in the place that Ezra calls Hell, to warme yourself there': it transpires from a witness statement that this was in August. As for Christ and the New Testament, he was accused of calling it

> the History of the Impostor Christ, and affirming him to have learned magick in Egypt, and that coming from Egypt into Judea, he picked up a few ignorant blockish fisher fellows whom he knew by his skill and [sic]

---

[11] *State Trials*, XIII, 917–20, 923–7, from NRS JC2/19, fols 294v–295v, 296v–298v. The originals of the latter in the High Court Minute Book, NRS JC6/14, fols 99v–103r, have the actual signatures of the witnesses. A handful of emendations have been introduced from the MS versions of the texts here and elsewhere. For the witnesses, see 'Matriculation Roll', I, 101 (Adam Mitchell, John Neilson, John Potter), 104 (Quintigernus Craig); Patrick Middleton does not appear. NRS JC26/78/1/4–7 comprise various executions of summons of witnesses, together with a list of witnesses which includes the following in addition to those whose evidence survives (with Middleton's name given as 'Midlemiss'): George Dalrymple, student of philosophy ('not ceited' since in Glasgow); Andrew Haliburtone, smith; William Eccfoord, officer, and his spouse Alison Oswald; Robert Monroe, 'officer to the wryters in Edinburgh'; James Craig, 'nephew to Mr Craig minister at Dudingstone at Sir Pat[rick] Homes'; John Hamilton, writer; Alexander Young, writer; Robert Hendersone, 'keeper of the Bibliotheck of the College of Edinburgh'; George Dicksone, tailor and Aikenhead's landlord, and his spouse Jane Elder; James Lafreice, writer; and Hugh Crafurd, former student and schoolmaster at Houston, Ayrshire ('not ceited'; cf. Craig, *A Lye*, p. 5; p. 8 of *A Lye* also refers to Richard Comlie as someone who could vouch for the author's innocence).

phisognomie, had strong imaginations, and that by the help of exalted imaginatione he play'd his pranks as you blashphemously terme the working of his miracles.

Aikenhead was said to have added 'that man's imaginatione duely exalted by airt and industry can do any thing, even in the infinite power of God', while his view of Moses was comparable to that of Christ. It was claimed that he had affirmed 'Moses, if ever you say ther was such a man, to have also learned magick in Egypt, but that he was both the better arteist and better politician than Jesus'.

Aikenhead was also reported to have rejected the doctrine of the Trinity, 'and say it is not worth any man's refutation'; Christ's status as at the same time God and man he considered 'as great a contradictione as Hircus Cervus', the mythical goat-stag, or as squaring the circle; while 'as to the doctrine of redemptione by Jesus, you say it is a proud and presumptuous devyce, and that the inventars therof are damned, if after this life ther be either rewaird or punishment'. The indictment further accused Aikenhead of claiming that the notion of a spirit was a contradiction, and maintaining 'that God, the world, and nature, are but one thing, and that the world was from eternity'. It was also alleged that 'you have lykwayes in discourse preferred Mahomet to the blessed Jesus, and you have said that you hoped to see Christianity greatly weakened, and that you are confident that in a short tyme it will be utterly extirpat' – by 1800, according to one of the witness statements on which the indictment was based.

* * *

The indictment against Aikenhead invoked two laws. One was an Act against blasphemy passed in 1661 by the first Scottish parliament of Charles II, which prescribed the death penalty for anyone who 'nor being distracted in his wits Shall rail upon or curse God, or any of the persones of the blessed Trinity'. A further Act passed in 1695 both confirmed this and also dealt with

> whoever hereafter shall in their writing or discourse, deny, impugn or quarrell, argue or reason, against the being of God, or any of the persons of the blessed Trinity, or the Authority of the Holy Scriptures of the old and new Testaments, or the providence of God in the Government of the World.

It was ordered that, on the first occasion, such an offender should be imprisoned and 'give publick Satisfaction in Sackcloth to the Congregation, within which the Scandal was committed'; on the second he should be fined; and on the third he should be executed 'as an obstinat Blasphemer'.[12]

Aikenhead's trial took place on 23 December 1696, when his case came before a jury composed of Edinburgh citizens; six of those summoned refused to serve, which possibly shows a degree of unease about the case on their part.[13] The witnesses were called and examined, and consideration was presumably also given to Aikenhead's 'Defences' against the indict-ment, which survive, and which allege various mitigating circumstances, including the fact that the opinions that he had expressed were those of the authors of books he had read, rather than his own, and that he was a minor (his twenty-first birthday would have fallen on 28 March 1697). It also referred to the existence of the 1695 Act and its provision that only those who were obstinate should be executed. From an account of the trial in a London paper we learn that, though Aikenhead's council 'had nothing further to say in his behalf, then desiring Mercy. The Prisoner excepted against his Witnesses, urging, that they were Socinians, and guilty of the same Crimes as they would endeavour to prove against him'.[14] This, however, was to no avail, and neither was the specific objection that he evidently made to one of the witnesses, Mungo Craig.[15] On 24 December – Christmas Eve – Aikenhead was found guilty of cursing and railing against God the Father and the Son, of denying Christ's incarnation and the Trinity, and of scoffing at the scriptures. He was thereupon condemned to death by hanging, evidently on the grounds that his transgression came under the terms of the 1661 Act and therefore

---

[12] *The Acts of the Parliaments of Scotland*, ed. T. Thomson and C. Innes, 12 vols (Edinburgh, 1814–75), VII, 202–3; IX, 386–7 (cf. VI, 208). The Acts are also printed in R. E. Florida, 'British Law and Socinianism in the Seventeenth and Eighteenth Centuries', in *Socinianism and Its Role in the Culture of the Sixteenth to Eighteenth Centuries*, ed. Lech Szczucki (Warsaw-Lódź, 1983), pp. 201–10 (pp. 207–8).

[13] *State Trials*, XIII, 920–3, 927, from NRS JC2/19, fols 296r and 298v, where the names and occupations of five of the six jurors who were 'unlawed' are given. See also the lists in JC26/78/1/8–9, which name the sixth juror; JC26/78/1/10 is the petition of one of those who failed to serve, William Menzies. JC26/78/1/14–15 are copies of the verdict and sentence, differing slightly from the printed version but forming the source of the accounts of the trial in British Library Harleian MS 6846, fols 398–9, and in Bodleian MS Locke b.4, fol. 91; the endorsement to JC26/78/1/14 refers to Aikenhead as 'Guilty of Horrid Blasphemy'.

[14] NRS JC26/78/1/13; *Protestant Mercury*, 1 January 1697 (no. 122). This therefore implies that Arnot, *A Collection*, pp. 326–7, was wrong to presume that Aikenhead had no legal representation, in which he is followed by various more recent authors. [However, on this matter see more recently Michael Graham, *The Blasphemies of Thomas Aikenhead* (Edinburgh, 2008), p. 102.]

[15] Craig, *A Lye*, p. 11. Aikenhead's objection was partly on the grounds of the malice displayed by Craig in publishing his first pamphlet, on which see this volume, p. 105.

merited immediate capital punishment, rather than the milder treatment of first offences prescribed in the more recent Act.

We come now to the question of whether and when Aikenhead repented of his offence, on which our sources are not altogether consistent. A newspaper report of his trial records how, after the sentence had been passed, he requested that its implementation be postponed, 'which occasioned the Court to ask, Whether it was in hopes to save his Life, or the better to prepare himself for Death?'[16] Earlier still, when Aikenhead was in prison but not yet convicted, he had submitted a petition (which survives) in which he protested his 'sorrow and remorse' for the words that he had uttered, claiming that he had simply repeated them from 'most villanous and atheisticall' books that he had read, which 'ought neither to be printed nor exposed to public view'. In addition, he gloried at length in having been born and educated in a country where the Gospel was so fully preached, affirming his belief in the immortality of the soul, the doctrine of the Trinity, the divine authority of the scriptures and 'the whole other principles of our holy Protestant religion'. As in his 'Defences', he also stressed that he was a minor. This petition survives in manuscript, titled 'The Supplication of Thomas Aikenhead'; it is mostly written in a clerical hand, but at the end Aikenhead has added 'And I doe hereby humbly refer my self to and bege your Lordships mercy and compassion upon the account of the premisses' and signed it.[17]

All this was reiterated in a further surviving petition, made to the Privy Council after his conviction. In this, he acknowledged the justice of the sentence for his 'blasphemous and wicked expressions', which 'ought not to be so much as named', but he repeated the mitigating circumstances of his minority and of his 'extravagances' having been prompted by the reading of 'some atheistical books'. He went on to request that his execution might be delayed 'that I may have the opportunity of conversing with godly ministers in the place, and by their assistance be more prepared for an eternal rest'.[18] In addition, the London *Protestant Mercury* records how, on the last Sunday of his life, Aikenhead made an appearance in the

---

[16] *Protestant Mercury*, 1 January 1697 (no. 122).
[17] NRS JC26/78/1/12, printed in *State Trials*, XIII, 921–3n. It is perhaps worth noting that in col. 922, the printed version accidentally omits the words 'atheisticall books, & did frequently presse upon me to repeat the' between 'reading of the said' and 'atheisticall principles' (it also omits 'Christian' between 'Protestant' and 'religion' in col. 923).
[18] *State Trials*, XIII, 927–8 (from Bodleian MS Locke b.4, fol. 97: see this volume, p. 104).

prison church, 'where he seem'd to be convinced of his fatal Error, and 'tis believed, he will accordingly be respited for some longer time'.[19]

The Privy Council minutes confirm that petitions by Aikenhead were submitted on 31 December and 7 January: both were said to have been 'Craveing a Repreyve', and both were 'read and refused'.[20] This was probably at least partly due to doubt as to the genuineness of his repentance, the London *Flying Post* reporting of these appeals: 'which their Lordships declared should be granted, if he would make any acknowledgment of his Errors, or repent of his Blasphemous and Wicked Tenets, which he refused to do'. This may seem at odds with the gushing profession of faith contained in Aikenhead's petitions, but it is quite possible that these were not really by him, but were composed on his behalf by ministers or lawyers, as commentators suggested a century ago and as is further implied by the fact that the one that survives in its original manuscript version is not in his hand.[21] The Privy Council's scepticism about the sincerity of Aikenhead's repentance was shared by one of the witnesses against him, Mungo Craig, who thought that he gave 'but little satisfaction' to the ministers who visited him while in gaol, and that he seemed unimpressed by the apologetic reading he was given.[22]

The *Flying Post* offers the following dramatic sequel. It claimed that, although on 7 January 'particularly' Aikenhead refused to repent, 'the next Day, being that of his Execution, he did acknowledge his Errors, and Atheistical Tenets, and owned the Being of a God, and the Merits of our Blessed Saviour; but the Council not having met that Day, the Sentence was Execute upon him'.[23] This cliff-hanging story is perhaps a little improbable; it was in any case denied by another commentator.[24] What matters here is that – despite his pleas for a postponement – on Friday, 8 January 1697, Aikenhead was taken from his prison cell in the old Tolbooth to 'the Galowlee betwixt Leith and Edinburgh', where he was executed. It was reported that 'He walk'd thither on Foot between a strong

---

[19] *Protestant Mercury*, 13 January 1697 (no. 125).

[20] NRS, PC4/2, fols 34r (31 December), 34v (7 Jan.). The petition of 31 December is reported in the *Post Boy*, 9 January 1697 (no. 262) and the *Protestant Mercury*, 8 January 1697 (no. 124); that of 7 January in the *Post Man*, 19 January 1697 (no. 265). On the latter, cf. William Lorimer, *Two Discourses* (London, 1713), pp. v–vi, and presumably also *Protestant Mercury*, 13 January 1697 (no. 125).

[21] *Flying Post*, 28 January 1697 (no. 267); *Macaulay on Scotland*, p. 35; Gordon, *Thomas Aikenhead*, pp. 9–10.

[22] Craig, *A Lye*, pp. 9, 11.   [23] *Flying Post*, 28 January 1697 (no. 267).

[24] Johnston to Locke, 27 February 1697, in *The Correspondence of John Locke*, ed. E. S. de Beer, 8 vols (Oxford, 1976–89), VI, 18.

Guard of Fuzileers, drawn up in two Lines', either in a deliberate display of the panoply of the state or because of genuine apprehension that popular sympathy for him might cause a disturbance. He was also accompanied to the gallows by ministers, and it was said that he died, Bible in hand, 'with all the Marks of a true Penitent'.[25]

Aikenhead left to posterity not only the memory of his execution and the events that had preceded it, but also two further documents which are certainly of his own composition: indeed, the fact that both are noticeably convoluted in style strengthens the likelihood that the more clearly written petitions were in fact penned for him. One was a letter to his friends, written on the day of his execution, in which he yet again reiterates his repentance, 'Being now wearing near the last moment of my time of living in this vain world'. The other was a 'Paper' or 'Speech' – called in one copy Aikenhead's 'Cygnea Cantio', his swan-song.[26] This is a fascinating but somewhat frustrating document, oscillating between lucidity and virtual incoherence, between repentance and an almost defiant outline of his heterodox notions, in a manner which bears witness to the tortured state that the young man's mind must have been in by this time.

In contrast to the incendiary nature of much of what was attributed to him by the indictment, here Aikenhead gave quite a profound account of how he had arrived at his sceptical opinions. He stressed his 'insatiable inclination to truth' from an early age as the reason why he challenged orthodoxy, rather in the manner of freethinkers of the eighteenth century. Like them, he also deliberately contradicted those who presumed that freethinkers devised their doctrines in order to justify immorality to which they had already committed themselves (indeed, one contemporary witness vouched for the fact that Aikenhead was 'not vicious, and extreamly studious').[27] He then proceeded to make a number of quite profound points. He spoke of his suspicion 'that a great part of morality (if not all)' was of purely human derivation. On the other hand, if an absolute morality did exist, then he questioned how it related to God, and accused of circular reasoning those who identified God with moral perfection and then defined such perfection in terms of the nature of God. He also

---

[25] *State Trials*, XIII, 927; *Post Man*, 19 January 1697 (no. 265). Cf. Lorimer, *Two Discourses*, p. vi; Macaulay, *History*, IV, 784.

[26] *State Trials*, XIII, 930–4 (from Bodleian MS Locke b.4, fols 99–101, 103–5). It is in the copy in Harleian MS 6846, fols 400–1, that it is described as 'Thomas Aikenhead his Cygnea Cantio'.

[27] Cf. David Berman, *A History of Atheism in Britain from Hobbes to Russell* (London, 1988), esp. ch. 8, sect. 1. For the comment on Aikenhead, see Anstruther to Cuningham, 26 January 1697, *State Trials*, XIII, 930.

rehearsed various quite ingenious arguments for the adequacy of natural as against revealed religion, arguing that the doctrine of providence itself contradicted revelation; lastly, he spoke of his difficulties with the doctrine of the Trinity, which he saw as tantamount to polytheism. He proceeded:

> these things I have puzled and vexed myself in, and all that I could learn therfrom, is, that I cannot have such certainty, either in natural or supernatural things as I would have. And so I desire all men, espechially ingenious young men, to beware and take notice of these things upon which I have splitt.

He ended by voicing the hope 'that my blood may give a stop to that rageing spirit of atheism which hath taken such footing in Brittain, both in practice and profession'.

* * *

Much of our evidence about the Aikenhead case derives from official records now preserved among the National Records of Scotland, but it is a testimony to the interest aroused by the affair at the time that various copies of these survive, especially of the indictment against Aikenhead, while multiple copies also exist of Aikenhead's 'Swan-Song' or 'Paper:' this was even cited by the Scottish theologian Thomas Halyburton as one of the texts that he deemed worthy of refutation alongside Lord Herbert of Cherbury and others in his treatise on the inadequacy of natural religion, posthumously published in 1714.[28] The fullest collection of material, which was the principal source of the early nineteenth-century published version of it, was that made by John Locke: this now survives in the Lovelace Collection in the Bodleian Library. Though Locke left no record of his opinion on the case, his interest in it is clear from the care with which he preserved and endorsed a whole series of relevant documents that he was sent with a covering letter by his friend, the Scottish politician,

---

[28] Thomas Halyburton, *Natural Religion Insufficient; and Reveal'd Necessary to Mans Happiness in His Present State* (Edinburgh, 1714), pp. 119–23. Halyburton cites the piece as *'Aikenhead's* Speech' in his 'Index of the Authors and Books quoted in this Treatise against *Deism'* (unpaginated, unsigned), but, contrary to what is suggested in *State Trials*, XIII, 938, this does not mean that it was printed. For other MS copies, see n. 26. For MS copies of the indictment, see Bodleian MS Locke b.4, fols 88–91, and British Library Harleian MS 6846, fols 398–9; fols 396–7 of MS 6846 is a further, inferior copy of this, and another copy is to be found in Edinburgh University Library, La.II.89, fols 222–3 (I am indebted to Roger Emerson for this reference). These copies derive from the version of the indictment in the process papers, NRS JC26/78/1/11, which is slightly different from that in the Books of Adjournal, JC2/19, printed in *State Trials*, XIII, 917–20.

James Johnston, Secretary of State from 1691 to 1696.[29] Apart from the legal documents and Aikenhead's letter and 'Paper', Locke also had copies of his two petitions, one of which does not otherwise appear to have survived, together with two other letters concerning the affair, one of which has hitherto been wholly ignored.[30]

Three other sources shed light on the case, all of them contemporary publications. One is the material in the English newspapers which I have already cited. The second is a lengthy retrospective account of the affair by a divine involved in it, William Lorimer.[31] Lastly, we have two pamphlets by Mungo Craig, one of the students who gave evidence against Aikenhead at his trial, the first of which came out while Aikenhead was in prison, and the second after his death. Interpretation of these documents is complicated by the bad blood that clearly existed between Aikenhead and his erstwhile colleague, which was exacerbated by Craig's public vindication of himself in this way. Aikenhead referred to Craig in his 'Paper', vindicating his innocence from the 'abominable aspersions' of Craig, 'whom I leave to reckon with God and his own conscience, if he was not as deeply concerned in those hellish notions, (for which I am sentenced) as ever I was'. Indeed James Johnston was almost certainly correct in suspecting that Craig was 'the decoy' who provided Aikenhead with the atheistical books from which he was supposed to have derived his opinions: though the name of this figure, who was identified in Aikenhead's first petition as one of the witnesses against him, was suppressed from the copy of the petition with which Locke was provided, it is inserted in the relevant place in the copy in the Justiciary papers.[32] This would explain Craig's anxiety to vindicate himself, particularly in his second pamphlet, *A Lye is No Scandal*,

[29] The originals now comprise MS Locke b.4, fols 86–106: on fols 107–8, see next note. For Johnston as the source of this material, see de Beer's attribution of the covering letter in Locke, *Correspondence*, VI, 17. In *State Trials*, XIII, 928, the letter is mistakenly attributed to Locke, and as a result it has been widely but incorrectly cited as revealing his views on the case. On the Locke MSS, presented to the Bodleian in 1947, see P. Long, *A Summary Catalogue of the Lovelace Collection of the Papers of John Locke in the Bodleian Library* (Oxford, 1959), esp. p. 42. Though the Aikenhead material now forms part of a volume of miscellaneous papers on politics and current affairs, I suspect that this arrangement is recent. An early nineteenth-century commentator on Locke's Aikenhead material described it as being 'In a bundle of MSS. on the subject of Toleration': Francis Horner, *Memoirs and Correspondence*, ed. Leonard Horner, 2 vols (London, 1843), I, 487.

[30] Bodleian MS Locke b.4, fols 107–8, endorsed 'letter Mr W. from Scotland upon burning the 7 witches'. This is a copy (lacking the postscript) of Robert Wylie to William Hamilton, 16 June 1697, now NRS GD103/2/3/17/1. On this, and the letters of Johnston and Anstruther, see further below. For the petition of which only Locke's copy survives, see n. 18.

[31] Lorimer, *Two Discourses*, pp. iv–vii. See further below.

[32] *State Trials*, XIII, 933, 922; Johnston to Locke, 27 February 1697, Locke, *Correspondence*, VI, 19; NRS JC26/78/1/12.

dated 15 January 1697 and subtitled 'a Vindication of *Mr. Mungo Craig*, From a Ridiculous Calumny cast upon him by *T. A.* who was Executed for Apostacy At *Edinburgh*, the 8 of *January*, 1697'. In it, he replied both to the accusation that he had corrupted Aikenhead and to the charge that it was he who had reported his fellow student to the authorities.[33]

Craig's first pamphlet comprises 'A Satyr against *Atheistical Deism*' in rhyming couplets 'With the Genuine Character of a Deist' – which, though a specimen of a well-established genre, was obviously aimed at Aikenhead – 'To which is Prefixt, *An account of* Mr Aikinhead's *Notions*, Who is now in Prison for the same Damnable Apostacy'. Craig's satire of Aikenhead's views is heavy-handed and somewhat tasteless, while the fact that he had an axe to grind evidently explains the moralising tone of the pamphlet, in which he poured scorn on the irreligious claims of 'scurvy *Wittlings*' before going on to assert the need for a strong line to be taken in defence of Christian orthodoxy and national honour. Indeed, if anyone called for vengeance in this affair, it was Aikenhead's fellow student, who urged the magistrates to be inspired by 'a Rational and Holy Flame' of Christian zeal, to 'attone with Blood, th'affronts of heav'n's offended throne'.[34] This itself is arguably symptomatic of the instinctive conformity of most students when placed under pressure, to which Aikenhead is so spectacular an exception. In his second pamphlet, Craig went on to criticise Aikenhead's swan-song as 'very unbecoming a dying Man in his Circumstances, being so far Stuff'd with the Affectation of a Bumbast and Airy Stile', while both are also interesting for the hints they give of the intellectual milieu from which Aikenhead emanated.[35]

* * *

Two major issues arise concerning Aikenhead's heterodoxy and its context: one is how he came to express the views that he did; the other is why he was treated as severely as he was, which involves looking at who advocated that this course be adopted and who took a more lenient line. The latter may be dispatched first, since it has attracted disproportionate attention in the past, particularly by those hostile to the role of the kirk in the affair. Thus Francis Horner, one of the founders of *The Edinburgh Review*, enjoined his heirs to preserve the Aikenhead case along with 'similar

---

[33] Craig, *A Lye*, esp. pp. 9–10, 15.

[34] Mungo Craig, *A Satyr against atheistical Deism* (Edinburgh, 1696), pp. 6, 10, 12–16 and elsewhere. On atheist 'characters', see this volume, pp. 45–6.

[35] Craig, *A Lye*, p. 9 and elsewhere.

documents from century to century, by way of proving, some thousand years hence, that priests are ever the same'.[36] Many other nineteenth-century commentators were inclined to see Aikenhead as 'this unhappy victim of priestly bigotry', though others rightly pointed out that he was sentenced by the justiciary, while the Privy Council was the body which had the ultimate say in the matter through their power of reprieve.[37] What conclusion should one draw on this vexed question?

At least three people who were close to the affair expressed their distaste for what happened to Aikenhead. One was William Lorimer, a minister domiciled in London who happened to be staying in Edinburgh at this point and who had preached a sermon to the chief magistrates while Aikenhead's trial was pending. Lorimer paid a series of pastoral visits to the youth while he was in gaol, in which Aikenhead was clearly subjected to a good deal of pious exhortation and in which Lorimer claimed that he showed genuine evidence of repentance. In his account of the affair, published in 1713, Lorimer was at pains to stress the force for moderation that he and other ministers had been, referring to an attempt to gain a reprieve for the student on the day before his execution made by himself and George Meldrum, Minister of Tron Church, the scene of one of Aikenhead's blasphemous outbursts. It was Lorimer's claim that 'the Ministers could not prevail with the Civil Government to pardon him', a majority of the Privy Council voting for Aikenhead's execution, 'that there might be a Stop put to the spreading of that Contagion of Blasphemy'.[38]

On the other hand, Lorimer could well be accused of special pleading, since it was evidently because his conduct in the Aikenhead case had been criticised that he felt impelled to issue this defence nearly two decades later. It is worth noting that the application for a reprieve to which Lorimer refers was rather late in the day, while it may well not be coincidental that both Lorimer and Meldrum were atypical of the Edinburgh clergy of the day, the former London-based and transient,

[36] Horner, *Memoirs and Correspondence*, I, 288.
[37] *The Christian Reformer; or, Unitarian Magazine and Review*, n.s. 12 (1856), 37. See also nn. 3–4 and J. H. Burton, *History of Scotland, from the Revolution to the Extinction of the Last Jacobite Insurrection*, 2 vols (London, 1853), I, 256–7; Robert Chambers, *Domestic Annals of Scotland from the Revolution to the Rebellion of 1745* (Edinburgh, 1861), p. 163; John Cunningham, *The Church History of Scotland*, 2nd ed., 2 vols (Edinburgh, 1882), II, 197–8; and W. L. Mathieson, *Scotland and the Union* (Glasgow, 1905), pp. 220–1. For contrasting views, see John Warrick, *The Moderators of the Church of Scotland from 1690 to 1740* (Edinburgh, 1913), pp. 100–2, and P. Hume Brown, *History of Scotland to the Present Time*, 3 vols (Cambridge, 1911), III, 31–2.
[38] Lorimer, *Two Discourses*, pp. iv–vii; *State Trials*, XIII, 925. On Lorimer and his role, see also Gordon, *Thomas Aikenhead*, pp. 19–26.

the latter an immigrant from Aberdeen. Though Lorimer vaguely asserted how 'I am sure the Ministers of the Establish'd Church us'd him with an affectionate Tenderness', this is specifically contradicted by one of our other witnesses, the privy councillor Lord William Anstruther. Anstruther claimed that he brought the matter to the vote in the Council but was told that clemency would only be possible if the ministers interceded for the victim: they, however, 'out of a pious tho I think ignorant zeal spok and preached for cutting him off'. He added how 'our ministers generaly are of a narow sett of thoughts and confined principles and not able to bear things of this nature'.[39]

Anstruther's views are revealing. As someone who was present at the Privy Council when Aikenhead was remitted for trial, he described him as 'an anomely, and monster of nature', while he was later to publish a generalised attack on 'atheism' in which he was conventionally disapproving of the phenomenon. He was certain that the matter was one for the Privy Council, accompanying the anticlerical sentiments already cited by adding: 'I am not for consulting the church in state affairs'. On the other hand, he considered capital punishment more appropriate for crimes against society than against God, and he was compassionate towards Aikenhead, whom he had visited in prison and 'found a work on his spirit', adding: 'I doe think he would have proven an eminent christian had he lived'.[40]

Another advocate of leniency was Locke's friend, James Johnston, who, as Secretary of State in the early 1690s, had been an active protagonist of a comprehensive Church and an opponent of Presbyterian extremism.[41] He argued that, despite the provision for severity made in the law of 1661, there were so many mitigating circumstances about Aikenhead's case that he should have been treated leniently, especially in the light of the milder penalties for a first offence prescribed in the more recent Act of 1695. Johnston questioned whether any of the sentiments of which Aikenhead was accused amounted to 'railing' and 'cursing' as defined in the 1661 Act; he noted the retractions in Aikenhead's petitions; he observed the youthfulness of the witnesses and the unreliability of Craig, in the light of his own involvement in the affair; and he denied that Aikenhead had seduced

[39] Lorimer, *Two Discourses*, p. v; Anstruther to Robert Cuningham, 26 January 1697, *State Trials*, XIII, 929–30. Cf. Robert Mylne's note on the copy of Craig's *Satyr against Atheistical Deism* in the Advocates' Library at Edinburgh, quoted in the supplement to Gordon's *Thomas Aikenhead*, p. 16.

[40] *State Trials*, XIII, 930; William Anstruther, *Essays, Moral and Divine* (Edinburgh, 1701), pp. 1–37 (this contains no reference to Aikenhead). For the attendance on 10 November 1696, see NRS PC1/51, p. 29.

[41] P. W. J. Riley, *King William and the Scottish Politicians* (Edinburgh, 1979), esp. pp. 81–2.

anyone. 'Laws long in dessuetude should be gently put in Execution', he wrote, 'and the first example made of one in circumstances that deserve no compassion, whereas here ther is youth, Levity, docility, and no designe upon others'.[42]

Johnston was by this time out of office, but that others in the Privy Council held similar views is suggested by the fact that, on 7 January, Aikenhead evidently came within a single vote of being granted a reprieve.[43] The views of the majority can be gauged only by their action, but clearly – like many in the early modern period – they took it for granted that the state should take a decisive role in defending Christian orthodoxy, and this is in line with what we know of the views of men like the Lord Advocate, Sir James Stewart, or the Chancellor, Sir Patrick Hume.[44] Indeed, it is almost certainly not coincidental that in January 1697 the Privy Council was responsible not only for the execution of Aikenhead but also for taking the initiative in the last major witch-hunt in Scotland, the affair of the witches of Renfrewshire, a juxtaposition noted by Macaulay, who spoke of 'two persecutions worthy of the tenth century'. Just as Christina Larner has argued that witch-hunting should be seen as an act of moral cleansing carried out jointly by Church and State, so the execution of Aikenhead should be similarly construed.[45]

Clerical attitudes towards Aikenhead are indicated by the fact that, although the General Assembly of the Church of Scotland was in session at Edinburgh from 2 to 12 January, no organised attempt appears to have been made to save the youth. Indeed, on 6 January 1697, while Aikenhead awaited his execution, the Assembly wrote to the King urging 'the vigorous execution' of the 'good laws' that existed to curb 'the abounding of impiety and profanity in this land'.[46] A more explicit commentary on the case was given in two letters, one to, and the other from, the minister Robert Wylie, and it is revealing that Wylie was by no means among the most extreme of Presbyterians of the day.[47] The first is a letter to Wylie written on the day

---

[42] Johnston to Locke, 27 February 1697, Locke, *Correspondence*, VI, 19. For comparable views, see Arnot, *Collection*, p. 327; David Hume, *Commentaries on the Law of Scotland*, 2 vols (Edinburgh, 1797), II, 518–19.

[43] *Post Man*, 19 January 1697 (no. 265).

[44] Chambers, *Domestic Annals*, pp. 135–6; George Brunton and David Haigh, *An Historical Account of the Senators of the College of Justice* (Edinburgh, 1832), pp. 451–61; see also Macaulay, *History*, IV, 782–3.

[45] Macaulay, *History*, IV, 181; Christina Larner, *Enemies of God: The Witch-Hunt in Scotland* (London, 1981).

[46] *Acts of the General Assembly of the Church of Scotland 1638–1842*, ed. T. Pitcairn et al. (Edinburgh, 1843), p. 258 (cf. pp. 261–2, 267).

[47] On Wylie, who had played an active role in the rising of the Covenanters in 1679 and who died in 1715, see *The Correspondence of the Rev. Robert Wodrow*, ed. T. McCrie, 3 vols

of the execution by the minister of the second charge at his parish of Hamilton, Alexander Findlater.[48] In the course of reporting on the proceedings of the General Assembly, Findlater wrote: 'I did see Aikinhead this day execute for his cursing railling against our Saviour calling him a Magician & that he hade Learned it in Aegypt but he abjured all his former errors & dyed penitently & I think G[od] was glorified by such ane awful & exemplary punishment'.

Wylie himself commented on the affair in retrospect, obviously in the light of the controversy that it aroused, in a letter to William Hamilton, Laird of Wishaw, dated 16 June 1697.[49] Interestingly, he juxtaposed a vindication of the correctness of the treatment of Aikenhead with a defence of the ensuing witch-hunt. Just as, on the question of witchcraft, he stood firmly by the 'Scripture Law', 'Thou shalt not suffer a witch to live', so he sought to vindicate the severity of the sentence against Aikenhead against what might be called the 'liberal' view of the matter; he associated this especially with the London 'wits', and he would doubtless not have been surprised to find it espoused by the Anglophile James Johnston.

Wylie was openly hostile to such attitudes. 'I have heard much of the censures past upon the Government here by some pious & charitable wits at London & elsewhere upon occasion of the sentence given against Aikenhead the Atheist,' he wrote:

> but when these Gentlemen understood, if they are capable of thinking or understanding any thing but a bold sparkish jest, That the Ground of that Wretches sentence was not, as I know some of them misrepresented it, a retracted errour of the Judgement, but a perverse malicious railing against the adorable object of christian worship, which simply inferrs Death without the quality and aggravation of [obstinat continuance] tho that also was in Aikenhead's case till after the sentence, and this most expresly by the first clause of Act. 21. parl. 1 Ch[arles] 2, And when these witty Criticks

---

(Edinburgh, 1842–3), I, 113–15, and Scott, *Fasti*, III, 260. For his moderate views and the way in which these were changing in the 1690s, see Wylie to the Duke of Hamilton, 11 December 1693, *Historical Manuscripts Commission (H. M. C.) Supplementary Report on the MSS of the Duke of Hamilton* (London, 1932), p. 129; Wodrow to James Wallace, 8 March 1701, in *Early Letters of Robert Wodrow, 1698–1709*, ed. L. W. Sharp (Scottish Historical Society, 3rd ser. 24, Edinburgh, 1937), pp. 154–5.

[48] Alexander Findlater to Robert Wylie, 8 January 1697, National Library of Scotland, Wodrow MSS 4to vol. 30, fols 244–5 [Letter no. 144]. The letter is not signed, but the fact that it is from Findlater is proved by the reference to 'our stipend' on fol. 244. I am grateful to Tristram Clarke for this point and to Trevor Pateman for initially drawing my attention to the letter. On Findlater, see Scott, *Fasti*, III, 262.

[49] NRS GD103/2/3/17/1; in l. 13 of the indented quotation, 'were' replaces 'are' deleted. See also this chapter, n. 30.

consider that Reason, common sense and good manners (their own Trinity) do require that no man should in the face of a people spitefully revile & insult the object of their adoration, and that a Christian could not be innocent who should rail at or curse Mahomet at Constantinople, and consequently that their pleadings against Aikenheads condemnation were most unjust & founded upon mistake of the case and matter of fact. One would think that after all this they should be more sparing & cautious, at such a distance & under such uncertainty of report in passing their little rash Judgements upon the late proceedings of this Government with reference to the witches in Renfrew.

A similar letter to Wylie's was published in the London *Flying Post*, where its author was identified only to the extent of saying that it came 'from so good a Hand, that we dare Vouch for the Truth of every Word on't'. This complained of 'false Representations' of the case – evidently also in England – and it included an epitome of the indictment against Aikenhead to illustrate how his expressions really had been

> so horrid that I should not desire they were made publick, if it were not to let the World know the Justice of our Proceedings in that Matter, which it seems some are so desirous to have any occasion to find fault with; for I am not willing to believe that there are any with you that out of favour to his wicked Principles exclaim at what is done against him.[50]

* * *

The background to such views is provided by the marked anxiety about heterodoxy to be found in Scotland in the 1690s, in the context of a sustained attempt by the kirk to achieve a truly godly society. In 1690, the newly re-established General Assembly had expressed concern about the 'dreadful atheistical boldness' of those who 'disputed the being of God and his Providence, the Divine authority of the Scriptures, the life to come, and immortality of the soul, yea, and scoffed at these things', while a further Act passed in January 1696 specifically associated such ideas with 'the Deists'.[51] Parliament's re-enactment of the 1661 law against blasphemy in 1695 is itself to be seen in the context of such concern, while 1696 saw the Privy Council ordering 'a kind of inquisition' of booksellers'

---

[50] *Flying Post*, 28 January 1697 (no. 267). It is probably not coincidental that the newswriter for the *Flying Post* was a Scottish Presbyterian, George Ridpath: see E. S. de Beer, 'The English Newspapers from 1695 to 1702', in *William III and Louis XIV: Essays 1680–1720. By and for Mark A. Thomson*, ed. Ragnild Hatton and J. S. Bromley (Liverpool, 1968), pp. 117–29 (p. 122). For a comparable attitude, cf. *Protestant Mercury*, 1 January 1697 (no. 122).

[51] Pitcairn, *Acts*, pp. 228, 253. Cf. Lorimer, *Two Discourses*, p. v.

shops in Edinburgh for books deemed 'Atheisticall, erronious or profane and vitious', which included the writings of the early seventeenth-century apostate Giulio Cesare Vanini and the Deist Charles Blount, together with Thomas Burnet's *Sacred Theory of the Earth*.[52]

One clue to the likely cause of such disquiet is provided by the attitudes and activities of the doctor and intellectual Archibald Pitcairne and his circle. Pitcairne was said at the time to be 'a professed Deist, and by many alledged to be ane Atheist . . . a great mocker at religion, and ridiculer of it', who produced two openly satirical attacks on the Presbyterian church in the 1690s.[53] In addition, it turns out that Aikenhead's was not the first but the second case of heterodoxy to come to the attention of the Scottish Privy Council in the autumn of 1696. The earlier one – which, though reported in the London papers at the time, has hitherto been almost wholly overlooked – involved a merchant's apprentice called John Frazer. Frazer was accused of arguing or reasoning against the being of a God, of denying the immortality of the soul and the existence of the Devil, and of ridiculing the divine origin of scriptures, affirming 'that they were only to freighten folks and to keep them in order': 'And when asked what religion he could be off that held such principles he answered of no religion at all but was just ane Atheist and that was all his religion'. On being confronted with these charges, however, Frazer immediately recanted fully and acknowledged the principles of Christianity, claiming – as Aikenhead was to do – that he had merely been repeating views expressed in a book that he had heard about, in this case Blount's *Oracles of Reason*, published in London in 1693. He added that he had also referred to another book, Grotius's *Of the Truth of the Christian Religion*, 'which was able to refute what any such Atheist was able to say'. The charge was found proven nonetheless, and he was ordered to be imprisoned and to give public satisfaction for his misdemeanour in sackcloth, as prescribed for a first offence under the 1695 Act: this he did over the next few months, finally being released on 25 February 1697.[54]

52 NRS PC 1/51, pp. 20, 28; *Protestant Mercury*, 28 October 1696 (no. 101), *Post Man*, 29 October 1696 (no. 230). The newspaper reports specifically link the initiative with the Frazer case: see below.

53 Robert Wodrow, *Analecta*, 4 vols (Edinburgh, 1842–3), II, 255 (see also I, 322–3, III, 307); Douglas Duncan, *Thomas Ruddiman: A Study of Scottish Scholarship in the Early Eighteenth Century* (Edinburgh, 1965), pp. 15–23. [See also this volume, ch. 6–7]. It is perhaps also worth noting that John Toland had been briefly at the University of Edinburgh in 1689–90: R. E. Sullivan, *John Toland and the Deist Controversy* (Cambridge, MA, 1982), p. 3.

54 NRS PC1/51, pp. 22–7, 130; PC4/2, fols 28v (13 October), 29r (15 October), 30v (26 November), 34r (31 December 1696), 37r (11 February), 38r (25 February 1697); *Protestant*

The contrast between the treatment of Frazer and Aikenhead is instructive, not least since – like Aikenhead in his 'Defences' – Frazer drew attention to the mild initial penalty for which the recent Act provided. Possibly Aikenhead suffered as he did simply because his was the second case in quick succession, suggesting that a firm line was needed to curb such dangerous tendencies. But what was almost certainly more important was that, whereas Frazer's doubts were alleged to have been divulged on one specific occasion, when in the company only of the couple with whom he lodged, Aikenhead's expression of extreme anti-Christian views was both outspoken and sustained. It was clearly this that outraged Robert Wylie, and there is more than a hint of proselytising in Aikenhead's open and provocative expression of his ideas, despite Johnston's claim to the contrary. The indictment against Aikenhead specifically accused him of having 'made it as it were your endeavour and work in severall compainies to vent your wicked blasphemies against God and our Saviour Jesus Christ, and against the holy Scriptures, and all revealled religione', reiterating how he uttered all this 'in severall companies without the least provocatione'.[55] In addition, Mungo Craig cited 'a considerable Number of Witnesses' who had 'heard him boast of the above mentioned ridiculous Notions', while Craig himself reported Aikenhead's assertion that 'all knowing Men' shared his views 'whatever they said to the contrary' and his claim to have converted 'a certain Minister of the Gospel' to his position.[56]

It was probably this that earned Aikenhead his severe sentence. It is symptomatic that Wylie believed that Aikenhead had been obstinate 'till after the sentence', while the author of the anonymous letter to the *Flying Post* believed that he had remained defiant till the day of his execution, and Craig implied that he had never repented at all.[57] Even if these commentators may have been mistaken about this – and in this connection the uncertainty about the extent and date of Aikenhead's repentance is significant – clearly their views and others' were affected by Aikenhead's manner, the way in which he expressed his doubts, and the effect that this had on those who heard them. The indictment was clearly intended to stress this, emphasising the 'reproachfull expressions' that the youth had

---

Mercury, 28 October 1696, 1, 8 January 1697 (nos. 101, 122, 124); *Post Boy*, 31 December 1696 (no. 262). See also Chambers, *Domestic Annals*, p. 147.

[55] *State Trials*, XIII, 919–20 (cf. the witness statements in cols 923–4); Locke, *Correspondence*, VI, 19.
[56] Craig, *A Satyr*, p. 3; *A Lye*, p. 9.
[57] *Flying Post*, 28 January 1697 (no. 267); Craig, *A Lye*, p. 9; for Wylie, see this chapter, p. 109. Cf. pp. 100–2, and Lorimer, *Two Discourses*, p. v, where it is stated that Aikenhead 'continued sullen and obstinate, I think for some Months'.

used towards the supreme objects of Christian worship, while Craig's statement alleged that Aikenhead's views about the New Testament were expressed 'in a scorning and jeiring manner'.[58]

Taking all this into account, one could argue that, for the authorities and, indeed, for many orthodox Christians of the day, what was significant about Aikenhead was less the exact nature of his statements and their intellectual coherence than the simple fact of his outrageous apostasy: it was essentially an act of anti-Christian revolt rather than a piece of pure thought. Johnston was being excessively precise in arguing that, of the words that Aikenhead was accused of uttering, only the accusation that Christ was an imposter (for which the only witness was Craig in any case) really constituted 'railing' and 'cursing' (it is interesting that the eighteenth-century historian Hugo Arnot, who took a similar line, construed this of a different comment[59]). Rather, I think, it was for his deliberate offensiveness that Aikenhead was convicted, the crucial factor being the affront caused to others.

This raises the issue of what was involved in the crime of blasphemy in this case, for the view of the offence expressed by Robert Wylie has something in common with the modern British legal definition, where the crucial issue is 'the manner in which the doctrines are advocated'.[60] Wylie's attitude was not identical with the modern view that 'the substance of the doctrines themselves', however damaging to Christianity, is irrelevant so long as it is soberly expressed: that was a development which had to await the nineteenth century. But the crucial point is that, in contrast to Johnston's and others' concern with the content of anti-Christian sentiment rather than its mode of presentation, Wylie and his associates evidently saw the essence of the crime of blasphemy as being met if – to cite a nineteenth-century judge's dictum – 'the tone and spirit is that of offence and insult and ridicule ... an appeal to the wild and improper feelings of the human mind, more particularly in the younger part of the community'.[61]

Undoubtedly, this aspect of the case is central to an understanding of why Aikenhead was treated as he was. It is also fundamental to the character of irreligion as it was perceived by contemporaries, who clearly expected this kind of aggressive oral assault on Christian orthodoxy.[62] The

---

[58] *State Trials*, XIII, 919, 926.   [59] Locke, *Correspondence*, VI, 19; Arnot, *Collection*, pp. 326–7.
[60] Quoted from Stephen's *Digest of the Criminal Law* by Lord Scarman in connection with the famous Whitehouse v. Lemon case: Law Commission Working Paper no. 79, *Offences against Religion and Public Worship* (London, 1981), p. 3.
[61] Ibid., p. 7.   [62] Cf. pp. 40, 50, 73.

implication of this was that, for them, it did not matter very much how coherent or original Aikenhead's statements were. Indeed, it is even possible that the accusations against Aikenhead did not comprise his actual views at all, but rather the smears of people outraged by the very notion of an assault on Christianity, who embroidered the case according to their expectations of what freethinkers were likely to say.[63] Certainly, much of what Aikenhead was accused of saying belonged to a standard repertoire of anti-Christian polemic, which recurs frequently in early modern character-isations of atheists and can be traced back to early Christian times – the accusation that Moses and Christ were magicians, for instance, or that religion was the device of 'politicians', or that the scriptures were unreli-able.[64] But it is equally likely that he *did* say these things, since even the clichés represent telling assaults on fundamental Christian principles, which Aikenhead ingeniously adapted in genuinely original ways. Moreover, it is worth noting that he did not deny making these state-ments. His only specific denial (in his farewell letter to his friends) was of having 'practised magick and conversed with devils': his blasphemous outbursts he acknowledged, only claiming that they were derived from books.[65]

What, however, was the relationship between the offensive oral out-bursts that brought Aikenhead to the attention of the authorities and the more serious streak represented especially by the 'Paper' that he wrote while awaiting execution? The latter contained the metaphysical specula-tions on the existence of an absolute morality and the like that were deemed worthy of refutation by Thomas Halyburton as if comprising a serious anti-Christian treatise, although Halyburton was rather disdainful of 'this inconsiderable *Trifler,* whose undigested Notions scarce deserve the Consideration we have given them'.[66] It is easy to presume that these sober thoughts must be Aikenhead's 'real' ideas and to write off his earlier and more outrageous outbursts as trivial and insignificant. But in fact a good case can be made for precisely the opposite evaluation, with Aikenhead's 'real' ideas being those that he expressed at liberty among his friends. It is the later statements of which one should surely be suspicious, issued as they were under the heavy influence of incarceration, indoctrination and despair, their very agenda perhaps being set by divines like William

[63] For a discussion of this possibility in another, comparable case, see David Wootton, *Paolo Sarpi: Between Renaissance and Enlightenment* (Cambridge, 1983), pp. 142–5 (where the Aikenhead case is noted).

[64] See pp. 39–40, 44, 47–8.   [65] *State Trials*, XIII, 934, 922n., 928, 933.

[66] Halyburton, *Natural Religion Insufficient*, p. 123 (and pp. 119–23).

Lorimer, who ministered to Aikenhead during his final weeks, and by the anti-atheist tracts that he was given to read at that stage, written by authors such as the English apologist, Sir Charles Wolseley.[67]

Even Aikenhead's account of the origins of his speculations, echoed by that which Lorimer gave 'in effect from his own Mouth', may deliberately have sanitised these by placing them in a respectable setting of Christian doubt: in that context, one would hardly have expected Aikenhead to claim anything other than that his 'doubtings and inquisitions' had resulted from the fact that he had 'been ever, according to my capacity, searching good and sufficient grounds whereon I might safely build my faith'. Especially predictable is Lorimer's neat account of Aikenhead's progress from initial doubt about the Trinity to questioning the divinity of Christ: 'and from his not being God, and yet assuming so much to himself, he concluded that he must have been the greatest Impostor that ever was in the World, and that the Christian Religion is a great Cheat imposed upon the World by cunning Men', a moral tale that Lorimer included in his text for the benefit of Socinians, who might be warned by the fate of 'that poor Man'.[68]

* * *

On the other hand, even if this is a very partial view of the progress of Aikenhead's apostasy, it is worth considering it as a clue to the source of his anti-Christian ideas, the next point to which I wish to turn. One thing is clear, that the experience of doubt with regard to even the most fundamental Christian doctrines was commonplace among the highly devout in the early modern period. What is more, the kind of arguments voiced in such contexts overlapped with the opinions associated with Aikenhead – for instance, the view that the scriptures were 'rather a Fable and cunning Story, then the holy and pure Word of God', or doubt about the existence of God, or the reality of the life to come.[69] Such notions are to be found in the spiritual autobiographies of various godly figures, and G. E. Davie has drawn a particular parallel between Aikenhead's apostasy and the experience of doubt of Thomas Halyburton, the very divine who was to take it upon

---

[67] Craig, *A Lye*, p. 11. [68] *State Trials*, XIII, 931, 934; Lorimer, *Two Discourses*, p. vii.

[69] John Bunyan, *Grace Abounding to the Chief of Sinners and The Pilgrim's Progress*, ed. Roger Sharrock (Oxford, 1966), esp. p. 33. Cf., for instance, Richard Baxter, *Reliquiae Baxterianae*, ed. N. H. Keeble, John Coffey, Tim Cooper and Tom Charlton, 5 vols (Oxford, 2020), I, 257–62, and Sir Simonds D'Ewes, *Autobiography and Correspondence*, ed. J. O. Halliwell, 2 vols (London, 1845), I, 251–4.

himself to refute Aikenhead's ideas. Davie writes how Halyburton 'in his youth, experienced a succession of similar sceptical crises, the last one (1696) contemporary with that of Aikenhead who could perhaps have been known to him personally'.[70]

Not only does Halyburton well illustrate the proclivity of the highly devout to such temptations; he also demonstrates how these might be encouraged by higher education and by reading dangerous books. Halyburton's inner doubts were exacerbated by attending university and studying theology, metaphysics and natural philosophy, which made him 'accustomed to subtle Notions, and tickled with them'. This fostered 'the natural Atheism of my Heart', suggesting 'contrary disquieting Arguments' that would not otherwise have occurred to him. In addition, when later reading the writings of the Deists in order to refute them, he found their theories unnervingly contagious.[71]

Leaving on one side the view of 'natural Atheism' that he expounds there, Halyburton's evaluation of the role of university education is certainly borne out by what we know of Aikenhead and his milieu. Aikenhead had been through most of the standard university arts course, and surviving notebooks and other sources show that the regents under whom he studied, Alexander Cunningham and William Scott, were typical of Scottish academics of their day in the way in which they cross-fertilized a basic scholastic framework with new ideas derived from philosophers like Descartes.[72] The influence of this blend on Aikenhead and his friends is well evidenced by the pamphlets of his one-time colleague, Craig. The quintessential 'Deist' whose character Craig sketched appears in the terminology of scholastic philosophy – '*An accidental aggregat of Contradictions actually existent*' – but Craig's familiarity with the ideas of Descartes and other modern natural philosophers is shown by his references to such topics as vortices and the notion of a world in the moon; one of the witnesses against Aikenhead similarly claimed that he likened Christ's ascension to 'a progresse to the world in [the] moon'.[73]

---

[70] Davie, *Scottish Enlightenment*, pp. 9–10.
[71] *Memoirs of the Life of the Reverend Mr. Thomas Halyburton* (Edinburgh, 1714), pp. 26–7, 41–6, 52.
[72] Shepherd, 'Philosophy and Science', pp. 68–70, 74–5, 99, 154, 175, 233 (on Cunningham), 126, 213, 221–2 (on Scott). On the course as a whole, see elsewhere in that dissertation and Christine Shepherd, 'The Arts Curriculum at Aberdeen at the Beginning of the Eighteenth Century', in *Aberdeen and the Enlightenment*, ed. J. J. Carter and J. H. Pittock (Aberdeen, 1987), pp. 146–54.
[73] Craig, *A Satyr*, pp. 1, 3, 12, 14 and elsewhere in this pamphlet and in Craig, *A Lye*; *State Trials*, XIII, 926.

This context undoubtedly explains much about Aikenhead's apostasy, from the point of view both of presentation and content. The disputations that traditionally comprised a significant part of the curriculum were notorious for making students 'pert and precocious', and Craig specifically remarked on Aikenhead's 'dexterity in that Art'.[74] In addition, the eclecticism typical of the late seventeenth century was commonly perceived to encourage sceptical attitudes: indeed, in his 'Paper' Aikenhead criticised his education in terms not so dissimilar from Halyburton's for failing to produce 'really sufficient' grounds for faith, while 'with the greatest facility sufficient ground could be produced for the contrair'. More important, much of what Aikenhead dealt with in that document is easily recognisable in the context of the university curriculum – particularly of the ethics classes that he would have had in his third year (1695–6) – including such topics as the relationship of divine and natural law and the morality of human actions.[75]

Aikenhead would also have been introduced to dangerous ideas on various subjects, which were widely canvassed, largely so as to assert the superior value of orthodox ones. Thus, the notions of Hobbes and, to a slightly lesser extent, Spinoza were regularly refuted in late seventeenth-century lectures, including the view that moral laws were of human rather than divine origin. It is symptomatic that Halyburton, who complained of the influence of these authors on 'our *young Gentry* and *Students*', considered Aikenhead's questioning of absolutes in morality a 'confus'd Discourse, which probably he learn'd from *Hobbs*'.[76] In addition, surviving lists of books purchased for the University of Edinburgh at this time show that quite questionable items were bought for the library, including Hobbes's works together with critiques of them, Charles Blount's translation of Philostratus's *Life of Apollonius of Tyaneus*, two copies of the heterodox *Letters Writ by a Turkish Spy*, Burnet's *Archaeologiae philosophiae* as well as his *Sacred Theory of the Earth*, and John Toland's *Christianity Not Mysterious*.[77] It is revealing in this connection that among the witnesses listed in connection with the case (though no evidence from him survives)

---

[74] Shepherd, 'Philosophy and Science', p. 30; Craig, *A Lye*, p. 4.
[75] Shepherd, 'Philosophy and Science', ch. 5; see also p. 47. Cf. *State Trials*, XIII, 930–4.
[76] Halyburton, *Natural Religion Insufficient*, pp. 31, 119–20.
[77] Edinburgh University Library, MSS Da.1.32 (fols 68, 75, 82, 134), Da.1.33 (fols 87,111), Da.1.34 (fols 1,7, 9). On the *Letters Writ by a Turkish Spy*, see David Wootton, 'New Histories of Atheism', in *Atheism from the Reformation to the Enlightenment*, ed. Michael Hunter and David Wootton (Oxford, 1992), pp. 13–53 (pp. 41–2).

was Robert Henderson, 'keeper of the Bibliotheck of the College of Edinburgh'.[78]

Aikenhead may have had access to private libraries too, and the full range of potentially unorthodox works with which his circle would have been familiar is illustrated by the account of the authors likely to be deployed by a quintessential 'Deist' in Mungo Craig's first pamphlet. First, and most obviously, there were the ancients – Aristotle for eternalism, and Epicurus for the denial of providence and the immortality of the soul, the idea that the world comprised a fortuitous concourse of atoms, and above all the advocacy of the pursuit of pleasure as the summum bonum. But equally important were the moderns. Descartes's 'Dubitation' was 'a chief Pillar of his Scepticism', while he also valued the French philosopher for confirming Epicurus's theories by showing how, '*Mater and motion being granted, all cou'd fall out as they are, without the concurrance of an inteligent Over-ruling Power*'. The 'Deist's' 'dearest darlings', however, were 'first the excellent Head-piece of *Malmsbury*' [i.e. Hobbes] and 'the incomparable' Spinoza, together with Blount's *Oracles of Reason* – '*Lucretius Redivivus*' – John Frazer's acquaintance with which in Edinburgh in 1696 has already been noted.[79] From this pot-pourri, Aikenhead could have derived any number of the opinions attributed to him, including both the metaphysical speculations in his 'Paper' and also various of the views associated with him in the indictment: that God and nature were identical, that the world was eternal, that the notion of spirit was nonsensical, or that the afterlife was unproven. There was also his lionising of reason as the supreme arbiter, and his stress on fraud in underwriting religion. All could be modishly found in books like Blount's and Spinoza's, but they could also trace their pedigree back to antiquity.

Indeed, in view of the wide availability of such dangerous ideas and the disputatiousness induced by academic training, it is perhaps surprising that there were not more Aikenheads. Certainly, Aikenhead appears to have found a receptive audience for his ideas among his friends, who, as he argued at his trial, were as much 'Socinians' as he.[80] It is also interesting that in 1699 the parliamentary commission for the Scottish universities listed

---

[78] NRS JC26/78/1/7. See this chapter, n. 11.

[79] Craig, *A Satyr*, p. 14 (I have read through his sarcastic emendations, e.g. of Blount's title as his '*Oracles of Nonsense*'). It is perhaps worth noting that Craig's 'Deist' 'has a very ill gust of Mr Lock's *Moral way of Demonstration*, however well he may please other parts of his works'.

[80] See p. 99. Cf. Lorimer, *Two Treatises*, p. v.

various ideas current among students that masters were to guard against, and that some of them overlap with notions voiced by Aikenhead, including excessive reliance on reason, the view that the world was eternal, and the denial of spirit.[81] But such concern apparently went no further on this or most other occasions, and virtually the only analogous case to Aikenhead's was that of Robert Hamilton of Aberdeen, whose Hobbesian opinions lost him his post in 1668.[82] In general, students did not go very far in developing the heterodox ideas with which they came into contact, instead conforming to the orthodox framework in which these were presented to them.

Much the same may be said of the experience of religious doubt of Halyburton and others. On the face of it, this may appear to have something in common with the case of Aikenhead, whose 'Paper' could be seen as an extreme specimen of the genre to which works like Halyburton's *Memoirs* belong: a struggle with anti-Christian doubt was thus recapitulated in the context of an assertion of repentance in the hope that others would be taught the counter-arguments with which the seductive appeal of these heterodox urgings might be repelled. Yet, once again, I think that one has to take into account the context of Aikenhead's 'Paper', and to avoid laying undue stress on this as against his earlier, more aggressive remarks. For there is a fundamental difference between the way in which Aikenhead and godly autobiographers like Halyburton handled their doubts and made use of the books at their disposal. Despite his inner struggle with anti-Christian arguments, there is no reason to believe that Halyburton would ever have contemplated a public expression of scepticism like Aikenhead's. For the godly, the experience of doubt was essentially personal and private: indeed, as we saw in Chapter 3, one of the problems that believers suffered from was a conviction that their doubts were unique, as with Elizabeth Wilkinson, who 'could not acquaint any with my condition. I did not think that it was so with any other, as it was with me'. Moreover, as was also there illustrated, John Bunyan, for one, distinguished the 'atheism' suffered by a believer like himself from outright apostasy, involving open, impenitent denial of God.[83]

In Aikenhead, by contrast, what one apparently sees is an aggressive nurturing of these anti-Christian sentiments into a cogent and coherent

[81] Shepherd, 'Philosophy and Science', pp. 305–6.
[82] Ibid., pp. 148, 200, 262–3, 307; *The Diary of Mr John Lamont of Newton, 1649–71*, ed. J. R. Murdoch (Edinburgh, 1830), pp. 207–8.
[83] Edmund Staunton, *A Sermon Preacht at Great Milton, at the Funeral of Elizabeth Wilkinson* (Oxford, 1659), p. 27; Bunyan, *Grace Abounding and Pilgrim's Progress*, esp. p. 72. See pp. 66–7, 68–9.

assault on Christianity, which all the evidence suggests that he propagated in a similar manner to that alleged of Christopher Marlowe in Elizabethan England, the case with which Aikenhead's is perhaps most directly comparable.[84] Moreover, there is a clear continuum between the 'serious' doubt of Aikenhead's 'Paper' and the aggressive free-thought of his publicly expressed views. In part, he dealt with the same issues, notably the Trinity, a topic of considerable concern in the 1690s: thus, while he instanced his doubts about this as a 'great point' in his 'Paper', one of the witnesses averred that he had heard Aikenhead speak about this 'oftner than any other thing'.[85] More important, however, is the ingenuity that Aikenhead deployed towards the ideas that he adopted. In the 'Paper' this is shown in various intriguing speculations – his view of the incompatibility of revelation and providence, for instance – while it is no less in evidence in the way in which he put materials to anti-Christian use in the public statements attributed to him by the indictment.

One particularly interesting theme is his stress on 'the power of the imagination' as a potential explanation of how Christ might have executed his miracles by natural means. This was a concept which derived from the natural magical tradition of the sixteenth century, a very flexible explanatory principle invoking mental forces not directly under conscious control that could either be 'occult' or effectively psychological in rationale.[86] The idea that miracles might be explained in these terms had been canvassed by Pietro Pomponazzi and, following him, by Giulio Cesare Vanini, at least one of whose works is known to have been in circulation in Edinburgh in the 1690s.[87] That views like these were to be expected from such men was stressed by the Cambridge Platonist Henry More, another author whose writings were certainly known to Aikenhead's circle, who was well aware of, and was hostile to, the ideas of Vanini and his 'bold Impiety and Prophaneness', and who complained of how 'the whistling Atheists impute all to *the natural power of Imagination*'.[88] Certainly, Aikenhead made good

---

[84] P. H. Kocher, *Christopher Marlowe* (Chapel Hill, 1946), ch. 2–3.

[85] *State Trials*, XIII, 932–3, 924. On the debate on this issue at the time, see esp. Sullivan, *John Toland*, ch. 3.

[86] See D. P. Walker, *Spiritual and Demonic Magic from Ficino to Campanella* (London, 1958), esp. pp. 76–84, 107–8.

[87] See *The Best of our Owne*, ed. W. T. Johnston (Edinburgh, 1979), p. 21, concerning a copy of Vanini's *De Admirandis* auctioned as part of the Balfour library in 1695. See also this volume, p. 111. On miracles, see esp. *Le Opere di Giulio Cesare Vanini*, ed. Luigi Corvaglia, 2 vols (Milan, 1933–4), I, 31–45.

[88] Craig, *A Lye*, pp. 11–12 (this also shows that Grotius was known to this group, as to Frazer: see this volume p. 111); Henry More, *An Explanation of the Grand Mystery of Godliness* (London, 1660), pp. 109, 335–6.

use of the heterodox potential of this idea to prove how 'our Saviour wrought no miracles but what any other man might have wrought by ane exalted fancie', and he went further than any of his predecessors in his cutting dismissal of Christ's miracles as 'pranks'.[89]

A similar picture can be found in the views attributed to Aikenhead concerning the Bible, and particularly the idea 'that Ezra was the inventer thereof'. This was an idea that Aikenhead could have derived from Spinoza's *Tractatus*, chapter 8 of which specifically made this claim. Alternatively, he could have picked it up from the *Critical History of the Old Testament* by the French divine Richard Simon, published in French in 1678 and translated into English in 1682, a copy of which had been bought for Edinburgh University Library earlier in the 1690s.[90] This canvassed a milder version of a similar theory in contradistinction to Spinoza's view, arguing that Ezra had been responsible for collecting and editing what survived of earlier Hebrew writings after the Babylonian Captivity.[91] But here again, Aikenhead surpassed any putative source in his aggressive taunt that the scriptures were 'Ezra's fables', 'by a profane allusione to Esop's fables', as the indictment put it.[92]

As for the rest of Aikenhead's allegations, these could perfectly easily have been derived from an alert and cynical reading of the biblical text, together with an ingenious embroidery of the old accusation that Christ and Moses were magicians and imposters.[93] Then, further jibes must have slipped off Aikenhead's tongue on the spur of the moment, as with 'the place that Ezra calls Hell'. The same is true of items reported by witnesses but not included in the indictment – for instance, his claim that 'the Revelatione was ane alchimy book for finding out the philosophers stone' or his comparison of the Jews with the Goths and Vandals.[94] Moreover, in a slightly convoluted way, I think it may be thus that one should read the 'Catalogue of the Works promised to the World by T. Aik[enhead] Gent.'

---

[89] *State Trials*, XIII, 924. An overlapping opinion attributed to Aikenhead by Craig in his witness statement is as follows: 'baptisme was a magicall ceremony that tyed children's imagination to that religion wherto they were baptised; and furder, if he were banished, he would make all Christianitie tremble, and would wryte against Christianity, and that if he or any other needed a familiar genius he could call for it': *State Trials*, XIII, 926–7.

[90] Edinburgh University Library, Da.1.33, fol. 115. Cf. MS Da.1.32, fol. 130.

[91] Richard Simon, *A Critical History of the Old Testament* (London, 1682), Preface and Book I, ch. 4.

[92] *State Trials*, XIII, 919–20.

[93] Ibid., XIII, 919–20, 923–7. See this volume, p. 114. There could be confusion in some of these claims: thus, one of the witnesses claimed that it was of Mahomet that Aikenhead said what the indictment associated with Moses: *State Trials*, XIII, 925, 919. Aikenhead himself appears to have confused Cyrus and Artaxerxes.

[94] Ibid., XIII, 925, 926.

included by Mungo Craig in his *Satyr against Atheistical Deism*, for through its rather pedestrian satire comes an echo of the actual ideas that Aikenhead was claimed to have uttered, which gives a real sense of their inventive bravado.[95]

In short, I see no reason why the more or less serious utterances in different contexts that have come down to us should not be construed as suggesting that Aikenhead had a complete 'system' of anti-Christian ideas. These would have included weighty philosophical notions like eternalism, the belief that God might be identified with nature, or the questioning of an absolute morality. But equally important, in view of the central role of the Bible in a strongly Protestant country like Scotland, was his attack on Holy Writ and its chief protagonists in the form of Moses and Christ. Clearly, different parts of this package were appropriate in different milieux: but that is no reason for doubting its coherence. Moreover, this helps to make sense of a facet of orthodox perceptions of heterodoxy at the time that to us may seem strange, namely, why contemporaries attached such significance to a bantering approach to Christianity, usually orally expressed. Not only does a close scrutiny of the material relating to Aikenhead indicate the continuum between this and his more serious ideas; it also indicates the sheer power of his gibes at Christianity, the resonances of which echo down the centuries. The reaction of the Scottish authorities may have been excessive, but they were arguably right to see the threat posed by this youth who aggressively asserted that 'within some hundreds of years the whole world would be converted to his opinion, and the Christian religion would be wholly ruined'.[96]

---

[95] Craig, *A Satyr*, p. 3. Cf. Craig, *A Lye*, pp. 4–5.
[96] *State Trials*, XIII, 925: this was averred by one of the witnesses, John Neilson.

CHAPTER 6

An Atheist Text by Archibald Pitcairne
Introduction to *Pitcairneana.*[*]

Archibald Pitcairne (1652–1713) was one of the most remarkable intellectuals of his age. His education was polymathic: having graduated with an MA at Edinburgh in 1671, he then studied divinity and law before travelling to France, where he became interested in medicine, gaining his MD from the University of Rheims in 1680. Then, after a notable encounter in 1692 with none other than Isaac Newton, he went on to become Professor of Medicine at Leiden before returning to Edinburgh, where he became extensively involved in medical debates. Pitcairne was also a committed Episcopalian and a thorn in the side of the Presbyterian establishment which dominated Scottish religious life at the time; in addition, he was a notable Latin poet. Lastly, his heterodox religious views have been the subject of attention, and in this connection particular significance attaches to the discovery in the Houghton Library at Harvard University of an overtly atheist text attributed to him, *Pitcairneana*, which had until recently been wholly unknown. All these aspects of him, and particularly the latter, will be the subject of the current chapter, which acts as an introduction to the complete text of *Pitcairneana* that follows in Chapter 7.

Let us start with Pitcairne's meeting with Newton, which clearly stemmed from the friendship that had developed in the 1680s between Pitcairne and the mathematician David Gregory, with whom he remained intimate for the rest of his life. Gregory clearly had a very high opinion of

[*] For help with my research on the manuscript of *Pitcairneana* and the man who donated it to Harvard, Henry Swasey McKean, I am grateful to Susan Halpert and the Reference Staff at Harvard University Archives. The following kindly read and commented on a draft of the article commenting on *Pitcairneana* that was originally published in the *Historical Journal*, 59 (2016), 595–607: Peter Anstey, Tristram Clarke, Roger Emerson, John Henry, Colin Kidd, Fred Lock, David Money, Alasdair Raffe, David Shuttleton, Reink Vermij, Paul Wood, Christopher Wright and two anonymous referees. I am also grateful to Alasdair Raffe for showing me the paper referred to in n. 13 prior to its publication and for various discussions of Pitcairne and his heterodox ideas.

Pitcairne, as is shown by the extent to which he copied out his friend's works in manuscript.[1] While Gregory began to study the work of Newton, Pitcairne was studying the writings of Italian authors like Giovani Alfonso Borelli and Lorenzo Bellini, who aspired to a reform of medicine by subjecting it to mathematical principles, something that Pitcairne was to develop much further, as we will see.[2] Pitcairne's momentous meeting with Isaac Newton occurred on 2–3 March 1692, when he was en route to taking up his new post at the University of Leiden (he seems to have met Newton twice, on successive days).[3] Gregory had established contact with Newton by this time, and he must have been responsible for the meeting. Moreover, it was to Gregory that Pitcairne transmitted the chief spoils of the encounter, a manuscript in Newton's own hand of his 'De Natura Acidorum', which, rather extraordinarily, Newton gave to Pitcairne, perhaps with a view to his vouchsafing it to Gregory. As is well known, this was a key document in Newton's evolving theory of matter, foreshadowing some of the ideas that were to be divulged in the *Opticks* in 1704, particularly in the 'Queries' at the end of that work. One presumes that Pitcairne was already sufficiently *au fait* with related ideas from his studies of the Italian iatromechanists for Newton to find him a fruitful interlocutor. It also seems likely that the accompanying notes on the corollaries to the initial paper were based on Pitcairne's recollection of the conversation that ensued: these survive only in a manuscript by Gregory, unlike the main statement of Newton's views, of which there is a duplicate manuscript version in the Macclesfield collection.[4]

Although Pitcairne was proud of this encounter, and although he was happy to invoke Newton in the mathematical theory of medicine for

---

[1] See, for example, the lengthy medical notes transcribed in Edinburgh University Library MS Dc.1.62. See also this chapter, nn. 3–5 for his copies of the material relating to Newton and Verwer.

[2] For general accounts, see Simon Schaffer, 'The Glorious Revolution and Medicine in Britain and the Netherlands', *Notes & Records of the Royal Society*, 43 (1989), 167–90; John Friesen, 'Archibald Pitcairne, David Gregory and the Scottish Origins of English Tory Newtonianism, 1688–1715', *History of Science*, 41 (2003), 163–91; Anita Guerrini, 'The Tory Newtonians: Gregory, Pitcairne, and their Circle', *Journal of British Studies*, 25 (1986), 288–311, and 'Archibald Pitcairne and Newtonian Medicine', *Medical History*, 31 (1987), 70–83; see also her account of Pitcairne in *ODNB*.

[3] See *The Correspondence of Isaac Newton*, ed. H. W. Turnbull et al., 7 vols (Cambridge, 1959–77), III, 205–14.

[4] The text is derived from Royal Society MS 247. For the further MS, see Cambridge University Library Add. MS 9597/2/18/81. On the significance of 'De Natura Acidorum', which was first published by John Harris in volume 2 of his *Lexicon Technicum* (London, 1710), see the reprinted version of that text with commentary in *Isaac Newton's Papers & Letters on Natural Philosophy*, ed. I. B. Cohen, 2nd ed. (Cambridge, MA, 1978), pp. 241–68, esp. pp. 255–8.

which he was to become renowned, his subsequent contacts with Newton do not seem to have amounted to very much. He was clearly intrigued both by Newton's matter theory and also by the rumours that he heard about Newton's religious views, and he must have been delighted by *Opticks*, including the 'Queries' appended to it, when it appeared in 1704. Indeed, in June 1706, by which time a Latin translation of the work had appeared to which Newton had made further additions, Pitcairne explained in a letter to the Dutch mathematician, Adriaan Verwer, how the 'mathematical chemistry' divulged in that book was stimulated 'meo sane rogatu', 'at my sober request', a rather astonishing claim that presumably alludes to his 1692 meeting with Newton.[5] Equally interestingly, in the same letter he also told Verwer that in the 'Queries' Newton 'demonstrates that all those who tried to prove God's existence by metaphysical arguments were atheists'. This could be seen as a rather loose reading of a passage in the Query that was to end up as no. 28, which had indeed first appeared in the 1706 Latin *Optice*.[6] On the other hand, Pitcairne added that this was something that he himself had long believed ('Id ego jam dudum credo'), and his imputation of the same view to Newton might have represented wishful thinking on his part.

That this was the case is suggested by a letter of 25 February of the same year to David Gregory, by then in England, in which Pitcairne wrote:

> For Gods Sake keep Sir Isaac Neuton at work, that wee may have the chymical business, his thoughts about God, more of vacuum which he promis'd to me at Cambridge, that of hardness or greatest attraction, (the matter of atomes) and elasticitie if he pleases. I am clear that metaphysics can never prove a Deity, and therefor think our churchmen here have no ground not to be Atheists.[7]

Note how he here states the second point as his own opinion, not Newton's, in contrast to his statement to Verwer later in the year that this view was to be found in the 'Queries'. Earlier, Pitcairne had more than once pestered Gregory for information about Newton's religious views,

---

[5] Pitcairne to Verwer, June 1706, Royal Society MS 247, fol. 73(1)v.
[6] See Query 28 (= 20 in 1706) in Newton, *Opticks* (Dover reprint, New York, 1979), p. 369: 'Later Philosophers banish the Consideration of such a Cause [i.e., of gravity] out of natural Philosophy, feigning Hypotheses for explaining all things mechanically, and referring other Causes to Metaphysicks'. Pitcairne's words to Verwer were: 'demonstrat Atheos esse eos omnes qui Metaphysicis argùmentis ostendere conantur esse Deum'.
[7] *The Best of Our Owne: Letters of Archibald Pitcairne, 1652–1713*, ed. W. T. Johnston (Edinburgh, 1979), p. 43.

and it is quite possible that he never actually obtained this and was left to work out the religious implications of Newtonianism for himself.[8] We will see in due course how in *Pitcairneana* (assuming it is by him), he took strong issue with Samuel Clarke, despite his Newtonian credentials, for attempting a metaphysical argument in favour of the deity. It is also interesting that, later in the same work, he quoted the Deist John Toland for his adaptation of Newtonian ideas to make motion intrinsic to matter – something to which Newtonians like Clarke were strenuously opposed, although Pitcairne (like Toland) almost certainly saw this as enhancing Newton's worldview rather than subverting it.[9]

A later letter to a medical contact, James Walkinshaw, illustrates Pitcairne's views on a related matter, the intervention by Newton's disciples (in at least some cases with Newton's tacit support) in the debate stemming from the publication of Thomas Burnet's *Sacred Theory of the Earth*, which was widely criticised for its unduly mechanistic view of the origins of the world. William Whiston, in his *New Theory of the Earth* of 1696, had attempted a riposte based on Newtonian principles, but another follower of Newton, John Keill, took issue both with Burnet and Whiston, arguing that 'no secondary causes without the interposition of Omnipotence' could have brought about the biblical flood.[10] Pitcairne considered that the implication of Keill's attempt to 'prove by geometrie that the deluge was a miracle' was 'That the rules of Attraction demonstrate by Sir Isaac are false'. He took a low view of Keill, whom he accused of trying to appease conservative religious thinkers and of failing to see 'That if Mr Whiston's i.e. Neuton thought was wrong, no deluge could have been', adding rather whimsically: 'Let the bees see to That, boy'.[11] (Pitcairne's dislike of Keill, a fellow Scot who had moved to England, was exacerbated by his suspicion that Keill had plagiarised the ideas of David Gregory.) Nevertheless, this episode, like his earlier encounter with Newton himself, is indicative of Pitcairne's engagement with the most up-to-date ideas of his day.

Moving now to other facets of Pitcairne, it was the medical theories that he expounded in his lectures at Leiden in 1692–3, which were published first there and then in a collected edition at Rotterdam in 1701, that made

---

[8] Ibid., pp. 19, 22.   [9] This volume, pp. 139–40, 155.
[10] See William Whiston, *New Theory of the Earth* (London, 1696) and John Keill, *An Examination of Dr Burnet's Theory of the Earth* (Oxford, 1698), pp. 178–9. For background, see J. E. Force, *William Whiston, Honest Newtonian* (Cambridge, 1985), ch. 2.
[11] Pitcairne to Walkinshaw, 27 December 1709, in Johnston, *Best of Our Owne*, pp. 56–7.

him famous.[12] He put forward a mechanical theory of the workings of the human body and the way in which therapies affected it. His ideas stemmed from William Harvey's demonstration of the circulation of the blood, the originality of which he had in fact defended, in a work published in 1688, against claims that this had already been known to the ancients.[13] On the basis of Harvey's work, and of ideas derived partly from the likes of Borelli and partly from Newton, he visualised the human body as a kind of hydraulic system, and it was thus that he explained illnesses and their appropriate cures. Bleeding, for instance, was seen as therapeutic because of the extent to which it transferred velocity from one part of the body to another, while various ailments were diagnosed in terms of an augmentation or privation of motion.[14] Such ideas were to prove widely influential in the early eighteenth century, forming the basis of a 'medical Newtonianism' which has been studied by Anita Guerrini, Theodore M. Brown and others.[15] Yet what characterises these writings is an extraordinary intellectual arrogance: I have sympathy with the view of them of the medical historian Lester S. King, who went so far as to describe Pitcairne as 'rather puerile in his approach' (though seeing this as a reason to try to understand him by placing him in context). King remarked on 'the rationalistic approach, the reasoning from fixed premises, the dependence on fragmentary evidence [and] the lack of detailed empirical study or critical evaluation of evidence' to be found in Pitcairne's medical writings.[16] Though others, like Guerrini and Brown, have tried to be more sympathetic, I still feel that medical Newtonianism was a strangely artificial phenomenon, imposing an

[12] See *The Works of Dr Archibald Pitcairne* (London, 1715), and his *Opera omnia* (The Hague, 1722, and subsequent editions). The latter also includes his *Elementa medicinæ physico-mathematica* (1717; English trans., 1718), which represents his Leiden lectures of 1692–3. For details of the Leiden editions, see Guerrini, 'Pitcairne and Newtonian Medicine', nn. 15, 22, 31–2; for the Rotterdam one, see Pitcairne, *Dissertationes medicæ* (Rotterdam, 1701). See further this volume, p. 136. On Pitcairne's Leiden period, see G. A. Lindeboom, 'Pitcairne's Leyden Interlude Described from the Documents', *Annals of Science*, 19 (1963), 273–84, and Rienk Vermij, 'The Formation of the Newtonian Philosophy: The Case of the Amsterdam Mathematical Amateurs', *British Journal for the History of Science*, 36 (2003), 183–200 (pp. 185–7).

[13] Pitcairne, *Solutio problematis de historicis; seu, inventoribus* (Edinburgh, 1688). For a commentary, see Alasdair Raffe, 'Archibald Pitcairne and Scottish Heterodoxy, c. 1688–1713', *Historical Journal*, 60 (2017), 633–57 (pp. 638–45).

[14] Pitcairne, *The Philosophical and Mathematical Elements of Physick* (London, 1718).

[15] Guerrini, 'Tory Newtonians' and 'Pitcairne and Newtonian Medicine'; T. M. Brown, 'Medicine in the Shadow of the *Principia*', *Journal of the History of Ideas*, 48 (1987), 629–48. On medical Newtonianism, see also R. E. Schofield, *Mechanism and Materialism: British Natural Philosophy in an Age of Reason* (Princeton, 1970), ch. 3, and Arnold Thackray, *Atoms and Powers: An Essay on Newtonian Matter-Theory and the Development of Chemistry* (Cambridge, MA, 1970), ch. 3.

[16] Lester S. King, *The Philosophy of Medicine: The Early Eighteenth Century* (Cambridge, MA, 1978), pp. 109–18, esp. 110, 116–17.

ostensibly mathematical rationale on a therapy that otherwise remained quite traditional. Yet Pitcairne's medical philosophy was very popular, being propagated by various physicians, many of them of Scottish descent, in early eighteenth-century England.[17] Pitcairne's writings were widely circulated in manuscript form, and his medical practice seems also to have been effective and well received.[18]

On the other hand, Pitcairne's views were controversial, and Edinburgh in the 1690s saw a ferocious debate, especially over the causes of fevers, about which Andrew Cunningham, Stephen Stigler and Anita Guerrini have written at length, in which the rationalistic medical theories of Pitcairne were pitted against a more empirical approach stemming from Thomas Sydenham.[19] At this time Pitcairne also got into a conflict over the proper method for the study of natural history with Sir Robert Sibbald, a patriarch of Scottish intellectual life who had previously patronised Pitcairne:[20] Pitcairne seems to have been an almost instinctive controversialist.

This is also evident in the part Pitcairne played in the bitter struggles between the Presbyterian kirk, which dominated the Scottish establishment and much of Scottish life at this time, and the Episcopalian minority, of which Pitcairne was one of the most vociferous spokesmen. In particular, he wrote two literary works that seem to have been no less potent for having circulated only in manuscript during his lifetime. One was *Babell*, a poem in rhyming couplets in the style of *Hudibras*, Samuel Butler's earlier satire of Puritanism. The other was a play, usually known as *The Assembly* (though Professor MacQueen, who recently re-edited it from a manuscript

---

[17] See Anita Guerrini, 'James Keill, George Cheyne, and Newtonian Physiology, 1690–1740', *Journal of the History of Biology*, 18 (1985), 247–66; 'The Tory Newtonians'; 'Newtonianism, Medicine and Religion', in *Religio Medici: Medicine and Religion in Seventeenth-Century England*, ed. O. P. Grell and Andrew Cunningham (Aldershot, 1996), pp. 293–312; *Obesity and Depression in the Enlightenment: The Life and Times of George Cheyne* (Norman, 2000); and D. E. Shuttleton, '"A Modest Examination": John Arbuthnot and the Scottish Newtonians', *British Journal for Eighteenth-Century Studies*, 18 (1995), 47–62.

[18] For manuscript copies, see, for example, Royal College of Physicians, Edinburgh, PIA/1 and PIA/2, Wellcome Library, London, MSS 3914, 3195, or Society of Antiquaries of London, MS 25. See also n. 1.

[19] See Andrew Cunningham, 'Sydenham versus Newton: the Edinburgh Fever Dispute of the 1690s between Andrew Brown and Archibald Pitcairne', in *Theories of Fever from Antiquity to the Enlightenment*, ed. W. F. Bynum and V. Nutton, *Medical History*, supplement no. 1 (London, 1981), pp. 71–98; Stephen M. Stigler, 'Apollo Mathematicus: A Story of Resistance to Quantification in the Seventeenth Century', *Proceedings of the American Philosophical Society*, 136 (1992), 93–126; Anita Guerrini, '"A Club of Little Villains": Rhetoric, Professional Identity and Medical Pamphlet Wars', in *Literature and Medicine during the Eighteenth Century*, ed. Marie Mulvey Roberts and Roy Porter (London, 1993), pp. 226–44.

[20] See Pitcairne's *Dissertatio de legibus historiae naturalis* (Edinburgh, 1696); for commentary on the dispute, see Robert Hepburn, *Dissertatio de scriptis Pitcarnianis* (London, [1715]), pp. 12–18.

version in broad Scots, prefers to call it *The Phanaticks*).[21] Both the poem and the play took as their theme the arrogance, stupidity and closed-mindedness of the Presbyterians and lost no opportunity to pour scorn on Pitcairne's adversaries in a manner that was calculated to provoke their ire. Pitcairne had a political agenda, since his support for the Episcopal church went with Tory and increasingly Jacobite views. His objection to Presbyterianism was not only its supposed dullness and anti-intellectualism but also its levelling tendency, while his stance was monarchist, elitist and unrepentantly intellectual.[22]

Pitcairne was also one of the most notable Latin poets of his day, and his verse has received fresh attention in recent years.[23] His enthusiasm for Latin verse composition was apparently shared by a coterie of like-minded friends who gathered in the slightly bohemian milieu that Pitcairne inhabited, not least the wine shops in Edinburgh at which he was said to hold court. Of these, the most notorious was one adjacent to St Giles's Church known as 'the Greppa' or 'Greping-Office', supposedly because you had to grope your way to it down a dark passage (the alternative is that 'Greppa' was the nickname of the proprietress).[24] It was apparently here that Pitcairne not only drank heavily but also carried out medical consultations, and an affectionate account of this was given over a century later by Robert Chambers in his *Traditions of Edinburgh* (1825). On the other hand, David Shuttleton has characterised Pitcairne's drinking circle as 'one of the most cosmopolitan intellectual groupings in late seventeenth-century

---

[21] See *Babell; A Satirical Poem, on the Proceedings of the General Assembly in the Year* MDCXCII, ed. G. R. Kinloch (Edinburgh, 1830). For the play, see Terence Tobin's edition of it as *The Assembly* (Lafayette, IN, 1972) and John MacQueen's Scottish Text Society edition under the title, *The Phanaticks* (Woodbridge, 2012), though it might be felt that this is a rather arbitrary choice of title and that *The Committee* (or *The Comitie*) would have been equally appropriate: see *The Phanaticks*, pp. xiii, lvii. On Pitcairne's further dramatic sketch, published in Kinloch, *Babell*, pp. 70–8, see John MacQueen, '*Tollerators and Con-tollerators* (1703) and Archibald Pitcairne: Text, Background and Authorship', *Studies in Scottish Literature*, 40 (2014), 76–104.

[22] This aspect of Pitcairne is well brought out in Bruce Lenman, *The Jacobite Risings in Britain 1689–1746* (London, 1980), pp. 223–5; Bruce Lenman, 'Physicians and Politics in the Jacobite Era', in *The Jacobite Challenge*, ed. Jeremy Black and Evelyn Cruickshanks (Edinburgh, 1988), pp. 74–91 (pp. 77–9); and Colin Kidd, 'The Ideological Significance of Scottish Jacobite Latinity', in *Culture, Politics and Society in Britain, 1600–1800*, ed. Jeremy Black and Jeremy Gregory (Manchester, 1991), pp. 110–30.

[23] See David Money's account of Pitcairne in his *The English Horace: Anthony Alsop and the Tradition of British Latin Verse* (Oxford, 1998), pp. 142–9; more recently, see John and Winifred MacQueen's invaluable edition of his *Latin Poems* (Assen and Tempe, AZ, 2009).

[24] Robert Chambers, *Traditions of Edinburgh* (new ed., Edinburgh, 1847), pp. 152–5. For the alternative, see MacQueen, *Latin Poems*, pp. 318–19.

Scotland', and it is perhaps significant that Chambers's account of the venue was largely based on Pitcairne's celebrations of it in Latin verse.[25]

Pitcairne's Latin poetry gives us more of a sense of his social milieu than we would gain by most other means. Some of the poems mourn the deaths of friends, including Mrs Henderson, proprietress of the 'Greping-Office', or Walter Denniston, who was involved in a drinking contest there. Others celebrate colleagues and family, while yet others commemorate Christian, and particularly Episcopalian, festivals; in addition, a significant group of verses are overtly Jacobite. The poems by Pitcairne's associates are comparable to his, and together they give a picture of an elitist, highly intellectual circle, cognisant with and often critical of political and cultural developments around them, congratulating themselves on their distinctness and superiority. No less revealing is the slightly idiosyncratic way in which these Latin verses were published: they were circulated in ephemeral, printed form, often in the form of single-sheet broadsides which were mainly produced by Robert Freebairn, a printer who was Pitcairne's protégé and disciple. Three main collections of these verse ephemera survive, one in Edinburgh, another in Oxford, and the third in Austin, Texas, while access to the poems themselves has now been greatly facilitated by the immaculate parallel text edition of them produced in 2009 by John and Winifred MacQueen.[26]

All these aspects of Pitcairne have received extensive scrutiny in recent years, while at the same time attention has also been paid to his religious views, though these remain elusive. In 2002, David Shuttleton gave an overview of Pitcairne's role in relation to the 'articulate irreligion' to be found in Edinburgh in the years around 1700, exemplified particularly by the trial and execution of Thomas Aikenhead in 1696–7.[27] Shuttleton

---

[25] David E. Shuttleton, 'Bantering with Scripture: Dr Archibald Pitcairne and Articulate Irreligion in Late Seventeenth-Century Edinburgh', in *The Arts of Seventeenth-Century Science*, ed. Claire Jowitt and Diane Watt (Aldershot, 2002), pp. 58–73 (p. 65); Chambers, *Traditions*, pp. 152–4.

[26] MacQueen, *Latin Poems*. For the publication of Pitcairne's verse, see David Foxon, *English Verse 1701–1750: A Catalogue of Separately Printed Poems with Notes on Contemporary Collected Editions*, 2 vols (Cambridge, 1975), esp. I, 577 and entries P294–409; see also this chapter, n. 46. The main collections are *Reliquiae Pitcairnianae* in Edinburgh Central Library; Bodleian Library, Oxford, Antiq. d. x. 7; and a series at the Harry Ransom Humanities Research Center, University of Texas, Austin, TX. For one of Pitcairne's disciples who was involved in this, Thomas Ruddiman, see Douglas Duncan, *Thomas Ruddiman: A Study in Scottish Scholarship of the Early Eighteenth Century* (Edinburgh, 1965), especially ch. 2, and 'Scholarship and Politeness in the Early Eighteenth Century', in *The History of Scottish Literature. Volume 2, 1660–1800*, ed. Andrew Hook (Aberdeen, 1987), pp. 51–63 (pp. 55–7; Pitcairne's *Assembly* is briefly discussed on pp. 194–5 of the same volume).

[27] Shuttleton, 'Bantering with Scripture'. On the Aikenhead case, see Chapter 5.

surveyed the evidence concerning contemporary reactions to Pitcairne, including the evaluation by the Presbyterian divine Robert Wodrow, which provide some of the most telling characterisations of him and his milieu. In 1711, in a tirade against the 'profanity' of his age, Wodrow wrote how: 'at Edinburgh, I hear Dr Pitcairn and several others doe meet very regularly evry Lord's Day, and read the Scripture, in order to lampoon and ridicule it'.[28] After Pitcairne's death two years later, Wodrow reiterated this and other accusations, characterising him as 'a professed Deist, and by many alledged to be ane Atheist, though he has frequently professed his belife of a God, and said that he could not deny a Providence'. Wodrow added that Pitcairne was 'a great mocker at religion, and ridiculer of it'. He acknowledged that Pitcairne was 'the most celebrated physitian in Scotland this age, and certainly a man of great skill', adding: 'He gote a vast income, but spent it upon drinking, and was twice drunk every day'.[29]

A further telling episode involving another Presbyterian divine, James Webster, occurred in 1712. Both Webster and Pitcairne were present at a book auction in Edinburgh in which there was spirited bidding for a copy of a deeply heterodox book, Charles Blount's edition of Philostratus's *Life of Apollonius*, whereas a copy of the Bible failed to attract bidders. Pitcairne quipped 'that it was no wonder it stuck in their hands for *verbum Dei manet in aeternum* [God's word remains eternal]'. Webster thereupon accused Pitcairne of overt irreligion. When another minister, John Pettigrew, greeted Pitcairne in the street with the words: 'Are you Dr Pitcairne, the atheist?', Pitcairne replied 'Yes', overlooking the latter part of the question. Realising that he had been wrong-footed, Pitcairne exclaimed: 'Oh, Pettigrew, that skull of yours is as deep as hell', to which the minister responded that he was glad to learn that Pitcairne had come to believe in hell. At that point the matter seems to have been dropped.[30]

As noted, the latter exchange occurred at a book auction that Pitcairne attended, and in this connection it is interesting that his library still survives in St Petersburg, having been acquired by Peter the Great for the nascent Russian Academy of Sciences. It is a remarkable assemblage, and from the listings of its content that are available, it is noticeable that, although it includes a comprehensive collection of the classics and of scientific and medical authors, it is noticeably thin on religious titles.

---

[28] Robert Wodrow, *Analecta*, 4 vols (Edinburgh, 1842–3), I, 322–3.
[29] Ibid., II, 255; see also Shuttleton, 'Bantering with Scripture', p. 63.
[30] For a full account, see Shuttleton, 'Bantering with Scripture', pp. 68–9. Cf. Wodrow, *Analecta*, III, 307, and James Erskine, Lord Grange, *Extracts from the Diary of a Senator of the College of Justice* (Edinburgh, 1843), pp. 13–14 and 101–10.

The normal staples of religious books in libraries of the period are almost completely lacking, whereas heterodox titles are noticeably present, including works such as Richard Simon's *Critical History of the Old and New Testament*, Antonie van Dale's *De Oraculis Ethnicorom Dissertationes Duæ* or Pierre Bayle's *Miscellaneous Reflections on the Comet of 1680*.[31]

As for Pitcairne's statements of his religious views, his poems, as we have already seen, celebrate Christian, and particularly Episcopalian festivals, though this was arguably more a sign of ideological allegiance than belief. There is just one composition by him that can be read as heterodox, a poem with a strongly Epicurean flavour which was widely circulated in manuscript and print, an English rendering of it being published by the eminent poet Matthew Prior.[32] In drawing attention to it, John and Winifred MacQueen have claimed that this 'more than anything else … was the cause of his reputation', which, though possible, seems a slight overstatement.[33] Another tantalising clue – in the context of Pitcairne's interest in Newton's religious views, as already discussed – is that in a letter of 1694 Pitcairne professed 'a vast propensitie to writ the Relligio mathematici, or Euclidis &c'. No such work survives, and it was apparently never composed. In any case, he went on: 'the paper (if ever I write it) shall be ane immortal confutation of poperie & of everything that smels of poperie', adding: 'it cannot be so printed me vivo. If I write it, I'l certainlie laugh in my grave if I can but understand then what a work there shall be made to answer it by those who'l not understand it'.[34]

Much more significant is Pitcairne's *Epistola Archimedis ad Regem Gelonem, Albæ Græcæ reperta anno æræ Christianæ 1688 (Epistle from Archimedes to King Gelo, found at Alba Graeca AD 1688)*, a strange text in Latin purporting to be a letter from Archimedes to the King of Syracuse, giving his views on religious matters, of which a full account has recently

---

[31] For the printed catalogue, see Edinburgh University Library MS La.III.629. For a transcript of the manuscript catalogue in St Petersburg, see National Library of Scotland MS Acc 8042. See also John H. Appleby and Andrew Cunningham, 'Robert Erskine and Archibald Pitcairne – Two Scottish Physicians' Outstanding Libraries', *The Bibliotheck*, 11 (1982), 3–16, and John H. Appleby, 'Archibald Pitcairne Re-encountered – a Note on his Manuscript Poems and Printed Library Catalogue', *The Bibliotheck*, 12 (1986), 137–9.

[32] MacQueen, *Latin Poems*, pp. 134–7 and 354–7. For Prior's version, see also *The Literary Works of Matthew Prior*, ed. H. Bunker Wright and Monroe K. Spears, 2 vols (Oxford, 1959), I, 396–7, and II, 923–4.

[33] MacQueen, *Latin Poems*, p. 354 (see also pp. 30, 254–7 and 436, for a reference to Arian/Socinian views).

[34] See Johnston, *The Best of Our Owne*, p. 18. For the claim in Pitcairne's play that mathematics led to infidelity, see MacQueen, *Phanaticks*, pp. 59 and 189–91.

been given by Alasdair Raffe.[35] This does indeed claim that geometrical reasoning should be applied even to religious matters, combining this with a fierce rejection of priestcraft and superstition, a mocking attitude towards Christian doctrines like the Trinity and a fascination with the role of religious lawmakers like Numa Pompilius.[36] It is undoubtedly a consciously heterodox work, which could be seen as presenting an outright attack on revealed religion, although (like much of Pitcairne's Latin verse) it is deliberately obscure.[37] Certainly, this is how the *Epistola* was read at the time by commentators like George MacKenzie, Earl of Cromarty, and the divine Thomas Halyburton: the latter devoted his entire inaugural lecture to a refutation of it in 1710, while the former regarded it as 'certainly a Piece hammered out of the Devil's Forge' which 'stricks [sic] at Christianity, in its Primitive Root'.[38] It is also revealing that, having apparently been printed at Pitcairne's behest at Amsterdam in 1706, there was an extended edition, evidently of *c.* 1712, which was reprinted at The Hague in 1716, when it came to the attention of the Huguenot savant, Prosper Marchand.[39] It thus

---

[35] *Epistola Archimedis ad Regem Gelonem* [n.p., n.d.]; Raffe, 'Pitcairne and Scottish Heterodoxy', pp. 646–53. It is perhaps worth noting here the British Library holding of this work, which comprises two versions, both in 8°, one comprising 15 pp., followed by an unpaginated errata leaf (BL 531.b.1(2)), and the other 48 pp. (BL 531.b.1(1)): the former lacks various passages that appear in the latter and it ends differently; it also contains various misprints which are emended in MS in the BL copy and are corrected in the 48 pp. version. Both are from the library of Sir Hans Sloane, and Pitcairne is identified as author in an MS note on the title page of both; the latter also has the inscription 'ex dono Auctore'. A further presentation copy of the 48 pp. version to Dr Richard Mead is now BL G16831. For the relationship between these and other printings of the text, see n. 39. There is also an MS copy of the shorter version in BL MS Sloane 2623, fols 61–73, though it is not linked with Pitcairne in extant catalogues. For an edition of this, see *Ein unächter Brief des Archimedes*, ed. G. Henning (Darmstadt, 1872) (though deducing that it is a composition of post-classical date, Henning completely misses the Pitcairne connection). A further MS copy of this version probably in the hand of David Gregory is in Edinburgh University Library, MS La. II. 36.

[36] *Epistola Archimedis* (48 pp. version), pp. 18–21, 35–44 and elsewhere.

[37] See the remarks to this effect in the article on Pitcairne in Pierre Bayle, *A General Dictionary, Historical and Critical*, ed. J. P. Bernard, Thomas Birch, John Lockman, et al., 10 vols (London, 1734–41), VIII, 419–22, on p. 421. The article, there attributed to 'a very intimate and learned friend of our Author', is in fact by Sir John Clerk of Penicuik: see the MS version in BL Add MS 4223, fols 146–7 (with covering letter dated 7 September 1738, BL Add MS 4223, fols 144–5).

[38] George MacKenzie, 1st Earl of Cromarty, *Synopsis Apocalyptica* (Edinburgh, 1708), 3rd pagination sequence, pp. iv–v; Thomas Halyburton, *Oratio inauguralis* (1710), in his *Natural Religion Insufficient; and Reveal'd Necessary to Man's Happiness in His Present State* (Edinburgh, 1714), pp. 1–24.

[39] For the 15 pp. and 48 pp. editions, see n. 35. For a further issue comprising 47 pp. at the Royal College of Physicians, Edinburgh, see Raffe, 'Pitcairne and Scottish Heterodoxy', p. 647. It is perhaps worth noting that a copy of this version was owned by Isaac Newton and is now at Trinity College, Cambridge, NQ.16.99¹: see John Harrison, *The Library of Isaac Newton* (Cambridge, 1978), p. 138 (no. 566). For the 1716 reprint, which comprises 16 pp., including the copy of it in Leiden University Library annotated by Marchand, see Raffe, 'Pitcairne and Scottish Heterodoxy', pp. 647–8, and Vermij, 'Formation of the Newtonian Philosophy', p. 192 n. 42.

entered the milieu of clandestine heterodox publishing in which the notorious *Treatise of the Three Impostors* was disseminated (and possibly composed), suggesting that Pitcairne's heterodox ideas stimulated a degree of interest and acceptance in the Netherlands that they never acquired in Britain.[40] In spite of all this evidence of Pitcairne's subversive activity, however, the consensus until recently – represented both by Anita Guerrini in her *Oxford Dictionary of National Biography* article on Pitcairne and endorsed by John and Winifred MacQueen in their edition of his *Latin Poems* – remained that, although his criticisms of the kirk led to charges of atheism, 'it is more likely that Pitcairne, like his friend Gregory, was a devoted, if not devout, Episcopalian'.[41]

* * *

All this, however, was changed by the discovery and subsequent publication of a new source to be found in a rather unexpected location, which had until then completely escaped the attention of Pitcairne scholars. This is a manuscript titled *Pitcairneana; Or Papers found in the Study of the late famous Physician, Doctor Archibald Pitcairn, and inscribed to the Preachers of the Boylean Lecture, but left out of his printed Works.* It is to be found in the Houghton Library at Harvard University, where its shelf mark is MS Eng 1114, and it came to light during a visit to the library on my part in September 2014 (until recently it was classified in the library's 'Amer' manuscript series, which may partly explain why it was long overlooked[42]). The manuscript was presented to Harvard on 18 January 1841 by Henry

---

[40] For the milieu, see Jonathan Israel, *Radical Enlightenment: Philosophy and the Making of Modernity 1650–1750* (Oxford, 2001), ch. 36; *Heterodoxy, Spinozism and Free Thought in Early Eighteenth-Century Europe: Studies on the 'Traité des trois imposteurs',* ed. Silvia Berti, Françoise Charles-Daubert and Richard H. Popkin (Dordrecht, 1996); *Le 'Traité des trois imposteurs' et 'L'esprit de Spinosa'. Philosophie clandestine entre 1678 et 1768,* ed. Françoise Charles-Daubert (Oxford, 1999); and Georges Minois, *The Atheist's Bible: The Most Dangerous Book that Never Existed,* English trans. (Chicago, 2012). Pitcairne's link to this milieu is indicated by the fact that his library (see this chapter, n. 31) contained a copy of Toland's *Adeisidaemon,* published at The Hague in 1709.

[41] *ODNB*; MacQueen, *Latin Poems,* esp. pp. 29–31. For a somewhat different assessment, see Roger Emerson, 'The Religious, the Secular and the Worldly: Scotland 1680–1800', in *Religion, Secularization and Political Thought: Thomas Hobbes to J. S. Mill,* ed. J. E. Crimmins (London, 1989), pp. 68–89 (p. 73): 'Pitcairne's beliefs are difficult to unravel, but he was hardly an ordinary or orthodox Episcopalian'. On the nature of Episcopalianism in the period, see Alasdair Raffe, *The Culture of Controversy: Religious Arguments in Scotland, 1660–1714* (Woodbridge, 2012). It is perhaps worth noting that Guerrini's view of the *Epistola Archimedis* in the *ODNB* is that it is 'a satire ostensibly of medical sects but in reality of presbyterianism' (in Guerrini, 'Archibald Pitcairne', p. 73, it is described as 'a savage satire of the Scots Presbyterians and medical methodists'); for the MacQueens' evaluation, see *Latin Poems,* pp. 30–1.

[42] I am grateful to Susan Halpert for this point.

Swasey McKean (1810–57), who had gained his AB at Harvard in 1828 and was tutor in Latin there from 1830 to 1835 before moving on to a career in civil engineering.[43] McKean was the son of Joseph McKean (1776–1818), who succeeded John Quincy Adams to become the second Boylston Professor of Rhetoric and Oratory at Harvard in 1809; he himself was the son of William McKean, born in Glasgow in 1739, a tobacconist who emigrated to the United States in 1763 and died in 1820.[44] This means that the *Pitcairneana* manuscript or its exemplar could have come from Scotland with William McKean, though obviously its Scottish links would have given it interest both for Joseph – who was quite a book collector, to judge from the catalogue of his library printed in 1818 – or his son; both men might also have been interested in Pitcairne as a Latin stylist.[45]

What, then, of the manuscript itself? The extant text is in a hand that seems to be of mid- to late eighteenth-century date, but there is no obvious reason why it should not derive from an earlier original, nor why this should not go back to Pitcairne's own time. As we will see, the most recent books cited in the work date from 1704–5, and there is nothing in it that is incompatible with a date of composition in Pitcairne's later years. Indeed, it shares various features with Pitcairne's known writings. Like many of them, it is short and pithy and, though it is in English whereas the bulk of Pitcairne's published writings were in Latin, it is worth noting that Pitcairne had himself earlier used the vernacular for the ecclesiastical polemics that he circulated in manuscript form. In any case, since the works cited are mainly in English, especially Samuel Clarke's Boyle Lectures, which form its principal target, it might have seemed strange not to write the text in the same language. As we will see, in its invocation

[43] See Joseph Palmer, *Necrology of Alumni of Harvard College 1851/2–1862/3* (Boston, 1864), pp. 141–3. There are various other manuscripts by McKean or associated with him at the Houghton or in the Harvard archives, including an annotated copy of George Ticknor's lectures on Spanish literature which includes a photograph of McKean and a biographical note on him based on that in Palmer's *Necrology* (HUC 8831.382.53).

[44] See Levi Hedge, *Eulogy on the Rev. Joseph McKean DD LLD, Boylston Professor of Rhetorick and Oratory* (Cambridge, MA, 1818), and William B. Sprague, *Annals of the American Pulpit* (2 vols, New York, 1857), II, 414–22. For a modern study that includes information on Joseph McKean's lectures, see Paul E. Ried, 'Joseph McKean: The Second Boylston Professor of Rhetoric and Oratory', *Quarterly Journal of Speech*, 46 (1960), 419–24. On William McKean, see also Joseph T. Buckingham, *Annals of the Massachusetts Charitable Mechanic Association, 1795–1892* (Boston, 1853), p. 173n.

[45] See *Catalogue of the Select Library of the Late Rev. Joseph McKean DD, LLD* (Boston, 1818): not surprisingly, *Pitcairneana* does not appear in this.

of 'Axioms' at the end, *Pitcairneana* partakes of the strongly Newtonian flavour of Pitcairne's medical writings, while its stress on 'bigotry' and 'superstition' echoes both his anti-Presbyterian satires and his *Epistola Archimedis*.

The work is presented as one found in Pitcairne's study at his death, but this, too, is perfectly feasible: the loyalty towards Pitcairne felt by many when he died is indicated by the numerous verse eulogies of him that appeared at that point.[46] A further sense of the kind of coterie in which a text like this would have been valued and preserved is given by the edition of Pitcairne's *Dissertationes medicæ* that his protégé Robert Freebairn brought out in 1713, with his 'Dissertatio de legibus historiae naturalis' and his 'Poemata selecta' appended (the edition contains a dedication by Pitcairne himself, who died on 23 October that year; it is dated 10 June, a special date for him as it was the Old Pretender's birthday).[47] This context would itself make sense of the claim that the document was found in Pitcairne's study, while the reference to its being 'left out of his printed Works' could allude to Freebairn's 1713 collection, the content of which was more than once reprinted in Latin and English.[48] Its title, ending in '-ana', alludes to a genre of books that had come to the fore in the seventeenth century, consisting of extracts from the conversation and writings of famous scholars like J. J. Scaliger, the subject of *Scaligeriana* (1666); though the content of *Pitcairneana* is rather different from such books, this reinforces the sense of its close linkage with Pitcairne.[49]

It is, of course, possible that one of his followers might have written the work and fathered it on the great man by using the old trope of claiming that it had been found posthumously among his papers. To examine this possibility, I investigated this circle, including both the authors of the elegies to Pitcairne and also Robert Hepburn, author of a rather deferential

[46] See Foxon, *English Verse*, K24 (Ker), K40–2 (Kincaid), R78 (Ramsay), and R329 (Ruddiman); there were also anonymous compositions (E214–15, O18) and elegies by George Davidson (D55) and John Wilson (W521), who have proved more elusive: Davidson (another poem by whom was published in 1717: Foxon, *English Verse*, entry D54) has not been identified, while John Wilson was perhaps the figure referred to in Charles Withers, 'Situating Practical Reason', in *Science and Medicine in the Scottish Enlightenment*, ed. Withers and Paul Wood (East Linton, 2002), pp. 54–78 (p. 64).

[47] See Archibald Pitcairne, *Dissertationes medicæ* (Edinburgh, 1713). There are two issues of this edition, one containing the 'Dissertatio de legibus historiae naturalis' and 'Poemata selecta', the other without them. For the significance of the date, see MacQueen, *Latin Poems*, pp. 248–9, 431–2.

[48] See n. 12.

[49] See Paul Korshin, 'The Development of Intellectual Biography in the Eighteenth Century', *Journal of English and Germanic Philology*, 73 (1974), 513–23 (pp. 519–22).

posthumous Latin account of his writings, just in case among these men might lurk the true author of *Pitcairneana*.[50] Although a lively bunch of budding intellectuals came to light, however, none seemed a particularly likely culprit. Thus, we have Thomas Ruddiman, who was to become Pitcairne's successor as the promoter of Latinate culture in Scotland;[51] Allan Ramsay, soon to emerge as a major literary figure in his own right and who presided over the 'Easy Club', a parallel social group to that around Pitcairne;[52] Robert Hepburn, whose *Dissertatio de scriptis Pitcarnianis* was addressed to Joseph Addison and who began a Scottish literary periodical in the mode of *The Spectator* and *The Tatler*;[53] John Ker, a schoolmaster and later Professor of Greek at Aberdeen and then of Latin at Edinburgh; the aristocrat and politician George Hay, Earl of Kinnoull; or the medical man, Thomas Kincaid.[54] Such sources as we have about these men reveal them to have been fervent Jacobites and Episcopalians, but I was unable to detect a hint of religious heterodoxy. It therefore seems much likelier, considering the philosophical sophistication of the work and Pitcairne's own track record earlier in his career, that he wrote it himself.[55] Indeed, one wonders whether his disciples might have been slightly shocked by the text, treasuring it as a memento of the great man but seeing it as suitable only for manuscript transmission rather than for print publication, and the same may also have been true of the McKeans in the godly environment of early nineteenth-century New England.

For what is extraordinary about the text is how overtly irreligious it is. When I first encountered it, it struck me as one of the most explicitly atheistic texts from the early eighteenth century that I had come across. This makes it significant regardless of its link or otherwise with Pitcairne. Its tone is apparent even from the witty and half-mocking opening address to the organisers of the well-known series of apologetic sermons founded under the will of Robert Boyle, offering them information on the privately expressed views of atheists that might otherwise be overlooked so that these could be confronted in the Boyle Lectures; it is equally evident from the remainder of

---

[50] Hepburn, *Dissertatio de scriptis Pitcarnianis*. For the elegies, see n. 46.
[51] See Duncan, *Thomas Ruddiman*, esp. ch. 2. Another unlikely candidate is David Gregory, who had died in 1708: for his religious views, see especially Friesen, 'Archibald Pitcairne', pp. 173–5.
[52] See *ODNB* and Duncan, *Thomas Ruddiman*, esp. pp. 75–80.
[53] See *ODNB* and MacQueen, *Latin Poems*, pp. 294–9 and 454.
[54] On Ker, see *ODNB*, and on him, Kinnoull and Kincaid see Duncan, *Thomas Ruddiman*, p. 19, and MacQueen, *Latin Poems*, pp. 41, 371–2, 396–7.
[55] Note how *Pitcairneana* might be seen to echo Pitcairne's sentiments quoted above in his letter to David Gregory of 25 February 1706 and his letter to Adriaan Verwer of June 1706: see p. 125.

the text, which is presented as a dialogue between *Incredulous*, a spokesman for an atheistic viewpoint, and his orthodox opponent, *Credulous*, in which the sceptical spokesman might throughout be seen as holding the upper hand. Indeed, from time to time he even adopts a rather disdainful approach towards his orthodox antagonist, as at one point where he says: 'You should have proved there was a God before you talked of his creating Power'.[56]

In its dialogue format, the text belongs to a well-established tradition going back to classical authors like Plato and Cicero, which had experienced a revival during the Renaissance. More specifically, it bears a resemblance to the confrontation between an atheist and a believer in George Berkeley's *Alciphron; Or the Minute Philosopher* (1732) which has often been seen as a revealing source of atheist views in the period, and which similarly claims access to private conversation as the key to understanding freethinking opinion. Largely for this reason, David Berman has gone so far as to describe Berkeley's treatment as 'perhaps the most searching contemporary account we have of free-thought in the seventeenth and early eighteenth century'.[57] Yet, though the opening address to *Pitcairneana* echoes *Alciphron* in claiming to present 'those Arguments . . . lately urged in Defence of his Opinions' by 'one, who calls himself a Free-thinker', the two works are quite different. This is because, whereas in Berkeley's book the atheist starts confidently but is ultimately comprehensively refuted by his orthodox antagonist, in *Pitcairneana* it is *Incredulous* who ends triumphant, effectively responding to his antagonist's promise of further arguments on behalf of orthodoxy by saying: 'Bring them on!' Indeed, one's suspicions that the opening address is to be read as tongue in cheek are aroused by its claim to have 'mentioned every Thing of Moment our Divines say on this Occasion' and thus 'to take away all Pretence of Cavilling', since the final phrase might be read as ambiguous as to which arguments are the most compelling; it might also be felt that the labelling of the orthodox interlocutor in the dialogue as *Credulous* is loaded in itself.

Moving to the dialogue proper, at the start we learn that the freethinker has become a sceptic while travelling abroad – which could, of course, be an autobiographical statement on Pitcairne's part, if it is really he that *Incredulous* represents – and this provides an opportunity for some telling relativist comments on his part, including a dismissal of the 'bigotry' that

---

[56] Since the text is quite brief, references for quotations from it will not be given in this commentary.
[57] David Berman, *George Berkeley: Idealism and the Man* (Oxford, 1994), p. 164. Cf. *The Works of George Berkeley, Bishop of Cloyne*, ed. A. A. Luce and T. E. Jessop, 9 vols (London, 1948–57), esp. III, 23–4, 32–3.

characterised traditional religions, with an aside on the encroachments of 'the most cunning Impostors' which echoes the writings by Pitcairne that have already been cited.[58] Such incisive comments recur throughout the dialogue, as where *Incredulous* complains about the baleful effects of 'Superstition', and perhaps reaching a climax when he refers to 'that inexhaustible Magazine of Inconsistencies, the Trinity'; it is also striking how *Incredulous* throughout distances himself from the Christian tradition that *Credulous* represents, speaking of 'your Divines' and 'your God', and complaining about the intolerance with which views like his were received (the perhaps surprising reference to 'our Divines' in the opening address could be seen as a kind of back-formation from this). Also notable is the outrage with which *Credulous* greets *Incredulous*'s opinions throughout, particularly near the start of the dialogue, as when he states: 'I hope your Inclination to Atheism will not carry you so far as to deny that there may be Beings of which we have no Ideas', or 'I can't bear your talking thus Blasphemously'.

In general, however, the debate is conducted at a high level of philosophical sophistication, and it seems appropriate here to give an account of the main topics covered and the authors invoked in connection with them, though this has been kept reasonably concise since readers can themselves relish the arguments from the transcript of the document that appears as Chapter 7. The first set of issues that is addressed concern space, matter and impenetrability, and particularly the question of whether it was possible for spiritual and non-spiritual bodies to occupy the same place: this had obvious implications for the existence or otherwise of God, which are debated at length by the orthodox and heterodox spokesmen. At this point, explicit reference is made to two thinkers, the Cambridge Platonist Henry More, whose *Enchiridion metaphysicum* (1671) had explicitly addressed the issue of the nature of spiritual beings, and Samuel Clarke, whose well-known Boyle Lectures of 1704, published the following year as *A Demonstration of the Being and Attributes of God*, had dealt at length with this and related matters.[59] In addition, *Incredulous* is critical of doctrines of

---

[58] The theme of a returning traveller is also to be found at the start of Pitcairne's play: MacQueen, *Phanaticks*, pp. 6–12.

[59] Insofar as works referred to in the text are documented in footnotes there, this will not be repeated here. However, it is perhaps worth noting that none of the works by Clarke, Hooke, More or Toland that are cited are to be found in Pitcairne's library (though other works by all four authors *are*; for other surprising lacunae, see Appleby and Cunningham, 'Robert Erskine and Archibald Pitcairne', p. 11); it may or may not be significant that a copy of Hooke's *Posthumous Works* was bought by the University of Edinburgh in 1712: see Edinburgh University Library MS Da.1.34, fol. 36.

God and the soul which he saw as of scholastic origin and which he associated with 'Immaterialists' – evidently meaning people like Clarke – whose conception of God he saw as framed 'out of the inconsistent Ideas of unextension and unsolidity'.[60]

The discussion then moves to the concept of eternity and the implication of this for ideas about the nature of God and the likelihood that he did indeed create the world at a finite point. Here, both *Credulous* and *Incredulous* quote passages from Clarke's *Demonstration of the Being and Attributes of God* in support of their position, while *Incredulous* alludes rather more archly to 'the Men he pretends to confute', a reference to Thomas Hobbes and Baruch Spinoza, who are specifically named as Clarke's chief adversaries on the title page of his book. At this stage in the argument, *Incredulous* puts forward a strong argument for eternalism, citing Cicero and other ancient philosophers to the effect that the perfection of the world was better explained by this than by a divine act of creation, though agreeing that the design argument at least had the advantage of exposing 'that absurd Notion of the Worlds being made by Chance', an evident allusion to Epicurean ideas.[61] This then leads to a discussion of the issue of whether motion was intrinsic to matter, on which a footnote invokes the Deist John Toland and his *Letters to Serena* (1704), which Samuel Clarke had sought to refute in his Boyle Lectures on the basis of Newtonian views. *Incredulous* implicitly aligns himself with views like Toland's on the grounds that those who saw the Newtonian principles of gravitation and attraction as intrinsic to matter could hardly see motion as separable from it.

This then leads to a final section in which the orthodox spokesman invokes as an argument against eternalism 'the late Progress of Arts and Sciences, and the small part of Time our Histories take in'. As ever, *Incredulous* has an answer, in this case concerning the challenge presented to a biblical timescale for the world by geological evidence like that invoked by Robert Hooke in his 'Discourse of Earthquakes', published in his *Posthumous Works* of 1705; he also refers to the great age of China.[62]

---

[60] For a discussion of Clarke and others as 'immaterialists', see Wayne Hudson, *Enlightenment and Modernity: The English Deists and Reform* (London, 2009), ch. 5.

[61] For a concern about eternalism on the part of more orthodox spokesmen, see George MacKenzie, Earl of Cromarty, *A Bundle of Positions* (London, 1705), especially the section comprising sig. D, and George Cheyne, *Philosophical Principles of Natural Religion* (London, 1705), esp. ch. 2.

[62] For the issues involved, see Rhoda Rappaport, *When Geologists Were Historians, 1665–1750* (Ithaca, 1997), esp. pp. 189–99. On China, see also Paolo Rossi, *The Dark Abyss of Time: The History of the Earth and the History of Nations from Hooke to Vico*, English trans. (Chicago, 1984), pt 2. For Pitcairne's view on contemporary geological debates see this volume, p. 126.

Incredulous rather interestingly took such evidence to support a catastrophist view of the history of a nonetheless eternal world, which he combined with an essentially cyclical view of human development: eras of great intellectual and other progress were succeeded by ages of barbarism. Claiming that 'Superstition has very much contributed to the Destruction of all true Knowledge', he blamed Christians as much as Mahometans for destroying the legacy of classical antiquity, while he also balanced the extraordinary civility of the Chinese against the primitiveness of savages still in the state of nature to suggest an almost random element in human development rather than any inexorable law of progress.[63]

At the end *Incredulous* has a peroration in which he recapitulates a number of his arguments, describing them as 'Axioms' in essentially Newtonian mode, as we have seen. *Credulous*, needless to say, replies that 'You triumph before Victory', promising to raise further arguments 'from Providence, from the Government of the World, and from the Impossibility of Matters thinking'.[64] One could well imagine much space being devoted to such themes, as was the case in other orthodox polemics of the period, but it might be felt that *Incredulous*'s views were by this time pretty clear and that little needed to be added to the position that he had already established. In any case, at this point the text ends with the word 'Finis'.

So where does this treatise stand within the philosophical traditions of the day, and particularly how is one to place the position of *Incredulous*, since that of *Credulous* is clearly intended to echo the views of orthodox thinkers, here reflected above all by Samuel Clarke? *Incredulous* is a Newtonian, but a Tolandian rather than a Clarkean one: Jeffrey Wigelsworth has recently helpfully reminded us that Toland's adaptation of Newtonianism to make motion intrinsic to matter was intended to enhance it rather than to subvert it, and the view that is being expressed here is, if anything, a more radical version of this.[65] Though it is perhaps surprising that the two philosophers who were seen as the chief exponents of the explicitly or implicitly

---

[63] There is a possible parallel with the disdain for the Hottentots shown at this point in a manuscript by Pitcairne in Edinburgh University Library, MS Dc.4.101, in which he attributed the greater proneness to disease of 'barbarous' countries, where 'the people are not polite' compared with northern nations, to their inferior personal hygiene.

[64] On the last topic, which is not discussed in *Pitcairneana*, see specifically John W. Yolton, *Thinking Matter: Materialism in Eighteenth-Century Britain* (Oxford, 1984). The other matters referred to were commonplaces of contemporary apologetic.

[65] J. R. Wigelsworth, *Deism in Enlightenment England: Theology, Politics and Newtonian Public Science* (Manchester, 2009), ch. 3, esp. pp. 78–81. Wigelsworth thus rejects the view of Toland as anti-Newtonian espoused by Margaret Jacob and others. See also Reink Vermij, 'Matter and Motion: Toland and Spinoza', in *Disguised and Overt Spinozism around 1700*, ed. Wiep van Bunge and Wim Klever (Leiden, 1996), pp. 275–88.

materialist systems that apologists like Clarke spent so much time refuting –
Hobbes and Spinoza – are here alluded to only as Clarke's antagonists,
Incredulous is clearly in sympathy with an essentially materialist view of the
world; no less central to his viewpoint is eternalism and the claim that the
perfection of nature was better explained in terms of that than of an act of
divine creation. Possibly most interesting is the rejection of the idea of
progress on the basis of catastrophist ideas taken from contemporary notions
about the geological history of the world, since historians have noted the
apologetic use to which progressivist arguments were beginning to be put at
this time, which *Incredulous* fiercely rejects.[66] Moreover, associated with this
is a regret about the damage done during the Dark Ages to the cultural
richness of classical antiquity which aligns *Incredulous* with the stance of a
kind of 'ancient' in the Ancients and Moderns controversy, though in
general Pitcairne is a figure who is more difficult to place in relation to that
than some commentators have realised.[67]

How, therefore, is this remarkable text to be interpreted? It is certainly
striking how overtly atheistic it is, using the dialogue form to allow its
sceptical interlocutor repeatedly to out-argue his orthodox opponent. But
what are we to make of its title and its claimed link with Pitcairne? The fact
that we only have a later copy makes it possible that it is not by Pitcairne at
all, though (as we have seen) both its terms of reference and its content are
coherent with its being written in the later years of Pitcairne's life. On the
other hand, in interpreting it, we need to be aware of Pitcairne's artfulness
as an author, the man who wrote *Babell*, his burlesque of Presbyterianism,
or the *Epistola Archimedis*, purporting to be an ancient discussion of
religious truth, and who showed a comparable virtuosity in his Latin
poems and the ingeniously subversive ways in which these were published.
Indeed, the clandestine milieu in which Pitcairne's *Epistola Archimedis*
circulated also offers a significant context. All this means that, though it
is possible that, through *Incredulous*, the new text presents Pitcairne's own

---

[66] See especially R. S. Crane, 'Anglican Apologetics and the Idea of Progress, 1699–1745', in his *The Idea of the Humanities and Other Essays Critical and Historical*, 2 vols (Chicago, 1967), I, 214–87, originally published in *Modern Philology*, 31 (1933–4).

[67] For a recent account of Pitcairne which places him in the context of the dated conceptual structure of R. F. Jones's *Ancients and Moderns* (2nd ed., St Louis, 1961), see MacQueen, *Latin Poems*, p. 363 (where Jones is cited) and elsewhere. It is unfortunate that, for all their erudition concerning the Latin culture of the period, the MacQueens seem unaware of critiques of Jones's views, for example, in Michael Hunter, *Science and Society in Restoration England* (Cambridge, 1981), especially ch. 6, and above all in J. M. Levine, 'Ancients and Moderns Reconsidered', *Eighteenth-Century Studies*, 15 (1981), 72–89, and *The Battle of the Books: History and Literature in the Augustan Age* (Ithaca, 1991).

views, it is equally possible that we are intended to remain unsure about this – that the objective of presenting what a true 'atheist' might say was rather intended primarily as a means of shocking the pious, and that Pitcairne's own position was a rationalist but essentially theistic one, as certain of his comments elsewhere suggest.[68]

This is a question that has to be left unresolved, since the answer to it seems to have gone with Pitcairne to his grave (which is in the churchyard of Greyfriars Church at Edinburgh). Either way, however, *Pitcairneana* provides a fascinating new insight into Pitcairne and his milieu. It also represents a striking contribution to the debates about the most fundamental philosophical issues that were exercising thinkers in the first decade of the eighteenth century, and deserves attention accordingly.

---

[68] See, for instance, his letter to Verwer, cited in n. 5. See also Raffe, 'Pitcairne and Scottish Heterodoxy'. It is also interesting to consider the views on related subjects of a one-time associate of Pitcairne's, George Cheyne, in his *Philosophical Principles*.

CHAPTER 7

The Text of Pitcairneana
Houghton Library, Harvard, MS Eng 1114

Pitcairneana;

Or Papers found in the Study of the late famous Physician, Doctor Archibald Pitcairn, and inscribed to the Preachers of the Boylean Lecture, but left out of his printed Works.

Reverend Sirs,

The Reason, as I humbly conceive, why the Lecture founded by Mr Boyle against Atheism has not all the Success pious Christians could wish, is that the Arguments with which Atheists in private attack the Being of a God, are unknown to You, whose Province it is to combat every Thing, which strikes at the Foundation of Religion. For which Reason I think I can't do greater Service to Religion in general, and to your Founders godly Design in particular, than to communicate to you those Arguments one, who calls himself a Free-thinker, lately urged in Defence of his

---

* The text is reproduced by courtesy of the Houghton Library, Harvard University. For a digital version, see http://nrs.harvard.edu/urn-3:FHCL.HOUGH:12939560. The MS comprises a formerly stitched paper book, like an exercise book, with coarse paper wrappers. The stitching now only survives at the inside of the central gathering, having come loose so that the folded leaves that make up the book are separate from one another. On the outside front cover, it is inscribed: 'Rec[eived] January 18. 1841 / Gift of / H. S. McKean Esq.' This is repeated at the top of the first page of the text. It is preserved in a slipcase, inside which is the bookplate: 'Harvard College Library the gift of H. S. McKean'. The MS is in a neat italic hand of mid- to late eighteenth-century date. It has a modern foliation at the bottom of the inner margin. Catchwords illustrate the continuity of the text. Each page has a pencil margin, within which 'C' or 'T' is written to denote the contributions to the dialogue. Before fol. 1 there is a leaf that is blank except for the old class marks, 'MS Amer 721' (this also appears to be deleted on the cover) and 'Cal. E. Dr. 4', on its verso. At the end, one page has been marked up with pencil margins after 'Finis'; there are then five wholly blank pages (i.e., verso of leaf with marked-up recto and 2 completely blank leaves, one conjugate with the opening blank leaf, the other with the leaf containing the title and preface). In the transcription that follows, page breaks have been denoted within soliduses; insertions above the line are denoted ‹thus› (these all appear to be trivial copying errors); and editorial interventions are enclosed in square brackets. Occasional flourishes at the ends of words, especially at line-ends, have been ignored; the usage of inverted commas on fol. 6 has been modernised, as has the list of 'Axioms' on fol. 12. Throughout the text, the word 'tho' has apostrophes at both the start and the end; here, the opening one has been silently ignored.

Opinions. I must own I had some Scruples of sending you this Discourse in so public a Manner, tho' the only Way I had of applying to You, 'till I considered that You, by being obliged to print Your Sermons against Atheism, are obliged, to print those very Arguments, tho' never so secretly conveyed, as soon as they come to Your Knowledge. And there is no Divine but would take it as a high Reflection to be thought so disingenuous as either to conceal, or misrepresent, the least Part of any of the /1v/ Arguments of the Atheists he writes against; since he knows that no Arguments except fully and fairly stated can be fully and fairly confuted. But, however, to take away all Pretence of Cavilling I have, in the following Conference, mentioned every Thing of Moment our Divines say on this Occasion; which, if not sufficient to answer all the Objections of this Free-thinker, plainly shows how necessary it is that they should be communicated to such learned Persons as I have the Honour to write to. /2/

The following Dialogue, between one I call Credulous, and the other Incredulous, began after this Manner.

Credulous. I am glad, Sir, to see you after so long an Absence return to us in Health, and likewise to understand that you have improved your Fortunes; but yet I should be extremely sorry you had stirred from Home, if it has been, as I am told, at the Expence of your Religion.

Incredulous. You know, Sir, that before I left you I was as great a Bigot as my Neighbours; but observing through the many Countries I have travelled that the People of all Religions are alike confident of their being in the Right, and that they alike build their Confidence on their Ancestors being supposed too knowing to be imposed on themselves, and too honest to impose on their Children, therefore they concluded what they taught them of their own Knowledge must be true; and that after the Truth was once received, there could be no Danger of losing it, because they could not but ⟨at⟩ all Times be able to distinguish between those Doctrines, Rites & Ceremonies that were handed down to them from Age to Age by their immediate Predecessors, and such Innovations as the most cunning Impostors would endeavour to obtrude on them as the Tradition of their Ancestors. This being the sole Motive of my embracing the Religion of my native Country, I found I could no longer rely on what served for the Support of all other Religions, and that I am now unavoidably obliged to examine all Points afresh, and should be extremely pleased if you, who have bent your Studies this Way, would be so charitable as to assist me in this grand Design. /2v/

C. With all my Heart. But what is it that sticks with You?

I. I can't doubt of the Existence of myself or of other Bodies, or that there is an infinity of Void or Room; (for that is the Idea I have of Space) for Bodies to move in; but, to speak Truth, I want Proof for the Existence of any other Beings.

C. This is very strange, since if you will but attend to the Dictates of your own Reason you may be as sure of the Existence of an infinite supreme Being as of your own. But the better to convince you, I would know what it is which makes you doubt of a Truth so universally received.

I. If your infinite, supreme Being exists every where, there can be no Room for any Thing else to exist; if he exists only somewhere, he cannot be infinite.

C. There are two sorts of Beings; one that is extended, and solid or impenetrable, which we call Body or Matter. The other unextended, unsolid or penetrable; which we call Spirit or immaterial Being. Now tho' we allow that neither of these two sorts of Beings can be in the same Place with a Being of the same Kind, yet we contend that they may be in the same Place with a Being of a different Kind; and consequently that God, tho' an infinite Spirit, may be in the same Part of Space with Body.

I. That we may understand one another, I ask you whether by an extended Being you do not mean a Being which is in some Part of Space; by solid and impenetrable, a Being which can't get into the Place of another Being without driving that out first; and by unextended a Being which is in no Part of /3/ Space; and by unsolid or penetrable, a Being which can exist in the same Place with another Being.

C. I must own I have no other Idea of those Words; nor do I find that any one has explained them otherwise.

I. If so, you then suppose God to be in no Place by making him unextended; and then by saying, he is unsolid you suppose him to be in the same Place with Body; which is making him extended and unextended, in a Place and in no Place at the same Time.

C. The learned Doctor Moore leaves unextension out of his Definition of Spirit whether finite or infinite; as carrying a manifest Repugnancy to all Being: But then he says a Spirit has a different Extension from Body.[1]

I. But since he can mean nothing by Extension either of Body or Spirit, but occupying some Part of Space, his saying Spirit has a different Extension from Body, and yet is in the same Place with Body, is saying Spirit is in and not in the same Place with Body. So that to save one Contradiction he runs into another. But is he the only Divine who makes Extension necessary to all Being?

C. Doctor Samuel Clark, who has wrote the best for the Existence of an infinite unsolid Being, supposes Extension to belong to all Beings whatever.[2]

---

[1] For Henry More's definition of spirit, see his *Enchiridion metaphysicum* (London, 1671), partially translated in Joseph Glanvill, *Saducismus triumphatus* (London, 1681), pp. 97–180. For a modern edition and translation see *Henry More's Manual of Metaphysics: A Translation of the Enchiridion metaphysicum (1679) with an Introduction and Notes*, ed. Alexander Jacob (Hildesheim, 1995).

[2] A reference to Samuel Clarke's *A Demonstration of the Being and Attributes of God* (London, 1705), especially pp. 27–74. A modern edition of this and other writings by Clarke with a commentary by Ezio Vailati was published in the Cambridge Texts in the History of Philosophy in 1998.

I. Those two then must think that all besides themselves do, in Effect, deny the Being of God; and that the Idol they worship is in a literal Sense truely Nothing.

C. I desire you to give us your Reasons why ⟨you⟩ suppose that no /3v/ two Beings can exist in the same Place or Space.

I. It is as much repugnant to our Notion of Being that two Things can be in the same Place at the same Time, as that one Thing can be in two Places at once. Two Things can no more have one Extension, than one Thing can have two Extensions. The same Reason which makes it evident that whatever exists must exist in some Space, must likewise convince us that no two Things can exist in the same Space. All our Notions of Identity and Diversity depend on the Impossibility of two Things being in the same Place; and consequently by conceiving Body and Spirit in the same Place, we, as having Nothing to distinguish them by, can't but conceive them to be the same Thing.

C. I grant you that if they were Beings of the same Sort we could not conceive them but as one and the same Being; but here we distinguish by one being solid or impenetrable and the other unsolid or penetrable.

I. How can you say that Body is impenetrable when you suppose it penetrable by Spirit? If we can't suppose Spirit can be in the same Place with Body except Body be in the same Place with Spirit, we must own they are both unsolid or penetrable. To say that Spirit is unsolid or penetrable but that Body is not, is to say that Spirit can be in the same Place with Body, but that Body can't be in the same Place with Spirit. But if they own they are alike unsolid or penetrable, since that is all we mean by these Words, so that we can't suppose them in the same Place without /4/ supposing them Beings of the same Sort, or alike penetrable to one another, and yet at the same Time we own that none but Beings of a different Kind can be in the same Place, how can you say that Spirit is not solid and impenetrable as Body; since you suppose every Spirit is so to Beings of it's own Kind, and Body you make to be penetrable to Beings of a different Kind.

C. Why may not Body and Spirit exist together as well as Body and Space?

I. The Idea we have of Space is that it is a Void or Room infinitely extended for Body to move in, and Body could not exist at all if it did not exist where there was Room for it to exist. But if you do not consider Spirit as the Void or Room in which Body exists, but a Being which itself exists in Space you cannot but allow it to take up some Part of Space. Now if two Beings, each of which when separate take up two Feet of Space, can so penetrate each other as that both shall take up but the same Space, either one of the Beings by this Penetration must be annihilated; or else the Parts of Space must penetrate each other, which, I suppose, you will grant to be an Opinion infinitely absurd.

If God and Body could exist together because one is unsolid and the other solid, yet God could not be infinite, or every where, because he could not be in the same Place with other unsolid Beings, as Angels, Souls, &c. So that upon your own Supposition you must give up all your finite unsolid /4v/ Beings, or else your single infinite one.

C. I hope your Inclination to Atheism will not carry you as far as to deny that there may be Beings of which we have no Ideas, and consequently unextended as well as unsolid Beings.

I. There may be, no doubt, many finite Beings of which we have no particular Ideas, but only the general Ideas of Being extended and solid; but this can be no ground to affirm that a Being can exist without Extension; or that two Beings can have but one Extension; or that there can be more than one infinite Being of the same Kind.

The Immaterialists frame a God out of the inconsistent Ideas of unextension and unsolidity and then charge those with very gross Thoughts who will not come into these contradictory Notions. So, (since a Contradiction is Nothing,) they first frame a God out of Nothing in order to make him afterwards frame all Things so.

C. I can't bear your talking thus Blasphemously.

I. I thought you charitably designed my Conversion; but can that be done except you permit me to put my Objections as strongly as I can: This your Love of Truth obliges me to do, but if you are angry I am silent.

C. Go on; and let me hear what you have further to say.

I. With Submission then, if the Doctrine of the Schools of the Souls being all in the Whole, and all in this, and all in that Part of the Body be a Contradiction, why is it not so to suppose the Godhead to be fully and compleatly in every Part of Space? Why should you, who not only /5/ suppose that two Beings may be in the same Place, but that one Being may be in a million of Places at once, boggle at Transubstantiation, or any other Absurdity?

C. We can't say that God is partly in this, and partly in that Place, because an infinite Being has no Parts.

I. On the contrary an infinite Being must have an infinity of Parts; tho' those Parts, there being no Room to divide them in, must be indivisible. Space has an infinity of Parts, but we can't seperate them even in Imagination. These Difficulties, you know, extremely perplex your Divines, and therefore they are forced to say God, tho' he acts every where, yet himself is no where; at least no where included and no where excluded. That his Center is no where, and his Circumference every where, and an hundred such like Expressions. And the Schools, to avoid what they apprehended to be greater Difficulties, say that God is *purus actus, mera forma* [pure action, mere form]; that his Immensity is a Point, his Eternity an Instant. And tho' they all affirm that the Idea of God is so clear that they have Reason to conclude it innate (which if it was it must be the same in all Men) yet no two of them are consistent with one another or with themselves, even when they do not mention that inexhaustible Magazine of Inconsistencies, the Trinity. And when they have run the Round of Contradictions then they gravely tell us, with the Fathers, that a true Knowledge of God is a perfect Ignorance of him.[3]

C. There may be Difficulties relating to the Essence of God /5v/ which cant be perfectly cleared, tho' his Existence is most manifest.

I. I am so ignorant as not to be able to distinguish between the Essence and the Existence of God; and those Difficulties relating to his Essence, which you own can't be perfectly cleared, are, in a great Measure, the Reason of my doubting of his Existence.

C. Tis impossible to account for the Existence of Things without having recourse to a self-existent Being, who created all Things out of Nothing.

I. That Things were created ought not to be admitted without Proof; because the Presumption is that Things have always existed after the manner they do at present; or, in other Words, that there has been a perpetual Succession of Causes & Effects.
    They, therefore, who maintain that there has been but one Being from Eternity, ought to prove it. And this admits of no other Proof but that it is a Contradiction; or repugnant to the Nature of all but one unsolid Being to have always existed. If Things may continue to Eternity I can't see how it is repugnant to their Nature to suppose they have existed from Eternity. In the Idea of Substance is contained subsisting by itself; and what can now subsist by itself (since the Nature of Substance is always the same) might have always ‹so› subsisted. I am to learn from you how it comes to be natural for one Substance so to subsist, and unnatural to all others.

C. I'll prove it to you from your own Confession: For if Things, as you say, have always existed as they do at present, they must always have a Beginning; and Things /6/ which have had a Beginning could not be from Eternity.

I. If Things always were and always had a Beginning there must be an infinity of Beginnings, which Infinity had no Beginning. A Reason which proves too much, proves Nothing at all. And this of yours were it conclusive would destroy eternal Duration; because every Period of Duration must have a Beginning, and what had a Beginning could not be from Eternity.

C. If every particular Man had a Beginning, must not the whole Species made up of those Particulars have a Beginning? Can the Whole have endured longer than all it's Parts?

I. This Sophistry strikes likewise at eternal Duration, since every Part or Period of it must have a Beginning, and if every Part has a Beginning, must not the Whole,

---

[3] In fact, this is a quotation from Pierre Charron, *Les trois veritez* (1594). See R. H. Popkin, *The History of Scepticism from Erasmus to Spinoza* (Berkeley and Los Angeles, 1979), p. 58.

made up of Parts, have a Beginning? By the same Argument you may destroy Eternity, *a parte post* ['for the part after', i.e., that part of time following a given instant]; for if every Part of Duration must have an End, how can the Whole be Endless?[4]

And by the same Reasoning it is impossible any Thing can be infinite, since all the Parts of it are every one of them finite.

Your Argument in Truth only holds, where the Parts are finite in Number; but where there is an infinity of Parts the Thing must be infinite, because there is no coming to an End of its Parts, tho' each Part be finite. An Author whose Boylean Lectures are esteemed to contain the best Proofs for the Being of God to be infinite says that "all the mataphysical [sic] Difficulties which arise from applying the Measures and Relations of Things finite to what is infinite, and from supposing /6v/ Things finite to be the Parts of Things infinite (when they really are not so, but only as mathematical Points to Quantity which have no Proportion at all) ought to be esteemed vain and of no Force".[5] If so, did not all who wrote on this Subject before him attack the Eternity of Things from such Arguments as ought to be esteemed vain and of no force?

C. "Either there has", says he, "always existed one unchangeable and independent Being from whom all other Beings have received their Original, or else there has been an infinite Succession of dependent Beings produced from one another in an endless Progression, without any original Cause at all."

"If we consider such an infinite Progression as one entire endless Series of dependent Beings it is plain the whole Series can have no Cause from without of its Existence, because in it are supposed to be included all Things which ever were: And 'tis plain it can have no Reason within of it's Existence, because no one Being in this infinite Succession is supposed to be self-existent or necessary. An infinite Succession of meerly dependent Beings without any original independent Cause is a Series of Things which have no Cause of Existence either within itself or without. It's an express Contradiction and Impossibility: It's supposing Something to be caused, and yet in the whole, it's absolutely caused by Nothing."[6] Can you refuse to assent to so plain a Demonstration?

I. Tho' your Author says he does not argue from the supposed Impossibility of an infinite Succession clearly considered in itself, yet his Arguments alike destroy all infinite Succession, because /7/ all such Succession not only supposes eternal Changes, but that in every Change the Effect, tho' ever so necessary, depends for it's Existence on it's Cause. And the Men he pretends to confute[7] maintain that the Matter of the Universe is self-existent, and that there is no Room for Causes

---

[4] For a discussion of eternity using the same commonplace tag, see John Locke, *Essay Concerning Human Understanding*, II.xvii.10.
[5] This is a quotation from Clarke's *Demonstration*, p. 22.   [6] Ibid., pp. 23–6.
[7] On the title page of his book, Clarke states that it is written 'More Particularly in Answer to Mr Hobbs, Spinoza, And their Followers'.

and Effects but in the Changes which are made, and, as they say, necessarily in the Position of Matter. Besides he not only owns the Infinity of Time, but likewise asserts that an eternal Duration, notwithstanding the Difficulties of conceiving it, is actually past. Now, if Omnipotency itself can't hinder the former Minute, or any other Period of Time from perishing before the present begins, your Author must, in spite of his boasted Demonstration, own an infinite Succession of what he can't but allow to be changeable, dependent, and perishable. And since all that can be said against an eternal Succession of Causes and Effects is included in this Argument, I shall show you that it is made up of Nothing but inconsistent Expressions; since I can no more join the Ideas of Endless and Entire than coming and not coming to an End. One completes the Idea of the Thing I am thinking of and the other supposes that impossible. So the Idea of the Whole supposes Nothing can be added, and the Idea of infinite Progression is a continual Addition without a Possibility of coming to the Whole; or to conclude in my Mind all the Beings that ever were this is fixing a standing Rule to a growing Measure. Nor can I consider whether an infinite Progression has an original Cause without considering it as finite, or having a Beginning. So that the Strength of this Demonstration lies in joining such Terms to /7v/ infinite Progression as makes it finite, and then arguing against it as such.

C. But tho' this Argument should not amount to a Demonstration, I hope you will not deny the Possibility of God's creating the Universe out of Nothing.

I. You should have proved there was a God before you talked of his creating Power. But letting that pass I am content to examine with you the Possibility of Creation. And you can't suppose the Universe to be created, except you suppose Space, as well as the Things in it, to be created. But Space having no Bounds, or Ends, cannot be created, since Creation supposes a Thing must have an End, otherwise there is no coming to an End of Creating it; and consequently whatever is created must come infinitely short of being Infinite or Boundless.

Besides we are so far from being able to conceive Space to be made by any Being whatever, that we must conceive it in [the] Order of Nature before all other Beings, since we must suppose a Space for them to exist in before we can suppose them to exist. And consequently Space must be supposed necessary to the Existence of all other Things, tho' no other Thing be necessary to it's Existence, since that could not but always exist tho' nothing else existed. And if, as your Writers pretend to prove, there could be but one necessary Being, it could not be your supposed Deity, since there is another Being necessary to his Existence. Nor could he be Omnipotent, since there is another infinite Being over which he has no manner of Power. Nor could he be All-sufficient for his Creatures or Himself, since /8/ without Space neither He nor They could exist. And it is in It that all Things live, move, and have their Being.

C. Tho' Space be an uncreated, eternal, and absolute independent Being, yet, sure, the Things that exist in Space may be made out of Nothing.

I. This is wholly inconceivable; because making supposes Something in being out of which another Thing is made, and all Operation supposes Something to operate upon.

Our Idea of Nothing consists in the Negation of all Being, Faculty, and Capability whatsoever, and consequently we can never suppose Nothing to become Something; that would be to suppose it Nothing and Something at the same Time. And if of Nothing, Nothing can be predicated, we can't so much as predicate of it a Possibility of becoming Something. If there is no Medium between Something and Nothing, and Nothing can't be the Subject out of which any Thing is made, whatever is made must be made out of some pre-existent Thing. *Ex Nihilo, Nihil fit* [Nothing comes from nothing] was an undisputed Axiom with all the antient Philosophers; and even your own Bible is not so absurd as to say any Thing was made out of Nothing; but affirms a Chaos, upon which your God, in new modelling of Things worked very hard for six Days together.

C. The true Notion of Creation is not forming Something out of Nothing, as out of a material Cause, but only bringing some Being into Being.

I. But notwithstanding you vary your Phrase the same Difficulties occur; since this must be bringing some Being into /8v/ Being out of Something or out of Nothing; but out of Nothing, Nothing can be taken. Besides does not bringing a Being into Being first suppose a Being, and after that suppose it brought into Being. Which is the same Blunder as in a certain Play, where Adam is brought upon the Stage going in great Hast to be created.[8]

C. Why may not a Being be brought into Being as well as the Figure of a Being be brought into Being?

I. Whoever expresses himself after that odd manner can only mean, Figure being nothing but the Extremity of the Parts of a Being, changing the Position of those Parts, and consequently here is Nothing produced but Motion.

C. Why may not Being begin to be as well as Motion?

I. In one Case not only the Mover and Moved, but the Medium for Body to move in are in Being. But in the other Case, as there is an infinite Distance between the two Extremes of Being and no Being, so there is no Medium, (tho' the infinite Distance could be got over) to pass from one Extreme to another. There is Nothing distinct from Being or not Being; and consequently no Beginning to be, or Beginning not to be: Or, in other Words, no Creation or Annihilation. Since there is a greater Distance between Something and Nothing, than between any two Beings or Modes of Being, is it not very odd that those who affirm God can't give Matter a Power of Thinking, nor divide an immaterial Being should yet contend

---

[8] The reference is obscure, though it could be to Georgius Macropedius's *Adamus* (1552), which Pitcairne might have encountered when at Leiden in the early 1690s. I am indebted to Jan Bloemendal and Sarah Knight for their advice on this point.

that he can make Nothing become Something? Can there be so much greater Opposition between twice Two and Five than between Being and no /9/ Being, as should oblige them to say that God, tho' he can't make twice Two to be Five, yet he can make no Number Five?

C. That twice Two should be Five is a Contradiction; and 'tis allowed on all Hands that God can't do a Contradiction.

I. Why can't God do a Contradiction?

C. Because a Contradiction is Nothing, and Nothing cant be the Subject of Divine Power. For which Reason he can neither make a Contradiction true or false, or build any Thing upon it, or draw any Thing from it.

I. Had you owned this at first you had saved me the Trouble of proving the Impossibility of drawing all Things from Nothing. And after this Concession I shall only add that if God and Body so infinitely differ, that there is not, according to the general Opinion, so much as Extension in common between them, how can one be the Cause and the other the Effect? Is it not saying Body is uncaused since there is Nothing in the Effect that is in the Cause? Can any Thing be more evident than that a Being cant give what it has not to give? And which it has not at all it can't have to give, and consequently that God having no Solidity could not give it.

C. Tho' God has it not really, yet he has it virtually.

I. That is saying God has a Virtue to bestow on another, which he has not Himself. Contrary to that self-evident Axiom *Nil dat quod non habet* [Nothing can give what it does not have]. Is Solidity a Perfection or an Imperfection?

C. It's an Imperfection. Because God who is without it would /9v/ otherwise want a Perfection which Body has.

I. If it be an Imperfection then Space, which is an infinite unsolid Being would be infinitely more perfect than Body. Besides if Solidity were an Imperfection how could you suppose it produced by an all-perfect Being? Or an all-good Being be at infinite Pains to add Imperfection to Being?

They who are against the Eternity of the Universe must yet be obliged to suppose that the Images of Things have been eternally in the Mind of that unsolid Being who framed them according to those Patterns. But is it not more natural to believe the Things themselves always to have existed than that the Images of the Things were before, nay eternally before the Things themselves? And if the common Notion is true that whatever is in God is God, these Images by being eternally and necessarily in God must be God Himself. Which is making God to be composed of the Images of Things; a great Part of which you must own to be solid, since what is unsolid can't be the Image or bear any Resemblance to that which is solid. And if this be not setting up Image worship I know not what is.

C. If these Arguments prove Creation impossible I grant it must [be] that Body or Matter, as well as Space has eternally and necessarily existed; yet even then we must suppose a God to put Things in such Order and Disposition as they are at present.

I. This without good Proof will not be admitted, since it is more natural to suppose that all the Parts of the Universe have always existed after the same Manner as at present /10/ than that one unsolid Part of it (for it can't be pretended your God is the Whole) should not only so exist, but have such Power over the rest as to destroy that natural Manner of Existence they had from Eternity and model them anew. But this can't be true as to Space, which all allow to be immutable.

C. If we had no other Proof of a God yet the admirable Order the material World is in sufficiently demonstrates it was put into that Order by an all-wise, all-powerful Being.

I. Whatever necessarily exists, could not but be from Eternity in the most perfect Manner its Nature is capable of, and putting it out of this proper and natural State must be putting it into an improper and unnatural State, which we can't conceive any other than a State of Confusion and Disorder. And therefore the antient Philosophers, particularly Cicero, thought the Perfection of the World was a Proof of its Eternity.[9] And consequently all the Arguments of your Divines on this Head, tho' they must be allowed to expose that absurd Notion of the Worlds being made by Chance, don't in the least affect it's Eternity. And they who suppose a Being which they make to be infinitely more perfect than the World to have existed from Eternity, one would think could not maintain that the Perfection of the World was an Argument against it's Eternity.

They who affirm that one Part of the Universe (which they call God) has infinite Perfections above the others, build their Opinion on his self-existence; but if that be common to the whole it can give no one Part any Advantage over the rest. And where there are several Beings independent of one another /10v/ in respect of their Existence there is no Reason to suppose one should be able to do every Thing on the other; without being reciprocally submitted to their Actions. And this even your Divines take to be so evident that they conclude their Cause desperate if they do not, tho' in direct Opposition to their Scriptures suppose all Things made out of Nothing.

C. If Matter was eternal yet Motion could not be so, because Matter is not capable of moving itself, and consequently there must be a Being distinct from Matter to give it that Order and Disposition it has at present, infinitely different from what it was when it was an inanimate Lump.

I. Since Matter is allowed to be indifferent as to Motion or Rest, is it not as easy to conceive it to have been from Eternity in Motion as in Rest? And Men are hard put to it when they suppose an immoveable Being to be the Mover of all Things.

---

[9] The reference is to Cicero's *De natura deorum*, and perhaps particularly the arguments of Cotta: see Cicero, *The Nature of the Gods*, trans. P. G. Walsh (Oxford, 1997).

The same Reason which proves Space to be incapable of giving Motion to, or stopping the Motion of Body, must likewise prove any other (could there be any other) infinite unsolid Body to be so.

C. But may not God, tho' like Space, an infinite unsolid, or immaterial Being, have Perfections that Space has not?

I. Space being an uncaused, independent, infinite, unsolid Being, must have all the Perfections belonging to the Nature of such a Being; and yet That, for want of Solidity can only be an infinite Void for Body to move in, without being able anywise to affect it. So that could we suppose any other infinite Being of the same Nature, unsolid and immaterial, we could only suppose it another infinite Void for Body to move in. /11/

C. Is it not more easy to conceive that God may be the Cause of the Motion of Matter; than that Matter may be the Cause of it's own Motion?

I. They are both alike inconceiveable. Because we can no more conceive that Matter can be moved by an unsolid Being, call it God or what you please; than that Matter can be the Cause of it's own Motion. If Motion is eternal as well as Matter,[10] it can no more be said that Matter caused Motion than that it caused itself, but both would be alike uncaused. If Motion was an unnatural State of Matter, there must be some Being distinct from Matter continually pushing it, because without it Matter would necessarily revert to its primitive State. But since it is allowed that Matter in Motion will continue in that State 'till put out of it, this shows that Motion is no unnatural State of Matter. And there is good Reason to think that no Part of Matter is perfectly at rest. And I can't see how they who suppose Gravitation and Attraction to be inseperable from Matter can suppose Motion, or at least a Tendency to it, to be seperable from any Part of it. And the Presumption is that those vast Bodies which have been for so many Thousand Years in Motion, without any but periodical Changes, have moved thus from Eternity. /11v/

If there is no Creator, or first Mover, all Things could not but exist in the Manner they do; since there could have been Nothing to have hindered their Existence, or make them exist otherwise than they do. They must then exist as necessarily as your imagined First Cause is supposed to do.

C. If the Earth had been eternal those Mountains which now rear their Heads so high would by Degrees have been washed down. Nor would such Inequalities have appeared on the Face of our Globe. Besides the late Progress of Arts and

---

[10] At this point an asterisk in the text keys to a footnote at the bottom of the page:

The ingenious Mr Toland, in his "Letters to Serena" has indeavoured to prove that *Motion* is an *essential* Property of all Matter; and if it be allowed that Matter exists *necessarily*, it will follow that *Motion* must have been *eternal*.

The reference is to Toland's *Letters to Serena* (London, 1704), which Clarke had attacked in his *Demonstration*, pp. 46–7 (incorrectly citing his target as Letter 3 when it is fact Letter 5).

Sciences, and the small Part of Time our Histories take in seem to conclude against the Eternity of the Earth.

I. Were this Matter doubtful such Arguments would scarce turn the Scale; since there may have been many great Changes in this Globe of which we know Nothing. And, Mr Hook, not to mention others, in his Posthumous Works, takes Notice of several of these Changes; how some Places have risen and others subsided; and makes it highly probable that Mountains owe their Origen to Earthquakes.[11] And he, and others, give us undeniable Proofs of Shells of Fishes, and sometimes such as belong to very distant Countries, being found deep under Ground, in high Places, and at a great Distance from the Sea. And they tell us of Ships and Anchors so found. That Quantity of Earth which is daily carried into the Rivers, must, in length of Time, cause very great Changes; and consequently there can be no Argument drawn from the Inequality of the Surface of the Earth against it's Eternity. And if by such Changes as these, or by War, Famine, Pestilence, or any /12/ other Accidents, the Men in any Country are reduced to a very small Number, Arts and Sciences, Learning and Books are lost, and the few Inhabitants, who then must be upon an Equality, have enough to do to get Food for themselves by digging the Earth or hunting Wild Beasts. If in a great Part of the West Indies the Inhabitants are but few and barbarously ignorant; while in other Places, as in China for Instance, the People are numerous and Arts, and Sciences have there flourished; as appears by their undoubted Histories, even before Moses's Deluge, this, in all probability can't be owing to the different Nature of the People, since Mankind are every where alike, but to some such Accidents. Not but that Superstition has very much contributed to the Destruction of all true Knowledge, and Christians, as well as Mahometans, out of their great Zeal, have destroyed an Infinity of Old Authors; so that it is a very great Accident that we have any Remains of Antiquity; and that those few Greek and Roman Authors which are still extant had not been destroyed by that Bigottry which confounded the Rest. Tho' by your Reasoning there is no way to account for the Ignorance of the Inhabitants of Soldania,[12] and many other such Countries, but by supposing they were created a very long Time after the more polite Nations.

By this Time I hope you see my Scruples are not so ill founded as you imagined, but built on such Axioms as, did they not clash with your Superstition would be incontestable. As,

- No two Beings can be in the same Place, nor the same Being in different Places at once.
- That there can be no more than one infinite Being of the same Sort.
- That out of Nothing, Nothing can /12v/ be produced.

[11] The reference is to Robert Hooke's *Posthumous Works*, ed. Richard Waller (London, 1705), especially pp. 279–450.

[12] At this point an asterisk in the text keys to a footnote at the bottom of the page:

Soldania is in the Hottentot's Country.

This refers to a passage in Locke's *Essay*, I.iv.8, in which the inhabitants 'at the Bay of *Soldania*' (Saldanha Bay in South Africa) were seen as exemplifying the state of nature.

- That no Being can give to another neither Motion, nor Solidity, or any Thing else which itself has not.
- That the Images of Things do not exist before the Things whose Images they are.

Tho' you have omitted Nothing that can be said for your Cause, your Notions are so sophistical that the very explaining the Terms under which they are couched sufficiently shows their Inconsistency; and therefore it is no Wonder you have Recourse to the grand Support of all Absurdities, Force, and make it almost every where Death to speak against your Opinion. Tho' of all the Arguments urged for the support of it, there is not one, except that lately written which I have considered, but what is given up by some of your own Writers.[13]

C. You triumph before Victory; and tho' you have artfully enough evaded what I have already urged for your Information, yet I do not doubt to produce such Arguments to you from Providence, from the Government of the World, and from the Impossibility of Matters thinking as shall make you ashamed of your Superstition.

I. You know I have an Ear always open to Reason; and as I heartily thank you for the Favour of this Conference, so I shall be very glad to hear what you have to say toMorrow on these Heads.

Finis.

---

[13] The meaning of the text is slightly obscure at this point, but it evidently alludes back to matters already dealt with.

CHAPTER 8

The Trial of Tinkler Ducket
Atheism and Libertinism in Eighteenth-Century England[*]

Tinkler Ducket was expelled from the University of Cambridge for atheism and immorality after a lengthy trial in the early months of 1739. A Fellow of Gonville and Caius College, Ducket had been ordained deacon in 1733 and priest in 1735, and was curate of Little Horkesley in Essex. His misdemeanours will become apparent in this chapter from the extensive documentation of the affair that survives, which has been frequently glanced at in the secondary literature but never properly written up.[1] Perhaps the most authoritative account of Ducket hitherto is the entry devoted to him by John Stephens in the *Dictionary of Eighteenth-Century British Philosophers* (1999), subsequently incorporated into *The Continuum Encylopedia of British Philosophy* (2006), which declared that Ducket was essentially 'a bad boy'.[2] Stephens's verdict may well be correct, as we will see, but there is nevertheless a good deal to be learned from looking at the case in detail, in terms partly of the incidence and nature of casual or not so casual irreligion among students and others in the early eighteenth century, and partly of the reaction to it by the powers that be, who in turn sensationalised and trivialised it in ways that will become

[*] I am grateful to Peter Anstey, Stephen Brogan, Geoffrey Cantor, Mark Goldie and Mark Statham for their helpful comments on a draft of this chapter. Jacqueline Cox kindly assisted me with the Ducket material in the university archives at Cambridge.
[1] Margaret C. Jacob, *The Radical Enlightenment: Pantheists, Freemasons and Republicans* (London, 1981), p. 174; John Gascoigne, *Cambridge in the Age of the Enlightenment* (Cambridge, 1989), pp. 135–6, 140; Wayne Hudson, *Enlightenment and Modernity: The English Deists and Reform* (London, 2009), p. 47; Jeffrey R. Wigelsworth, *Deism in Enlightenment England: Theology, Politics, and Newtonian Public Science* (Manchester, 2009), pp. 1–2; Robert G. Ingram, *Reformation without End: Religion, Politics and the Past in Post-Revolutionary England* (Manchester, 2018), pp. 25–7 (who cites many of the sources deployed here, though without commenting on their intricacies and discrepancies).
[2] John Stephens, 'Tinkler Ducket (*c.* 1711–*c.* 1774)', in *The Dictionary of Eighteenth-Century British Philosophers*, ed. John W. Yolton, John Valdimir Price and John Stephens, 2 vols (Bristol, 1999), I, 295–6, reprinted in *The Continuum Encyclopedia of British Philosophy*, ed. Anthony Grayling, Andrew Pyle and Naomi Goulder, 4 vols (London, 2006), II, 899.

apparent in the course of this chapter. Here, an account will be given of the various records of Ducket's trial that exist, collating their content and exploring the significance of the discrepancies between them.[3] Then, we may draw some broader conclusions about the overall significance of the case.

It was, in fact, a strangely protracted affair, since the key document that incriminated Ducket was a letter written four years earlier than it actually came to light. This was dated 3 October 1734 and was addressed to another Fellow of Caius, Stephen Gibbs. In it, Ducket gloried in having reached 'the Top, the *ne plus ultra*', of atheism. Yet it was only in January 1739 that the letter actually materialised, having been dropped in the courtyard at Caius, obviously with malicious intent – though it is not clear by whom – where it was picked up by James Burrough, esquire-bedell and later Master of the college.[4] It was this belated discovery that triggered the proceedings against Ducket over the next three months with which we will be concerned in this chapter.

This is arguably significant in itself for suggesting that, although we rarely hear about views like Ducket's, they were not uncommon – that, as John Gascoigne has suggested in connection with this and a comparable Oxford case, 'there were other dons who shared their principles but not their misfortune in being publicly exposed'.[5] That this was so is certainly suggested by the prime Oxford incident to which Gascoigne there alludes, that of Nicholas Stevens, which had occurred in 1728. This only came to light due to the suicide of one of those involved in it, Robert Jennens, a relative by marriage of the High Church Earl of Aylesford, which obviously raised the profile of the case.[6] Letters from Stevens were discovered in Jennens's desk and subsequently published as *Two Letters from a Deist to his Friend, Concerning the Truth and Propagation of Deism, In Opposition to*

---

[3] For convenience, these are listed in a separate Appendix.

[4] Throughout this paper, identifications of Cambridge figures have been verified by the use of J. and J. A. Venn, *Biographical History of Gonville and Caius College*, 2 vols (Cambridge, 1898) and *Alumni Cantabrigienses* [to 1751], 4 vols (Cambridge, 1922–7).

[5] Gascoigne, *Cambridge*, p. 136.

[6] For the best account of the case see V. H. H. Green, 'Religion in the Colleges 1715–1800', in *The History of the University of Oxford*, vol. 5, ed. L. S. Sutherland and L. G. Mitchell (Oxford, 1986), pp. 425–67 (pp. 435–7). See also W. R. Ward, *Georgian Oxford: University Politics in the Eighteenth Century* (Oxford, 1958), pp. 145–6. Both depend heavily on *H. M. C. Portland*, VII, 467–70. For reference to the case in the Chancellor's Court papers see Bodleian CC Papers 1728/101:1–3; see also the Court Act Book, Bodleian Hyp/A/57, fol. 107.

Christianity, with Remarks by the Revd. Samuel Wesley, which make interesting, if not very lucid, reading.[7]

We need to dwell for a moment on the Oxford case, because the letters intriguingly open by boasting their author's success in making converts to the cause of heterodoxy through the use of the copy of Pierre Bayle's *Dictionary* in the Bodleian Library. It continues with a rather convoluted advocacy of Bangorianism as an alternative to overt irreligion – an allusion to the views of Benjamin Hoadly, Bishop of Bangor, who downplayed the sacerdotal role of the church – advocating a degree of subterfuge which reduced the commentator on the pamphlet, Samuel Wesley, to paroxysms of rage. It also ranges more widely, modishly comparing metaphysical propositions 'upon the *Newtonian* scheme' with 'the *Berkleian*': indeed, there were those who blamed an undue preoccupation with mathematics for the heterodoxy that is in evidence in the whole affair.[8] On the other hand, the pamphlet also goes on to boast of converting a colleague to irreligion as a cure for the uneasiness caused 'when pleasure and Christianity come in competition', thus suggesting an element of the moral misdemeanour that also arose in the Ducket case.[9] When confronted with the accusations against him, Stevens initially fainted; subsequently he abandoned Oxford and took a medical degree at Leiden.[10] The Oxford establishment seems to have shown little interest in the content of his views. Instead, the chief controversy that arose in connection with the episode concerned the issuing of a 'Programma' urging teachers to take more care over the reading that they prescribed to their charges, which was contested by those who resented this central interference in the pastoral responsibilities of college tutors.[11]

Perhaps the most interesting aspect of the affair concerned the prior affiliations of those involved in it, since it turned out that the students in question were not extreme Whigs, as might have been expected from

---

[7] *Two Letters from a Deist to his Friend, Concerning the Truth and Propagation of Deism, In Opposition to Christianity, with Remarks* (London, 1730).

[8] Ibid., esp. pp. 1, 2–4, 13; Letter of R. Downes, 24 January 1738/9, in Joseph Spence, *Anecdotes, Observations and Characters, of Books and Men*, ed. Samuel Weller Singer (London, 1820), pp. 386–8.

[9] *Two Letters*, p. 19.

[10] *H. M. C. Portland*, VII, 468; R. W. Innes Smith, *English-Speaking Students of Medicine at the University of Leyden* (Edinburgh, 1932), p. 223.

[11] For the Programma dated 2 December 1728, see Bodleian GA Oxon b. 111, fol. 39. For the controversy over it, see *H. M. C. Portland*, VII, 469–70; Thomas Hearne, *Remarks and Collections*, ed. C. E. Doble, D. W. Rannie and H. E. Salter, 11 vols (Oxford, 1885–1921), X, 71, 86; and Thomas Tanner to Edmund Gibson, 26 November 1728, University of St Andrews Library Special Collections msBX5199.G6 (ms 5248).

contemporary polemics. On the contrary, the unfortunate suicide, Jennens, was said to be '*high Church even to Superstition*', while Stevens himself was 'once so thorough a Tory or even Jacobite, that he sometime kept back from taking his degree on account of dissatisfaction about taking the oaths'.[12] By contrast, we know relatively little about the former affiliations of Ducket and his Cambridge peers, except for their evident enthusiasm for *The Craftsman* – they were said to be 'strenuous Patriots' – thus aligning them with the ethos of Bolingbroke and others against Walpole and the Robinocracy.[13] Indeed, the original incriminating letter of 1734 contained a postscript referring to a response to 'the Ministerial Writers' which inspired 'Caleb D'Anvers' (the fictional editor of *The Craftsman*) to a riposte denying knowledge of the author involved, Samuel Strutt; this led to a further, rather inconclusive exchange of letters in *The Gentleman's Magazine* in April and May 1739, after the Ducket affair had been concluded, which is chiefly significant for attempting to distance *The Craftsman* itself from the irreligious views that Ducket had expressed.[14] However, at this point we are getting slightly ahead of ourselves, so let us revert to the incriminating letter itself.

Various copies of this survive, despite the fact that, when confronted with it in January 1739, Ducket 'did by force and violence seize the said scandalous paper or Letter and tear the same into peices with intent utterly to destroy the same'.[15] It was addressed to Stephen Gibbs at Wymondham in Norfolk, where he was evidently vacationing (his father was a farmer there), and it opened with pleasantries about the receipt of a guinea and of partridges. It then went on to refer to a Caius student and mutual friend, Robert Pate, who had gone incognito to London – though it was uncertain 'when he'll have Power to break from the Arms of his Charmer'. However,

[12] Tanner to Gibson, 26 November 1728.

[13] See the classic study by Isaac Kramnick, *Bolingbroke and His Circle: The Politics of Nostalgia in the Age of Walpole* (Ithaca, 1968). For the quotation, see Tunstall to the Earl of Oxford, 3 February 1739, BL Add. MS 4253, fol. 88.

[14] The Ducket letter was originally published in *The Daily Gazetteer*, no. 1187 (11 April 1739), accompanied by a hostile comment by 'A. B.' The riposte from D'Anvers, dated 11 April 1739, is printed in *The Gentleman's Magazine*, 9 (1739), p. 198. Then, *The Gentleman's Magazine* published the Ducket letter in ibid., p. 203, referring to D'Anvers' response, to which a further response by 'A. B.' appeared in ibid., pp. 203–4 (reprinted from *The Daily Advertiser*, 21 April 1739), with a further reply from D'Anvers in ibid., p. 249 (reprinted from *The Craftsman*, no. 669, 5 May 1739). Strutt, who died in 1737, is mentioned in various of the letters. For his heterodox dealings in London circles, see also *Selections from the Journals and Papers of John Byrom*, ed. Henri Talon (London, 1950), pp. 113–14, 127–8 (and for his death, ibid., p. 172).

[15] This is stated in the 'Articles' against Ducket, V.C. Ct. 1.99 (5–6). The defaced original letter evidently survives as ibid., no. 7. See Appendix, no. 1.

his place was being taken at 'the Tunns today' by Edward Votier, another student, 'who is as great a Heroe in the Cause of Truth'. Ducket also wished well to a further mutual friend, Will Bale. Then, however, the letter contains the incriminating passage which is worth quoting at length:

> As to any farther Progress in Atheism, I was arriv'd at the Top, the *ne plus ultra*, before I enjoy'd the Beatific Vision (the Night I was born by the Spirit from you)[16] being fix'd & immoveable in the Knowledge of the Truth, to which I attain'd by means of that infallible Guide the *Philosophical Enquiry*; & I'm glad to hear, what I did not at all doubt of, that it wou'd equally enlighten your Understanding; & am perswaded that you see the necessary Connection between every Proposition, & consequently that the Points in Debate are strictly demonstrated. If any material Objections should arise, which is barely a possible Supposition, I beg you wou'd consult me, or some other able Minister of the Word of Truth, to the quieting of your Conscience, & avoiding all Scruple & Doubt.

> I was inexpressably happy with the most adorable & omniscient Father Strutt, his Brother, Whitehead, Windle, &c. compleatly fulfilling the Scene propos'd in his Letter.

The letter then outlines various travels around East Anglia on Ducket's part over the previous few days, prior to his being 'oblig'd to return to College to pray'. He added: 'I've sent you one Song as a Taste of our Mirth';[17] he also stated that he had received a letter from the Master of the college, obliging him to return to Little Horkesley, Essex, where he was curate, next Tuesday, and how he hoped to see Gibbs at the college 'about the 5th of November'. There was then the postscript about *The Craftsman* that has already been referred to, which additionally refers to female acquaintances of the two men. However, let us deal with the main content of the quoted passage.

---

[16] Tunstall, in his letter to Oxford of 18 March 1739 (BL Add. MS 4253, fol. 93v), explained that this alluded to Strutt's horse, which was called the Holy Ghost. In the copy of the letter in *The Daily Gazetteer* 'by' appears as 'in' in this passage, and there are other very minor discrepancies between the different versions of the text which have not been recorded here. It is perhaps worth noting, however, that in the copy of the letter made by 'C. T.' (perhaps Charles Tuck, Bursar of Caius) and dated 'about the 5th or 6th of Jan: 1738[/9]' in V.C. Ct. 1.99 (8) and other manuscript versions derived from it, the words 'As to' are followed by a blank space of the length of a word and a descender: there is a hole in the original (V.C. Ct. 1.99 (7)) at this point and, since the missing word or words cannot be reconstructed, it seems best to ignore them.

[17] In forwarding a copy of the letter to Oxford, James Tunstall noted of this song that it was 'too blasphemous to be inserted': BL Add. MS 4253, fol. 93v. In a subsequent letter dated 6 May, he reported on his further enquiries concerning it: 'The truth is, there are in it such abundancy of blasphemy & such a scarcity of Wit, that people either have not thought it worth their while to procure it, or are ashamed to remember it', though he apparently did include a 'specimen' to give an idea of its 'profaneness' (fols 96v–7).

The 'infallible Guide' to which Ducket refers is *A Philosophical Enquiry into the Physical Spring of Human Actions, and the Immediate Cause of Thinking*, published anonymously in 1732 but generally attributed to the little-known writer Samuel Strutt, of the Inner Temple. Strutt had earlier written *A Defence of the Late Learned Dr Clarke's Notion of Natural Liberty: In Answer to Three Letters Wrote by him to a Gentleman at the University of Cambridge, on the Side of Necessity* (1730), in which his name appeared on the title page. We do not need to go into detail about these pamphlets and their context here – a useful account of them has been provided by John Yolton – but the essential thrust of the *Philosophical Enquiry* was materialistic and determinist, explicitly influenced by such authors as John Toland and Anthony Collins, and it was clearly for this that it appealed to Ducket.[18] It was presumably for the same reason that it appealed to William Windle, another student at Caius who was in fact forced to publish *An Enquiry into the Immateriality of Thinking Substances, Human Liberty, and the Original of Motion* in 1738 to vindicate himself from holding views like Strutt's – in other words, prior to Ducket's trial, and suggesting that unease about such ideas already existed, though it is not otherwise evidenced.[19] The other main figure referred to in the letter was Paul Whitehead, a notorious litterateur who wrote oppositionist satires and was later secretary to the infamous Hell-Fire Club.[20] No wonder Ducket wanted to destroy the document!

We then move to the proceedings against Ducket by a court comprising the Vice-Chancellor and the heads of houses of the university, which were set in train by a ponderous set of ten 'Articles'.[21] These are wordy and legalistic, evidently in an attempt to leave no loopholes in establishing the

[18] John W. Yolton, *Thinking Matter: Materialism in Eighteenth-Century Britain* (Oxford, 1984), ch. 7. On p. 151, n. 20, Yolton expresses slight doubt as to Strutt's authorship of the 1732 treatise, but this is repeatedly confirmed in the documents relating to the Ducket case.

[19] Windle, *Enquiry into the Immateriality of Thinking Substances, Human Liberty, and the Original of Motion* (London, 1738). For comments on the work see Yolton, *Thinking Matter*, pp. 42, 151 n. 21.

[20] See *ODNB*; Geoffey Ashe, *The Hell-Fire Clubs: A History of Anti-Morality*, revised ed. (Stroud, 2000), esp. pp. 121–4; Evelyn Lord, *The Hell-Fire Clubs: Sex, Satanism and Secret Societies* (New Haven and London, 2008), esp. pp. 103–4. The letter also refers to Strutt's brother, on whom see this chapter, n. 40.

[21] V.C. Ct. 1.99 (5–6). This is one of the extant ancillary documents relating to the case, whereas the original *acta curiae* for 1739 do not survive (see Appendix, no. 1). The Vice-Chancellor's court was responsible for discipline in the university: see John Twigg, *The University of Cambridge and the English Revolution, 1625–88* (Woodbridge, 1990), p. 5. The ancillary documents also include various formal summons to Ducket and to two witnesses, Stephen Gibbs (the recipient of the 1734 letter) and John Scotman, another Fellow of Caius, who does not otherwise appear in the proceedings (1–4).

fact of Ducket's 'being and declaring yourself an Atheist and your endeavouring to seduce others into many wicked and erroneous Opinions'; that this was in contravention of the objectives of the University of Cambridge of which he was a member; and that it was therefore appropriate for him to receive due punishment for his misdemeanour.[22] The promoter was Thomas Eglington, a Fellow of Caius, and proceedings opened on 21 February 1739 under the auspices of the deputy Vice-Chancellor, the astronomer Roger Long, Master of Pembroke, when Ducket was not present, and matters were therefore deferred until 9 March. On that occasion, now in the presence of the Vice-Chancellor, John Whalley, Master of Peterhouse, the accused acknowledged authorship of the offending letter and his status as a member of the university, hence making him subject to the jurisdiction of the court, but denied the charge of atheism and its propagation.[23]

However, things then took a somewhat different turn with the introduction as a witness against Ducket of Mary Richards, a widow of Ewell Hall, near Kelvedon, Essex. It appears that, after becoming acquainted with her about two and half years earlier, Ducket had made sexual advances to her in her bedchamber, calling her 'his pretty little mistress' and declaring that 'That was the time to make him happy'. When she objected 'That such a Compliance would be criminal without Matrimony; & render her liable to Damnation', he replied

> that Matrimony was Priestcraft, & the Invention of Men in Power, however highly dignified; that she made a mere Bugbear of God to think that he wou'd punish his Creatures for gratifying the Passions, he had implanted in them: that instead of a Sin, her Compliance would be the highest Act of Benevolence.

What is more, if she was worried about getting pregnant, he had 'a Sovereign Remedy which were Drops to avoid Child-bearing'. A letter from Ducket to Mrs Richards was produced in which he asserted 'the Reasonableness of my Request', urging her 'by the strongest Dictates of Reason & Nature to grant it' due to 'the Sincerity of my Passion for you'.

---

[22] It is presumably this that explains why long strings of months and years are given as the parameters of the offences committed.

[23] The narrative that follows is taken from the various copies of the lost *acta curiae* relating to the case: see Appendix. There are some minor discrepancies between these which in general it is has not seemed worth itemising: for instance, apart from the disagreement between them as to whether Ducket said 'Marriage was Priestcraft' or 'only Priestcraft', as given by all the sources (nos 2–6) except Cole and its derivatives (nos 7–9), the latter omit the phrase about 'his pretty little mistress'.

Indeed, he went on: 'These are selfevident Truths, therefore whatever Doctrines we may meet with contrary to them, we cannot but be certain are the Forgeries of crafty & designing Villains, however dignify'd by Authority'.[24]

This was a bit of a bombshell, and it was clearly contrived by the authorities. Ducket was forced to admit that he had indeed stated that 'Matrimony was Priestcraft', though he had not used the more provocative phrase, 'only Priestcraft', as averred in many reports on the case. Moreover, although under examination he made 'some impertinent Interrogatories' concerning Mrs Richards's evidence, it was recorded that she 'pertinently answered' them. Clearly, someone had seen that the best way to trap Ducket and divest him of any public sympathy was to compound his guilt by condemning him of actual immorality. Moreover, as the Cambridge antiquary, Thomas Baker, presciently noted at the time, in this the authorities were following a precedent effectively established by an earlier Cambridge atheism case, that of Daniel Scargill, which had occurred in 1668.[25] As we saw in Chapter 4, Scargill, like Ducket half a century later, had clearly been something of a loose cannon, airing dangerously hetero-dox views in public orations at the university.[26] But, as Jon Parkin has so effectively demonstrated, what most damaged him was the claim that he was not only a devotee of Hobbes but also a libertine – that 'agreeably unto which principles and positions' he had 'lived in great licentiousness, swearing rashly, drinking intemperately, boasting myself insolently, cor-rupting others by my pernicious principles and example, to the high Dishonour of God, the Reproach of the University, the Scandal of Christianity, and the just offence of mankind' – a claim that was dissem-inated through the *Recantation* of his views that was published and given wide circulation.[27] Parkin demonstrates how this was a propaganda coup for the orthodox, which was reinforced in the 1670s by the notorious case of the Earl of Rochester, so that the association of Hobbesianism and libertinism became commonplace.[28] It should be added that, though there were rumours of sexual impropriety on Scargill's part, this was nothing to

---

[24] For the letter, see V.C. Ct. 1.99 (18–19) and Tunstall to Oxford, 11 March 1739, BL Add. MS 4253, fols 91v–2. In the former, 'selfevident' is preceded by 'Truths', deleted, and 'Villains' is preceded by 'men', deleted.

[25] Tunstall to Oxford, 23 January, 3 February 1739, BL Add. MS 4253, fols 86v, 87v.

[26] See pp. 77–8.

[27] *The Recantation of Daniel Scargill, Publickly Made before the University of Cambridge, in Great St Maries, July 25, 1669* (Cambridge, 1669), pp. 3–4.

[28] Above, p. 82.

the overt sexual element that entered into the Ducket case. He might well have seemed finished.

In fact, however, Ducket proceeded to indulge in a careful defence of himself, taking the form of 'a premeditated Speech, which he spoke with a good Grace & great Intrepidity'. It is perhaps symptomatic of the way in which opinion on the case was moving in the light of the allegations of Mary Richards that many accounts of the trial simply ignore this interesting oration, while we learn from one commentator on the affair, James Tunstall, Fellow of St John's and later Public Orator to the university, that Ducket's invocation of 'benevolence', both in his speech and in his alleged approach to Mrs Richards, 'made some mirth in the Court'. Tunstall noted of the speech: 'It is allowed to have been well composed, tho' the Topics were injudiciously selected, & shewed him to be full as much, if not more, concerned to assert the innocency of his former Error, as the sincerity of his Conversion'.[29] More than one version of it survive, which differ slightly, evidently due to being taken down verbatim: the differences are mainly in the order in which the components appear, the content being much the same, so a reconstruction will be attempted.[30]

First, Ducket made the striking claim 'That Reason was the sovereign Guide of all Mankind; that Freedom of Thought, & private Judgement were the Right of every one'. To support this he quoted John Locke – almost certainly alluding to Locke's famous claim in the chapter on enthusiasm added to the fourth edition of the *Essay*, that 'Reason must be our last Judge and Guide in every Thing' – together with a further figure, identified in one version of the speech as the latitudinarian divine, Gilbert Burnet, and in another as Joseph Butler, author of *The Analogy of Religion, Natural and Revealed, to the Constitution and Course of Nature* (1736), whom Ducket was indeed to cite later.[31] He continued: 'That if Reason leads to Atheism, there is as much Virtue in that as in the contrary persuasion, provided there has

---

[29] Tunstall to Oxford, 11 March 1739, BL Add. MS 4253, fols 89v–90, 92v (including fol. 89v for the fact that, since the speech was pre-prepared, it 'therefore did not enter into the particulars of the Evidence').

[30] See Appendix for the versions recorded by Grey (no. 5), Cole (nos 7–9) and Tunstall (no. 6): the latter appears to be independent of the Grey/Cole one.

[31] Locke, *Essay Concerning Human Understanding*, IV. xix. 14. For the other figure involved, Cole and its derivatives (Appendix, nos 7–9) have 'Bp Burnet' (and are quoted for this in Gascoigne, *Cambridge*, p. 135) whereas Grey (no. 5: Cambridge U.L. Ee.6.43, fol. 12v) has 'Butler'; Tunstall (no. 6) cites no authority at this point. It is unclear what passage in Burnet's voluminous writings Ducket might have had in mind, assuming that his name is correctly given: for Butler, see n. 33.

been the same Impartiality in the Inquiry. That for his part he was not sensible, that he had not used that Impartiality; & possibly he might have believed more, had he reasoned less.' He then turned to the issue of morality:

> That whereas some had thought, that Atheism destroyed all moral Obligations, he thought them mistaken: since an Atheist might be influenced by the innate principle of Benevolence, a moral sense, & the Relation of things; & himself had felt the force of these principles, having all along entertained a great Veneration for & an high Opinion of the Excellency of Virtue. That tho' Atheism inferred Fatality & Materialism; yet that these were consistent with the Ideas of Morality: for which he cited some passages of Bishop Butler's Book *Analogy* &c.[32]

It should perhaps be added that Ducket had a valid point – that Butler in his *Analogy* did indeed raise issues to do with the relative autonomy of moral principles in relation to theistic ones, also arguing for the paramountcy of reason along the lines that Ducket indicated. It is additionally interesting that Ducket echoes Butler's language in parts of his book in the use of such terms as 'Benevolence', 'Virtue' and 'Fatalism'.[33] Indeed, it could be argued that Ducket had rightly picked up on what has sometimes been called the 'atheological' tendency in Butler's thought, itself stemming from the claims for a natural morality independent of Revelation that had earlier been put forward by the Earl of Shaftesbury in his *Inquiry Concerning Virtue or Merit* (1699) and, before him, by Pierre Bayle.[34]

One account of the speech then goes on to note that Ducket 'complained of a certain Bishop, (who is supposed to be Dr Gooch) for telling

---

[32] This is from Tunstall's version: BL Add. MS 4253, fol. 90 (Appendix, no. 6); Grey and Cole and its derivatives (nos 5, 7–9) have much the same content, though the point about how 'if he had examined less, he had believed more' appears later in the speech. In a subsequent passage Tunstall added that in his speech Ducket 'attempted to shew, that Atheism did not leave us destitute of moral principles, since the operations of this affection, the sense of the Beauty of Virtue, & the Perception of the Relations of things, might nevertheless continue, the Influence of which principles he had himself experienced, when he had the misfortune to be in that state': ibid., fol. 92v.

[33] See Joseph Butler, *The Analogy of Religion* (London, 1736). For discussions of the work that indicate the ambivalence in Butler's approach that would have appealed to Ducket, see the classic account by Sir Leslie Stephen, *History of English Thought in the Eighteenth Century*, 3rd ed., 2 vols (London, 1902), I, ch. 5, and, more recently, *Joseph Butler's Moral and Religious Thought: Tercentenary Essays*, ed. Christopher Cunliffe (Oxford, 1992); Isabel Rivers, *Reason, Grace, and Sentiment: A Study of the Language of Religion and Ethics in England, 1660–1780*, 2 vols (Cambridge, 1991–2000), II, ch. 3, esp. pp. 215–26; and Lori Branch, 'Bishop Butler', in *The Oxford Handbook of English Literature and Theology*, ed. Andrew Hass, David Jasper and Elisabeth Jay (Oxford, 2009), pp. 590–606.

[34] See Thomas Dixon, *From Passions to Emotions: The Creation of a Secular Psychological Category* (Cambridge, 2003), p. 81 and elsewhere in ch. 3. See also this volume, pp. 11–12.

him, "That atheistical Principles must necessarily proceed from a depraved Will'": this evidently oral intervention by Thomas Gooch, the then Master of Caius, is not otherwise documented.[35] Ducket also 'corrected Mr Addison for affirming, "That Atheists ought to be whipt out of Society"', an allusion to a passage in *The Tatler* for 24 December 1709, in which, in a disquisition about irreligion, the famous essayist objected especially to 'the grave Disputant, that reads and writes, and spends all his Time in convincing himself and the World, that he is no better than a Brute, [who] ought to be whipped out of a Government, as a Blot to a civil Society, and a Defamer of Mankind'.[36]

Ducket then expressed remorse, claiming

> That he had not long been in the Atheistic Persuasion before he became convinced of the necessity of Religion both to the Good of the Public & the Comfort of every private person; since nothing could be more melancholy than the Horror of Insensibility & the prospect of forlorn Nature, subject to Chance & without the Direction of Wisdom. That he was likewise soon persuaded of his Error, & firmly believed the Truth of Religion, & Christianity in particular, being of Opinion, that there can be no Medium between a Christian & an Atheist.[37]

He added that: 'For his own Love of Virtue, & strong Attachment to it, during the dark Scene of his Atheism, he appeals to all his Friends who conversed with him, & to his Exercises in the Public Schools, if (as he modestly express'd himself) "they were not long since justly forgotten".'[38] He ended by asserting:

> That the Sincerity of his Professions, which he so solemnly made should not be called in question, and lastly he hoped, that the Punishment he had already undergone by the Usage he had met with, the Loss of the good Opinion of others, & his appearing in that place, might be esteemed sufficient.[39]

---

[35] This appears only in the Grey/Cole version of the speech and the derivatives of the latter (Appendix, nos 5, 7–9), and not the Tunstall one (no. 6). For Gooch, see *ODNB* – his published output was limited to a handful of conventional sermons.

[36] *The Tatler*, ed. D. F. Bond, 3 vols (Oxford, 1987), II, 170.

[37] BL Add. MS 4253, fol. 90v (Appendix, no. 6); there is a related passage in the Grey/Cole version and the derivatives of the latter (Appendix, nos 5, 7–9). Ducket here possibly echoes similar sentiments expressed by Addison in *The Spectator*, ed. D. F. Bond, 5 vols (Oxford, 1965), III, 431.

[38] This is from the Grey/Cole version and the derivatives of the latter (Appendix, nos 5, 7–9).

[39] This reverts to Tunstall's version (no. 6), though Grey/Cole and the derivatives of the latter have a comparable passage.

All this was apparently 'mixed now & then with some sharp Reflections upon his Prosecutors', which can hardly have helped his case, and neither did the witnesses who were now called, since, although attestations were provided by William Windle and Stephen Gibbs to the effect that Ducket had changed his mind about the merits of Strutt's materialist arguments, Charles Tuck, Bursar of Caius, rather complicated matters by deposing that, when Gibbs had been shown the letter of October 1734, Gibbs 'said that he knew the Defendant to be an Atheist, and being asked why he never attempted to reclaim the Defendant answered "I thought the Defendant to be too tenacious of his Principles to be disputed with"'. This conversation had taken place the previous January, when the letter had come to light. Ducket was then allowed to call in 'Jonathan May of Colchester Peruque-Maker [who] being sworn, deposeth, That he knows the Defendant, and that he knows nothing amiss of him in regard to his Character, or heard any thing'. It was agreed that other witnesses should be summoned for a further meeting of the court a week later, though Ducket was dissuaded from calling the incendiary figure of Whitehead and others. The proceedings were then adjourned for a week.[40]

Come 16 March, the witnesses were called as planned, including Robert Pate, MA, although an objection was made to his 'Incapacity & Incompetency' due to his role in the affair. Pate 'deposeth that He has known the Defendant 12 Years, that He has often heard Him discourse against the being of a God about 5 years ago – That the Defendant told Him, that he was led into the Principles of Atheism by a Book, entitled, *The Philosophical Enquiry*'. There was then some slightly fruitless logomachy as to just what Ducket had claimed that he did or did not believe, both at the time when he wrote the incriminating letter and since, and how far this was due to his reading of Strutt's book. There was also the issue of whether Ducket had committed atheistic opinions to writing, which Pate denied, though agreeing that Ducket *had* 'expressed his Disbelief of a God or his Belief in the Principles of Atheism in company' – although the court was left slightly unclear about where or how long ago.[41]

That line of enquiry having ended slightly inconclusively, consideration now turned to evidence received remotely from Henry Cornelison, Esq., of

---

[40] This is mainly from the John Rylands and Baker/Grey accounts, Appendix, nos 2–5, which are fuller at this point than either Tunstall or Cole and its derivatives, nos 6–9, though it is the latter that name Whitehead and an attorney named Strutt, brother of the author of *A Philosophical Enquiry* (who had himself died in 1737).

[41] This continues from the John Rylands and Baker/Grey accounts, which are fuller than Tunstall's and Cole's and its derivatives.

Boxted Lodge, Essex, described by James Tunstall as 'the chief Man' in the parish of Little Horkesley where Ducket was curate. To him, two sets of interrogatories were put, one supplied by Ducket, the other by his prosecutors, and Cornelison's responses were relayed to the court by two local clerics who were entrusted with interrogating him. Both sets of inquiries related to Ducket's orthodoxy, involving such questions as: 'Did you ever hear him oppose the Principles of Religion, for Instance, the Being of God, or a future State in any Conversation?', to which Cornelison responded in the negative. He was also asked whether he would 'knowingly have entertained and encouraged any Clergyman who declared himself an Atheist', to which he effectively responded: 'Of course not'.[42]

No further witnesses were called, and on the whole things might have seemed to be going Ducket's way, but again he stirred things up: he 'asserted the Justness of his former Defence, & endeavoured to invalidate the Evidence, by throwing unjust Reflections upon Mrs Richards's Character; but withall, alledg'd that His Conversations with her were so far from tending to Atheism, that They supposed the being of a God'. He then went even further: 'he threw out many injurious Reflections upon His Prosecutors, and concluded, by telling his Judges, That no Court, but that of the Inquisition, would be satisfied with Such Evidence'.[43] At that point, the court adjourned till 23 March.

On the 23rd, the court initially met at the Law Schools as previously but it proved inquorate due to the non-appearance of William Towers, Master of Christ's; ostensibly this was in protest at the absence from the proceedings of Thomas Gooch, the Master of Caius, though the antiquary William Cole found Towers an altogether rather difficult figure.[44] To make up the necessary quorum, the meeting was therefore adjourned to the Master's Lodge at Trinity so that the ailing but indomitable scholar

---

[42] These interrogatories and ancillary documents appear in C.C. Ct. 1.99 (9–17) (Appendix, no.1), with copies in the John Rylands version (no. 2) and in the Grey account (no. 5), in the latter case perhaps having been copied (like Ducket's speech) from the account of the case recorded by Philip Williams. Tunstall and Cole and its derivatives merely summarise them (nos 6–9). The documents in C.C. Ct. 1.99 include both drafts and fair copies of the interrogatories (9–10, 12–13); Whalley's formal request to the local clergymen involved, Stephen Newcomen of Boreham and George Stubbs of Kelvedon, to execute the task (11); and their signed and sealed responses (14–17). For Tunstall's comment, see Tunstall to Oxford, 18 March 1739, BL Add. MS 4253, fol. 93. There is some confusion in the sources between Boxted and Braxted, Essex.

[43] This part of the proceedings fails to appear in the John Rylands, Baker and Smith versions (Appendix, nos 2–4) as against Grey and Cole and its derivatives (nos 5, 7–9); Tunstall's comments (no. 6) are more generalised.

[44] Tunstall to Oxford, 24 March 1739, BL Add. MS 4253, fol. 94 (Tunstall states that the meeting would have taken place at the Physic School, in contrast to the other accounts). For Cole's account of Towers, see vol. 20 of his Collections, BL Add. MS 5821, fols 78–9.

Richard Bentley could attend. Indeed, this was one of his last public appearances: he was virtually incapacitated in his last years, dying in 1742. The scholar Conyers Middleton quipped in a letter to his patron, Lord Hervey, how this adjournment of the case to Bentley's parlour 'gave him the honor of ending his life as it began with the demolition of Atheism' – an allusion to Bentley's famous series of Boyle Lectures in 1692, often seen as one of the classic anti-atheist polemics of the era.[45] One aspect of the encounter is revealing. According to Bentley's early nineteenth-century biographer, J. H. Monk, 'tradition in the University still records a jest then uttered by Bentley'. Enquiring of those present 'which was the atheist?', and on being directed to Ducket, 'a small and spare personage', Bentley exclaimed: 'What! is that the atheist? I expected to have seen a man as big as Burrough the beadle', alluding to the portly figure of the university's esquire-bedell.[46] Once again, we see the impact of the anti-atheist stereotype at work in this expectation that the classic freethinker would be a florid *bon-viveur*.

More to the point, however, were the proceedings against Ducket for the crime of atheism, when John Whalley, the Vice-Chancellor, 'expatiated upon the Heinousness of the Crime, as destructive of all Religion, & all social Happiness', found Ducket guilty of it and proposed expulsion. Needless to say, Ducket responded 'That he must think this Sentence, both cruel & unjust', which stimulated one of those present, William Greaves, Fellow of Clare and Commissary of the university, to 'move for his Commitment, as having offered the greatest Insult to the Court that was ever heard of, & which no Court in the World wou'd bear with Impunity'. Evidently sensing that his time was up, Ducket begged pardon and the motion was dropped. Instead, he asked for a copy of the court's acts, to which the Vice-Chancellor responded that he could have anything he wanted in a legal way, and the court broke up.[47] His expulsion from the university was ratified by a Latin declaration declaring him guilty of 'gravissimi Atheismi criminis', while Ducket was also suspended from his cure in Essex by the Bishop of London.[48]

---

[45] Middleton to Hervey, 25 March 1739, BL Add. MS 32458, fol. 98.

[46] J. H. Monk, *Life of Richard Bentley*, 2nd ed., 2 vols (London, 1833), II, 394. Concerning Ducket's appearance, Cole noted that he was 'a thin spare Man, of a florid red Complexion': BL Add. MS 5822, fol. 93v.

[47] This appears in most of the accounts that include the proceedings on 23 March (i.e., Appendix, nos 5, 7–9). However, Smith (no. 4) and Tunstall (no. 6) give slightly less detail.

[48] Tunstall to Oxford, 23 March, 6 May 1739, Add. MS 4253, fols 95v, 97. For a summary of the proceedings signed by the Vice-Chancellor and the eight heads of house see V.C. Ct. 1.99 (20–1); for a reference to Ducket's earlier ordination, see Ingram, *Reformation without End*, p. 39 n. 10

James Tunstall reported that it was not thought that Ducket would make an appeal to Westminster Hall and, although it was reported that he was 'printing his Speech in his own Vindication', this did not materialise. Tunstall added: ''Tis thought he will apply himself to physic' – perhaps like the Oxford renegade, Nicholas Stevens, whom we encountered earlier in this chapter – though Tunstall went on: 'however, one of his Friends gave out, that he would apply himself to a way much more advantageous than that of the Gown'.[49] This turned out to be the diplomatic service, and Ducket is to be found in a succession of posts between 1739 and 1746 as secretary to the British ambassadors to Sweden, Russia, Poland and Berlin, presumably because anticlerical Whigs in government were not averse to cocking a snook at university clerics. Thereafter he was to be found in Turin and in Venice, while he was chancellor at Constantinople from 1769 until his dismissal for a 'flagrant breach of confidence' in 1773, which is the last we hear of him.[50] So perhaps, at least until his indiscretion in Constantinople, Ducket had the last laugh.

Here, however, we may return to the reaction to him, which tended to sensationalism in language and attitude. Commentators could not resist embroidering their sources: we have already seen how many versions of the proceedings give Ducket's words to Mary Richards as 'Matrimony was only Priestcraft', whereas in fact he probably did not use the word 'only'. Similarly, Cole's 'Account' completely unwarrantedly added 'supreme' to the word 'top' in Ducket's description in his 1734 letter to Gibbs of how he had reached 'the Top, the *ne plus ultra*', of atheism, while Zachary Grey can also be observed spicing things up while composing his version of Ducket's defence speech, altering 'opinion' to the much stronger word 'Delusion' when describing Ducket's views.[51] It was all a matter of increasing the shock and horror of Ducket's supposed atheism, the nature and extent of which was not really discussed at all; it is revealing that Ducket's defence speech, including his telling allusions to Butler's *Analogy*,

---

[49] Tunstall to Oxford, 6 May 1739, BL Add. MS 4253, fol. 97 ('to him' is deleted after 'advantageous'). See also his letter of 24 March, Add. MS 4253, fol. 94v, for a comparable comment.

[50] D. B. Horn, *British Diplomatic Representatives 1689–1789*, Camden Society 3rd series, vol 46 (London, 1932), pp. 92, 114, 124, 143, 154; John Ingamells, *A Dictionary of British and Irish Travellers in Italy 1701–1800* (New Haven and London, 1997), p. 316. See also Sir G. F. Duckett, *Duchetiana; or Historical and Genealogical Memoirs of the Family of Ducket, from the Norman Conquest to the Present Time* (London, 1874), p. 366.

[51] See Appendix, no. 7 (fol. 91), followed by the copies in nos 8–9; no. 5 (fol. 12v) (this could, however, be a copying error, as with his change of wording in the passage concerning Addison on fol. 13).

was simply ignored and does not even appear in some accounts of the trial. Clearly, the sexual innuendo concerning Mary Richards was the last straw, and it is interesting to find that, when James Tunstall recorded that there was a rumour in May 1739 that two of Ducket's associates were to be prosecuted, he noted: 'whether the Crime to be charged is of a moral or speculative nature, is not yet known. It is remarkable in these Gentlemen, that they have been thoroughly consistent with themselves, & have not taken Liberties in speculation only'.[52]

Here, a revealing parallel may be found in the case of the notorious freethinker, Matthew Tindal, whose *Rights of the Christian Church* (1706) had presented a legalistic critique of Anglican views on the relations of church and state with wide implications, as Dmitri Levitin has demonstrated, and who subsequently published *Christianity as Old as the Creation* (1730).[53] For Tindal was dogged by persistent attempts at character assassination, reaching a climax in the pamphlet, *The Religious, Rational, and Moral Conduct of Matthew Tindal, LL.D.* (1735). As V. H. H. Green has put it: 'Though in fact an abstemious man, Tindal's supposed lack of moral principles was considered a natural sequel to his unbelief'.[54] Not only was Tindal accused of various sexual misdemeanours against which his protagonists have felt the need to defend him, but this was mixed up with accusations of crypto-Catholicism, and with allusions to the Earl of Rochester and even to the notorious Henry Atherton, convicted of sodomy in the early seventeenth century.[55]

The point is that the argument that atheists were axiomatically immoralists was convenient to the orthodox because it made it possible to avoid serious discussion of the heterodox ideas of the figures involved. In a way, it was an effective ploy. Whether it actually worked, however, is another question. William Cole noted Ducket's later subscription to a work by the antiquary Joseph Ames, whom he considered an equally outrageous freethinker,[56] and the complaints of the orthodox might lead one to

---

[52] Tunstall to Oxford, 6 May 1739, BL Add. MS 4253, fol. 97.
[53] Dmitri Levitin, 'Matthew Tindal's *Rights of the Christian Church* (1706) and the Church–State Relationship', *Historical Journal*, 54 (2011), 717–40.
[54] Green, 'Religion in the Colleges', p. 435.
[55] *The Religious, Rational, and Moral Conduct of Matthew Tindal, LL.D.* (London, 1735). For discussion, see esp. Stephen Lalor, *Matthew Tindal, Freethinker: An Eighteenth-Century Assault on Religion* (London, 2006), ch. 1. On Atherton, see Peter Marshall, *Mother Leakey and the Bishop: A Ghost Story* (Oxford, 2007).
[56] BL Add. MS 5831, fol. 175v.

believe that irreligious views were rampant: indeed, this was the thrust of three pastoral letters issued by Bishop Gibson around 1730, to which Tindal in fact responded.[57] Perhaps Ducket was right in his evident indignation at the way in which he was treated. He was being made a scapegoat for a phenomenon of much wider cultural significance.

[57] *The Bishop of London's Pastoral Letter to the People of his Diocese* (London, 1728); *The Bishop of London's Second Pastoral Letter* ... (London 1730); *The Bishop of London's Third Pastoral Letter* ... (London, 1731); [Matthew Tindal], *An Address to the Inhabitants of the Two Great Cities of London and Westminster* (London, 1728); [Matthew Tindal], *A Second Address* ... (London, 1730).

The Accounts of Ducket's Trial

The various accounts of the trial are as follows:

1. Vice-Chancellor's Court, Cambridge. Though the *acta curiae* relating to the case do not survive, a full series of ancillary documents is extant in Cambridge University archives, V.C. Ct. 1.99. These comprise the incriminating 1734 letter itself and a copy of it (7–8); various formal summons issued by the Vice-Chancellor, John Whalley, both to Ducket himself and to Stephen Gibbs and John Scotman as witnesses (1–4); the 'articles' against Ducket (5–6); a series of documents relating to the interrogation of Henry Cornelison (9–17); Ducket's letter to Mary Richards (18–19); and the record of the final verdict, signed by Whalley and eight college heads (20–1). There is no record of Ducket's speech.

2. John Rylands Library GB 133 Eng MS 1169 (purchased from Clogher Diocesan Library in 1953 and now bound with a collection of eighteenth-century trial pamphlets), fols 1–9. This version gives not only a full text of the 'articles' against Ducket (fols 1–2) and the original 1734 letter (fol. 9) but also a transcript of the *acta curiae* entries relating to the case, though only those for 21 February and 9–16 March (fols 3–5v; that for 23 March is missing). These items are all in a uniform scribal hand. Details of the interrogatories to Cornelison then appear in a different hand (fols 7–8), while an account of the proceedings on 23 March is added in a much later one (fol. 5v). Again, there is no record of Ducket's speech.

3. Thomas Baker's account of the trial, Cambridge University Library MS Mm.1.51 (formerly Baker MS 40), fols 38–9. This comprises a transcript of the *acta curiae* entries relating to the trial, within which the 'articles' are alluded to but not quoted in full. It lacks Ducket's speech, the Cornelison interrogatories and the events of 23 March, ending the account of the proceedings on 16 March on fol. 39 with

the marginal note: 'The rest I have not, But Mr Ducket was expell'd, at a meeting ‹or Court›, at Trinity College, Dr Bentley present.' The 1734 letter appears separately in the volume at fol. 131.

4. John Smith's copy of the trial, Gonville and Caius College MS 621/ 457, item 8, pp. 164–80, part of a series of notes and extracts by this future Master of Caius. This is copied from Baker's account, with the 1734 letter appearing at the start (pp. 164–6). On pp. 179–80 details of the events on 23 March are added in another hand. Ducket's speech and the Cornelison interrogatories do not appear.

5. Zachary Grey's account, Cambridge University Library MS Ee.6.43, fols 3–14. This opens with the 1734 letter, going on to quote the *acta curiae* at length, including the verdict on 23 March. It also includes the Cornelison interrogatories, together with Ducket's speech, the latter taken from 'an abstract of This Tryal in the hand writing of Dr *Philip Williams* then President of *St Johns College Cambridge*' (fol. 12v). Williams's manuscript does not appear to survive.

6. James Tunstall's account of the entire affair in a series of letters to the Earl of Oxford dated 23 January to 6 May 1739, in a transcript by Thomas Birch, British Library Add. MS 4253, fols 86–97. The 1734 letter is merely summarised, but a copy of it (now missing) was sent with the letter of 18 March (fol. 92v). This is a full and independent narrative, with a version of Ducket's speech which differs slightly from that in Grey (no. 5) and in Cole and its derivatives (nos 7–9), presumably due to the way in which it was taken down at the time. It also includes a transcript of Ducket's letter to Mary Richards (fols 91v–2), but the Cornelison interrogatories and the 'articles' against Ducket are merely summarised.

7. William Cole's account of the trial in British Library Add. MS 5822, fols 90v–4 (vol. 21 of Cole's Cambridgeshire Collections). This starts by quoting the 1734 letter in full, introduced by a note explaining that it was found by Burrough. There is then a full 'Account of the Tryal of Tinkler Ducket' which is derived from a version 'wrote all in Dr Williams's Hand, who possibly might also be the Composer of it', which is evidently the account of the trial also used by Grey (above, no. 5). In contrast to nos 2 and 5, this refers only briefly to the interrogation of Cornelison, but it *does* include Ducket's speech. At the end is a note about Ducket's appearance, about Windle (see p. 163) and about Towers (see p. 170). In a subsequent volume of Cole's collections, Add. MS 5831 (vol. 30), fols 175v–6, is a note about Ducket's subscription to Ames's *Typographical Antiquities*,

providing Cole with an opportunity for a tirade against Ames as a freethinker, together with an extract from a letter of Waterland of 31 Jan. 1739 with Cole's notes on it, in which he records that he was present at the trial. Cole uses much underlining throughout, which I have ignored in my transcripts.

8. James Bentham's account of the trial in Cambridge University Library Add. MS 2961, fols 6–15, part of a collection of transcripts of *c.* 1785 by this cleric and historian of Ely Cathedral, who was evidently interested in the case due to its link with Wymondham, of which he held the living (see *ODNB*). This is clearly derived from Cole's, which is exactly reproduced with very minor changes except for a lacuna on fol. 12, where the words 'his disbelief of the Conclusiveness of the Arguments in The Philosophical Enquiry & that he has heard him since that Time acknowledge' are omitted, evidently due to miscopying.

9. Account of the trial in British Library Add. MS 32502 (Family of North Miscellaneous Papers), fols 80–2. A further exact copy of Cole's account, except that it ends with the proceedings on 16 March and does not include those for 23.

CHAPTER 9

Conclusion

At this point it is appropriate to try to draw some general conclusions from the various case studies that we have surveyed in the course of this book. What overall view comes to light from these varied instances? Are any conclusions available about the contrasting state of affairs in Scotland and England as we enter the period of the Enlightenment, and what more general deductions may be drawn concerning irreligion and the attitude towards it on the part of the orthodox in this pivotal period?

As we have seen, atheistic ideas were predominantly orally expressed, and clearly it was prudent to restrict the extent to which knowledge of them came to the attention of a wider public. One can well understand the reaction of Tinkler Ducket when the letter that provided written incrimination of him came to light, who 'did by force and violence seize the said scandalous paper or Letter and tear the same into peices with intent utterly to destroy the same'.[1] The most obvious instance of the disastrous consequences of a full investigation of a case of atheism is provided by the case of Thomas Aikenhead, whose shocking execution still echoes down the centuries.

But what is striking in retrospect is that – in contrast to the godly doubters whom we encountered in Chapter 3, who genuinely seem to have kept their reservations to themselves or to a very limited circle – atheists could not resist trumpeting their views, as we hear over and over again in the evidence against them. Such opinions were expressed 'openly and impudently' (as with the 1599 atheist with whom we opened this book), or propounded 'in severall companies without the least provocatione', as was claimed concerning Aikenhead; it was similarly stated of Christopher Marlowe a century earlier that 'almost into every company he cometh he perswades men to Atheism'.[2] Again and again, we hear the strong assurance that, as was indicated in the Introduction, characterises the

[1] See p. 161.   [2] See pp. 1, 40, 50, 112.

figures with whom we have been concerned throughout this book: not for them the anxious uncertainty displayed by the godly, with which their views have sometimes mistakenly been conflated.

Perhaps the most striking instance of this almost obsessive desire on the part of an atheist openly to promote his heterodox opinions in oral form concerns not a British case but a continental one, that of the peripatetic Italian apostate, Giulio Cesare Vanini.[3] In his published books, Vanini was careful to hedge his bets, weaving a tapestry of often derivative opinions suggesting an irreligious stance but carefully ensuring that these were refuted by counter-arguments. Orally, however, he was much less discreet, permitting himself great freedom of speech, particularly among young and impressionable auditors. In the words of one report, 'he mocked all that is sacred and religious. He held the Incarnation of Our Lord in abhorrence, he knew no God, he attributed everything to chance'. What made things worse was his attempt to inculcate such views in 'the young who had only just left school and who, by their great youth, were the most susceptible to new opinions'.[4] It is ironic that those who prosecuted Vanini in Toulouse in 1619 were not even aware of his identity as the author of his published books, the offence for which he was tried being the oral propagation of blasphemous ideas, often to virtual strangers. But the result was a spectacular *auto-de-fé*, in which he at last trumpeted his apostasy 'and died an atheist'.[5]

Vanini was especially unwise to allow this to occur in Toulouse, which was a notorious bastion of conservative religious opinion. Aikenhead was equally unlucky in voicing his opinions in a milieu that had all the mechanisms in place for swift and effective retribution, in terms of the legislative structure that existed and the alliance of churchmen and politicians glad to make an example of their unfortunate young victim. Matters were made worse by the particularly disastrous circumstances that had befallen the city of Edinburgh, and the Scottish economy generally, in 1696; this appeared to illustrate God's wrath with the country, as Michael Graham has well indicated in his account of the episode.[6] Equally, the

---

[3] For the most recent account, see Adam Horsley, *Libertines and the Law: Subversive Authors and Criminal Justice in Early Seventeenth-Century France* (Oxford, 2021), ch. 3. For earlier studies, see the writings cited by Horsley, esp. pp. 102, nn. 3–4, and 103, nn. 9–10, and Nicholas Davidson, '"Le plus beau et le plus meschant esprit que ie aye cogneu": Science and Religion in the Writings of Giulio Cesare Vanini, 1585–1619', in *Heterodoxy in Early Modern Science and Religion*, ed. John Brooke and Ian MacLean (Oxford, 2005), pp. 59–79.
[4] Horsley, *Libertines and the Law*, p. 127.   [5] Ibid., pp. 134–6, 157, 170–2.
[6] Michael F. Graham, *The Blasphemies of Thomas Aikenhead* (Edinburgh, 2008), esp. ch. 3.

hostile reactions that the case elicited in England clearly indicate the contrast between the two countries, in that the relative homogeneity of Scottish public life at the time, which made possible Aikenhead's execution, contrasted with the more diffuse state of affairs in England, where outrage was easy to express but difficult to implement in practice, something that we will explore more fully in the course of this Conclusion.

With Pitcairne, on the other hand, we encounter a more nuanced picture than that which occurred in the Aikenhead case, enabling him to survive the rumours that circulated concerning his heterodoxy and to die peacefully in 1713. By comparison with the poorly established student, Pitcairne enjoyed a secure profession in terms of his successful medical practice. Moreover, although he made enough enemies in the course of his career, these were balanced by equally loyal allies among his Episcopalian and Jacobite friends. When it came to irreligion, Pitcairne knew how far it was prudent to go in terms of the dissemination of the heterodox ideas that he held. Of course, we cannot be certain that *Pitcairneana* is by him or that he actually held the views expressed in it by the spokesman 'Incredulous'. On the other hand, even giving expression to these would be striking enough, in that its author literally thought the unthinkable – to a greater extent than almost any predecessor or than many of his successors.

Leaving that to one side, however, it is notable how Pitcairne organised the circulation of the milder heterodox views that he expressed in his *Epistola Archimedis*. For one thing, his sojourn in the Netherlands in the 1690s had evidently attuned him sufficiently to the currents of ideas in that country for him to understand that a Dutch publisher rather than a British one was more appropriate to circulate his questionable views and to draw them to the attention of like-minded intellectuals. Beyond that, it is striking to note that he actually donated inscribed presentation copies of the work to two leading English medical men who we know were sympathetic to somewhat heterodox and Deistic religious views, Richard Mead and Sir Hans Sloane: these are the copies of the work now surviving in the British Library, which thus imply a kind of subversive network in action that is revealing in itself.[7]

On the question of whether the state of affairs in Scotland encouraged occasional cases of irreligion as much as was the case in England in this period, the jury is out. Richard Burridge certainly claimed that he was

---

[7] See pp. 133–4 and p. 133, n. 35. For Mead's and Sloane's religious views, see Michael Hunter, *The Decline of Magic: Britain in the Enlightenment* (New Haven and London, 2020), ch. 5.

'most civilly entertain'd' in both Glasgow and Edinburgh, where he may have advanced outrageous ideas similar to those that had 'poison'd the Understanding' of his auditors at Cambridge a few years earlier, though exactly what he said is frustratingly unclear.[8] It is also notable that no less a figure than the Deist John Toland spent time in Edinburgh around 1690, where he 'seems to have sought notoriety through public displays of heterodoxy and esoteric learning'.[9] Moreover, there are other hints of freethinking elements in Scottish culture in this period. For instance, there is a strange episode recorded in the *Diary* of James Erskine, Lord Grange, thus adding to the extreme complexity of the intellectual career of this slightly maverick figure that has been sketched by Ian Bostridge.[10] In 1699 Erskine spent a storm at sea writing bawdy poems modelled on those of Lord Rochester, taking the view that 'my Religion was at ane end', and expressing 'a great esteem' for Jean Le Clerc in Amsterdam and the way in which he 'thought freely', having shaken off the prejudices displayed by Erskine's Presbyterian compatriots; only later was he to turn into a deeply religious Scottish particularist, best known for his opposition to the Witchcraft Bill in 1736.[11]

Equally interesting is the case of the budding intellectual George Turnbull, whose earliest extant letter, dated 1718, proclaimed: 'I am a Freethinker, and I glory in the character'. This was addressed to none other than John Toland, whose sojourn in Edinburgh twenty years earlier has just been noted, and who was one of the authors who had been cited by Pitcairne in *Pitcairneana*.[12] Subsequently, Turnbull was to exchange various letters with Robert, Viscount Molesworth, a close colleague of Toland's, in which he lionised the Earl of Shaftesbury and others, and the attitude of Toland and Molesworth towards the orthodox consensus against which Turnbull reacted in his early years is perhaps revealed by their derisive comments on the incompetence and credulity of Martin Martin in his *Description of the Western Islands of Scotland*, their annotated copy of which still survives and has been the subject of scrutiny by the late

---

[8] Richard Burridge, *Religio Libertini* (London, 1712), pp. 15, 19

[9] Robert E. Sullivan, *John Toland and the Deist Controversy* (Cambridge, MA, 1982), p. 3; Graham, *Blasphemies of Aikenhead*, pp. 27–8

[10] See Ian Bostridge, *Witchcraft and Its Transformations, c. 1650–c. 1750* (Oxford, 1997), pp. 184–92.

[11] James Erskine, Lord Grange, *Extracts from the Diary of a Senator of the College of Justice* (Edinburgh, 1843), pp. 78–84; Bostridge, *Witchcraft*, pp. 184–92.

[12] George Turnbull, *Education for Life: Correspondence and Writings on Religion and Practical Philosophy*, ed. M. A. Stewart and Paul Wood (Indianapolis, 2014), pp. 3–4; see also pp. 5–14. For Pitcairne's use of Toland's *Letters to Serena*, see this volume, p. 155.

Justin Champion and myself.[13] On the other hand, Turnbull, too, was subsequently to revert to a more orthodox position, even publishing an attack on the Deist Matthew Tindal.[14] Such examples of youthful flirtation with freethinking ideas are nevertheless illuminating, suggesting that, behind its ostensibly orthodox façade, Scotland already harboured more seeds of change than might otherwise be apparent.[15]

Turning now to the state of affairs in England, the situation is somewhat ambiguous. Expressions of disquiet about the commonness of atheistic sentiments proliferated throughout this period. Thus, the Boyle Lectures continued, including series with titles like *The Pretended Difficulties in Natural or Reveal'd Religion No Excuse for Infidelity* or, more succinctly, *Against Atheists*; the outrage that irreligious views caused is illustrated, for example, by the claim that the South Sea Bubble was sent as a chastisement by God for the nation's apostasy.[16] It is also worth pointing to the laws that existed, there as in Scotland, proscribing the expression of heterodox opinion, perhaps notably the Blasphemy Act of 1698, passed with considerable support within Parliament and aimed particularly at anti-Trinitarian opinion, though its remit included anyone who 'by writing, printing, teaching, or advised speaking' should 'deny the Christian religion to be true'.[17] The background to this has been provided by John Spurr in an insightful essay which points to the widespread concern that existed about 'scoffing' at religion – that veritable avalanche of comment hostile to 'priestcraft' and its works aimed (in his words) 'to puncture certainties and raise unsettling thoughts, often in a witty turn', which helps to explain the anxiety about atheism that we have encountered throughout this book. The difficulty was that ridicule was hard to answer: in the words of the Boyle Lecturer Samuel Clarke, '*Banter* is not capable of

---

[13] See Justin A. I. Champion, 'Enlightened Erudition and the Politics of Reading in John Toland's Circle', *Historical Journal*, 49 (2006), 111–41; Michael Hunter, *The Occult Laboratory: Magic, Science and Second Sight in Late Seventeenth-Century Scotland* (Woodbridge, 2001), pp. 29–31, and *The Decline of Magic*, pp. 54–6.

[14] See Turnbull, *Education for Life*, esp. pp. 171–215.

[15] For the suggestion of a comparable context for Hume see John S. Warren, 'Shining a Light in Dark Places, Part II', *Global Intellectual History*, 3 (2018), 1–46 (pp. 25–9).

[16] The sermons in question were by Brampton Gurdon, 1721–2 and Ralph Heathcote, 1763 (the full title of which is *A Discourse upon the Being of God: Against Atheists*); R. G. Ingram and A. W. Barber, '"The Warr … against Heaven by Blasphemors and Infidels": Prosecuting Heresy in Enlightenment England', in *Freedom of Speech, 1500–1850*, ed. Ingram, Jason Peacey and Barber (Manchester, 2020), pp. 151–70 (p. 154).

[17] David Hayton, 'Moral Reform and Country Politics in the Late Seventeenth-Century House of Commons', *Past & Present*, 128 (1990), 48–91; Eloise Davies, 'English Politics and the Blasphemy Act of 1698', *English Historical Review*, 135 (2020), 804–35. For the Act see 9 William III c. 35, in *Statutes of the Realm*, ed. Alexander Luders et al., VII (London, 1820), p. 409.

being answered by *Reason*. Instead, as Spurr points out, 'scoffing had to be converted into the offence of blasphemy' so that the aid of the civil magistrate might be invoked in suppressing irreligion of this kind.[18]

Yet it is ironic that the 1698 Act was never actually used in practice. Instead, cases of blasphemy were prosecuted under the common law, following the precedent established by Lord Chief Justice Hale in the late seventeenth century, when he famously stated that 'Christianity is parcel of the laws of England; and therefore to reproach the Christian religion is to speak in subversion of the law'.[19] On the other hand, an attempt to supplement this by introducing a further piece of legislation in 1721 met with widespread resistance, even from bishops like White Kennett and Edmund Gibson, who were far from clear that such laws were effective in controlling the expression of opinion, and who argued that such measures smacked of popery.[20] Moreover, it has been pointed out that the actual use of blasphemy prosecution was puzzlingly random: in the words of Leonard W. Levy, 'no rational explanation exists for the seemingly haphazard targeting of victims'.[21]

Indeed, in the early eighteenth century, a state of affairs existed which was somewhat paradoxical. Thus we have the case of Richard Burridge, whose prosecution for blasphemy seems capricious and rather arbitrary, and who in any case survived this to capitalise on his reputation as a redeemed sinner, relishing his jousts with eminent bishops on doctrinal issues.[22] No less revealing, if more serious in its consequences, was the episode involving the unfortunate cleric Thomas Woolston, who was successfully prosecuted for blasphemy and was under house arrest when he died.[23] There can be no doubt that Woolston sailed far too close to the wind in his outspoken critique of the biblical miracles, the offensiveness of

[18] John Spurr, 'The Manner of English Blasphemy, 1676–2008', in *Religion, Identity and Conflict in Britain*, ed. S. J. Brown, Frances Knight and John Morgan-Guy (Farnham, 2013), pp. 27–46 (pp. 32, 34); Samuel Clarke, *A Discourse Concerning the Unchangeable Obligations of Natural Religion* (London, 1706), p. 31.

[19] Elliott Visconsi, 'The Invention of Criminal Blasphemy: *Rex v. Taylor* (1676)', *Representations*, 103 (2008), 30–52. On the history of the crime of blasphemy, see also G. D. Nokes, *A History of the Crime of Blasphemy* (London, 1928).

[20] Ingram and Barber, '"Warr . . . against Heaven by Blasphemors and Infidels"'.

[21] L. W. Levy, *Blasphemy: Verbal Offense against the Sacred, from Moses to Salman Rushdie* (New York, 1993), p. 291.

[22] See this volume, pp. 90–2.

[23] See Levy, *Blasphemy*, pp. 308–15; William H. Trapnell, *Thomas Woolston: Madman and Deist?* (Bristol, 1994); Roger D. Lund, 'Irony as Subversion: Thomas Woolston and the Crime of Wit', in *The Margins of Orthodoxy*, ed. Lund (Cambridge, 1995), pp. 170–94, and *Ridicule, Religion and the Politics of Wit in Augustan England* (Farnham, 2012), pp. 201–9; James A. Herrick, *The Radical Rhetoric of the English Deists: The Discourse of Skepticism, 1680–1750* (Columbia, SC, 1997), ch. 4;

his gibes at which, and even at Christ's resurrection, is evident. His aim was, in his own words, 'to shew that the story of many of *Jesus*'s Miracles is literally absurd, improbable and incredible', but he went about this in an almost ribald manner that was calculated to upset the orthodox.[24] Indeed, more than almost any other case – not only in this period but in any other – the prosecution of Woolston illustrates the extent to which the law of blasphemy was used to protect the feelings of Christian believers. It should be added that, whatever Woolston's own intentions, there can be no doubt that his cutting gibes would have provided entertainment, not to say ammunition, for those of an irreligious persuasion, as commentators on the case, like Bishop Gibson, made clear.[25] Yet it is paradoxical that there can be no question that, for all his hostility to the ecclesiastical establishment, Woolston's intentions in his attacks were sincerely pious: he aimed to establish the authentic, allegorical meaning of the episodes in question as 'a Christian and a true Believer of the Religion of Christ, though I may have some different Conceptions from other Men about it'.[26] It is an extraordinary episode, but one that throws only tangential light on the actual incidence of atheism with which we have here been concerned.

Hardly less revealing, however, is the case of Tinkler Ducket, the subject of the final substantive chapter of this book. For one thing, Ducket's successful diplomatic career following his run-in with the Cambridge authorities shows that other sections of society disdained the narrow clerisy associated with the ancient universities, suggesting a tolerance or at least indifference towards the expression of irreligious views that is significant in itself. It is equally interesting how little publicity the affair received at the time: though Ducket's incriminating letter was published in more than one contemporary periodical, it was accompanied by only the sketchiest of information about his expulsion from the university.[27] No less revealing is the evidence provided by the way in which the episode itself was transacted.

Laura M. Stevens, 'Civility and Skepticism in the Woolston–Sherlock Debate over Miracles', *Eighteenth-Century Life*, 21 (1997), 57–70; Michael Suarez, '"The Most Blasphemous Book that ever was Publish'd": Ridicule, Reception, and Censorship in Eighteenth-Century England', in *The Commonwealth of Books*, ed. Wallace Kirsop (Melbourne, 2007), pp. 46–77; and Wayne Hudson, *Enlightenment and Modernity* (London, 2009), ch. 3.

[24] Thomas Woolston, *A Discourse on the Miracles of Our Saviour* (London, 1727), p. 21.
[25] [Edmund Gibson], *The Bishop of London's Pastoral Letter to the People of His Diocese* (London, 1728), p. 27.
[26] Thomas Woolston, *Mr Woolston's Defence of his Discourses on the Miracles of Our Saviour. Part 1* (London, 1729), p. 15.
[27] See this volume, p. 161, n. 14.

For one thing, it is telling that 'Atheism' was throughout reified with a capital 'a' as an object of repulsion, something 'wicked and erroneous', which yet was never engaged with or discussed, as surely ought to have been the case in an academic setting. Ducket's delinquency was simply taken as a given, his guilt evidently being confirmed in the eyes of those involved by his moral turpitude as revealed by his illicit approach to Mary Richards – thus itself showing the insidious effect that all the talk of 'practical atheism' had had over the years. The result was simply to close down discussion of the serious matters that Ducket tried to raise in his defence speech.

What is equally significant is the complacency of which the case gave evidence. Those involved platitudinously informed Ducket that atheism 'must necessarily proceed from a depraved Will'; they also 'expatiated upon the Heinouness of the Crime, as destructive of all Religion, & all social Happiness'.[28] Moreover, this went with a rather self-satisfied advocacy of a bland, theistic worldview, as was well exemplified by Joseph Addison, the spokesman for orthodoxy with whom Ducket actually took issue in his defence speech. The passage to which Ducket objected occurs in no. 111 of *The Tatler*, where Addison gave a tirade in favour of the virtues of religion, in contrast to

> the Works of a few solemn Blockheads, that meet together with the Zeal and Seriousness of Apostles, to extirpate common Sense, and propagate Infidelity. These are the Wretches, who, without any Show of Wit, Learning, or Reason, publish their crude Conceptions with an Ambition of appearing more wise than the rest of Mankind, upon no other Pretence, than that of dissenting from them.

'There is not a more ridiculous Animal than an Atheist in his Retirement', he continued, holding up by contrast the 'wise Man, that lives up to the Principles of Reason and Virtue ... taking in the System of the Universe, observing the mutual Dependance and Harmony, by which the whole Frame of it hangs together, beating down his Passions, or swelling his Thoughts with magnificent Idea's of Providence'.[29] Similar views are to be found throughout Addison's other writings, notably *The Spectator*, which proved so popular throughout the eighteenth century; this contained such sentiments as that 'Infidelity has been attack'd with so good Success of late Years, that it is driven out of all its Outworks' or that 'the Zeal of spreading Atheism is, if possible, more absurd than Atheism it self'.[30]

---

[28] See pp. 168, 171.
[29] Joseph Addison, *The Tatler*, ed. D. F. Bond, 3 vols (Oxford, 1987), II, 170–1.
[30] Joseph Addison, *The Spectator*, ed. D. F. Bond, 5 vols (Oxford, 1965), II, 230, 232 and elsewhere.

It is interesting that Addison here attributes to his putative atheists the very proselytising quality, the assurance, which we have been at pains to stress throughout this book. But what is more telling is his complete disdain for them, his complacent sense of the invincibility of the theistic synthesis with which he countered their views. Here, one is reminded of the famous, equally self-satisfied comments of Edmund Burke in his *Reflections on the Revolution in France* (1790) concerning those 'whom the vulgar, in their blunt, homely style, commonly call Atheists and Infidels': 'Who, born within the last forty years, has read one word of Collins, and Toland, and Tindal, and Chubb, and Morgan, and that whole race who called themselves Freethinkers?'[31] Burke had no doubt of the fundamental and unshakeable religiosity of English society, continuing: 'We know, and what is better we feel inwardly, that religion is the basis of civil society, and the source of all good and of all comfort', citing Cicero's *De Legibus* in support of this. Of course, the reaction to the French Revolution which he there heralded did indeed instil much sentiment of a comparably conformist and anti-radical nature. But the point here is that Burke's view reflected the same complacency as Addison's, and his optimism was premature.

In fact, as we move through the eighteenth century we find an increasing number of people who seem to have adopted arguments of the kind of which Burke disapproved, not only in France, of course, where by this time the floodgates had been opened, but also in Britain.[32] Thus we have the astonishingly outspoken atheist tract, *The Origin of Moral Virtue and Religion Arraigned* (1745), to which Roger Maioli has recently drawn attention, while a further open expression of atheistic views came slightly later from Matthew Turner in his *Answer to Dr Priestley's Letter to a Philosophical Unbeliever* (1782), as has been indicated by David Berman.[33] Meanwhile we have the initially slightly hesitant but ultimately much more influential religious writings of David Hume, while the tradition of iconoclasm towards orthodox belief arguably reached its climax with Thomas Paine and his outspoken *Age of Reason* (1794–5).[34] Well-known authors like

---

[31] Burke, *Reflections on the Revolution in France,* 6th ed. (London, 1790), pp. 132–4.

[32] For France, see such studies by Alan Kors as his *D'Holbach's Coterie* (Princeton, 1976) and 'The Atheism of d'Holbach and Naigeon' in *Atheism from the Reformation to the Enlightenment*, ed. Michael Hunter and David Wootton (Oxford, 1992), pp. 273–300. More recently, see Charles Devellennes, *Positive Atheism: Bayle, Meslier, D'Holbach, Diderot* (Edinburgh, 2021).

[33] See Roger Maioli, 'The First Avowed British Atheist: Lord Hervey?', *Eighteenth-Century Studies*, 54 (2021), 357–79; David Berman, *A History of Atheism in Britain: From Hobbes to Russell* (London, 1988), pp. 110–20. See also this volume, p. 3.

[34] See Berman, *History of Atheism in Britain*, esp. ch. 4–5.

these were accompanied by other, more shadowy figures, such as the antiquary Joseph Ames, said to have fancied himself as 'an *esprit fort* in matters of religion, so much as even to question the existence of a Deity', or the physician William Cheselden, about whom similar suspicions were recorded by the memorialist Joseph Spence.[35] In addition, we hear of virtuosi like Martin Folkes, who (according to the antiquary William Stukeley) was 'in matters of religion an errant infidel & loud scoffer' and whose views apparently had real influence on leading aristocrats.[36] Moreover, at this point we encounter an even larger group whose opinions seem to have verged on Deism, including doctors like Sir Hans Sloane and Richard Mead, the recipients of Pitcairne's subversive *Epistola Archimedis*, whose views on the implausibility of ostensibly supernatural phenomena aligned them with the more sceptical of clerics of the day.[37] It was only a matter of time before the floodgates were opened and a non-theistic outlook became at least thinkable as an alternative to orthodoxy.

This takes us back to the pioneers with whom this book has been concerned. There did not need to be many atheists to suggest the idea that such figures were rampant. Robert Boyle frankly confessed that, in all his dealing with those suspected of harbouring such beliefs, he had only 'met two or three speculative and resolved atheists', but he nevertheless felt that 'the territory of infidelity' was not 'so narrowly circumscribed, as most men take it to be' – thus alluding to the more general mindset encouraging atheistic attitudes that was indicated in the Introduction.[38] It could be left to other, less fastidious champions of orthodoxy, like the Calvinist divine John Edwards, to pick up and exaggerate the rare examples of which a man like Boyle was aware and to imagine 'constant *Cabals* and *Assemblies* of Profess'd Atheists', gnawing at the fabric of religion in late seventeenth-century London.[39] As with the state of affairs classically outlined by Alan Kors in

---

[35] Francis Grose, *The Olio*, 2nd ed. (London, 1796), p. 134–5 (the sceptical Grose put this down to affectation on Ames's part, but see also William Cole's view: this volume, pp. 173, 176–7); Spence, *Observations, Anecdotes and Characters of Books and Men*, ed. J. M. Osborn, 2 vols (Oxford, 1966), I, 208 (cf. his notes showing a comparable curiosity about Garth, Bolingbroke and others, for example, I, 127, 209, 267, 344).

[36] David B. Haycock, *William Stukeley: Science, Religion and Archaeology in Eighteenth-Century England* (Woodbridge, 2002), p. 227. Cf. Anna Marie Roos, *Martin Folkes, 1690–1754, Newtonian, Antiquary, Connoisseur* (Oxford, 2021), pp. 124–8.

[37] Hunter, *Decline of Magic*, esp. ch. 5.

[38] *The Works of Robert Boyle*, ed. Michael Hunter and Edward B. Davis, 14 vols (London, 1999–2000), XII, 482; see this volume, pp. 19–21.

[39] Edwards, *Some Thoughts Concerning the Several Causes and Occasions of Atheism* (London, 1695), p. 128

relation to France and also summarised in the Introduction, the symbiosis of the imagined and the real could be left to work its insidious effect.[40]

Here, it is important to stress once again the assurance with which our atheists put forward their views. It was above all their confidence, their appeal to reason and 'common sense', their cynical, opportunist stance, their apparent disregard for the just deserts promised to sinners in the afterlife, their overall iconoclasm and refusal to be impressed by erudition and tradition, their generally sarcastic, dismissive demeanour, that at the same time alarmed and incensed contemporaries. Not for them the thoughtful dubitation of questioning Christians; rather, these atheists actively proselytised in favour of their viewpoint. Again and again in this book we have encountered such attitudes, representing an amalgam of the affective and the cognitive, a blend of emotion and intellect, which at the same time had real power and potential menace.

Leaping forward in period, let us quote Edward Royle in his *Victorian Infidels*:

> Just as Christian belief can be, and often is, founded on an emotional response in a given situation, to be confirmed later by intellectually satisfying 'evidences', so infidelity seems to have frequently been inspired by disgust with the Church and moral revulsion against Christian doctrines, and then sustained by a growing intellectual conviction of the rightness of such a rejection.[41]

The key thing here is the sense of inner conviction that such men experienced, a 'gut feeling' that there was something defective about the orthodox position that was so strenuously urged against them, even if it did not necessarily have an explicit intellectual foundation, and this resonates with the findings of the current volume. The point that needs to be stressed, however – returning to one of the principal themes of this book – is that this is a history not of doubt but of certainty, and this point is crucial, in contrast to those who have mistakenly seen 'doubt' as the essence of the matter. These men simply knew that they were right and acted accordingly. In doing so, they were often subjected to significant risk to their lives and reputation – as seen in Aikenhead's execution and Ducket's expulsion from Cambridge – though in the case of Pitcairne

---

[40] See pp. 5, 22–3.
[41] Edward Royle, *Victorian Infidels: The Origins of the British Secularist Movement 1791–1866* (Manchester, 1974), p. 108.

his prudent circumspection meant not only that he survived unscathed but that we cannot even be sure that *Pitcairneana* is actually by him or that he held the extreme opinions voiced by its aptly-named protagonist, 'Incredulous'. Nevertheless, the views expressed there are as breathtakingly radical as those voiced openly by Marlowe and Aikenhead. In retrospect, these pioneers deserve to be celebrated for taking a heroic stand against the prevailing orthodoxy. Their story should be better known.

Bibliography

MANUSCRIPT SOURCES

Cambridge, Gonville and Caius College

MS 621/457, item 8, pp. 164–80: John Smith's copy of Ducket trial.

Cambridge University Archives

V.C. Ct.1–99 (1–21): Vice-Chancellor's Court Loose Papers: Documents relating to the trial of Tinkler Ducket, 1738/9.

Cambridge University Library

Add. MS 2961, fols 6–15: James Bentham's copy of Cole's account of Ducket trial.
Add. MS 9597/2/18/81: manuscript of Newton's 'De Natura Acidorum'.
MS Ee.6.43, fols 3–14: Zachary Grey's account of Ducket trial.
MS Mm.1.51 (formerly Baker MS 40), fols 38–9: Thomas Baker's account of Ducket trial (with the 1734 letter at fols 131–2).

Cambridge, MA, Harvard University Archives

HUC 8831.382.53: copy of George Ticknor's lectures on Spanish literature annotated by H. S. McKean, including a photograph of McKean and a biographical note on him based on that in Palmer's *Necrology*.

Cambridge, MA, Houghton Library

MS Eng 1114: the manuscript of *Pitcairneana*; for a digital version, see http://nrs.harvard.edu/urn-3:FHCL.HOUGH:12939560.

Edinburgh, National Library of Scotland

MS Acc 8042: transcript of manuscript catalogue of Pitcairne's library in St Petersburg.

MS 7028, fol. 27v: Marquess of Tweeddale to James Johnston, 17 February 1694.
Wodrow MSS 4to vol. 30, fols 244–5 [Letter no. 144]: Alexander Findlater to Robert Wylie, 8 January 1697.

Edinburgh, National Records of Scotland

CC8/8/77, fols 126v–8: will of James Aikenhead.
GD103/2/3/17/1: Robert Wylie to William Hamilton, 16 June 1697.
JC2/19: High Court of Justiciary Books of Adjournal, 1693–9.
JC6/14: High Court of Justiciary Minute Book, 1693–1701.
JC26/78/1/1–14: High Court of Justiciary Process Papers for Aikenhead case.
OPR 685/1/8: Baptism Register, Parish of Edinburgh, 1675–80.
PC1/51: Privy Council Register of Acta, 1696–9.
PC4/2: Privy Council Minute Book, 1696–9.

Edinburgh, Royal College of Physicians

PIA/1 and PIA/2: Pitcairne medical manuscripts.

Edinburgh University Library

Da.1.32–3: Matriculation Receipts and Disbursements, 1667–93.
Da.1.34: General Book of Disbursements, 1693–1719.
Dc.1.62: notes on Pitcairne's 'Praxis'.
Dc.4.101–3: medical and other notes by Pitcairne.
La.II.89, fols 222–3: copy of indictment against Aikenhead.
La.II.36: transcript of Pitcairne's *Epistola Archimedis*.
La.III.629: printed catalogue of Pitcairne's library.
'Matriculation Roll of the University of Edinburgh. Arts, Law, Divinity. Transcribed by Dr Alexander Morgan, 1933–4' (typescript), vol. 1 (1623–1774).

London, British Library

Add. MS 4223, fols 144–7: Sir John Clerk of Penicuik's account of Pitcairne with covering letter to Thomas Birch dated 7 September 1738.
Add. MS 4253, fols 86–97: James Tunstall's account of Ducket trial in letters to the Earl of Oxford, 23 January to 6 May 1739; transcript by Thomas Birch.
Add. MS 5821, fols 78–9 (vol. 20 of Cole's Cambridgeshire Collections): William Cole's account of William Towers.
Add. MS 5822, fols 90v–4 (vol. 21 of Cole's Cambridgeshire Collections): William Cole's account of Ducket trial.
Add. MS 5831, fols 175v–6 (vol. 30 of Cole's Cambridgeshire Collections): further notes by Cole.
Add. MS 32458, fol. 98: Conyers Middleton to Lord Hervey, 25 March 1739.

Add. MS 32502 (Family of North Miscellaneous Papers), fols 80–2: account of Ducket trial.

Harleian MS 6846, fols 396–401: copies of indictment against Aikenhead and related documents, including his 'Cygnea Cantio'.

Harleian MSS 6848–9 and 6853: manuscripts relating to Marlowe: see Constance B. Kuriyama, *Christopher Marlowe: A Renaissance Life* (Ithaca, 2002), appendix.

Harleian MS 6849, fols 183–90: MS of Cerne Abbas enquiry.

Harleian MS 7042, fols 193–236: transcripts by Thomas Baker.

Sloane MS 2623, fols 61–73: copy of Pitcairne's *Epistola Archimedis*.

London, The National Archives

SP 12/83, fols 114–15: 'Agaynst the Atheysts', 1571.

SP 12/151, fols 102, 109, 118: accusations by Charles Arundel against the Earl of Oxford, 1581.

STA 8/59/11, memb. 2: case of Robert Blagden of Keevil.

London, Royal Society

MS 247: Gregory volume.

London, Society of Antiquaries

MS 25: Pitcairne medical manuscript.

London, Wellcome Library

MSS 3914, 3195: Pitcairne medical manuscripts.

Manchester, John Rylands Library

GB 133 Eng MS 1169, fols 1–9: account of Ducket trial.

Oxford, Bodleian Library

CC Papers 1728/101:1–3: Chancellor's Court Papers, 1728.

GA Oxon b. 111, fol. 39: Programma dated 2 December 1728.

Hyp/A/57, fol. 107: Court Act Book, 1728.

MS Add D 105, fols 70–1: John Wallis to Thomas Tenison, 30 November 1680.

MS Locke b.4, fols 86–106: papers relating to the Aikenhead case.

MS Locke b.4, fols 107–8: copy of Robert Wylie to William Hamilton, 16 June 1697 (NRS GD103/2/3/17/1).

Antiq. d. x. 7: collection of Pitcairne's Latin poems, printed and manuscript.

St Andrews, University of St Andrews Library Special Collections

msBX5199.G6 (ms 5248): Thomas Tanner to Edmund Gibson, 26 November 1728.

Wiltshire Record Office

Diocese of Salisbury Dean's Presentments, 1607–9 (10), fol. 66: case against John Derpier.

York, Borthwick Institute

HC CP 1637/3: case before York High Commission against Peter Vavasour, 1637.

PRIMARY SOURCES

Abernethy, John, *A Christian and Heavenly Treatise Containing Physicke for the Soule*, 3rd ed. (London, 1630).

Adams, Thomas, *A Commentary or Exposition upon the Divine Second Epistle Generall [of] St. Peter* (London, 1633).

Workes (London, 1630).

Addison, Joseph, *The Spectator*, ed. D. F. Bond, 5 vols (Oxford: Clarendon Press, 1965).

The Tatler, ed. D. F. Bond, 3 vols (Oxford: Clarendon Press, 1987).

Ames, William, *An Analyticall Exposition of Both the Epistles of the Apostle Peter* (London, 1641).

Anstruther, William, *Essays, Moral and Divine* (Edinburgh, 1701).

Arnot, Hugo, *A Collection and Abridgement of Celebrated Criminal Trials in Scotland* (Edinburgh, 1785).

Ascham, Roger, *English Works*, ed. W. A. Wright (Cambridge: Cambridge University Press, 1904).

Aubrey, John, *Brief Lives with an Apparatus for the Lives of Our English Mathematical Writers*, ed. Kate Bennett, 2 vols (Oxford: Oxford University Press, 2015).

Bacon, Francis, *The Essayes or Counsels, Civill and Morall*, ed. Michael Kiernan (Oxford: Clarendon Press, 1985).

Bacon, Nathaniel, *A Relation of the Fearefull Estate of Francis Spira* (London, 1638, and various later editions).

Baxter, Richard, *The Reasons of the Christian Religion* (London, 1667).

Reliquae Baxterianae: or Mr Richard Baxter's Narrative of the Most Memorable Passages of His Life and Times, ed. N. H. Keeble, John Coffey, Tim Cooper and Tom Charlton, 5 vols (Oxford: Oxford University Press, 2020).

Bayle, Pierre, *A General Dictionary, Historical and Critical,* ed. J. P. Bernard, Thomas Birch, John Lockman et al., 10 vols (London: 1734–41).

  Miscellaneous Reflections, Occasion'd by the Comet Which appear'd in December 1680, English trans., 2 vols (London, 1708).

Beard, Thomas, *The Theatre of Gods Judgements* (London, 1597; 3rd ed., London, 1631).

Bentley, Richard, *Correspondence,* ed. Christopher Wordsworth, 2 vols (London, 1842).

  Works, ed. Alexander Dyce, 3 vols (London, 1836–8).

Berkeley, George, *Works,* ed. A. A. Luce and T. E. Jessop, 9 vols (London: Nelson & Sons, 1948–57).

Blount, Charles, *Anima Mundi: Or, an Historical Narration of the Opinions of the Ancients Concerning Man's Soul after This Life: According to Unenlightened Nature* (London, 1679).

  The First Two Books, of Philostratus, Concerning the Life of Apollonius Tyaneus (London, 1680).

  Great Is Diana of the Ephesians: Or, The Original of Idolatry, together with the Politick Institution of the Gentiles Sacrifices (London, 1680).

  Miracles, No Violations of the Laws of Nature (London, 1683).

  The Oracles of Reason (London, 1693).

Boyle, Robert, *Correspondence,* ed. Michael Hunter, Antonio Clericuzio and Lawrence M. Principe, 6 vols (London: Pickering & Chatto, 2001).

  Workdiaries of Robert Boyle, The (www.livesandletters.ac.uk//wd/view/text_ed/ WD1_ed.html).

  Works, ed. Michael Hunter and Edward B. Davis, 14 vols (London: Pickering & Chatto, 1999–2000).

Breton, Nicholas, *The Good and the Badde* (London, 1616).

Brunton, George, and Haigh, David, *An Historical Account of the Senators of the College of Justice* (Edinburgh, 1832).

Buckingham, Joseph T., *Annals of the Massachusetts Charitable Mechanic Association, 1795–1892* (Boston, 1853).

Bunyan, John, *Grace Abounding to the Chief of Sinners,* ed. Roger Sharrock (Oxford: Clarendon Press, 1962), reprinted with *The Pilgrim's Progress* in the Oxford Standard Authors series (1966).

  Grace Abounding with Other Spiritual Biographies, ed. John Stachniewski and Anita Pacheco, World's Classics (Oxford: Oxford University Press, 1998).

Burke, Edmund, *Reflections on the Revolution in France,* 6th ed. (London, 1790).

Burnet, Gilbert, *Some Passages of the Life and Death of the Right Hon. John, Earl of Rochester, Who Died the 26th of July, 1680* (London, 1680).

Burridge, Richard, *Religio Libertini: Or, The Faith of a Converted Atheist* (London, 1712).

Burton, J. H., *History of Scotland, from the Revolution to the Extinction of the Last Jacobite Insurrection,* 2 vols (London, 1853).

Burton, Robert, *The Anatomy of Melancholy,* ed. T. C. Faulkner, N. K. Kiessling and R. L. Blair, 6 vols (Oxford: Clarendon Press, 1989–2000).

Butler, Joseph, *The Analogy of Religion, Natural and Revealed, to the Constitution and Course of Nature* (London, 1736).

Calendar of State Papers Domestic, 1601–3 (London, 1870).

Carlson, Leland H., ed., *The Writings of John Greenwood and Henry Barrow, 1591–3*, Elizabethan Nonconformist Texts, VI (London: Allen & Unwin, 1970).

Carpenter, John, *A Preparative to Contentation* (London, 1597).

Chambers, Robert, *Domestic Annals of Scotland from the Revolution to the Rebellion of 1745* (Edinburgh, 1861).

Traditions of Edinburgh, new ed. (Edinburgh, 1847).

Character of a Coffee-House, with the Symptomes of a Town-Wit, The (London, 1673).

Cheyne, George, *Philosophical Principles of Natural Religion* (London, 1705).

Christian Reformer; or, Unitarian Magazine and Review, The, n.s. 12 (1856).

Cicero, *The Nature of the Gods*, trans. P. G. Walsh (Oxford: Oxford University Press, 1997).

Clarke, Samuel, *A Demonstration of the Being and Attributes of God* (London, 1705). Also Ezio Vailati, ed., *Cambridge Texts in the History of Philosophy* (Cambridge: Cambridge University Press, 1998).

Clarke, Samuel, *A Discourse Concerning the Unchangeable Obligations of Natural Religion* (London, 1706).

Cobbett, W., Howell, T. B. et al., eds., *A Complete Collection of State Trials*, 34 vols (London, 1809–28).

Corderoy, Jeremy, *A Warning for Worldlings* (London, 1608).

Craig, Mungo, *A Lye Is No Scandal* ([Edinburgh], 1697).

A Satyr against Atheistical Deism (Edinburgh, 1696).

Crichton, Andrew, *Converts from Infidelity*, 2 vols (Edinburgh, 1827).

Cromarty, George MacKenzie, 1st Earl of, *A Bundle of Positions* (London, 1705).

Synopsis Apocalyptica (Edinburgh, 1708).

Cudworth, Ralph, *The True Intellectual System of the Universe* (London, 1678).

Cuffe, Henry, *The Differences of the Ages of Mans Life* (London, 1607).

Cunningham, John, *The Church History of Scotland*, 2nd ed., 2 vols (Edinburgh, 1882).

D'Ewes, Sir Simonds, *Autobiography and Correspondence*, ed. J. O. Halliwell, 2 vols (London, 1845).

Daily Gazetteer, no. 1187 (11 April 1739).

[Darrell, John], *Triall of Maist. Dorrell, The* (Middelburg, 1599).

Dove, John, *A Confutation of Atheisme* (London, 1605).

Dunton, John, *The Life and Errors* (London, 1705).

Edwards, John, *Some Thoughts Concerning the Several Causes and Occasions of Atheism* (London, 1695).

Edwards, Thomas, *Gangraena: Or a Catalogue and Discovery of Many of the Errours, Heresies, Blasphemies and Pernicious Practices of the Sectaries of this Time* (London, 1646; reprinted Exeter: The Rota and the University of Exeter, 1977).

[Eliot, John], *Mr John Eliot, Called, Doctor of Medicine, His Last Speech and Advice to the World, At His Suffering, March 9, 1694* (Edinburgh, 1694).

Ellis, Havelock, ed., *Christopher Marlowe*, The Mermaid Series (London, 1887).

Firth, C. H, and Rait, R. S., eds., *Act and Ordinances of the Interregnum, 1642–1660*, 3 vols (London: HMSO, 1911).

Fitzherbert, Thomas, *The Second Part of a Treatise Concerning Policy, and Religion* ([Douai], 1610).

Flying Post (London, 1696–7).

Fotherby, Martin, *Atheomastix* (London, 1622).

Fuller, Thomas, *The Holy State and the Profane State* (Cambridge, 1642).

Gardiner, Samuel, *Doomes-Day Booke* (London, 1606).

Gastrell, Francis, *The Certainty and Necessity of Religion in General* (London, 1697).

Gentleman's Magazine, 9 (1739).

Gibbens, Nicholas, *Questions and Disputations Concerning the Holy Scripture* (London, 1601).

[Gibson, Edmund], *The Bishop of London's Pastoral Letter to the People of His Diocese* (London, 1728).

    The Bishop of London's Second Pastoral Letter . . . (London, 1730).

    The Bishop of London's Third Pastoral Letter . . . (London, 1731).

Gilpin, Richard, *Daemonologia Sacra; or, A Treatise of Satan's Temptations* (London, 1677).

Glanvill, Joseph, *A Blow at Modern Sadducism in Some Philosophical Considerations about Witchcraft* (London, 1668).

    Plus Ultra: Or the Progress and Advancement of Knowledge Since the Days of Aristotle (London, 1668).

    Seasonable Reflections and Discourses in Order to the Conviction, & Cure of the Scoffing, & Infidelity of a Degenerate Age (London, 1676).

Gordon, John, *Thomas Aikenhead: A Historical Review*, 3rd ed (London, 1856).

Gosson, Stephen, *The Trumpet of Warre* (London, 1598).

Grange, James Erskine, Lord, *Extracts from the Diary of a Senator of the College of Justice* (Edinburgh, 1843).

Greenham, Richard, *Workes*, ed. H. Holland, 3rd ed. (London, 1601).

Grose, Francis, *The Olio,* 2nd ed. (London, 1796).

Gurdon, Brampton, *The Pretended Difficulties in Natural or Reveal'd Religion No Excuse for Infidelity* (London, 1723).

'H. L., a Lay-Man', *The Second Spira, Being a Fearful Example of F. N. An Atheist, Part the Second* (London, 1693).

Hale, W. H., *A Series of Precedents and Proceedings in Criminal Causes* (London, 1847).

Hall, Joseph, *Works*, new ed., ed. Philip Wynter, 10 vols (Oxford, 1863).

Halyburton, Thomas, *Memoirs of the Life of the Reverend Mr. Thomas Halyburton* (Edinburgh, 1714).

    Natural Religion Insufficient; and Reveal'd Necessary to Man's Happiness in His Present State (Edinburgh, 1714).

Harris, John, *The Atheistical Objections, Against the Being of God and His Attributes* (London, 1698).
 Immorality and Pride, the Great Causes of Atheism (London, 1698).
Hawarde, John, *Les Reportes del Cases in Camera Stellata, 1593–1609*, ed. W. P. Baildon (London, 1894).
Hearne, Thomas, *Remarks and Collections*, ed. C. E. Doble, D. W. Rannie and H. E. Salter, 11 vols (Oxford, 1885–1921).
Heathcote, Ralph, *A Discourse upon the Being of God: Against Atheists* (London, 1763).
Hedge, Levi, *Eulogy on the Rev. Joseph McKean DD LLD, Boylston Professor of Rhetorick and Oratory* (Cambridge, MA, 1818).
Henning, G., ed., *Ein unächter Brief des Archimedes* (Darmstadt, 1872).
Hepburn, Robert, *Dissertatio de scriptis Pitcarnianis* (London, [1715]).
Heywood, Oliver, *Autobiography and Diaries*, ed. J. H. Turner, 4 vols (Brighouse and Bingley, 1882–5).
Heywood, Thomas, *A True Discourse of the Two Infamous Upstart Prophets* (London, 1636).
Hill, Adam, *The Crie of England* (London, 1595).
Historical Manuscripts Commission, *Manuscripts of His Grace the Duke of Portland*, 10 vols (London: H. M. C., 1891–1931).
 Supplementary Report on the MSS of the Duke of Hamilton (London: H. M. C., 1932).
Hobbes, Thomas, *Correspondence*, ed. Noel Malcolm, 2 vols (Oxford: Clarendon Press, 1994).
[Hobbes, Thomas], *Memorable Sayings of Mr. Hobbes* ([London, 1680]).
Holland, Philemon, trans., *The Historie of the World. Commonly Called, The Naturall Historie of C. Plinius Secundus* (London, 1601).
Hooke, Robert, *Posthumous Works*, ed. Richard Waller (London, 1705).
Hooker, Richard, *Of the Laws of Ecclesiastical Polity*, ed. A. S. McGrade, 3 vols (Oxford: Oxford University Press, 2013).
Horner, Francis, *Memoirs and Correspondence*, ed. Leonard Horner, 2 vols (London, 1843).
Hull, John, *Saint Peters Prophesie of These Last Daies* (London, 1610).
 The Unmasking of the Politike Atheist, 2nd ed. (London, 1602).
Hume, David, *Commentaries on the Law of Scotland*, 2 vols (Edinburgh, 1797).
Hunter, Michael, ed., *Robert Boyle by Himself and His Friends* (London: Pickering & Chatto, 1994).
Jackson, Thomas, *London New-Yeeres Gift* (London, 1609).
Johnston, W. T., ed., *The Best of Our Owne: Letters of Archibald Pitcairne, 1652–1713* (Edinburgh: Saorse Books, 1979).
Keill, John, *An Examination of Dr Burnet's Theory of the Earth* (Oxford, 1698).
Laing, D., ed., *Historical Notices of Scotish Affairs. Selected from the Manuscripts of Sir John Lauder of Fountainhall*, 2 vols (Edinburgh, 1848).
Locke, John, *Correspondence*, ed. E. S. de Beer, 8 vols (Oxford: Clarendon Press, 1976–89).

Essay Concerning Human Understanding (cited by book/chapter).

Longstaffe, W. H. D., ed., *The Acts of the High Commission Court within the Diocese of Durham*, Surtees Society, 34 (Durham, 1858).

Lorimer, William, *Two Discourses* (London, 1713).

Lorrain, Paul, *Popery Near A-Kin to Paganism and Atheism* (London, 1712).

Lyly, John, *Euphues: The Anatomy of Wit and Euphues & His England*, ed. M. W. Croll and H. Clemons (London: Routledge 1916).

Macaulay, T. B., *The History of England*, 5 vols (London, 1849–61).

MacIntosh, J. J., ed., *Boyle on Atheism* (Toronto: University of Toronto Press, 2005).

Manningham, Thomas, *Two Discourses* (London, 1681).

[McCrie, Thomas], *Macaulay on Scotland: A Critique Republished from 'The Witness'* (Edinburgh, n.d.).

[McKean, Joseph], *Catalogue of the Select Library of the Late Rev. Joseph McKean DD, LLD* (Boston, 1818).

Meres, Francis, *Palladis Tamia. Wits Treasury* (London, 1598).

Monk, J. H., *Life of Richard Bentley*, 2nd ed., 2 vols (London, 1833).

More, Sir George, *A Demonstration of God in His Workes* (London, 1597).

More, Henry, *An Explanation of the Grand Mystery of Godliness* (London, 1660).

More, Henry, *Enchiridion metaphysicum* (London, 1671), partially translated in Joseph Glanvill, *Saducismus triumphatus* (London, 1681), pp. 97–180; see also *Henry More's Manual of Metaphysics: A Translation of the Enchiridion metaphysicum (1679) with an Introduction and Notes*, ed. Alexander Jacob (Hildesheim: Olms, 1995).

Mornay, Phillippe Duplessis, *A Woorke Concerning the Trewnesse of the Christian Religion*, trans. Sir Philip Sidney and Arthur Golding (London, 1587).

Morton, Thomas, *A Treatise of the Nature of God* (London, 1599).

Mosse, Miles, *Ivstifying and Saving Faith Distinguished from the Faith of the Devils* (Cambridge and London, 1614).

Murdoch, J. R., ed., *The Diary of Mr John Lamont of Newton, 1649–71* (Edinburgh, 1830).

Nashe, Thomas, *Works*, ed. R. B. McKerrow, 2nd ed., 5 vols (Oxford: Blackwell, 1958).

Newton, Isaac, *Correspondence*, ed. H. W. Turnbull et al., 7 vols (Cambridge: Cambridge University Press, 1959–77).

Opticks, Dover reprint (New York: Dover, 1979).

Papers & Letters on Natural Philosophy, ed. I. B. Cohen, 2nd ed. (Cambridge, MA: Harvard University Press, 1978).

Nicholls, William, *A Conference with a Theist* (London, 1696).

Nichols, Josias, *An Order of Houshold Instruction* (London, 1596).

The Plea of the Innocent (London, 1602).

Origen: Contra Celsum, trans. Henry Chadwick (Cambridge: Cambridge University Press, 1953)

Pagitt, Ephraim, *Heresiography*, 5th ed. (London, 1654).

Palfreyman, Thomas, *The Treatise of Heavenly Philosophie* (London, 1578).

Palmer, Joseph, *Necrology of Alumni of Harvard College 1851/2–1862/3* (Boston, 1864).

Parsons, Robert, *A Christian Directorie Guiding Men to their Salvation* ([Louvain], 1585).

[Parsons, Robert], *An Advertisement Written to a Secretarie of My L. Treasurers of Ingland* ([Antwerp], 1592).

Perkins, William, *Workes*, 3 vols (Cambridge, 1608–9).

Pitcairne, Archibald, *The Assembly*, ed. Terence Tobin (Lafayette, IND: Purdue University Studies, 1972).

　Babell; A Satirical Poem, on the Proceedings of the General Assembly in the Year MDCXCII, ed. G. R. Kinloch (Edinburgh, 1830).

　Dissertatio de legibus historiae naturalis (Edinburgh, 1696).

　Dissertationes medicæ (Edinburgh, 1713).

　Dissertationes medicæ (Rotterdam, 1701).

　Elementa medicinæ physico-mathematica (London, 1717; Eng. trans., 1718).

　Epistola Archimedis ad Regem Gelonem (various editions).

　Latin Poems, ed. John and Winifred MacQueen (Assen: Royal Van Gorcum, and Tempe, AZ: Arizona Center for Medieval and Renaissance Studies, 2009).

　Opera omnia (The Hague, 1722, and subsequent editions).

　The Phanaticks, ed. John MacQueen (Woodbridge: Scottish Text Society, 2012).

　Solutio problematis de historicis; seu, inventoribus (Edinburgh, 1688).

　The Works of Dr Archibald Pitcairne (London, 1715).

Pitcairn, T. et al., eds., *Acts of the General Assembly of the Church of Scotland 1638–1842* (Edinburgh, 1843).

Post Boy (London, 1696–7).

Post Man (London, 1696–7).

Price, Daniel, *Sauls Prohibition Staide* (London, 1609).

Primaudaye, Pierre de la, *The Second Part of the French Academic,* trans. Thomas Bowes (London, 1594).

Prior, Matthew, *Literary Works*, ed. H. Bunker Wright and Monroe K. Spears, 2 vols (Oxford: Clarendon Press, 1959).

Protestant Mercury (London, 1696–7).

Ritson, Joseph, *Observations on the Three First Volumes of the History of English Poetry* (London, 1782).

Rochester, John Wilmot, Earl of, *Letters*, ed. Jeremy Treglown (Oxford: Blackwell, 1980).

　Works, ed. Harold Love (Oxford: Oxford University Press, 1999).

Rogers, Thomas, *The Catholic Doctrine of the Church of England*, ed. J. J. S. Perowne (Cambridge: Parker Society, 1854).

Roll of Edinburgh Burgesses and Guild-Brethren 1406–1700 (Edinburgh: Scottish Record Society, 59, 1929).

Satan His Methods and Malice Baffled (London, 1683).

[Sault, Richard], *A Conference Between a Modern Atheist, and His Friend. By the Methodizer of the Second Spira* (London, 1693).

(attrib.), *The Second Spira: Being A Fearful Example of An Atheist, Who Had Apostacised from the Christian Religion, and Dyed in Despair at Westminster December 8. 1692* (London, 1693) and '30th edition' (London, [1719]).

[Scargill, Daniel], *The Recantation of . . ., Publickly Made before the University of Cambridge, in Great St Maries, July 25, 1669* (Cambridge, 1669).

Shaftesbury, Anthony Ashley Cooper, 3rd Earl of, *Characteristics of Men, Manners, Opinions, Times*, ed. Lawrence E. Klein (Cambridge: Cambridge University Press, 1999).

Sidney, Sir Philip, *The Countess of Pembroke's Arcadia*, ed. Maurice Evans (Harmondsworth: Penguin, 1977).

Simon, Richard, *A Critical History of the Old Testament* (London, 1682).

Singer, S. W., ed., Marlowe and Chapman's *Hero and Leander* (London, 1821).

Smith, Henry, *Gods Arrowe against Atheists* (London, 1593).

Smith, John, *The Judgment of God upon Atheism and Infidelity, in a Brief and True Account of the Irreligious Life and Miserable Death of Mr. George Edwards* (London, 1704).

Smith, Samuel, *The Great Assize*, 3rd impression (London, 1618).

Spence, Joseph, *Anecdotes, Observations and Characters, of Books and Men*, ed. Samuel Weller Singer (London, 1820).

  Observations, Anecdotes and Characters of Books and Men, ed. J. M. Osborn, 2 vols (Oxford: Clarendon Press, 1966).

Spicer, John, *The Sale of Salt* (London, 1611).

Sprague, William B., *Annals of the American Pulpit*, 2 vols (New York, 1857).

Sprat, Thomas, *The History of the Royal Society of London* (London, 1667).

Statutes of the Realm, ed. Alexander Luders et al., 10 vols. (London, 1810–28)

Staunton, Edmund, *A Sermon Preacht at Great Milton, 1654, at the Funeral of Elizabeth Wilkinson* (Oxford, 1659).

Stephens, John, *Satyrical Essayes Characters and Others* (London, 1615).

Stillingfleet, Edward, *A Letter to a Deist in Answer to Several Objections against the Truth and Authority of the Scriptures* (London, 1677).

Strutt, Samuel, *A Defence of the Late Learned Dr Clarke's Notion of Natural Liberty: In Answer to Three Letters Wrote by him to a Gentleman at the University of Cambridge, on the Side of Necessity* (London, 1730).

  A Philosophical Enquiry into the Physical Spring of Human Actions, and the Immediate Cause of Thinking (London, 1732).

Talon, Henri, ed., *Selections from the Journals and Papers of John Byrom* (London: Rockcliffe, 1950).

Tenison, Thomas, *A Sermon Concerning the Folly of Atheism* (London, 1691).

Thomson, T., and Innes, C., eds., *The Acts of the Parliaments of Scotland*, 12 vols (Edinburgh, 1814–75).

[Tindal, Matthew], *An Address to the Inhabitants of the Two Great Cities of London and Westminster* (London, 1728).

  A Second Address . . . (London, 1730).

  Religious, Rational, and Moral Conduct of Matthew Tindal, LL.D., The (London, 1735).

Toland, John, *Letters to Serena* (London, 1704).

[Trosse, George], *The Life of the Revd. George Trosse*, ed. A. W. Brink (Montreal: McGill-Queens University Press, 1974).

Turnbull, George, *Education for Life: Correspondence and Writings on Religion and Practical Philosophy*, ed. M. A. Stewart and Paul Wood (Indianapolis: Liberty Fund, 2014).

Vanini, Giulio Cesare, *Le Opere*, ed. Luigi Corvaglia, 2 vols (Milan: Società Anonima Editrice Dante Alighieri, 1933–4).

Vaughan, William, *The Golden-Grove, Moralised in Three Books* (London, 1600).

Veron, John, *A Fruteful Treatise of Predestination* (London, [1561]).

Wagstaffe, John, *The Question of Witchcraft Debated*, 2nd ed. (London, 1671).

Weemes, John, *A Treatise of the Foure Degenerate Sonnes* (London, 1636).

Wesley, John, *Letters*, ed. John Telford, 8 vols (London: Epworth Press, 1931, reprinted 1960).

[Wesley, Samuel, ed.], *Two Letters from a Deist to his Friend, Concerning the Truth and Propagation of Deism, in Opposition to Christianity, with Remarks* (London, 1730).

West [Wast], Elizabeth, *Memoirs, or Spiritual Exercises* (Edinburgh, 1724).

Whiston, William, *A New Theory of the Earth* (London, 1696).

Wilkins, John, *Of the Principles and Duties of Natural Religion* (London, 1678).

Willobie His Avisa, ed. G. B. Harrison (London: John Lane, The Bodley Head, 1926).

Windle, William, *Enquiry into the Immateriality of Thinking Substances, Human Liberty, and the Original of Motion* (London, 1738).

Wingfield, John, *Atheisme Close and Open, Anatomized*, 2 pts (London, 1634).

Wodrow, Robert, *Analecta*, 4 vols (Edinburgh, 1842–3).
  Correspondence, ed. T. McCrie, 3 vols (Edinburgh, 1842–3).
  Early Letters of . . ., 1698–1709, ed. L. W. Sharp (Edinburgh: Scottish Historical Society, 3rd ser. 24, 1937).

Wolseley, Sir Charles, *The Unreasonablenesse of Atheism Made Manifest* (London, 1669).

Wood, Anthony, *Life and Times*, ed. Andrew Clark, 5 vols (Oxford, 1891–1900).

Woolston, Thomas, *A Discourse on the Miracles of Our Saviour* (London, 1727).
  Mr Woolston's Defence of his Discourses on the Miracles of Our Saviour. Part 1 (London, 1729).

Woolton, John, *A Treatise of the Immortalitie of the Soule* (London, 1576).

Wotton, William, *Reflections upon Ancient and Modern Learning* (London, 1694).

SECONDARY SOURCES

Aldridge, A. O, 'Shaftesbury and the Deist Manifesto', *Transactions of the American Philosophical Society*, n.s. 41 (1951), 297–385.

Alexander, Nathan, 'Defining and Redefining Atheism: Dictionary and Encyclopedia Entries for "Atheism" and Their Critics in the Anglophone

World from the Early Modern Period to the Present', *Intellectual History Review*, 30 (2020), 253–71.

Allen, D. C., *Doubt's Boundless Sea: Skepticism and Faith in the Renaissance* (Baltimore: Johns Hopkins Press, 1964).

Andrews, Frances, Methuen, Charlotte, and Spicer, Andrew, eds., *Doubting Christianity: The Church and Doubt*, Studies in Church History 52 (Cambridge, Cambridge University Press, 2016).

Appleby, John H., 'Archibald Pitcairne Re-encountered: A Note on His Manuscript Poems and Printed Library Catalogue', *The Bibliotheck*, 12 (1986), 137–9.

Appleby John H., and Cunningham, Andrew, 'Robert Erskine and Archibald Pitcairne – Two Scottish Physicians' Outstanding Libraries', *The Bibliotheck*, 11 (1982), 3–16.

Arnold, John H., *Belief and Unbelief in Medieval Europe* (London: Hodder Arnold, 2005).

Ashe, Geoffrey, *The Hell-Fire Clubs: A History of Anti-Morality*, revised ed. (Stroud: Sutton Publishing, 2000).

Augustine, Matthew C., and Zwicker, Steven N., eds., *Lord Rochester in the Restoration World* (Cambridge: Cambridge University Press, 2015).

Axtell, J. L., 'The Mechanics of Opposition: Restoration Cambridge v. Daniel Scargill', *Bulletin of the Institute of Historical Research*, 38 (1965), 102–11.

Aylmer, G. E., 'Unbelief in Seventeenth-Century England', in *Puritans and Revolutionaries: Essays in Seventeenth-Century History Presented to Christopher Hill*, ed. D. H. Pennington and Keith Thomas (Oxford: Clarendon Press, 1978), pp. 22–46.

Bahlman, D. W. R., *The Moral Revolution of 1688* (New Haven: Yale University Press, 1957).

Bakeless, John, *The Tragicall History of Christopher Marlowe*, 2 vols (Cambridge, MA: Harvard University Press, 1942).

Bennett, H. S., *English Books and Readers, 1558–1603* (Cambridge: Cambridge University Press, 1965).

Berman, David, 'Deism, Immortality, and the Art of Theological Lying', in *Deism, Masonry and the Enlightenment*, ed. J. A. Leo Lemay (Newark: University of Delaware Press, 1987), pp. 61–78.

'Disclaimers as Offence Mechanisms in Charles Blount and John Toland', in Michael Hunter and David Wootton, eds., *Atheism from the Reformation to the Enlightenment*, pp. 255–72.

George Berkeley: Idealism and the Man (Oxford: Clarendon Press, 1994).

A History of Atheism in Britain: From Hobbes to Russell (London: Croom Helm, 1988).

'The Repressive Denials of Atheism in Britain in the Seventeenth and Eighteenth Centuries', *Proceedings of the Royal Irish Academy*, 82 (1982), 211–46.

Berti, Silvia, Charles-Daubert, Françoise, and Popkin, Richard H., eds., *Heterodoxy, Spinozism and Free Thought in Early Eighteenth-Century Europe: Studies on the 'Traité des trois imposteurs'* (Dordrecht: Kluwer, 1996).

Bianca, Concetta, 'Per la Storia del Termine "Atheus" nel Cinquecento: Fonti et Traduzioni Greco-Latine', *Studi Filosofici*, 3 (1980), 71–104.

Bostridge, Ian, *Witchcraft and Its Transformations, c. 1650–c. 1750* (Oxford: Clarendon Press, 1997).

Bourke, Joanna, *Fear: A Cultural History* (London: Virago, 2005).

Boyce, Benjamin, *The Theophrastan Character in England to 1642* (Cambridge, MA: Harvard University Press, 1947).

Branch, Lori, 'Bishop Butler', in *The Oxford Handbook of English Literature and Theology*, ed. Andrew Hass, David Jasper and Elisabeth Jay (Oxford: Oxford University Press, 2009), pp. 590–606.

Bray, Alan, *Homosexuality in Renaissance England* (London, 1982; new ed., New York: Columbia University Press, 1995).

Brie, Friedrich, 'Deismus und Atheismus in der Englischen Renaissance', *Anglia*, 48 (1924), 54–98, 105–68.

Briggs, W. D., 'On a Document Concerning Christopher Marlowe', *Studies in Philology*, 20 (1923), 153–9.

Brown, T. M., 'Medicine in the Shadow of the *Principia*', *Journal of the History of Ideas*, 48 (1987), 629–48.

Buckley, George T., *Atheism in the English Renaissance* (Chicago, 1932; reprinted New York: Russell & Russell, 1965).

Buckley, Michael J., *Denying and Disclosing God: The Ambiguous Progress of Modern Atheism* (New Haven and London: Yale University Press, 2004).

   At the Origins of Modern Atheism (New Haven and London: Yale University Press, 1987).

Budd, Susan, 'The Loss of Faith. Reasons for Unbelief among Members of the Secular Movement in England, 1850–1950', *Past and Present*, 36 (1967), 106–25.

   Varieties of Unbelief: Atheists and Agnostics in English Society 1850–1960 (London: Heinemann, 1977).

Bullivant, Stephen, and Ruse, Michael, eds., *The Cambridge History of Atheism*, 2 vols (Cambridge: Cambridge University Press, 2021).

Burns, N. T., *Christian Mortalism from Tyndale to Milton* (Cambridge, MA: Harvard University Press, 1972).

Burtt, Shelley, 'The Societies for the Reformation of Manners: Between John Locke and the Devil in Augustan England', in Lund, ed., *Margins of Orthodoxy*, pp. 149–69.

Busson, Henri, 'Les Noms des Incrédules au XVIᵉ Siècle', *Bibliothèque d'Humanisme et Renaissance*, 16 (1954), 273–83.

Cameron, J. K., 'Scottish Calvinism and the Principle of Intolerance', in *Reformatio Perennis*, ed. B. A Gerrish (Pittsburgh: Pickwick Press, 1981), pp. 113–28.

   'Theological Controversy: A Factor in the Origins of the Scottish Enlightenment', in *The Origins and Nature of the Scottish Enlightenment*, ed. R. H. Campbell and A. S. Skinner (Edinburgh: John Donald, 1982), pp. 116–30.

Champion, Justin A. I., 'Enlightened Erudition and the Politics of Reading in John Toland's Circle', *Historical Journal*, 49 (2006), 111–41.

   The Pillars of Priestcraft Shaken: The Church of England and Its Enemies, 1660–1730 (Cambridge: Cambridge University Press, 1992).

Republican Learning: John Toland and the Crisis of Christian Culture, 1696–1722 (Manchester: Manchester University Press, 2003).

Charles-Daubert, Françoise, ed., *Le 'Traité des trois imposteurs' et 'L'esprit de Spinosa'. Philosophie clandestine entre 1678 et 1768* (Oxford: Voltaire Foundation, 1999).

Clark, Stuart, 'Inversion, Misrule and the Meaning of Witchcraft', *Past & Present*, 87 (1980), 98–127.

 Thinking with Demons: The Idea of Witchcraft in Early Modern Europe (Oxford: Clarendon Press, 1997).

 'Wisdom Literature of the Seventeenth century: A Guide to the Contents of the "Bacon-Tottel" Commonplace Books', *Transactions of the Cambridge Bibliographical Society*, 6 (1976), 291–305.

Cohen, Stanley, *Folk Devils and Moral Panics: The Creation of the Mods and Rockers* (London: McGibbon & Kee, 1972).

Collins, Jeffrey R., 'Early Modern England', in Bullivant and Ruse, *Cambridge History of Atheism*, 1, pp. 202–22.

 The Allegiance of Thomas Hobbes (Oxford: Oxford University Press, 2005).

Collins, Kenneth J., 'Assurance', in *The Oxford Handbook to Methodist Studies*, ed. W. J. Abraham and J. E. Kirby (Oxford: Oxford University Press, 2009), pp. 602–17.

Collinson, Patrick, 'A Comment: Concerning the Name Puritan', *Journal of Ecclesiastical History*, 31 (1980), 483–88.

 The Elizabethan Puritan Movement (London: Jonathan Cape, 1967).

 English Puritanism (London: Historical Association, 1983).

 The Religion of Protestants: The Church in English Society 1559–1625 (Oxford: Clarendon Press, 1982).

Crane, R. S., 'Anglican Apologetics and the Idea of Progress, 1699–1745', in his *The Idea of the Humanities and Other Essays Critical and Historical*, 2 vols (Chicago: University of Chicago Press, 1967), I, 214–87, originally published in *Modern Philology*, 31 (1933–4).

Cunliffe, Christopher, ed., *Joseph Butler's Moral and Religious Thought: Tercentenary Essays* (Oxford: Clarendon Press, 1992).

Cunningham, Andrew, 'Sydenham versus Newton: the Edinburgh Fever Dispute of the 1690s between Andrew Brown and Archibald Pitcairne', in *Theories of Fever from Antiquity to the Enlightenment*, ed. W. F. Bynum and V. Nutton (*Medical History*, supplement no. 1, London: Wellcome Institute for the History of Medicine, 1981), pp. 71–98.

Curtis, T. C., and Speck, W. A., 'The Societies for the Reformation of Manners: A Case Study in the Theory and Practice of Moral Reform', *Literature and History*, 3 (1976), 45–64.

Dabbs, Thomas, *Reforming Marlowe: The Nineteenth-Century Canonisation of a Renaissance Dramatist* (Lewisburg: Bucknell University Press, 1991).

Danchin, F. C., 'Etudes Critiques sur Christopher Marlowe', *Revue Germanique*, 9 (1913), 566–87, with commentary in *Revue Germanique*, 10 (1914), 52–68.

Davidson, Nicholas, 'Christopher Marlowe and Atheism', in *Christopher Marlowe and English Renaissance Culture*, ed. Darryll Grantley and Peter Roberts (Aldershot: Scolar, 1996), pp. 129–47.

'"Le plus beau et le plus meschant esprit que ie aye cogneu": Science and Religion in the Writings of Giulio Cesare Vanini, 1585–1619', in *Heterodoxy in Early Modern Science and Religion*, ed. John Brooke and Ian MacLean (Oxford: Oxford University Press, 2005), pp. 59–79.

'Unbelief and Atheism in Italy, 1500–1700' in Michael Hunter and David Wootton, eds., *Atheism from the Reformation to the Enlightenment*, pp. 55–85.

Davie, G. E., *The Scottish Enlightenment* (London: Historical Association, 1981).

Davies, Eloise, 'English Politics and the Blasphemy Act of 1698', *English Historical Review*, 135 (2020), 804–35.

Davis, Edward B., 'Boyle's Philosophy of Religion', in *The Bloomsbury Companion to Robert Boyle*, ed. Jan-Erik Jones (London: Bloomsbury Academic, 2020), pp. 257–82.

Davis, J. C., *Fear, Myth and History: The Ranters and the Historians* (Cambridge: Cambridge University Press, 1986).

Davis, J. C., MacGregor, J. F., Capp, Bernard, Smith, Nigel and Gibbons, B. J., 'Fear, Myth and Furore: Reassessing the "Ranters"' (Debate), *Past and Present*, 129 (1990), 79–103, and 140 (1993), 155–210.

de Beer, E. S., 'The English Newspapers from 1695 to 1702', in *William III and Louis XIV: Essays 1680–1720. By and for Mark A. Thomson*, ed. Ragnild Hatton and J. S. Bromley (Liverpool: Liverpool University Press, 1968), pp. 117–29.

Delany, Paul, *British Autobiography in the Seventeenth Century* (London: Routledge & Kegan Paul, 1969).

Dent, C. M., *Protestant Reformers in Elizabethan Oxford* (Oxford: Oxford University Press, 1983).

Devellennes, Charles, *Positive Atheism: Bayle, Meslier, d'Holbach, Diderot* (Edinburgh: Edinburgh University Press, 2021).

Dixon, Thomas, *From Passions to Emotions: The Creation of a Secular Psychological Category* (Cambridge: Cambridge University Press, 2003).

Drummond, A. L., and Bulloch, James, *The Scottish Church, 1688–1743: The Age of the Moderates* (Edinburgh: St Andrew Press, 1973).

Duckett, Sir G. F., *Duchetiana; or Historical and Genealogical Memoirs of the Family of Ducket, from the Norman Conquest to the Present Time* (London: John Russell Smith, 1874).

Duncan, Douglas, 'Scholarship and Politeness in the Early Eighteenth Century', in *The History of Scottish Literature. Volume 2, 1660–1800*, ed. Andrew Hook (Aberdeen: Aberdeen University Press, 1987), pp. 51–63.

Thomas Ruddiman: A Study in Scottish Scholarship of the Early Eighteenth Century (Edinburgh: Oliver & Boyd, 1965).

Ellensweig, Sarah, *The Fringes of Belief: English Literature, Ancient Heresy, and the Politics of Freethinking, 1660–1760* (Stanford: Stanford University Press, 2008).

Elton, W. R., *King Lear and the Gods* (San Marino, CA: Huntington Library, 1966).

Emerson, Roger, 'The Religious, the Secular and the Worldly: Scotland 1680–1800', in *Religion, Secularization and Political Thought: Thomas Hobbes to J. S. Mill*, ed. J. E. Crimmins (London: Routledge, 1989), pp. 68–89.

English Short Title Catalogue: http://estc.bl.uk/.

Erdozan, Dominic, *The Soul of Doubt: The Religious Roots of Unbelief from Luther to Marx* (Oxford: Oxford University Press, 2016).

Erikson, K. T., *Wayward Puritans: A Study in the Sociology of Deviance* (New York: John Wiley & Sons, 1966).

Febvre, Lucien, *The Problem of Unbelief in the Sixteenth Century: The Religion of Rabelais*, trans. Beatrice Gottlieb (Cambridge, MA: Harvard University Press, 1982).

Florida, R. E., 'British Law and Socinianism in the Seventeenth and Eighteenth Centuries', in *Socinianism and Its Role in the Culture of the Sixteenth to Eighteenth Centuries*, ed. Lech Szczucki (Warsaw-Łódź: Polish Academy of Sciences, 1983), pp. 201–10.

Force, J. E., *William Whiston, Honest Newtonian* (Cambridge: Cambridge University Press, 1985).

Foster, J., *Alumni Oxonienses, 1500–1714*, 4 vols (Oxford: Parker & Co., 1891–2).

Foxon, David F., *English Verse 1701–1750: A Catalogue of Separately Printed Poems with Notes on Contemporary Collected Editions*, 2 vols (Cambridge: Cambridge University Press, 1975).

Friesen, John, 'Archibald Pitcairne, David Gregory and the Scottish Origins of English Tory Newtonianism, 1688–1715', *History of Science*, 41 (2003), 163–91.

Gascoigne, John, *Cambridge in the Age of the Enlightenment* (Cambridge: Cambridge University Press, 1989).

Gibson, Marion, *Possession, Puritanism and Print: Darrell, Harsnett, Shakespeare and the Elizabethan Exorcism Controversy* (London: Pickering & Chatto, 2006).

Ginzburg, Carlo, *The Cheese and the Worms: The Cosmos of a Sixteenth-Century Miller*, English trans. (London: Routledge & Kegan Paul, 1980).

Graham, Michael F., *The Blasphemies of Thomas Aikenhead: Boundaries of Belief on the Eve of the Enlightenment* (Edinburgh: Edinburgh University Press, 2008).

'Kirk in Danger: Presbyterian Political Divinity in Two Eras', in *The Impact of the European Reformation*, ed. Bridget Heal and O. P. Grell (Aldershot: Ashgate, 2008), pp. 167–86.

Green, Ian, *The Christian's ABC: Catechisms and Catechising in England c. 1530–1740* (Oxford: Clarendon Press, 1996).

Green, V. H. H., 'Religion in the Colleges 1715–1800', in *The History of the University of Oxford, vol. 5, The Eighteenth Century*, ed. L. S. Sutherland and L. G. Mitchell (Oxford: Clarendon Press, 1986), pp. 425–67.

Greenblatt, Stephen J., 'Invisible Bullets: Renaissance Authority and its Subversion', *Glyph; Johns Hopkins Textual Studies*, 8 (1981), 40–61, reprinted in Greenblatt, *Shakespearean Negotiations: The Circulation of Social*

Energy in Renaissance England (Berkeley and Los Angeles: University of California Press, 1988), pp. 21–65.

Sir Walter Ralegh: The Renaissance Man and His Roles (New Haven and London: Yale University Press, 1973).

Greenough, C. N., *A Bibliography of the Theophrastan Character in English* (Cambridge, MA: Harvard University Press, 1947).

Greyerz, Kaspar von, *European Physico-Theology (1650–c. 1760) in Context: Celebrating Nature and Creation* (Oxford: Oxford University Press, 2022).

Guerrini, Anita, 'Archibald Pitcairne and Newtonian Medicine', *Medical History*, 31 (1987), 70–83.

'"A Club of Little Villains": Rhetoric, Professional Identity and Medical Pamphlet Wars', in *Literature and Medicine during the Eighteenth Century*, ed. Marie Mulvey Roberts and Roy Porter (London: Routledge, 1993), pp. 226–44.

'James Keill, George Cheyne, and Newtonian Physiology, 1690–1740', *Journal of the History of Biology*, 18 (1985), 247–66.

'Newtonianism, Medicine and Religion', in *Religio Medici: Medicine and Religion in Seventeenth-Century England*, ed. O. P. Grell and Andrew Cunningham (Aldershot: Scolar, 1996), pp. 293–312.

Obesity and Depression in the Enlightenment: The Life and Times of George Cheyne (Norman: University of Oklahoma Press, 2000).

'The Tory Newtonians: Gregory, Pitcairne, and their Circle', *Journal of British Studies*, 25 (1986), 288–311.

Haigh, Christopher, *The Plain Man's Pathways to Heaven: Kinds of Christianity in Post-Reformation England* (Oxford: Oxford University Press, 2007).

Harries, Richard, 'Rochester's "Death-Bed Repentance"', in *That Second Bottle: Essays on John Wilmot, Earl of Rochester*, ed. Nicholas Fisher (Manchester: Manchester University Press, 2000), pp. 191–6.

Harrison, John, *The Library of Isaac Newton* (Cambridge: Cambridge University Press, 1978).

Haycock, David B., *William Stukeley: Science, Religion and Archaeology in Eighteenth-Century England* (Woodbridge: Boydell Press, 2002).

Hayton, David, 'Moral Reform and Country Politics in the Late Seventeenth-Century House of Commons', *Past & Present*, 128 (1990), 48–91.

Hecht, Jennifer Michael, *Doubt: A History* (New York: Harper San Francisco, 2003).

Hempton, David, *Evangelical Disenchantment: Nine Portraits of Faith and Doubt* (New Haven and London: Yale University Press, 2008).

Herrick, James A., *The Radical Rhetoric of the English Deists: The Discourse of Skepticism, 1680–1750* (Columbia: University of South Carolina Press, 1997).

Hill, Christopher, 'Freethinking and Libertinism: The Legacy of the English Revolution', in Lund, ed., *Margins of Orthodoxy*, pp. 54–70.

'Irreligion in the "Puritan" Revolution', in *Radical Religion in the English Revolution*, ed. J. F. McGregor and Barry Reay (Oxford: Oxford University Press, 1984), pp. 191–211.

Honan, Park, *Christopher Marlowe: Poet and Spy* (Oxford: Oxford University Press, 2005).

Horn, D. B., *British Diplomatic Representatives 1689–1789*, Camden Society 3rd series, 46 (London: Camden Society, 1932).

Horsley, Adam, *Libertines and the Law: Subversive Authors and Criminal Justice in Early Seventeenth-Century France* (Oxford: Oxford University Press, 2021).

Hotson, Leslie, *Shakespeare versus Shallow* (London: Nonesuch Press, 1931).

Houston, R. A., *Social Change in the Age of Enlightenment: Edinburgh, 1660–1760* (Oxford: Clarendon Press, 1994).

Hudson, Wayne, 'Atheism and Deism Demythologized', in Hudson, Lucci and Wigelsworth, eds., *Atheism and Deism Revalued,* pp. 13–23.

The English Deists: Studies in Early Enlightenment (London: Pickering & Chatto, 2009).

Enlightenment and Modernity: The English Deists and Reform (London: Pickering & Chatto, 2009).

Hudson, Wayne, Lucci, Diego, and Wigelsworth, J. R., eds., *Atheism and Deism Revalued: Heterodox Religious Identities in Britain, 1650–1800* (Farnham: Ashgate, 2014).

Hume Brown, P., *History of Scotland to the Present Time*, 3 vols (Cambridge: Cambridge University Press, 1911),

Hunter, Michael, 'Appendix: Boyle and the Sects', *History of Science*, 33 (1995), 86–92, reprinted in Hunter, *Scrupulosity and Science*, pp. 51–7.

Boyle: Between God and Science (New Haven and London: Yale University Press, 2009).

Boyle Studies: Aspects of the Life and Thought of Robert Boyle (1627–91) (Farnham: Ashgate, 2015).

'Casuistry in Action: Robert Boyle's Confessional Interviews with Gilbert Burnet and Edward Stillingfleet, 1691', *Journal of Ecclesiastical History*, 44 (1993), 80–98, reprinted in Hunter, *Scrupulosity and Science*, pp. 72–92.

'The Conscience of Robert Boyle: Functionalism, "Dysfunctionalism" and the Task of Historical Understanding', in *Renaissance and Revolution*, ed. J. V. Field and F. A. J. L. James (Cambridge: Cambridge University Press, 1993), pp. 147–59, reprinted in Hunter, *Scrupulosity and Science*, pp. 58–71.

The Decline of Magic: Britain in the Enlightenment (New Haven and London: Yale University Press, 2020).

The Occult Laboratory: Magic, Science and Second Sight in Late Seventeenth-Century Scotland (Woodbridge: Boydell Press, 2001).

Robert Boyle (1627–91): Scrupulosity and Science (Woodbridge: Boydell Press, 2000).

'Robert Boyle's Blasphemous Thoughts and "Flashy Emanations": Newly Discovered Evidence', *The Seventeenth Century*, 34 (2019), 601–14.

'Science and Heterodoxy: An Early Modern Problem Reconsidered', in *Reappraisals of the Scientific Revolution*, ed. David C. Lindberg and Robert S. Westman (Cambridge: Cambridge University Press, 1990), pp. 437–60, reprinted in Hunter, *Science and the Shape of Orthodoxy*, pp. 225–44.

Science and the Shape of Orthodoxy: Intellectual Change in Late Seventeenth-Century Britain (Woodbridge: Boydell Press, 1995).

Science and Society in Restoration England (Cambridge: Cambridge University Press, 1981).

Hunter, Michael, and Wootton, David, eds., *Atheism from the Reformation to the Enlightenment* (Oxford: Clarendon Press, 1992).

Ingamells, John, *A Dictionary of British and Irish Travellers in Italy 1701–1800* (New Haven and London: Yale University Press, 1997).

Ingram, Martin, *Church Courts, Sex and Marriage in England, 1570–1640* (Cambridge: Cambridge University Press, 1987).

Ingram, Robert G., *Reformation without End: Religion, Politics and the Past in Post-Revolutionary England* (Manchester: Manchester University Press, 2018).

Ingram, Robert G., and Barber, Alex W., '"The Warr... against Heaven by Blasphemors and Infidels": Prosecuting Heresy in Enlightenment England', in *Freedom of Speech, 1500–1850*, ed. Ingram, Jason Peacey and Barber (Manchester: Manchester University Press, 2020), pp. 151–70.

Innes Smith, R. W., *English-Speaking Students of Medicine at the University of Leyden* (Edinburgh: Oliver & Boyd, 1932).

Israel, Jonathan, *Enlightenment Contested: Philosophy, Modernity and the Emancipation of Man 1670–1752* (Oxford: Oxford University Press, 2006).

The Enlightenment that Failed: Ideas, Revolution, and Democratic Defeat 1748–1830 (Oxford: Oxford University Press, 2019).

Radical Enlightenment: Philosophy and the Making of Modernity 1650–1750 (Oxford: Oxford University Press, 2001).

Jacob, J. R., *Robert Boyle and the English Revolution* (New York: Burt Franklin, 1977).

Jacob, Margaret C., *The Newtonians and the English Revolution 1689–1720* (Hassocks: Harvester Press, 1976).

The Radical Enlightenment: Pantheists, Freemasons and Republicans (London: Allen & Unwin, 1981).

Jacquot, Jean, 'Thomas Harriot's Reputation for Impiety', *Notes and Records of the Royal Society*, 9 (1952), 164–87.

Jesseph, Douglas M., *Squaring the Circle: The War between Hobbes and Wallis* (Chicago: University of Chicago Press, 1999).

Johnstone, Nathan, *The Devil and Demonism in Early Modern England* (Cambridge: Cambridge University Press, 2006).

Jones, R. F., *Ancients and Moderns: A Study of the Rise of the Scientific Movement in Seventeenth-Century England*, 2nd ed. (St Louis: Washington University Studies, 1961).

Keeble, N. H., *Richard Baxter: Puritan Man of Letters* (Oxford: Clarendon Press, 1982).

Kendall, Roy, *Christopher Marlowe and Richard Baines* (Madison, NJ: Fairleigh Dickinson University Press, 2003).

'Richard Baines and Christopher Marlowe's Milieu', *English Literary Renaissance*, 24 (1994), 507–52.

Kidd, Colin, 'The Ideological Significance of Scottish Jacobite Latinity', in *Culture, Politics and Society in Britain, 1600–1800*, ed. Jeremy Black and Jeremy Gregory (Manchester: Manchester University Press, 1991), pp. 110–30.

King, Lester S., *The Philosophy of Medicine: The Early Eighteenth Century* (Cambridge, MA: Harvard University Press, 1978).

Klein, Lawrence, *Shaftesbury and the Culture of Politeness: Moral Discourse and Cultural Politics in Early Eighteenth-Century England* (Cambridge: Cambridge University Press, 1994).

Kocher, P. H., *Christopher Marlowe: A Study of his Thought, Learning and Character* (Chapel Hill: University of North Carolina Press, 1946).

Science and Religion in Elizabethan England (San Marino, CA: Huntington Library, 1953).

Kors, Alan Charles, *Atheism in France 1650–1729. Volume 1: The Orthodox Sources of Disbelief* (Princeton: Princeton University Press, 1990).

'The Atheism of d'Holbach and Naigeon' in Hunter and Wootton, eds., *Atheism from the Reformation to the Enlightenment*, pp. 273–300.

D'Holbach's Coterie (Princeton: Princeton University Press, 1976).

Epicureans and Atheists in France, 1650–1729 (Cambridge: Cambridge University Press, 2016).

Naturalism and Unbelief in France, 1650–1729 (Cambridge: Cambridge University Press, 2016).

Korshin, Paul, 'The Development of Intellectual Biography in the Eighteenth Century', *Journal of English and Germanic Philology*, 73 (1974), 513–23.

Kramnick, Isaac, *Bolingbroke and His Circle: The Politics of Nostalgia in the Age of Walpole* (Ithaca: Cornell University Press, 1968).

Kuriyama, Constance B., *Christopher Marlowe: A Renaissance Life* (Ithaca: Cornell University Press, 2002).

Lake, Peter, 'Anti-Popery: The Structure of a Prejudice', in *Conflict in Early Stuart England: Studies in Religion and Politics*, ed. Richard Cust and Ann Hughes (London: Longman, 1989), pp. 72–106.

'Anti-Puritanism: The Structure of a Prejudice', in *Religious Politics in Post-Reformation England*, ed. Lake and Kenneth Fincham (Woodbridge: Boydell Press, 2006), pp. 80–97.

'The Historiography of Puritanism', in *The Cambridge Companion to Puritanism*, ed. Paul C. H. Lim and John Coffey (Cambridge: Cambridge University Press, 2008), pp. 346–71.

Lalor, Stephen, *Matthew Tindal, Freethinker: An Eighteenth-Century Assault on Religion* (London: Continuum, 2006).

Larner, Christina, *Enemies of God: The Witch-Hunt in Scotland* (London: Chatto & Windus, 1981).

Larsen, Timothy, *Crisis of Doubt: Honest Faith in Nineteenth-Century England* (Oxford: Oxford University Press, 2006).

Law Commission Working Paper no. 79, *Offences against Religion and Public Worship* (London: H. M. S. O., 1981).

Lefranc, Pierre, *Sir Walter Ralegh, Ecrivain: l'oeuvre et les ideés* (Paris: Libraire Armand Colin, 1968).

Lenman, Bruce, *The Jacobite Risings in Britain 1689–1746* (London: Eyre Methuen, 1980).

'Physicians and Politics in the Jacobite Era', in *The Jacobite Challenge*, ed. Jeremy Black and Evelyn Cruikshanks (Edinburgh: John Donald, 1988), pp. 74–91.

Levine, J. M., 'Ancients and Moderns Reconsidered', *Eighteenth-Century Studies*, 15 (1981), 72–89.

The Battle of the Books: History and Literature in the Augustan Age (Ithaca: Cornell University Press, 1991).

Levitin, Dmitri, *Ancient Wisdom in the Age of the New Science. Histories of Philosophy in England, c. 1640–1700* (Cambridge: Cambridge University Press, 2015).

'Matthew Tindal's *Rights of the Christian Church* (1706) and the Church–State Relationship', *Historical Journal*, 54 (2011), 717–40.

Levy, Leonard W., *Blasphemy: Verbal Offense against the Sacred, from Moses to Salman Rushdie* (New York: Alfred A. Knopf, 1993).

Treason against God: A History of the Offense of Blasphemy (New York: Schoeken Books, 1981).

Lim, Paul C. H. 'Atheism, Atoms, and the Activity of God: Science and Religion in Early Boyle Lectures, 1692–1707', *Zygon*, 56 (2021), 143–67.

Mystery Unveiled; The Crisis of the Trinity in Early Modern England (Oxford: Oxford University Press, 2012).

Lindeboom, G. A., 'Pitcairne's Leyden Interlude Described from the Documents', *Annals of Science*, 19 (1963), 273–84.

Long, P., *A Summary Catalogue of the Lovelace Collection of the Papers of John Locke in the Bodleian Library* (Oxford: Oxford University Press, 1959).

Lord, Evelyn, *The Hell-Fire Clubs: Sex, Satanism and Secret Societies* (New Haven and London: Yale University Press, 2008).

Lucci, Diego, and Wigelsworth, Jeffrey R., '"God does not act arbitrarily, or interpose unnecessarily": Providential Deism and the Denial of Miracles in Wollaston, Tindal, Chubb and Morgan', *Intellectual History Review*, 25 (2015), 167–89.

Lund, Roger D., 'Irony as Subversion: Thomas Woolston and the Crime of Wit', in *The Margins of Orthodoxy*, pp. 170–94.

ed., *The Margins of Orthodoxy: Heterodox Writing and Cultural Response, 1660–1750* (Cambridge: Cambridge University Press, 1995).

Ridicule, Religion and the Politics of Wit in Augustan England (Farnham: Ashgate, 2012).

Lurbe, Pierre, 'La réfutation de l'athéism par Richard Bentley', in *La question de l'athéism au dix-huitieme siècle*, ed. Sylvia Taussig and Pierre Lurbe (Turnhout: Brepols, 2004), pp. 157–72.

Lynch, Andrew, and Broomhall, Susan, eds., *The Routledge History of Emotions in Europe, 1100–1700* (London: Routledge, 2020).

MacDonald, Michael, '*The Fearful Estate of Francis Spira*: Narrative, Identity and Emotion in Early Modern England', *Journal of British Studies*, 31 (1992), 32–61.

MacQueen, John, '*Tollerators and Con-tollerators* (1703) and Archibald Pitcairne: Text, Background and Authorship', *Studies in Scottish Literature*, 40 (2014), 76–104.

Maioli, Roger, 'The First Avowed British Atheist: Lord Hervey?', *Eighteenth-Century Studies*, 54 (2021), 357–79.

Malcolm, Noel, *Aspects of Hobbes* (Oxford: Clarendon Press, 2002).

Mandelbrote, Scott, 'The Religion of Thomas Harriot', in *Thomas Harriot: An Elizabethan Man of Science*, ed. Robert Fox (Aldershot: Ashgate, 2000), pp. 246–79.

Manning, Gillian, 'Rochester's *Satyr Against Reason and Mankind* and Contemporary Religious Debate', *The Seventeenth Century*, 8 (1993), 99–121.

Marsh, Christopher, *Popular Religion in Sixteenth-Century England* (Basingstoke: Macmillan, 1998).

Marshall, John, *John Locke, Toleration and Early Enlightenment Culture* (Cambridge: Cambridge University Press, 2006).

Marshall, Peter, *Mother Leakey and the Bishop: A Ghost Story* (Oxford: Oxford University Press, 2007).

Mathieson, W. L., *Scotland and the Union: A History of Scotland from 1695 to 1747* (Glasgow: James Maclehose & Sons, 1905).

McEwen, Gilbert D., *The Oracle of the Coffee House. John Dunton's 'Athenian Mercury'* (San Marino, CA: Huntington Library, 1972).

McLachlan, H. J., *Socinianism in Seventeenth-Century England* (Oxford: Oxford University Press, 1951).

Minois, Georges, *The Atheist's Bible: The Most Dangerous Book that Never Existed*, English trans. (Chicago: University of Chicago Press, 2012).

Mintz, Samuel I., *The Hunting of Leviathan: Seventeenth-Century Reactions to the Materialism and Moral Philosophy of Thomas Hobbes* (Cambridge: Cambridge University Press, 1962).

Money, David K., *The English Horace: Anthony Alsop and the Tradition of British Latin Verse* (Oxford: Oxford University Press for the British Academy, 1998).

Mortimer, Sarah, *Reason and Religion in the English Revolution: The Challenge of Socinianism* (Cambridge: Cambridge University Press, 2010).

Mosse, G. L., *The Holy Pretence: A Study of Christianity and Reason of State from William Perkins to John Winthrop* (Oxford: Blackwell, 1957).

Mullan, D. G., *Narratives of the Religious Self in Early-Modern Scotland* (Farnham: Ashgate, 2010).

Nash, David, *Acts against God: A Short History of Blasphemy* (London: Reaktion Books, 2020).

'The Uses of a Martyred Blasphemer's Death: The Execution of Thomas Aikenhead, Scotland's Religion, the Enlightenment and Contemporary Activism', in *Law, Crime and Deviance Since 1700: Micro-Studies in the History of Crime*, ed. Anne-Marie Kilday and David Nash (London: Bloomsbury Academic, 2017), pp. 19–35.

Nicholl, Charles, *The Reckoning: The Murder of Christopher Marlowe* (London: Jonathan Cape, 1992; 2nd ed., London: Vintage, 2002).

Nokes, G. D., *A History of the Crime of Blasphemy* (London: Sweet & Maxwell, 1928).

Oxford Dictionary of National Biography (ODNB), ed. H. C. G. Matthew and Brian Harrison, 60 vols (Oxford: Oxford University Press, 2004), also available online.

Oxford English Dictionary (OED), 2nd ed., prepared by J. A. Simpson and E. S. C. Weiner, 20 vols (Oxford: Clarendon Press, 1989), also available online.

Palmer, D. J., 'Marlowe's Naturalism', in *Christopher Marlowe*, ed. Brian Morris (London: Ernest Benn, 1968), pp. 151–75.

Parkin, Jon, 'Hobbism in the Later 1660s: Daniel Scargill and Samuel Parker', *Historical Journal*, 42 (1999), 85–108.

Taming the Leviathan: The Reception of The Political and Religious Ideas of Thomas Hobbes in England 1640–1700 (Cambridge: Cambridge University Press, 2007).

Parks, Stephen, *John Dunton and the English Book Trade* (New York: Garland Publishing, 1976).

Pennington, Richard, *A Descriptive Catalogue of the Etched Work of Wenceslaus Hollar, 1607–77* (Cambridge: Cambridge University Press, 1982).

Phillipson, N. T. 'Culture and Society in the Eighteenth-Century Province: The Case of Edinburgh and the Scottish Enlightenment', in *The University and Society*, ed. Lawrence Stone, 2 vols (Princeton: Princeton University Press, 1974), II, 407–48.

Popkin, R. H., *The History of Scepticism from Erasmus to Spinoza* (Berkeley and Los Angeles: University of Los Angeles Press, 1979).

Prouty, C. T., *George Gascoigne* (New York: Columba University Press, 1942).

Quinn, D. B., and Shirley, J. W., 'A Contemporary List of Hariot References', *Renaissance Quarterly*, 22 (1969), 9–26.

Raab, Felix, *The English Face of Machiavelli: A Changing Interpretation, 1500–1700* (London: Routledge & Kegan Paul, 1964).

Rack, Henry D., *Reasonable Enthusiast: John Wesley and the Rise of Methodism*, 3rd ed. (London: Epworth, 2002).

Raffe, Alasdair, 'Archibald Pitcairne and Scottish Heterodoxy, c. 1688–1713', *Historical Journal*, 60 (2017), 633–57.

The Culture of Controversy: Religious Arguments in Scotland, 1660–1714 (Woodbridge: Boydell Press, 2012).

Rappaport, Rhoda, *When Geologists Were Historians 1665–1750* (Ithaca: Cornell University Press, 1997).

Redwood, John, *Reason, Ridicule and Religion: The Age of Enlightenment in England 1660–1750*, revised ed. (London: Thames & Hudson, 1996).

Ried, Paul E., 'Joseph McKean: The Second Boylston Professor of Rhetoric and Oratory', *Quarterly Journal of Speech*, 46 (1960), 419–24.

Riggs, David, *The World of Christopher Marlowe* (London: Faber & Faber, 2004).

Riley, P. W. J., *King William and the Scottish Politicians* (Edinburgh: John Donald, 1979).

Rivers, Isabel, *Reason, Grace, and Sentiment: A Study of the Language of Religion and Ethics in England, 1660–1780*, 2 vols (Cambridge: Cambridge University Press, 1991–2000).

Robertson, John, *The Case for Enlightenment: Scotland and Naples 1680–1760* (Cambridge: Cambridge University Press, 2005).

Roos, Anna Marie, *Martin Folkes, 1690–1754, Newtonian, Antiquary, Connoisseur* (Oxford: Oxford University Press, 2021).

Rosenwein, Barbara, *Generations of Feeling: A History of Emotions, 600–1700* (Cambridge: Cambridge University Press, 2016).

Rossi, Paolo, *The Dark Abyss of Time: The History of the Earth and the History of Nations from Hooke to Vico*, English trans. (Chicago: University of Chicago Press, 1984).

Royle, Edward, *Victorian Infidels: The Origins of the British Secularist Movement 1791–1866* (Manchester: Manchester University Press, 1974).

Ryrie, Alec, *Being Protestant in Reformation Britain* (Oxford: Oxford University Press, 2013).

'Reformation', in *Cambridge History of Atheism, vol. 1*, ed. Bullivant and Ruse, pp. 183–201.

'Seeking the Seekers', *Studies in Church History*, 57 (2021), 185–209.

Unbelievers: An Emotional History of Doubt (London: William Collins, 2019).

Schaffer, Simon, 'The Glorious Revolution and Medicine in Britain and the Netherlands', *Notes & Records of the Royal Society*, 43 (1989), 167–90.

Schofield, R. E., *Mechanism and Materialism: British Natural Philosophy in an Age of Reason* (Princeton: Princeton University Press, 1970).

Scott, Hew, *Fasti Ecclesiae Scoticanae,* new ed., 7 vols (Edinburgh: Oliver and Boyd, 1915–28).

Shagan, Ethan H, *The Birth of Modern Belief: Faith and Judgment from the Middle Ages to the Enlightenment* (Princeton: Princeton University Press, 2018).

The Rule of Moderation: Violence, Religion and the Politics of Restraint in Early Modern England (Cambridge: Cambridge University Press, 2011).

Shepherd, Christine M., 'The Arts Curriculum at Aberdeen at the Beginning of the Eighteenth Century', in *Aberdeen and the Enlightenment*, ed. J. J. Carter and J. H. Pittock (Aberdeen: Aberdeen University Press, 1987), pp. 146–54.

'Philosophy and Science in the Arts Curriculum of the Scottish Universities in the Seventeenth Century' (Unpublished PhD thesis, Edinburgh, 1975).

Sheppard, Kenneth, *Anti-Atheism in Early Modern England 1580–1720. The Atheist Answered and His Error Confuted* (Leiden: Brill, 2015).

Sheppard, Kenneth, 'Atheism, Apostacy, and the Afterlives of Francis Spira in Early Modern England', *The Seventeenth Century*, 27 (2012), 410–34.

Shoemaker, Robert B., *Prosecution and Punishment: Petty Crime and the Law in London and Rural Middlesex, c.1660–1725* (Cambridge: Cambridge University Press, 1991).

Shuttleton, D. E., '"A Modest Examination": John Arbuthnot and the Scottish Newtonians', *British Journal for Eighteenth-Century Studies*, 18 (1995), 47–62.

Shuttleton, D. E., 'Bantering with Scripture: Dr Archibald Pitcairne and Articulate Irreligion in Late Seventeenth-Century Edinburgh', in *The Arts of Seventeenth-Century Science*, ed. Claire Jowitt and Diane Watt (Aldershot: Ashgate, 2002), pp. 58–73.

Sirota, Brent S., *The Christian Monitors: The Church of England and the Age of Benevolence 1680–1730* (New Haven and London: Yale University Press, 2014).

Smith, Nigel, 'The Charge of Atheism and the Language of Radical Speculation, 1640–60', in Hunter and Wootton, eds., *Atheism from the Reformation to the Enlightenment*, pp. 131–58.

Perfection Proclaimed: Language and Literature in English Radical Religion 1640–60 (Oxford: Clarendon Press, 1989).

Spurr, John, 'The Manner of English Blasphemy, 1676–2008', in *Religion, Identity and Conflict in Britain: From the Restoration to the Twentieth Century*, ed. S. J. Brown, Frances Knight and John Morgan-Guy (Farnham: Ashgate, 2013), pp. 27–46.

The Restoration Church of England 1646–89 (New Haven and London: Yale University Press, 1991).

Stephen, Sir Leslie, *History of English Thought in the Eighteenth Century*, 3rd ed., 2 vols (London: Smith, Elder & Co., 1902).

Stephens, John, 'Tinkler Ducket (*c.* 1711–*c.* 1774)', in *The Dictionary of Eighteenth-Century British Philosophers*, ed. John W. Yolton, John Valdimir Price and John Stephens, 2 vols (Bristol: Thoemmes Press, 1999), I, 295–6, reprinted in *The Continuum Encyclopedia of British Philosophy*, ed. Anthony Grayling, Andrew Pyle and Naomi Goulder, 4 vols (London: Continuum, 2006), II, 899.

Stevens, Laura M., 'Civility and Skepticism in the Woolston–Sherlock Debate over Miracles', *Eighteenth-Century Life*, 21 (1997), 57–70.

Stigler, Stephen M., 'Apollo Mathematicus: A Story of Resistance to Quantification in the Seventeenth Century', *Proceedings of the American Philosophical Society*, 136 (1992), 93–126.

Stone, J. M., 'Atheism under Elizabeth and James I', *The Month*, 81 (1894), 174–87.

Strathmann, Ernest A., 'Robert Parsons's Essay on Atheism', in *Joseph Quincy Adams Memorial Studies*, ed. J. G. McManaway, G. E. Dawson and E. E. Willoughby (Washington, D.C.: Folger Shakespeare Library, 1948), pp. 665–81.

Sir Walter Ralegh: A Study in Elizabethan Skepticism (New York: Columbia University Press, 1951).

Suarez, Michael, '"The Most Blasphemous Book that Ever Was Publish'd": Ridicule, Reception and Censorship in Eighteenth-Century England', in *The Commonwealth of Books*, ed. Wallace Kirsop (Melbourne: Monash University, 2007), pp. 48–77.

Sullivan, Robert E., *John Toland and the Deist Controversy: A Study in Adaptations* (Cambridge, MA: Harvard University Press, 1982).

Sutherland, James, 'Burridge the Blasphemer', in Sutherland, *Background for Queen Anne* (London: Methuen, 1939), pp. 3–32.

Tarantino, Giovanni, 'Collins's Cicero, Freethinker', in Hudson, Lucci and Wigelsworth, eds., *Atheism and Deism Revalued*, pp. 81–99.

Taranto, Pascal, *Du déism à l'athéisme: La libre-pensée d'Anthony Collins* (Paris: Editions Champion, 2000).

Taylor, Charles, *A Secular Age* (Cambridge, MA: Harvard University Press, 2007).

Thackray, Arnold, *Atoms and Powers: An Essay on Newtonian Matter-Theory and the Development of Chemistry* (Cambridge, MA: Harvard University Press, 1970).

Thomas, Keith, *Religion and the Decline of Magic: Studies in Popular Beliefs in Sixteenth and Seventeenth Century England* (London: Weidenfeld & Nicolson, 1971, reprinted Harmondsworth: Penguin, 1978).

Tilmouth, Christopher, *Passion's Triumph over Reason: A History of the Moral Imagination from Spenser to Rochester* (Oxford: Oxford University Press, 2007).

Tipson, Baird, 'A Dark Side of Seventeenth-Century English Protestantism: The Sin against the Holy Ghost', *Harvard Theological Review*, 77 (1984), 301–30.

Trapnell, William H., *Thomas Woolston: Madman and Deist?* (Bristol: Thoemmes Press, 1994).

Tucker Brooke, C. F., *The Life of Christopher Marlowe and the Tragedy of Dido Queen of Carthage* (London: Methuen, 1930).

Turner, Simon, *The New Hollstein: German Engravings, Etchings and Woodcuts 1400–1700: Wenceslaus Hollar*, parts 1–9, ed. Guilia Bartram (Ouderkerk aan den Ijssel: Sound and Vision Publishers, 2009–12).

Twigg, John, *The University of Cambridge and the English Revolution, 1625–88* (Woodbridge: Boydell Press, 1990).

Urry, William, *Christopher Marlowe and Canterbury* (London: Faber & Faber, 1988).

Usher, R. G., *The Rise and Fall of the High Commission* (Oxford: Clarendon Press, 1913; 2nd ed., introduced by P. Tyler, 1968).

Venn, J. and Venn, J. A., *Alumni Cantabrigienses* [to 1751], 4 vols (Cambridge: Cambridge University Press, 1922–7).

Biographical History of Gonville and Caius College, 2 vols (Cambridge: Cambridge University Press, 1898).

Vermij, Reink, 'The Formation of the Newtonian Philosophy: The Case of the Amsterdam Mathematical Amateurs', *British Journal for the History of Science*, 36 (2003), 183–200.

'Matter and Motion: Toland and Spinoza', in *Disguised and Overt Spinozism around 1700*, ed. Wiep van Bunge and Wim Klever (Leiden: Brill, 1996), pp. 275–88.

Visconsi, Elliott, 'The Invention of Criminal Blasphemy: *Rex v. Taylor* (1676)', *Representations*, 103 (2008), 30–52.

Walker, D. P., 'Atheism, the Ancient Theology and Sidney's *Arcadia*', in *The Ancient Theology* (London: Duckworth, 1972), pp. 132–63.

Spiritual and Demonic Magic from Ficino to Campanella (London: Warburg Institute, 1958).

Ward, W. R., *Georgian Oxford: University Politics in the Eighteenth Century* (Oxford: Clarendon Press, 1958).

Warren, John S., 'Shining a Light in Dark Places, Parts I and II', *Global Intellectual History*, 2 (2017), 268–307; 3 (2018), 1–46.

Warrick, John, *The Moderators of the Church of Scotland from 1690 to 1740* (Edinburgh: Oliphant, Anderson & Ferrier, 1913).

Watkins, Owen C., *The Puritan Experience* (London: Routledge & Kegan Paul, 1972).

Whitmarsh, Tim, *Battling the Gods: Atheism in the Ancient World* (New York: Alfred A Knopf, 2015).

Wiener, C. Z., 'The Beleaguered Isle. A Study of Elizabethan and Early Stuart Anti-Catholicism', *Past & Present*, 51 (1971), 27–62.

Wigelsworth, Jeffrey R., *Deism in Enlightenment England: Theology, Politics, and Newtonian Public Science* (Manchester: Manchester University Press, 2009).

Withers, Charles, 'Situating Practical Reason: Geography, Geometry and Mapping in the Scottish Enlightenment', in *Science and Medicine in the Scottish Enlightenment*, ed. Withers and Paul Wood (East Linton: Tuckwell Press, 2002), pp. 54–78.

Wootton, David, 'Lucien Febvre and the Problem of Unbelief in the Early Modern Period', *Journal of Modern History*, 60 (1988), 695–730.

'New Histories of Atheism', in Hunter and Wootton, eds., *Atheism from the Reformation to the Enlightenment*, pp. 13–53.

Paolo Sarpi: Between Renaissance and Enlightenment (Cambridge: Cambridge University Press, 1983).

'Unbelief in Early Modern Europe', *History Workshop Journal*, 20 (1985), 82–100.

Yolton, John W., *Thinking Matter: Materialism in Eighteenth-Century Britain* (Oxford: Blackwell, 1984).

Index

Abernethy, John, 54
Adams, John Quincy, 135
Adams, Thomas, 36, 41, 44
Addison, Joseph, 137, 168, 185–6
Aikenhead, Thomas, 1–3, 28–30, 61, 67, 71–2,
    93, 130, 179–80, 188–9
    Defences, 99–100, 112
    Letter, 102, 104, 114
    Paper, 102–5, 114, 117–20
    petitions, 100–2, 104, 107
    views expressed by, 96–8
Aikenhead, James, 95–6
Aldrich, Simon, 49n
Alexander, Sir William, 54
Allen, Don Cameron, 14
Allen, Hannah, 67, 69
Allen, Thomas, 25, 49, 51
Ames, Joseph, 173, 176–7, 187
Ames, William, 41
Ancients and Moderns controversy, 142
Anne, Princess, 89
Anstruther, Lord William, 107
anti-Catholicism, 37, 56, 90, 132, 173
Apollonius of Tyaneus, 79, 117, 131
Aristotle and Aristotelianism, 22, 38–9, 45, 87, 118
Arnot, Hugo, 113
Ascham, Roger, 38, 40, 43
atheism
    definition of, 4, 22, 37–8, 41, 73
    and moral obligation, 102, 167
    practical, 11–12, 16–17, 21, 32, 38, 41–2, 50,
        74, 173, 185
    repressive denial of, 17–18
atheists
    assurance of, 15–16, 21, 28, 32, 57, 67,
        178–9, 186, 188
    characteristics of, 2, 19–20, 39, 50
Atherton, Henry, 173
Aubrey, John, 25
Aylesford, Earl of, 159
Aylmer, Gerald, 84

Bacon, Francis, 34, 42
Baines, Richard, 26–7, 34, 36n, 47, 50, 67
Baker, Thomas, 27, 35n, 165, 175
Baldwin, John, 35
Bale, Will, 162
Bancroft, Richard, 1, 35, 50, 67
Barlow, Thomas, 5, 63, 66
Barrow, Henry, 23
Baxter, Richard, 12–13, 58–9, 64–7, 69
Bayle, Pierre, 11, 32, 132, 160, 167
Beard, Thomas, 26, 34, 36, 43–4, 47, 85
Bedford, Arthur, 15
Bellini, Lorenzo, 124
Bentham, James, 177
Bentley, Richard, 9–10, 75, 82, 92, 171, 176
Berkeley, George, 138, 160
Berman, David, 3n, 6, 17–18, 138, 186
Bernard, Edward, 82
Beza, Theodore, 86
Bible, attacks on, 2, 25, 30, 39, 44, 48–9, 59, 61,
        65, 81, 88, 97, 99, 110–12, 115, 121, 131
Birch, Thomas, 64, 176
Blagden, Robert, 49, 51
blasphemy, 29, 58, 74, 90, 92, 94–6, 106, 183–4
    definition of, 113
blasphemy acts, 98, 100, 107, 109–11, 182
Blount, Charles, 10–11, 28, 78–80, 85, 111,
        117–18, 131
Bolingbroke, Viscount, 161, 187n
Boreel, Adam, 62
Borelli, Giovani Alfonso, 124, 127
Boyle, Robert, 5, 8, 18, 19–21, 61–5, 67–9, 71,
        75, 79, 82, 187
Boyle Lectures, 4, 9–10, 16, 20, 75, 80, 82, 92,
        134–5, 137, 139, 144, 150, 171, 182
Breton, Nicholas, 45
Brown, Adam, 31
Brown, Theodore M., 127
Browne, Sir Thomas, 59
Buckley, George T., 6
Bunyan, John, 15, 58–9, 68–70, 119

Burghley, Lord Treasurer, 51
Burke, Edmund, 186
Burnet, Gilbert, 4n, 5, 63, 71, 80, 166
Burnet, Thomas, 111, 117, 126
Burridge, Richard, 28, 88–92, 180, 183
Burrough, James, 159, 171
Burton, Robert, 3, 53
Butler, Joseph, 166–7, 172
Butler, Samuel, 128

Calvin, John, 86
Cambridge
  Gonville and Caius College, 158–9
  Jesus College, 91, 181
  Trinity College, 170, 176
  Vice-Chancellor's court, 1, 163, 175
Castellio, Sebastian, 86
Celsus, 44
Cerne Abbas enquiry, 23–5, 35, 49, 51, 54
Chambers, Robert, 129
Champion, Justin, 182
character books, 45–6, 56, 76, 105
Charron, Pierre, 149n
Cheselden, William, 187
Cheyne, George, 140n, 143n
Chillingworth, William, 59
China, 140, 156
Christ, attacks on, 2, 10, 27, 44, 47, 49, 59, 61,
  68, 71, 79, 97–9, 112–15, 121–2, 184
Chubb, Thomas, 11, 186
Cicero, 43, 138, 140, 154, 186
Clark, Stuart, 4, 45
Clarke, Samuel, 5n, 16, 92, 126, 135, 139, 141,
  146, 150, 155n, 163, 182
Clarkson, Lawrence, 59, 70, 76
Clerk, Sir John, 133n
Clogher Diocesan Library, 175
Cole, William, 170, 171n, 172–3, 176, 187n
Collins, Anthony, 10–11, 31, 163, 186
Collinson, Patrick, 56
Comby, 83
Comlie, Richard, 97n
Compton, Henry, 92
Corderoy, Jeremy, 39–40, 42
Cornelison, Henry, 169–70, 175–6
Craftsman, The, 161–2
Crafurd, Hugh, 97n
Craig, James, 97n
Craig, Mungo, 97n, 99, 101, 104–5, 107, 112,
  116, 118, 122
Crichton, Andrew, 64
Cromarty, George MacKenzie, Earl of, 133,
  140n
Cudworth, Ralph, 7–8, 16, 75
Cunningham, Alexander, 96, 116

Cunningham, Andrew, 128

D'Anvers, Caleb, 161
D'Ewes, Sir Simonds, 52, 69
Dalrymple, George, 97n
Darrell, John, 1
Davidson, George, 136n
Davie, G. E., 115
Davis, J. C., 22, 34n
Deism, 10–11, 31, 55, 82, 105, 111, 116, 131,
  159–60, 187
Denniston, Walter, 130
Derpier or Deryner, John, 49–50
Descartes, Rene, 5, 116, 118
Diagoras, 43, 86
Dicksone, George, 97n
doubt, 13–15, 18, 28, 42, 52, 57–8, 60–2, 64,
  67, 71, 115, 119, 178, 188
Dove, John, 36, 39
Ducket, Tinkler, 1–2, 32, 184–5, 188
  articles against, 163–4, 175
  diplomatic posts, 172, 184
  Letter, 159, 161–4, 169, 172, 175, 178,
    184
  Speech, 166–9, 172, 175, 185
Dunton, John, 83–4

Eccfoord, William, 97n
Edinburgh, 29, 31, 94, 128, 179
  book trade, 110–11, 131
  Galowlee, 101
  Grassmarket, 30
  Greping-Office, 129
  Greyfriars churchyard, 143
  University of, 90–1, 94, 96, 117, 181
  University of, library, 121
Edwards, George, 85–8
Edwards, John, 3, 10, 187
Edwards, Thomas, 70, 76
Eglington, Thomas, 164
Elder, Jane, 97n
Eliot, John, 30
Ellesmere, Lord Chancellor, 23
Ellis, Havelock, 27
emotions, history of, 18, 57, 75
Epicurus, 43, 87, 118, 132, 140
Episcopalians, Scottish, 31, 123, 129, 132, 134,
  137, 180
eternalism, 38–9, 87–8, 118–19, 140, 142, 149,
  153
Euclid, 132
Ezra, 2, 97, 121

Family of Love, 53
Febvre, Lucien, 6–7

Findlater, Alexander, 109
Fineaux or Finis, Thomas, 49
Fisher, Robert, 47, 50–1
Fitzherbert, Thomas, 41
Flying Post, 101, 110
Folkes, Martin, 187
Fotherby, Martin, 39–40
Frazer, John, 2n, 31, 111, 118
Freebairn, Robert, 130, 136
freethinkers, 5, 9, 28, 39–41, 55, 77, 79, 102, 114, 138, 144, 171, 173, 180–1, 186
Fuller, Thomas, 36, 41–2

Gardiner, William, 49–50
Garth, Sir Samuel, 187n
Gascoigne, John, 159
Gastrell, Francis, 17
Gauden, John, 62
Gentleman's Magazine, The, 161
Gibbens, Nicholas, 47
Gibbs, Stephen, 159, 161, 163n, 169, 172, 175
Gibson, Edmund, 171, 174, 183–4
Gilpin, Richard, 66, 69
Ginzburg, Carlo, 95
Glanvill, Joseph, 6, 9, 16, 76
Glasgow, University of, 90–1, 181
Gloucester, Duke of, 89
Golding, Arthur, 43
Gooch, Thomas, 168, 170
Graham, Michael F., 29, 31, 179
Grange, James Erskine, Lord, 181
Greaves, William, 171
Green, V. H. H., 173
Greenham, Richard, 36, 53
Greenwood, John, 23
Gregory, David, 123–6, 133n, 134, 137n
Grey, Zachary, 172, 176
Grose, Francis, 187n
Grotius, Hugo, 111
Guerrini, Anita, 127–8, 134
Gurdon, Brampton, 182n

Hacket, William, 23
Hale, Lord Chief Justice, 183
Haliburtone, Andrew, 97n
Hall, Joseph, 36, 46
Halyburton, Thomas, 30, 61, 103, 114–16, 119, 133
Hamilton, John, 97n
Hamilton, Robert, 119
Hamilton, William, 109
Harries, Richard, 81
Harriot, Thomas, 26, 54–5
Harris, John, 19–20, 80
Harvey, William, 127

Heathcote, Ralph, 182n
Hebrews, Epistle to the, 16, 68–9
Hecht, Jennifer Michael, 14
Hell-Fire Club, 163
Henderson, Mrs, 130
Henderson, Robert, 97n, 118
Hepburn, Robert, 136–7
Herbert of Cherbury, Lord, 79, 103
Hervey, Lord, 3, 171
Heywood, Elizabeth, 61
High Commission, 23, 35, 50
Hill, Christopher, 76
Hoadly, Benjamin, 160
Hobbes, Thomas, 28, 77–9, 80–2, 117–19, 140, 142, 150n, 165
Hobbism, 28, 77–8, 82
Holland, Philemon, 54
Hollar, Wenceslaus, 79
Hooke, Robert, 139n, 140, 156
Hooker, Richard, 4, 24, 36, 38, 40, 45
Horner, Francis, 105
Houghton Library, Harvard, 31, 123, 134, 144n
Hull, John, 44
Hume, David, 29, 186
Hume, Sir Patrick, 108
Hyde, Robert, 24, 48n

imagination, power of, 120
Inquisition, Spanish, 36, 170
irreligion, casual, 25, 51, 57, 158

Jacob, Margaret C., 6
Jacobitism, 91, 129–30, 137, 161, 180
James I, 4
James II, 89
James, St, 90
Jennens, Robert, 159, 161
John Rylands Library, 175
Johnston, James, 104, 107, 109, 112–13

K., M., 59
Keill, John, 126
Kennett, White, 183
Ker, John, 137
Kincaid, Thomas, 137
King, Lester S., 127
Kinnoull, George Hay, Earl of, 137
Kocher, Paul H., 26–7, 48
Kors, Alan, 5, 7, 187
Kuriyama, Constance, 26
Kyd, Thomas, 34, 48n, 53

Lafreice, James, 97n
Larner, Christina, 108
Le Clerc, Jean, 181

Leiden, University of, 123–4, 126, 152n, 160
Leo X, 43
Letters Writ by a Turkish Spy, 117
Levitin, Dmitri, 8, 173
Levy, Leonard W., 6, 183
libertinism, 12, 16, 60, 78, 81–2, 85, 158, 165
Little Horkesley, 158, 162, 170–1
Locke, John, 88, 103–4, 118n, 150n, 156n, 166
London
    British Library, 133n, 180
    British Library, Harleian MSS, 24, 27, 35n
    coffee-houses, 20, 73, 82
    Inns of Court, 83
    Star Chamber, 35, 47, 50
    Westminster Hall, 82, 172
Long, Roger, 164
Lorimer, William, 104, 106–7, 114–15
Lorrain, Paul, 90
Lucian, 43, 89
Lucretius, 43, 89, 118
Luther, Martin, 68, 86, 90
Lyly, John, 38, 44

Macaulay, Lord, 94, 108
Machiavelli, Niccolo, 40, 43, 54
MacIntosh, J. J., 19
MacQueen, John and Winifred, 130, 132, 134
Macropedius, Georgius, 152n
Mahomet, 98, 110
Mahometans, 141, 156
Maioli, Roger, 3, 186
Marchand, Prosper, 133
Mark, St, 63
Marlowe, Christopher, 2, 23, 26–9, 34, 36, 38,
    47–50, 55, 57–9, 67, 71, 120, 178, 189
Marprelate Tracts, 23
Martin, Martin, 181
Martinique, 89
May, Jonathan, 169
McKean, Henry Swasey, 134–5, 137, 144n
McKean, Joseph, 135, 137
McKean, William, 135
Mead, Richard, 133n, 180, 187
Meldrum, George, 106
Mennochio, 95
Menzies, William, 99n
Meres, Francis, 53
Mersenne, Marin, 3
Mews, Peter, 92
Middleton, Conyers, 171
Middleton, Patrick, 97n
miracles, 71, 79, 81, 86, 98, 120–1, 126, 183–4
Mitchell, Adam, 97n
Molesworth, Robert, Viscount, 181
Monk, J. H., 171

Monroe, Robert, 97n
Montaigne, Michel de, 59
More, Henry, 120, 139, 146
More, Sir George, 36, 42
Moreton, William, 91–2
Morgan, Thomas, 11, 186
Mornay, Phillippe Duplessis, 43
mortalism, 24, 40, 49, 51, 53, 65, 83, 110–11,
    118
Morton, Thomas, 45
Moses, attacks on, 44, 47, 49, 98, 114, 121–2
Mosman, George, 30–1
Muggletonians, 70, 76

Nash, David, 29
Nashe, Thomas, 3, 36, 40, 43
Neilson, John, 97n, 122n
New England Company, 62
Newcomen, Stephen, 170n
Newport, Francis, 84
Newton, Sir Isaac, 123–7, 132, 133n, 140–1, 160
Nichols, Josias, 37, 42, 46
Nicolson, Daniel, 30

Oliver (Thomas Allen's servant), 25, 49
Origen, 44
Origin of Moral Virtue and Religion Arraigned, 3,
    186
Osborne, Francis, 59–60
Oswald, Alison, 97n
Oxford
    Bodleian Library, 103, 160
    Magdalen College, 89
    Programma (1728), 160
    St John's College, 83
Oxford, Edward de Vere, Earl of, 48n
Oxford, Edward Harley, Earl of, 176

Pagitt, Ephraim, 34n, 76
Paine, Thomas, 186
Palfreyman, Thomas, 37, 43
Parkin, Jon, 77–8, 165
Parsons, Robert, 25, 38, 48n
Pate, Robert, 161, 169
Paul, St, 49
Perkins, William, 36
Peter the Great, 131
Pettigrew, John, 131
Pitcairne, Archibald, 1–3, 31, 88, 111, 180–1,
    188–9
    Assembly, The, 128, 136
    Babell, 128, 136, 142
    Epistola Archimedis ad Regem Gelonem, 31,
        132–4, 136, 142, 180, 187
    Latin poetry, 129–30, 133, 136, 142

Pitcairne, Archibald (cont.)
  library, 131–2, 139n
  medical writings, 124, 126–8, 136
  milieu, 129, 136–7
  religious views, 130–1, 132
Pitcairneana, 2–3, 31, 88, 123, 134, 144–57,
    180–1, 189
Plato, 138
Pliny, 43, 54
Pocock, J. G. A., 74
Pompilius, Numa, 133
Pomponazzi, Pietro, 120
Potter, John, 97n
Presbyterianism, English, 23, 75
Presbyterianism, Scottish, 31, 93, 105, 108,
    110–11, 123, 128–9, 181
Pringle, Mrs, 30
Prior, Matthew, 132
Protagoras, 43
Protestant Mercury, 100
Puckering, Sir John, 23, 35, 53
Puritanism, 22, 56
Pythagoreans, 87

Quakers, 62, 70, 75–6

Raffe, Alasdair, 133
Ralegh, Carew, 24–5, 51
Ralegh, Sir Walter, 23–6, 35, 48n, 53,
    58–9
Ramsey, Allan, 137
Ramsey, Helen (née), 95
Ranters, 22, 34n, 68, 70, 75
Redwood, John, 6
Reformation, impact of, 13–14, 53, 86
Revelation, Book of, 121
Richards, Mary, 164–5, 166, 170, 172, 175, 185
Richardson, Ralph, 80
Ridpath, George, 110n
Ritson, Joseph, 27
Rochester, John Wilmot, Earl of, 2, 5, 28, 80–2,
    89, 165, 173, 181
Rogers, John, 70
Rogers, Thomas, 43
Royal Society, 62
Royle, Edward, 188
Ruddiman, Thomas, 130n, 137
Ryrie, Alec, 14–15, 18–19, 28, 57–63, 66–8, 70,
    72

Sault, Richard, 83–4
Scaliger, J. J., 136
Scargill, Daniel, 77–8, 165
science, 8–9, 20, 54, 89
scoffing, 17, 21, 40–1, 73, 92, 182

Scotland
  free-thought in, 180–1
  National Records of, 103
  Privy Council, 1, 96, 100, 106–8, 111
Scotman, John, 163n, 175
Scott, William, 96, 116
Second Spira, 30n, 83–4
sectaries, 23–4, 34–5, 55, 62, 70, 75–6
Seekers, 59, 62, 70
Shaftesbury, Earl of, 11, 167, 181
Shagan, Ethan, 14, 74
Sheppard, Kenneth, 74
Shuttleton, David, 129–30
Sibbald, Sir Robert, 128
Sidney, Sir Philip, 38, 43
Simon, Richard, 121, 132
Sin against the Holy Ghost, 63, 68, 71
Singer, S. W., 27n
Sloane, Sir Hans, 133n, 180, 187
Smith, Henry, 24
Smith, John (Master of Caius), 176
Smith, John (physician), 83
Smith, John (Vicar of West Ham), 85, 88
Smith, Samuel, 37
Societies for the Reformation of Manners, 74, 85
Socinians, 9–10, 99, 115, 118
Soldania, 86, 88, 156
South Sea Bubble, 182
Spence, Joseph, 187
Spinoza, Baruch, 29, 79–80, 82, 117–18, 121,
    140, 142, 150n
Spira, Francesco, 68, 83
Sprat, Thomas, 8
Springett, Mary, 59
Spurr, John, 182
Staunton, Edmund, 69
Stephens, John, 158
Stevens, Nicholas, 32, 159–61, 172
Stewart, Sir James, 108
Stigler, Stephen, 128
Stillingfleet, Edward, 63, 71, 85
Stremar, Christopher, 25n
Strutt (brother of Samuel), 162, 169n
Strutt, Samuel, 161–3, 169
Stubbs, George, 170n
Stukeley, William, 187
Sutherland, Sir James, 88, 92
Sydenham, Thomas, 128
Sylvester, Matthew, 65
Symonds, John Addington, 27n

Taylor, Jeremy, 74
Tenison, Thomas, 11, 16, 77, 81, 92
Theodorus, 43, 86
Thomas, Keith, 57–60, 62, 72

Thynne, Charles or John, 25, 49
Tindal, Matthew, 11, 31, 173, 182, 186
Toland, John, 10–11, 31, 111n, 117, 126,
    140–1, 155n, 163, 181, 186
Toulouse, 179
Towers, William, 170, 176
Treatise of the Three Impostors, 134
Trinity, critiques of, 10, 30, 98–9, 103, 115,
    120, 133, 139, 148, 182
Trosse, George, 61, 72
Tuck, Charles, 162n, 169
Tunstall, James, 162n, 166, 167n, 170, 172–3,
    176
Turnbull, George, 181
Turner, Jane, 71
Turner, John, 5
Turner, Matthew, 3n, 186

Ussher, James, 64

van Dale, Antonie, 132
Vanini, Guilio Cesare, 80, 111, 120, 179
Varro, 86
Vaughan, William, 34, 47
Vavasour, Peter, 50
Verwer, Adriaan, 125
Votier, Edward, 162

Wagstaffe, John, 5, 9, 28, 77
Walker, Brian, 50
Walkinshaw, James, 126
Wallis, John, 77, 81
Walpole, Horace, 3
Walpole, Sir Robert, 161
Warren, John S., 29
Waterland, Daniel, 177
Webster, James, 131

Wesley, John, 15
Wesley, Samuel, 159–60
West, Elizabeth, 61
Whalley, John, 164, 170n, 171, 175
Wharton, Thomas, 27
Whiston, William, 126
Whitehead, Paul, 162–3, 169
Wiener, Carol Z., 56
Wigelsworth, Jeffrey, 141
Wigglesworth, Michael, 59
Wilkinson, Elizabeth, 67, 69, 119
Williams, John, 91
Williams, Philip, 170n, 176
Willis, Thomas, 31n
Wilson, John, 136n
Wilwood, Harvey, 80
Windle, William, 162–3, 169, 176
Wingfield, John, 38, 42, 61
Winstanley, Gerrard, 59
wit, 20, 30, 40, 50, 53, 73, 81, 109,
    182
witchcraft, 4, 9, 45, 55, 77, 108–9
    Act (1736), 181
Wodrow, Robert, 131
Wollaston, William, 11
Wolseley, Sir Charles, 8, 115
Wood, Anthony, 30, 83
Woolston, Thomas, 183–4
Woolton, John, 53
Wootton, David, 7
Wotton, William, 75
Wylie, Robert, 108–10, 112–13

Yolton, John, 163
Young, Alexander, 97n

Zwingli, Ulrich, 86